China and the Wireless Undertow

Technicities
Series Editors: Ryan Bishop, Winchester School of Art, University of Southampton and Jussi Parikka, Aarhus University and FAMU, Prague

The philosophy of technicities: exploring how technology mediates art, frames design and augments the mediated collective perception of everyday life.

Technicities will publish the latest philosophical thinking about our increasingly immaterial technocultural conditions, with a unique focus on the context of art, design and media.

Editorial Advisory Board
Marie-Luise Angerer, Benjamin Bratton, Sean Cubitt, Daphne Dragona, Matthew Fuller, Yuriko Furuhata, Olga Goriunova, Yuk Hui, Jin Huimin, Akira Mizuta Lippit, Shaoling Ma, Claudia Mareis, Gunalan Nadarajan, elin o'Hara slavick, Robert Pietrusko, Tania Roy, Susan Schuppli, Christina Vagt, Geoffrey Winthrop-Young.

Published
Lyotard and the Inhuman Condition: Reflections on Nihilism, Information and Art
Ashley Woodward

Critical Luxury Studies: Art, Design, Media
Edited by John Armitage and Joanne Roberts

Cold War Legacies: Systems, Theory, Aesthetics
Edited by John Beck and Ryan Bishop

Fashion and Materialism
Ulrich Lehmann

Queering Digital India: Activisms, Identities, Subjectivities
Edited by Rohit K. Dasgupta and Debanuj DasGupta

Zero Degree Seeing: Barthes/Burgin and Political Aesthetics
Edited by Ryan Bishop and Sunil Manghani

Rhythm and Critique: Technics, Modalities, Practices
Edited by Paola Crespi and Sunil Manghani

Photography Off the Scale: Technologies and Theories of the Mass Image
Edited by Tomáš Dvořák and Jussi Parikka

The Informational Logic of Human Rights: Network Imaginaries in the Cybernetic Age
Josh Bowsher

Art and Technology in Maurice Blanchot
Holly Langstaff

China and the Wireless Undertow: Media as Wave Philosophy
Anna Greenspan

Reconfiguring the Portrait
Edited by Abraham Geil and Tomáš Jirsa

www.edinburghuniversitypress.com/series/TECH

China and the Wireless Undertow

Media as Wave Philosophy

Anna Greenspan

EDINBURGH
University Press

Edinburgh University Press is one of the leading university presses in the UK. We publish academic books and journals in our selected subject areas across the humanities and social sciences, combining cutting-edge scholarship with high editorial and production values to produce academic works of lasting importance. For more information visit our website: edinburghuniversitypress.com

Edinburgh University Press Ltd
13 Infirmary Street,
Edinburgh, EH1 1LT

First published in hardback by Edinburgh University Press 2023

Typeset in 11/13 Adobe Sabon by
IDSUK (DataConnection) Ltd

A CIP record for this book is available from the British Library

ISBN 978 1 3995 1973 1 (hardback)
ISBN 978 13995 1974 8(paperback)
ISBN 978 1 3995 1975 5 (webready PDF)
ISBN 978 1 3995 1976 2 (epub)

Contents

For
Louis Greenspan
1934–2018

In this space there is not only my vision of you, but information from Moscow Radio that's being broadcast at the present moment and the seeing of somebody from Peru. All the radio waves are just the same kind of waves, only longer waves. And then the radar from the airplane, which is looking at the ground trying to figure out where it is, is coming through this room at the same time. Plus the X-rays, and cosmic rays, and all these other things, the same kind of waves, exactly the same waves, but shorter, faster, or longer, slower, exactly the same thing. So this big field, this area of irregular motions of an electric field of vibration contains this tremendous information, and IT'S ALL REALLY THERE, that's what gets you! . . . So all these things are going through the room at the same time, which everybody knows, but you've got to stop and think about it to really get the pleasure about the complexity, the INCONCEIVABLE nature of nature.

Richard Feynman, BBC interview, July 1983

The sea was indistinguishable from the sky, except that the sea was slightly creased as if a cloth had wrinkles in it. Gradually as the sky whitened a dark line lay on the horizon dividing the sea from the sky and the grey cloth became barred with thick strokes moving, one after the another, beneath the surface, following each other, pursuing each other, perpetually. As they neared the shore the bar rose, heaped itself, broke and swept a thin veil of white water across the sand. The wave paused, and then drew out again, sighing like a sleeper whose breath comes and goes unconsciously [. . .]

Virginia Woolf, *The Waves*, 1931

On the waves, there is nothing but waves.

Carl Schmitt, *The Nomos of the Earth*, 1950

Series Editors' Preface

Technological transformation has profound and frequently unforeseen influences on art, design and media. At times technology emancipates art and enriches the quality of design. Occasionally it causes acute individual and collective problems of mediated perception. Time after time technological change accomplishes both simultaneously. This new book series explores and reflects philosophically on what new and emerging *technicities* do to our everyday lives and increasingly immaterial technocultural conditions. Moving beyond traditional conceptions of the philosophy of technology and of techne, the series presents new philosophical thinking on how technology constantly alters the essential conditions of beauty, invention and communication. From novel understandings of the world of technicity to new interpretations of aesthetic value, graphics and information, Technicities focuses on the relationships between critical theory and representation, the arts, broadcasting, print, technological genealogies/histories, material culture and digital technologies and our philosophical views of the world of art, design and media.

The series foregrounds contemporary work in art, design and media while remaining inclusive, in terms of both philosophical perspectives on technology and interdisciplinary contributions. For a philosophy of technicities is crucial to extant debates over the artistic, inventive and informational aspects of technology. The books in the Technicities series concentrate on present-day and evolving technological advances, but visual, design-led and mass mediated questions are emphasised to further our knowledge of their often-combined means of digital transformation.

The editors of Technicities welcome proposals for monographs and well-considered edited collections that establish new paths of investigation.

Ryan Bishop and Jussi Parikka

K-Waves

1780s

1805

1845

1873-5

1896

1929

1946-8

1973

2000

2020

1
Europe
Coal, iron, steam

- 1832 Faraday's discovery of electromagnetic waves
- 1842 Treaty of Nanjing
- 1844 First telegraphic message

2
Europe
Railways, steamships, the telegraph

- 1865 The telegraph reaches China
- 1871 Chinese telegraph code
- 1881 Nietzsche's idea of Eternal Return
- 1883 China takes control of its telegraphic lines
- 1884 The synchronization of World Time with Greenwich as the zero point
- 1896 Marconi receives a patent for the radio

3
Europe & USA
The Electric Age

- 1898 'Zhongxue wei ti, Xixue wei yong; The Hundred Day Reform; The Death of Tan Sitong
- 1902 Rudyad Kipling's story Wireless'
- 1905 Albert Einstein 'Annus Mirabilis'
- 1906 The multinational Wireless Spectrum adopts a plan to divide the electromagnetic spectrum
- 1910 Yang Wenhui establishes the Buddhist Research Society in Nanjing
- 1911 Fall of the Qing Dynasty
- 1932 Xiong Shili publishes the New Treatise on Consciousness Only

4
USA & Asia
The Electronic Age

- 1967 The first Atomic clock
- 1976 The Apple 1
- 1977 The launch of the first text satellite for GPS
- 1979 First generation of cell phones; The beginning of Opening and Reform.
- 1980 Shenzhen established as a Special Economic Zone
- 1987 Founding of Huawei
- 1988 CCTV airs River Elegy
- 1997 Geramie Barme coins the term The Great Firewall
- 2000 Beidou launches its first satellite; China enters the WTO

5
China
The Wireless Age

- 2004 Mediatek introduces a turnkey solution that facilitates the production of shanzhai phones
- 2009 Youtube and Twitter banned in China
- 2010 Google leaves China
- 2011 Wechat is launched
- 2018 Wechat reaches 1 billion users; Meng Wanzhou's Arrest
- 2019 Shanghai's Hongkou district claims to be the first area in the world with full 5G connectivity
- 2020 Gengzi; The Covid 19 Pandemic
- 2022 Shanghai Lockdown

Key Terms

Body Electric
A term linking microcosm to macrocosm. The electric energy that permeates both the human organism and the body of the Earth.

Cultivation 修 (Xiu) Nourishing Life 養生 (Yangsheng)
An ethic and embodied practice that implicates both the internal and external world. For Mou Zongsan, cultivation is the path towards Awakening or Intellectual Intuition.

Constant Transformation 恆轉 (Hengzhuan)
The idea of continuous change, fundamental to the wave ontology of Xiong Shili.

Contraction and Expansion 翕闢 (Xi/Pi)
Concepts found in the Yijing and made use of by Xiong Shili. The rhythmic forces of productive power that are responsible for both mental and material manifestations.

Ether 以太 (Yitai)
The medium of cosmic interconnectedness; central to the philosophy of Tan Sitong.

Occult Materialism
A philosophical outlook, prevalent in the nineteenth century, that linked the unseen power of electricity to forces of the occult.

Qi 氣
The vital force or energy of the cosmos. The central principle of Chinese medicine, Taichi and other Qi Gong practices.

Ren 仁
A central Confucian virtue, often translated as 'benevolence' or 'humaneness'. Critical to the thought of Tan Sitong.

Sentient City
A bottom-up, distributed form of urban intelligence that can be contrasted with the Smart City, which is characterised by top-down control.

Shanzhai 山寨
An anarchic culture and mode of cell phone production, based on the copy, which emerged from the street markets and urban villages of Shenzhen.

Ten Thousand Things 萬物 (Wanwu)
A Chinese religio-philosophical term for the myriad nature of manifest reality.

Ti/Yong 體/用
A conceptual pair prominent in Daoist, Buddhist and Confucian philosophy mobilised by nineteenth-century scholar officials to help conceptualise the relationship of Chinese tradition to modern technology.

Transcendental Materialism
The idea that the *a priori* conditions of experience are found in the material world rather than located in the mind of the rational subject.

Yijing 易經 (The Book of Changes)
One of the oldest and most important of China's classical texts; integral to the philosophy of Xiong Shili.

Yin/Yang 陰陽
Twinned elemental forces which serve as a foundation for Chinese cosmology.

Yogacara
The Buddhist 'Nothing but Consciousness School' whose modern revival in the nineteenth century made an enormous impact on both Tan Sitong and Xiong Shili.

Zone
A site of exteriority that is used strategically in the realm of politics and socio-economics; a demarcation of the outside in science fiction and philosophy.

Key Characters

Liang Qichao 梁啟超 (1873–1929)
One of China's most prominent modernist reformers. A friend of Tan Sitong who helped disseminate his writings after his death.

Meng Wanzhou 孟晚舟 (1972–)
The CFO of Huawei and the daughter of the company's founder Ren Zhengfei. Meng was arrested in Canada during a dispute between China and America over the future of 5G.

Mou Zongsan 牟宗三 (1909–95)
Widely considered one of China's most important philosophers. His work synthesises New Confucianism with Buddhist and Kantian thought. A student of Xiong Shili.

Wang Fuzhi 王夫之 (1619–92)
A neo-Confucian philosopher and proponent of the School of Vital Stuff; an important precursor to the thought of Tan Sitong, Xiong Shili and Mou Zongsan.

Tan Sitong 譚嗣同 (1865–98)
A key figure in the 1898 reforms whose writings connect the science of electricity and the ether with traditional Chinese thought.

Xiong Shili 熊十力 (1885–1968)
The 'father' of New Confucianism. A teacher of Mou Zongsan.

Zhang Zhidong 張之洞 (1837–1909)
A late Qing government official who advocated modernisation and reform. His slogan 'Chinese learning for essence, Western learning for practice' 中學為體西學為用 (*Zhongxue wei ti, Xixue wei yong*) aimed to formulate a particular relationship between Chinese culture and modern machines.

Acknowledgements

This book has taken a long time to write and, after so many years, it has become very hard to untangle its many influences.

I have been exceedingly fortunate in my mentors and allies at NYU in New York, most especially Lisa Gitelman and Marita Sturken. I also want to thank Krishnendu Ray, Clay Shirky, Dan O'Sullivan and Angela Zito.

I am enormously grateful for the supportive leadership at NYU Shanghai, particularly Dean Maria Montoya and Provost Joanna Waley Cohen. My colleagues and students in the program for Interactive Media Arts at NYU Shanghai have managed to foster a remarkably positive work environment that is able to withstand even the most trying of times.

For guidance on the writing process, I turned to my old friends Michelle Murphy and Silvia Lindtner, who both directed me to Alan Klima and the helpful writing practices and community he has developed at Academic Muse. I also want to thank Silvia for the research we did together with David Li on the *shanzhai* culture of Shenzhen, and for introducing me to the talented editor Heath Sledge.

This book has benefited enormously at various stages from the invaluable input of Amy Ireland who has corrected small details, offered insightful advice on conceptual structure and helped me articulate the project's large intellectual scope.

I read fragments of philosophers in Chinese with the aid of a very smart and patient teacher, Jiani Lian. Yifan Hu, a gifted friend and former student, helped with some final editing and designed the K-wave diagram at the front of the book. I am also thankful for the copy-editing help of Tian Tian Wedgwood Young and Feifan Li.

I have enjoyed working with Benjamin Bratton over the past few years and am extremely grateful to him for introducing me to the wonderfully generous and supportive editors of the Technicities Series at Edinburgh University Press, Ryan Bishop, Jussi Parikka and Carol Macdonald.

I have workshopped the book at various stages and have had many influential conversations with friends and colleagues in China, Europe and North America. I want to thank them for pointing to relevant writings, asking insightful questions, suggesting various directions and offering guidance as I think through ideas. I have especially appreciated comments by Bogna Konior, David Perry, Weixian Pan, Xuenan Cao, Monika Lin, Rodolfo Cossovich, Lu Teng, Lu Zhao, Lena Scheen, Duane Corpis, Jonathan Soffer, Almaz Zelleke, Allison de Fren, Deepti Gupta, Carlos Rojas, Joshua Neves, Jefferey Wasserstrom, Katherine Hayles, James Miller, Zhen Zhang, Suzanne Livingston, Steve Goodman and Lawrence Lek.

Amy Goldman has helped with the book, along with much else in my life.

A special thanks also goes to Brad Weslake for his meticulous notes on a draft of my manuscript and for our many discussions in the Philosophy and Neuroscience reading group and in the class we co-teach on the Philosophy of Technology.

My life as a scholar is enormously enriched by my regular 10 a.m. phone calls with Francesca Tarocco, and I am thankful for our ongoing conversation, which now spans many years, on culture, history, philosophy and religion.

I am continually inspired by the intense creativity of my family – my mother Sheila, my brother Jeremy, my children Max and Zoe and always and especially Nick.

This book is dedicated to my father Louis. I remember discussing an outline with him in a coffee shop on one of our final outings before he died. He was as wise and thoughtful as ever. I am forever thankful for his companionship.

Preface

Since I first came to Shanghai two decades ago, the urban landscape has been utterly transformed. I have watched as the city built more than a dozen new subway lines, two of the world's highest towers and thousands of skyscrapers. Vast neighbourhoods have been torn down and reconstructed. Countless new parks and museums have miraculously appeared. Streets that were once lined with cheap dumpling and noodle stands now house hyper-designed boutiques and bars. The year I arrived it was announced that the city would host the 2010 World Expo. The event, which occurred on the heels of the 2008 Beijing Olympics, was promoted as part of 'China's coming out party'. Shanghai, at the dawn of the millennium, was ambitiously reanimating itself as a hub of cosmopolitan modernity. In doing so, it manifested a complex urban futurism, which my previous book, *Shanghai Future*, explored.[1]

This book was inspired by a transformation in the city's media landscape, a change that is more subtle, but no less profound. In 2002 Shanghai still had attended public telephone booths. These were often housed in small, decrepit buildings, commonly found at the entrance to a lane. They were easily identified by the oversized orange telephones that were placed on a shelf outside the main window. Patrons leaned inside to speak with the agent/s (in my neighbourhood, an elderly couple), who operated the phone and sold prepaid and long-distance phone cards.

Every day government newspapers were posted on public boards in parks and in residential communities. In the mornings old people would gather around to read and discuss the main headlines. Magazine stands were located every couple of blocks. The kiosks sold newspapers, magazines, cartoons, small toys, drinks and sweets that school children would buy at the end of the day. Foreign news was harder to find. Although the Internet was available and censorship was relatively limited, the landlines were still slow and unreliable. Expats and travellers tended to frequent the business centres of five-star hotels where they could pick up copies of the *New York*

Times or *Wall Street Journal*. Out-of-date issues of magazines such as *Newsweek*, *Time* and *The Economist* could often be found in the stores and stalls that traded in pirated DVDs.

In my initial years in China I used a silver Motorola to make phone calls and send text messages. Unlike today, street stalls sold SIM cards with Chinese phone numbers that could be installed without registration. As the Beijing Olympics and the World Fair drew closer, smartphones arrived. The city was soon flooded with both big-name brands (Apple opened its huge pilot store to great fanfare in Shanghai's Pudong district in 2010) as well as the pirated phones 山寨機 (*shanzhai ji*) that had started to pour out of the markets of Shenzhen.

By the second decade of the twenty-first century, one could already sense that the mediasphere in Shanghai was leapfrogging ahead. Landing at Toronto airport every summer, I started to joke that the only real way to tell that one had entered North America was by comparing the size of everyone's phones (Asian phones were substantially more compact). By 2020 life in Shanghai had become unnavigable without a mobile device. Although by law vendors had to accept cash, in practice, in many places, mobile payments were the only way to shop. Taxis didn't stop for anyone one who didn't hail them with an app. Alipay and Wechat, the two e-commerce and messaging super apps, were ubiquitous. With the outbreak of the coronavirus pandemic and the implementation of the health registration code it became literally impossible to enter or move around China without a smartphone that could generate a green QR code. The visible urban landscape had become entirely immersed in invisible wireless waves.

This book has been written primarily for those who are interested in our contemporary media environment. Its argument, at the most basic level, is a simple one: China and the current epoch of wirelessness are intimately intertwined. To understand the present technological era, therefore, requires an engagement with China. My hope is that the book will also appeal to those who know China well, and that my own engagement with Chinese technological modernity will succeed in presenting what might seem familiar in a new light.

It has become common for media scholars in the West to turn to earlier thinkers to help conceptualise the contemporary media environment (see, for example, Mark Hansen's work on Alfred North Whitehead or Adrian Mackenzie's work on William James).[2] This book is based on a synthesis of media theory from Europe and America and modern Chinese thought. It focuses specifically on the work of three critical figures in modern Chinese intellectual history: Tan Sitong 譚嗣同 (1865–98), Xiong Shili 熊十力 (1885–1968) and Mou Zongsan 牟宗三 (1909–95).[3] In exploring their ideas alongside those of media theorists from the West, the book develops a wave philosophy[4] that posits a cosmo-ontology, which enables new ways of thinking about our current wireless age.

It is now over two years since the first Covid-19 outbreak began in Wuhan. The world has become dramatically and unexpectedly closed and Shanghai's cosmopolitanism seems increasingly precarious. In this hardening atmosphere, 'China' is often equated with the authoritarian power of the State – an association eagerly put forward by both the Chinese Communist Party (CCP) and the *New York Times*. Yet the question of what we mean – or rather the many things we mean – by 'China' has long been contested, both by the country's own historians and in the rich scholarship of the Sinophone diaspora.[5] Literary scholar David Wang remarks that the question, 'What is China?', which is clichéd but fundamental, returns again and again in the field of Chinese studies.[6] Responses are wide, varied and fiercely debated. Is China a political entity, a cultural continuity, a national imaginary, a linguistic collective, an essentialising identity? Is its locality, culture or ethnicity singular or multiple? 'Language, culture, civilization, people, nation, polity – how does one describe, interpret, and understand "China"?'[7]

My own approach to these questions, like that of a number of recent theorists, involves returning to a time in the late nineteenth and early twentieth centuries at the end of the Qing Empire and the beginning of the modern state.[8] This was an immensely fertile period intellectually, with a multiplicity of rich and nuanced ideas about the country and its culture, and their relation to technological modernity.[9] China was in an extremely unsettled state. Thinkers of the period grappled with how to integrate knowledge and practices that had consolidated over centuries with an emerging world that was becoming thoroughly dependent on electric machines. In doing so, a number of them began to articulate a philosophy of the wave. Although this perspective belonged to a marginalised subcurrent of late Qing thought, it produces a conceptual line that connects with our current wireless age in ways that provide rich, nuanced and novel understandings of contemporary China and its profound effect in shaping the technologies of the twenty-first-century world.

Notes

1. Anna Greenspan, *Shanghai Future: Modernity Remade* (New York: Oxford University Press, 2014).
2. Mark Hansen, *Feed Forward: On the Future of Twenty-First-Century Media* (Chicago: University of Chicago Press, 2015); Adrian Mackenzie, *Wirelessness: Radical Empiricism in Network Cultures* (Cambridge, MA: MIT Press, 2010).

3. For non-native Chinese speakers, the possibility of making these connections is only very recent. Although I did read large sections of primary texts in the original, with the invaluable help of a Classical Chinese teacher, much of my engagement with these thinkers was made possible due to new translations. Mou Zongsan's work, for example, has only begun to be translated into English. Jason Clower's *Late Works of Mou Zongsan* appeared in 2014, while John Makeham's translation of Xiong Shili's *New Treatise on the Uniqueness of Consciousness* came out in 2015. My hope is that this book lies on the cusp of a period of intensive translation, which, like those of the past, will open up new lines of comparative thought and fertile moments of intellectual exchange.

4. The most common character for wave in the texts I am working with is *bo* 波. This is also the character used to describe electric waves 電波 (*dian bo*). Xiong Shili also uses the character *ou* 漚. Both terms connote froth, ripples or bubbles. Larger waves are more often referred to as *lang* 浪. For more on Xiong Shili's use of *ou* 漚, see John Makeham, 'Xiong Shili and the *Treatise on Awakening Mahāyāna Faith* as Revealed in *Record to Destroy Confusion and Make My Tenets Explicit*', in *The Awakening of Faith and New Confucian Philosophy*, ed. John Makeham (Leiden: Brill, 2021).

5. Zhaoguang Ge, *What is China? Territory, Ethnicity, Culture, and History*, trans. Michael Gibbs Hill (Cambridge, MA: Harvard University Press, 2018); Shu-mei Shih, Chien-hsin Tsai and Brian Bernards, eds, *Sinophone Studies: A Critical Reader* (New York: Columbia University Press, 2013).

6. David Der-wei Wang, 'Sailing to the Sinophone World: On Modern Chinese Literary Cartography', public lecture at Cambridge University, 2014, https://www.youtube.com/watch?v=2F5ZdEyMgA8.

7. Ien Ang, *On Not Speaking Chinese: Living Between Asia and the West* (London: Routledge, 2001), 37.

8. Shaoling Ma, *The Stone and the Wireless: Mediating China, 1861–1906* (Durham, NC: Duke University Press, 2021).

9. Although this book uses the language of modernity, I take the point raised by Andrew Jones in his book *Developmental Fairy Tales* that historically it was more common for people to refer instead to terms such as 'development' and 'growth' (*fazhan*, 發展, *fada*, 發達). Andrew Jones, *Developmental Fairy Tales: Evolutionary Thinking and Modern Chinese Culture* (Cambridge, MA: Harvard University Press, 2011), 15.

Introduction: Historical Waves, Electric Waves, Wave Philosophy

In the late nineteenth century, when Heinrich Hertz first proved the existence of electromagnetic frequencies, he could see no practical purpose for his experiments. 'It's of no use whatsoever', he is reported to have said. 'This is just an experiment that proves Maestro Maxwell was right, we just have these mysterious electromagnetic waves that we cannot see with the naked eye. But they are there.' Today, these invisible vibrations provide a communication channel that is occupied by an increasing number of smart devices embedded in all aspects of life. At the beginning of the twentieth century radio used the airwaves to broadcast telegraphic signals across the sea; by the century's end, the mobile phone was spreading across the planet faster than any device in history; and now, in the twenty-first century, 5G networks consisting of wearables and the Internet of Things promise a web of billions of interconnected objects. Our electromagnetic atmosphere has intensified, powering a machinic realm that grows ever more ubiquitous, autonomous and sentient.

Nowhere is this more so than in urban China, where a hyper-dense network of mobile devices has completely transformed everyday existence. Mobile phones are used to access the largest e-commerce platforms in the world. QR codes are omnipresent and form the semiotic of a vast sharing economy that includes bikes, umbrellas and phone chargers. WeChat, the immensely popular messaging app found on every mobile phone, is used to talk to friends, colleagues and business partners.[1] Mobile payment platforms, built by tech giants Alibaba and Tencent, have become so successful that everyone from fruit sellers to street beggars has stopped using cash. During the coronavirus pandemic, mammoth Internet platforms joined with government services to create a 'sensing layer' of QR codes and mobile phone signals, which were used as an extremely effective epidemiological tool to manage the disease throughout China's megacities.[2]

China is thus deeply entwined in the intensification of wireless waves. By the second decade of the twenty-first century, China and this mutating media environment have become thoroughly entangled. Outside China the alliance provokes fear: the threat of a temporal, technological and geographical concurrence seems to grow ever darker and more dystopian, as planetary computation is envisioned as becoming subject to a single transcendent authority – a master switch controlled by Beijing. This 'techno-orientalist fabrication of China as a distant authoritarian society in the future with vast resources at its disposal' has been both reinforced and accelerated by the expansion of techno-authoritarian rule that consolidated after the outbreak of Covid-19.[3] In the aftermath, the techno-autocrats gained enormous new powers. Sinophobia and technophobia have become almost indistinguishable.

Yet there is an alternative notion of Sinofuturism that eludes these narratives by incorporating a complex temporal twist. In his 2016 video essay *Sinofuturism*, simulation artist Lawrence Lek defines Sinofuturism as a 'science fiction that already exists'. His strategy is to embrace the cultural stereotypes of China as a name-less, faceless swarm. Rather than resist the impression of China as a machinic society, his speculative, hyperstitional[4] essay positively takes up the computational characteristics of Chinese culture, such as copying, gaming and the tireless capacity for work. Implicit in this embrace is a challenge to the timeline. *Sinofuturism* functions as 'a retrospective manifesto' for a distributed movement made from a multiplicity of flows. 'I propose', says the film's narrator, 'that Sinofuturism is a form of Artificial Intelligence', spread across billions of people and things.

This apparent affinity between China and modern technology, however, is really quite new. Sinofuturism – at least in certain formu-lations – belongs to a particular historical epoch. In the nineteenth century, when the planet first electrified, Chinese culture was consid-ered to be incompatible with the rapid pace of technological change. Many within China resisted the new media, treating it as a foreign invasion – a form of exotic modernisation that was associated with the West. Alongside this rejection, however, was a profound attempt to contend with modernity. China's early encounter with electronic media in the late nineteenth and early twentieth centuries generated a moment of great intellectual ferment. There were intense debates around cultural compatibility as scholar officials of the late Qing dynasty and early Republican period sought to reconcile older Chinese cultural traditions with the use of new technologies that had just landed on their shores.

Techno-culture is ultimately rooted in cosmology. As such it involves a model of time. The idea that the trajectory of modern technology follows a progressive advance, for example, is bound to the eschatological temporality encoded in the Abrahamic religious traditions. The possibility of a Chinese cosmotechnics, as philosopher Yuk Hui has written, necessarily involves an alternative conception of time.[5] In its richest conceptualisations, Sinofuturism does not simply imply a change in the future, but rather involves a shift in the notion of the future as such. This book uses the idea or figure of the wave to reimagine the relationship between China and wirelessness. It focuses on waves of various scales, from the long slow rhythms of techno-cultural history to the high-speed frequencies of electromagnetic machines, and argues that now, in the fifth long cycle of techno-capitalist time, with the rollout of fifth-generation cellular networks, these two kinds of waves, which occupy radically different frequencies, converge. It is within this fifth wave concurrence that China's geopolitical rise has become increasingly intermeshed with the infrastructure of our wireless world. Wave cosmo-ontology further contends that these empirical, concrete and phenomenal manifestations are the expression of a deeper, more intrinsic reality, which is characterised by a continuous wave-like change.

5G

In a world composed of waves, individuation is best understood in terms of events – a singular momentary disturbance that causes long-range ripple effects. Theoretical physicist Carlo Rovelli details such a vision in his book *The Order of Time*. He describes a world that does not consist of people and things but is composed instead of countless events – something that *occurs*, not something that *is*. 'Even things that are most "thing-like"', he writes, 'are nothing more than long events.' All that we think of as stable, permanent and hard 'is in reality a complex vibration of quantum fields, a momentary interaction of forces, a process that for a brief moment manages to keep its shape, to hold itself in equilibrium before disintegrating in dust'. Our world, says Rovelli, 'is not so much made of stones as of fleeting sounds, or of waves moving through the sea'.[6] Philosopher Gilles Deleuze, writing about the 'process philosophy' of Alfred North Whitehead, outlines a similar way of looking at the world. Whitehead's lectures on *Process and Reality*, which were given in the wake of Einstein's revolution in physics, evoke a fluid cosmology made up entirely of occasions. For Whitehead the world is made up of 'events, and nothing but events: happenings rather than things, verbs rather than nouns, processes rather than substances'.[7] Events or occasions, 'passages of Nature', are the components of reality.[8] Deleuze's book A *Thousand Plateaus*, which he co-authored with Félix Guattari, is structured around a series of threshold events, each of which is marked by a date. Dates, the authors contend, indicate a mode of individuation that is different from a place, a person, a thing. 'A season, a winter, a summer, an hour, a date have perfect individuality lacking nothing, even though this individuality is different from that of a thing or a subject.'[9] Dates are the semiotic of events.

1 December 2018. Two critical episodes, purportedly unrelated, coincide. The first was a much-anticipated meeting in Argentina at the tail end of the Asia Pacific Economic Summit between the then presidents of China and the United States, Xi Jinping 習近平 and Donald Trump. Little of substance was discussed, but there was hope that a friendly sign between the leaders of these two giant nations – one waxing, one waning – would signal the beginning of an end to a trade war that had been escalating for months. On the same day, in a more backstage but ultimately more pivotal incident, Meng Wanzhou 孟晚舟, chief financial officer and deputy chairwoman of Huawei, one of the largest and most important telecom companies in the world, was arrested at Vancouver airport in Canada for extradition to the US. Meng, who is the daughter of Huawei's founder Ren Zhengfei 任正非 and was widely seen as the successor to one of China's most powerful IT firms, was accused of bank fraud in relation to an alleged shell company charged with violating the American embargo in Iran.

Lurking in the background of these concurrent events was China's intensifying role in the infrastructure of fifth-generation wireless media. Techno-capitalism – as the very term 5G signals – arrives in waves. The first generation of mobile technology, which could only make and receive phone calls, was launched in Tokyo in 1979. Since then, a new generation of cellular networks has been introduced every decade. Each generation uses faster technology capable of accessing higher frequencies of the electromagnetic spectrum, which open new channels of communication. 2G allowed for text as well as voice calls. 3G, which was unveiled at the turn of the millennium, was based on an even more radical innovation. In enabling mobile data, 3G networks powered the global spread of smartphones that quickly came to alter even the most intimate details of everyday life. 4G, which was used throughout the 2010s, shifted the user experience by enabling the streaming of content. The rollout of 5G, however, which will take place throughout the 2020s, heralds an even more revolutionary mutation.

Fifth-generation networks provide the platform for a new mode of wireless communication in which everything is online all the time. '5G is much more transformative than the shift from 3G to 4G', states Paul Triolo, an expert in the geopolitics of technology.[10] More significant than faster download speeds for consumer mobile networks is the massive scope of machine-to-machine communications, which enable autonomous vehicles, roboticised factories and ubiquitous Augmented Reality (AR). Huawei's Future Network Team envisions a 5G-enabled 'Network 2030' in which 'all things are connected, all things are sensing, and all things are intelligent'. Online experience is imagined as a fully immersive environment populated by holographic avatars, like remote robot surgeons, which are capable of touch as well as sight and sound. In analysing Huawei's projections, theorist Edmund Berger writes of this transition as a shift away from the primacy of the optical regime that characterises Web 2.0 towards a new 'tactile network', which produces a more haptic space for telepresence, enabling a richer participation in the sensory realm.[11] 5G is what is facilitating the spread of metaverse and cryptographic technologies embedded in the emergence of Web 3.0.

China's relation to 5G is guided by an ardent techno-nationalism that has global ambitions. The country's approach to 5G networks emerged from – but also in contrast to – the attitude it took to the rollout of 3G, which was much more internally focused.[12] Having previously failed to impact global mobile network standards, 'no country', says Triolo, 'has devoted more effort in preparing the ground for 5G than China'.[13] Of special note is the extent to which China's investment in 5G outpaced America's. A report by Deloitte states that 'since 2015, China outspent the United States by approximately $24 billion in wireless communications infrastructure and built 350,000 new sites, while the United States built fewer than 30,000'. In 2017 China Tower, the largest telecom tower operator in the world, added almost 500 new sites per day. It built more towers in three months than US tower companies and carriers had added in the previous three years. The 'United States', Deloitte reports, 'underspent China in wireless infrastructure by $8 billion to $10 billion per year since 2015'. Due to network effects and first mover advantage, the report concludes, China 'may be creating a 5G tsunami, making it near impossible to catch up'.[14]

The most powerful force in this tsunami is Huawei 華為. At the time of Meng's arrest, Huawei was the only company in the world capable of producing 'all the elements of a 5G network, at scale and at cost'.[15] Huawei, Triolo explained, is 'almost unique amongst the global players in that it can produce all elements of the network from handsets to data centers to everything in between'.[16] The company worked hard to gain a voice in the setting of global standards, challenging the control of licensing arrangements that had long been held by giant legacy companies in Europe and America (Qualcomm, Ericsson, Nokia). Huawei's goal was to position itself at the forefront of a new global infrastructure, slated to cost hundreds of billions of dollars.

More than any other IT firm, Huawei came to be associated with the nationalism embedded in China's global technological aspirations. Yet it did not start out that way. The company was founded in 1987 by Ren Zhengfei. In telling his own biography, Ren, a notoriously secretive figure, stresses his upbringing in a small town in Guizhou, one of China's poorest provinces. His formative period occurred during the Cultural Revolution, when 'there was chaos almost everywhere'.[17] His father, a school teacher, was denounced as a 'Capitalist Roader'. It was during this period that Ren served in the army as an engineer. He left the military just as China began its process of Reform and Opening, going to work in a state-owned enterprise (SOE) in Shenzhen.

According to Ren, Huawei was registered with a total investment of 21,000 rmb, money that he and his wife borrowed from family and friends. Unlike many of his competitors, Ren did not start off by partnering with a foreign firm. As a private company, moreover, Huawei, at least initially, was not particularly favoured by the government banks. Instead, the company used the typical Shenzhen formula of copying and reverse engineering, assembling routers in the markets that were surfacing in and around *Huaqiangbei* 華強北. It focused its attention where others weren't looking, operating in the cracks of the global economy. In adopting these tactics, Huawei was influenced by the *shanzhai* culture of the 1980s and the intimate ties that were being formed between the hyper-metropolis on the Pearl River Delta and the explosive growth of wireless machines.[18] While China's mainstream telecom companies concentrated on the large cities and more built-up areas, Huawei saw an opportunity in neglected, underdeveloped rural regions. It got its start by testing its telecom infrastructure in the remote north-east. In company mythology it is said that Ren followed the Maoist guerrilla strategy of 'surrounding the city with the countryside'. A similar approach was followed in its international expansion. Huawei focused first on developing countries in Asia, Latin America and Africa. By 2018 it had expanded into 170 countries, with more than 13,000 suppliers from around the world.

In the mid-1990s the pendulum swung, and the company gained substantial government support such that by the dawn of 5G, Huawei was closely aligned with the state. Ren Zhengfei, who has a background in the People's Liberation Army, and fosters a highly disciplined and cryptic corporate culture, is assumed to have deep links with the Party. Suspicions were confirmed after Meng's detention prompted a series of harsh retaliatory moves by the Chinese government, including the detention and severe sentencing of Canadians in China.[19] Huawei became a critical part of Xi Jinping's 'Made in China 2025' policy, which aimed at increasing self-reliance in emerging areas of high tech, and was widely seen as one of the lightning rod issues in the trade tensions between China and the US. In 2019 long-time tech watcher Jeremy Goldkorn noted that Huawei had become an avatar for the threat of the Chinese state's looming technological dominance.[20]

In the aftermath of Meng's arrest global distrust of Huawei intensified, especially in America, where the suspicions and accusations against the company reached fever pitch. Meng's indictment triggered a turning point, a sudden realisation that the rise of China and the advance of wireless media were inextricably linked. Crucial government decisions on contracts and investments were imminent, and there was a growing sentiment that whoever dominated the 5G networks would gain a critical technological, economic and military edge. On 25 February 2019 the *New York Times* ran a podcast, which began: 'The US believes whoever controls 5G will have a global advantage for decades to come – the fear is that China is already there.'[21]

Amid this growing anxiety there was an extensive push to boycott Huawei products due to a perceived risk of espionage. The Americans led a forceful offensive, threatening a blanket ban and repercussions for any country that allowed Chinese telecoms to play a role in the construction of their communication infrastructure. The campaign against Huawei focused on security, stressing the surveillance capacities of the new technology amid China's growing authoritarianism. Fears started to mount of a new war that would begin with the unplugging of a country's communications grid. Wireless platforms built by Huawei, the US warned, would ultimately be controlled by the Communist Party.[22] Speaking at the Munich security conference in 2019, then Vice President Mike Pence tried to persuade Europe to exclude Chinese telecoms, stating: 'We cannot ensure the defense of the West if our allies grow dependent on the East.'[23] Huawei, which only months before had been little known outside China, gained immense worldwide notoriety amid talk of decoupling global supply chains and the beginning of a new Cold War. The international clash between China and the United States over 5G seemed to anticipate a broader impending technological and geopolitical transition of power. Commenting in the *New Yorker*, Jiayang Fan compared Meng's case to that of the Chinese villager Lin Weixi, whose death in 1839 at the hands of British merchant sailors is said to have sparked the Opium War. 'How the nations involved choose to proceed at this juncture, two hundred years later', she concluded ominously, 'may come to define the terms of Sino-American engagement for many years to come.'[24]

The convergence of China and wireless media constitutes an event composed through a series of nested vibrations. The catalytic episode of the arrest of Huawei's CFO, which marked the moment the world recognised that the growth of China was intertwined with the arrival of fifth-generation wireless media, created ripple effects in an ongoing and profound geopolitical struggle both within and beyond China. The event, writes Deleuze, 'is a vibration with an infinity of harmonics or submultiples, such as an audible wave, a luminous wave, or even an increasingly smaller part of space over the course of an increasingly shorter duration'.[25] From the high-speed frequencies of electromagnetic media to the long, slow cycles of capitalist time, all these waves ultimately follow the rhythms of a still more enveloping and elemental pulsation.

The Fifth Wave

China and cellular technology have long been aligned. 1979 not only marked the beginning of the first generation of cellular networks, it was also the year that China unveiled its policies of Reform and Opening 改革開放 (*gai ge kai fang*). Mobile phones started to infiltrate the planet at precisely the same moment that Shenzhen, the southern coastal city on the Pearl River Delta, was declared a Special Economic Zone. Since then, the mushrooming megacity has established itself as a global hub: the place where most of the world's wireless devices are made. The city's phenomenal growth has become one of the most vital manifestations of China's remarkable rise. It is positioned at the heart of the conjunction between a rising China and the world's increasing immersion in electromagnetic vibrations. This confluence, which has been intensifying for decades, is culminating in the resonance between fifth-generation mobile technology and techno-capitalism's fifth long cycle. China's recent upswing, then, comes not as the linear advance of a neglected or backward region, but rather through a planetary ebb and flow that has come to subsume global modern history.

There is a vast literature analysing capitalist temporality as a series of involuted cycles of various lengths. The shortest, the Kitchin business cycle of 3–5 years, is nested inside the Juglar or major economic cycle of 7–11 years, which in turn is enveloped by the Kuznet swing of 15–25 years. The longest is the Kondratiev cycle, or K-wave, which lasts approximately half a century. The idea of the K-wave originated in the 1935 essay 'The Long Waves in Economic Life' by Russian economist Nikolai Kondratiev (1892–1938), who posited the existence of the long cycle through an analysis of price. 'The idea that the dynamics of economic life in the capitalist social order is not of a simple and linear but rather of a complex and cyclical character is nowadays generally recognized', he begins. 'Science, however, has fallen far short of clarifying the nature and the types of these cyclical, wave-like movements.'[26] Kondratiev's contribution was to argue that in addition to the shorter cycles already acknowledged, there is 'reason to assume the existence of long waves of an average length of 50 years'.[27] These slow frequencies of the modern world economy give shape to historical time.

The idea of the long wave was made famous by the economist Joseph Schumpeter, whose work examines the cyclical nature of the capitalist system. Schumpeter's analysis was opposed to neo-classical economics, in which mathematical modelling favoured a 'normal' state of equilibrium. He was deeply critical of a static economic theory that privileged the ideal of self-reproduction. Instead, he insisted, there was a dynamic oscillating force that pushed the economy in and out of equilibrium. 'We wish to distinguish definite periods in which the system embarks upon an excursion away from equilibrium', he wrote, 'and equally definite periods in which it draws toward equilibrium.'[28]

The capitalist economy is produced through rhythmic fluctuation; inherent swings or pulsations that make capitalism more like a living organism than a stable object. Schumpeter advocated what he called 'evolutionary economics', a theory that emphasises instability and transformation over permanence and continuity. Capitalism develops through mutations, which regularly disrupt the constant equilibrium. For Schumpeter, the economy is a process, not a thing. This ongoing development does not adhere to a consistent rate of change; rather it is marked by intermittent upheavals, studded with sudden bursts of excitement and catastrophe: '[e]volution is a disturbance of existing structures that is more like a series of explosions than a gentle, though incessant, transformation'.[29]

In aligning his ideas with the theory of the long wave, Schumpeter suggests that these periodic fluctuations, which generate evolutionary growth, follow a recognisable pattern that was described by Kondratiev in his investigation of the fifty-year cycle.[30] For Schumpeter these cycles are endogenous. They have no external causation. 'Cycles are not, like tonsils, separable things that might be treated by themselves', he insisted, 'but are, like the beat of the heart, of the essence of the organism that displays them.'[31] For Schumpeter, then, capitalism is like a living entity. The rise and fall of K-waves are its pulse.

Schumpeter did not just seek to detect economic waves. His aim was to determine their cause. How, he asks, does the economic system generate its inherent transformational force? For Schumpeter, write Freeman and Louçã in a now classic text on cyclical theory, 'it is irrelevant to explain cycles as fluctuations over a trend if the basic historical process, which generates the trend and the cycle itself, is unexplained'. This issue, they note, had vexed Kondratiev's whole academic life and work.[32] Schumpeter's own response was emphatic. Change was not caused by external disturbances such as war or natural disasters, but was rather intrinsic to the working of the economic organism itself.[33] According to Schumpeter, the fundamental source of this essential mutation was technological change. In the economic history of capitalist society, it was innovation that stood out as 'the outstanding fact'.[34] Wave theory, then, provides an exposition of modern capitalism that places machinic transformation at its heart.[35]

One of the critical observations of the Kondratiev cycle is that technological change is not uniformly distributed through history, but rather tends to cluster in accordance with the wave. Innovation ripples through the economy, beginning with certain sectors, in certain places, at certain times. 'Industrial change is never harmonious advance', wrote Schumpeter; instead its 'progress proceeds by jerks and rushes'.[36] Innovation occurs through discontinuous swarms, which are not evenly spread through time, but tend to gather around a revolutionary technology, whose deployment catalyses multiple, overlapping, feedback effects.[37] In illustrating this point, wave theorist Carlota Perez points to the IT revolution, which began with an initial constellation of technologies that clustered around microprocessors (and other integrated semiconductors), 'calculators, games, civil and military miniaturizing and digitalizing of control instruments and others'. This was followed by 'an overlapping sequence of minicomputers and personal computers, software, telecoms and Internet that have each opened new systems trajectories, while being strongly interrelated and interdependent'.[38] Tight feedback loops – both technological and economic – strengthen the overlapping interconnections.

One of the most important insights of cyclical theory is that the transformative technologies that spark these chains of related innovation tend to establish themselves in the downturn of the cycle.

In these moments of 'decreasing returns, falling investments, and exhaustion of material advancement', new inventions, often already long established, begin to disseminate.[39] As the wave's initial upward curve starts to decline, novelty becomes sparse, and there is less to attract investment. The whole system loses momentum. At this point two complementary tendencies kick in: first, in a process that echoes the Kuhnian analysis of scientific change, 'innovations that are "out of joint" with the character of the dominant paradigm begin to accumulate'; at the same time 'financial capital goes into a searching pattern. It is this convergence that helps set the conditions for the next upswing.'[40] The resulting intensive metamorphosis involves widespread and often painful adjustment. 'A new cluster of technologies will arrive on the economic stage during the downswing of a long wave', explain Peter Hall and Paschal Preston. 'Their general introduction will, however, be delayed by the need for wider socio-economic and political changes, entailing major and even agonizing transformation in the structure of society.'[41] The establishment of new technologies, infrastructures and industries revolutionises everything that comes in their wake. It is this, according to the Schumpeterian theory of the long wave, that lays the foundations for the subsequent upsurge.

> A railroad through new country, i.e., a country not yet served by railroads, as soon as it gets into working order upsets all conditions of location, all cost calculations, all production functions within its radius of influence; and hardly any way of doing things which have been optimal before remain so afterwards.[42]

At the start of each K-wave, then, is a technological paradigm shift that severely challenges the old order, giving shape to the next fifty years. Perez describes the rhythm of the continuously evolving system as follows:

> Each *great surge of development* involves a turbulent process of diffusion and assimilation. The major incumbent industries are replaced as engines of growth by new emerging ones; the established technologies and the prevailing paradigm are made obsolete and transformed by the new ones; many of the working and management skills that had been successful in the past become outdated and inefficient demanding unlearning, learning and relearning processes. Such changes in the economy are very disturbing of the social status-quo and have each time accompanied the explosive growth of new wealth with strong polarising trends in the income distribution. These and other imbalances and tensions, including a major financial bubble and its collapse, result from the technological upheaval and end up creating conditions

that require an equally deep transformation of the whole institutional framework. It is only when this is achieved and the enabling context is in place that the full wealth creating potential of each revolution can be deployed.[43]

Creative Destruction, Schumpeter's most famous doctrine, depicts these cyclical disturbances, which began with the Industrial Revolution and have, ever since, structured the whole 'organic' process of capitalist time. 'Industrial mutation – if I may use the biological term – that incessantly revolutionizes the economic structure from within, incessantly destroying the old one, incessantly creating a new one. This process of Creative Destruction is the essential fact about capitalism.'[44]

The cyclic theory postulates a rhythm of time. As such it involves both a retrospective and a predictive analysis. Yet history that is still unfolding is almost impossible to ascertain. Time is transcendental and therefore, by its nature, obscure. Our immersion in technical mutation, moreover, only becomes clear retrospectively. At the beginning of the telegraph, the telephone or the Internet nobody could know all the disruptive changes that these new machinic infrastructures would bring. For all these reasons, the idea of the K-wave, a fifty-year cycle of time, is necessarily speculative. Since Schumpeter's death, moreover, the theory has been questioned, deepened and enriched by an enormous amount of critique and debate. There remains a great deal of contention over the very existence of the waves, which only subsist in heterodox corners of economics that are comfortable entertaining non-standard and unpopular beliefs. Even among those who support the idea, there is great contestation about the length of cycles and their precise dating, whether they are fixed or variable, the types of innovation that serve as their causal mechanism, the role of organisations and social institutions, and the critical function of the state. In describing this intellectual history, Hall and Preston contend that interest in the concept itself has come in waves.[45]

The details of K-waves are, therefore, inherently hard to decipher. Theoretical differences lead to discrepancies over dates. The vertical axis on any graph is not based on a fixed metric that can track technological diffusion. The messiness ensures that cycles are not exact. Nevertheless, the theory proposes a pattern, which, crucially, encompasses space as well as time.

According to the cyclical theory, techno-capitalism's global spread is internal to the time of the wave. In their review of the theory, Hall and Preston track how temporal cycles of innovation follow a planetary geography. This idea of a 'geography of innovation' is borrowed in part from Perez, who has shown that surges of development, which begin with what she calls 'big bangs' in places where the revolution originally takes shape, tend to diffuse unevenly from core to peripheral zones. Each wave or techno-economic paradigm has a different core. The fortunes of the main industrial nations have waxed and waned as K-waves ripple across the Earth. Capitalism, notes system theorist Immanuel Wallerstein, 'is essentially one process with the whole world as its stage'.[46] At the start of the first Kondratiev cycle, Britain was the 'workshop of the world'. By the end of the second wave, industrial manufacturing had begun to relocate to America. Manchester was as much the 'cradle and the symbol of the Age of Steam' as 'Silicon Valley has been for the microelectronics revolution'.[47] The capacity for innovation, then, switches from region to region and city to city as each new wave of technological platforms rises, breaks and falls: first in Britain, then Germany, America, Japan and the Asian tigers. Cyclical theory contends that China's own modernity is subsumed by the rhythms of global techno-capitalism. Its own processes of development are internal to the wave.

The first Kondratiev wave, at the start of the Industrial Revolution, is generally said to have begun in the 1780s, with an upswing lasting approximately twenty-five years. This initial cycle, which had Britain at its centre, was based on core technologies of coal, iron and steam. During the downturn of the first wave, which lasted until the mid-1840s, foundations were laid for a new planetary infrastructure consisting of steel railways, steamships and the telegraph.

These platforms served to power the second wave, which is generally said to have lasted from the latter half of the 1840s to the late 1890s. In this period, the heart of technological change began to shift from Britain to Germany and America. Again, revolutionary technology was introduced in the final decades of the cycle. In 1876 Alexander Graham Bell was granted a patent for the telephone. In 1879 Thomas Edison lit up his laboratory at Menlo Park with the incandescent light bulb. In 1886 Karl Benz was granted a patent for the modern car. In 1896, at the bottom of the wave, Marconi received a patent for the radio, 'the first patent ever issued for a Hertzian wave'.[48]

The dissemination of these revolutionary technologies and the socio-economic and machinic mutations that came in their wake energised the third wave, the electric age, which is most commonly dated from the mid-1890s to just after the Second World War, with a peak right before the 1929 crash. The downswing of the third K-wave brought the mass industrialisation of electronics and the beginnings of digital computing.

The transistor, which was invented at Bell labs in 1947 as the wave was hitting its trough, was, as Hall and Preston write, 'without doubt one of the technological keys that opened the fourth Kondratiev'.[49] From the very start of the fourth cycle information technology became 'one of the true carrier waves of world economic development'.[50] The oil crises and the end of the gold standard in the early 1970s triggered the downswing that ended the long fourth Kondratiev boom. During the downturn, in the latter decades of the twentieth century, the telephone and the computer converged. This coincided with the deindustrialisation of America as electronic manufacturing was outsourced to Asia.

At this point the timing of cycles becomes even more speculative. It is plausible to date the end of the fourth wave to sometime around the turn of the millennium, with the bursting of the dot-com bubble. In this interpretation of the theory, we have now entered the fifth K-wave, the wireless wave, to which China is so intimately tied. The early 2020s, when 5G is set to roll out, occurs just as the fifth wave is hitting its crest. If the pattern holds, the new technological platform of high-speed electromagnetic vibrations will host the evolutionary mutations that normally accompany a downturn, which is due to end sometime in the middle of the twenty-first century.

The concurrence of the fifth Kondratiev cycle and the implementation of 5G involves the coming together of two types of waves, which occur at radically different scales. K-waves give shape to historical time. Their long, slow cycles take more than half a lifetime to complete. As they gradually crest and break over and through geographical regions, they subsume planetary space into the undulating rhythms of time. The high-frequency electromagnetic waves generated by 5G, on the other hand, constitute an immersive field of vibrating energy, which operates in fragments of time too small to perceive. The relationship between China and wireless media is determined by the interference of these two distinct temporalities. The ongoing rise and fall of K-waves provides the technological, economic and geopolitical contextualisation, while the high-speed frequencies of 5G constitute a new media environment that forms the abstract infrastructure of daily life.

Media Infrastructure

Infrastructure inhabits a position at the edges of perception, occupying a zone on the borderlands between the seen and the unseen. Critical infrastructure studies has sought to untangle this relationship, unveiling that which seeks to remain concealed. Yet the call by infrastructure studies to 'make the invisible visible' reaches a kind of limit point with the inherent imperceptibility of electromagnetic waves. The vibrational body of wirelessness forms an unseen infrastructure that, while highly technological, is also absolutely natural. This elemental media constitutes a transcendental plane, an abstract layer that conditions our experiences of the world.

Certain large-scale infrastructure projects such as the astonishing marvels of bridges or dams, for example, have long been designed to be noticed, even to awe. This tendency reaches a pinnacle in the spectacle of the TV tower. In the words of Lisa Parks:

> Television towers from Berlin to Tokyo, from Stockholm to Tehran, were designed precisely to be seen and admired from near and far. . . Jutting hundreds of feet into the sky, TV towers are capped with visitors' centres, restaurants/bars and viewing platforms, encouraging people to tour these infrastructure sites and glimpse what the world looks like from a transmitter's perspective.[51]

Materialist media theory,[52] which interrogates electronic communication less for 'what people say with it' than for 'how it works', contends that it is the overt display of these towers that matters most.[53] The importance of London's iconic GPO Tower, for example, which was built in the 1960s to support microwave aerials, comes less from the content being delivered than from the fact of its delivery. As Marshall McLuhan argued long ago, the machines of the information age – radio, telephone, television and computers – are best exemplified by electric light: a 'medium without a message'.[54] Illuminated by the empty purity of light, it becomes clear that the true significance of new technologies is the electric environment itself, which subsumes and transforms the world simultaneously. 'Environments', McLuhan insists, 'are not just containers, but are processes that change the content totally.'[55]

In no city is the visual presence of the TV tower more evident than in Shanghai. The Oriental Pearl Radio and TV Tower, which stands at the heart of the finance centre of Lujiazui, was completed in 1994, only two years after Deng Xiaoping's tour of the South, which marked the opening of Shanghai to the world. The building, which occupies a large plot near the banks of the Huangpu River, is impossible to miss. The 'Pearl Orient', as it is known, rises from a gigantic steel tripod, which supports a tower of eleven bright pink and steel silver balls. Its deliberately archaic sci-fi structure recalls Toronto's CN Tower, which was built in the 1970s, Berlin's Television Tower, which was completed in 1969, and the Seattle Space Needle, which was constructed as a landmark for the 1962 World Fair. Shanghai's extravagant TV tower deliberately embraced an archaic sci-fi architecture and thus became a main marker of the metropolis's bombastic celebration of a retrofuturist aesthetic. Still today, the Pearl Orient is one of the city's most iconic buildings and is used to symbolise the enthusiastic futurity embedded in the urban core.

In contrast to the hyper-visibility epitomised by the TV tower, much infrastructure is marked by a salient obscurity. Partly this has to do with the scale of infrastructure projects, which makes them difficult to grasp in their entirety. Their non-human proportions are temporal as well as spatial. According to Paul Edwards, 'Outside rare moments of creation or major transitions' – the heightened attention to the coming of 5G provides a particularly potent example – 'infrastructures change too slowly for most of us to notice, the stately pace of infrastructural change is part of their reassuring stability. They exist, as it were, chiefly in historical time.'[56]

This intrinsic imperceptibility, however, is accentuated by a deliberate cover-up. The concealment of our everyday surroundings – its building and upkeep – takes work. 'Infrastructures, normally taken for granted and an unspoken part of the background, must nonetheless be managed, negotiated, navigated, and made to work as a part of the environments and practices that they support.'[57] They only recede into the background through a continual, laborious maintenance regime that stays hidden in order to work.

This sense of infrastructure as an open secret – pipes and sewers, wires and towers that are everywhere apparent but still somehow hidden – is shared, as a kind of unwritten rule, among those who are already familiar with a particular landscape. To those who come from outside, this supposedly invisible backdrop is starkly apparent. Visitors to Shanghai, for example, who have walked the city's unreconstructed lanes, cannot help but notice the chaotic mass of twisted wires that are used to dry laundry, blankets and meat. For those on the inside, complicit in the play of the unseen, however, the tangled lines of the electricity and telecommunications grid fade into the background of daily life. Being taken for granted is a key sign that infrastructure is working well. 'Mature technological systems – cars, roads, municipal water supplies, sewers, telephones, railroads, weather forecasting, buildings, even computers in the majority of their uses – reside in a naturalized background', notes Edwards. They are 'as ordinary and unremarkable to us as trees, daylight, and dirt. Our civilizations fundamentally depend on them, yet we notice them mainly when they fail, which they rarely do.'[58] Infrastructure is thus only truly unveiled when it breaks down or falls apart.

The Internet seems particularly prone to this dynamic of disguise. Few pay attention to the physical systems of information distribution, with their wires, cables, plugs, settings, standards and protocols. Concentration on the 'physicality of the virtual' runs counter to a popular discourse of deterritorialised dematerialisation that has long surrounded digital technology, from Negroponte's famous formula 'from atoms to bits' to the placelessness implied in the naming of 'the cloud'.[59] Today, more than grids of pipes and wires, infrastructure includes 'pools of microwaves beaming from satellites and populations of atomized electronic devices that we hold in our hands'.[60]

The intention of critical infrastructure studies has been to interrupt this process of masking by paying attention to bridges, highways, power grids, railways, telephone lines and plumbing.[61] Susan Star thus begins her influential article 'The Ethnography of Infrastructure' with a 'call to study boring things'.[62] In heeding this call, media theorists draw awareness to 'the clunky visibility of wireless', which is deliberately camouflaged by a 'politics of infrastructural invisibility'.[63] 'Most people are socialized to know very little about the infrastructures that surround them in everyday life, whether electrical systems, sewer pipes or broadcast networks', writes Lisa Parks. 'Not only are people socialized to be unaware of such systems; infrastructures are often designed purposefully to be invisible or transparent, integrated with the built environment, whether submerged underground, covered by ceilings and walls, or camouflaged as "nature".'[64] In order to expose this 'strategy of concealment'[65] there is a deliberate scrutiny of mobile phone towers, antennae, undersea cables and fibre optic links. The stated aim of these explorations is to make 'the invisible visible', so as to see beyond the moments of breakdown and unearth the dynamics of power that are embedded in the masquerade.

Uncovering the obscurity of infrastructure has political as well as ethical implications. Large-scale technical structures are owned and operated by governments, militaries and megacorporations. They are shaped and characterised by entrenched socio-economic systems of labour, maintenance and repair. In crystallising institutional structures in an intricate web of concealment and visibility, they manifest complex systems of power and control. To counter this tendency, scholars and activists have cultivated what Shannon Mattern calls an 'infrastructural intelligence', consisting of popular writings and a plethora of 'apps and data visualizations, soundwalks and speculative design workshops, DIY manuals and field guides, urban dashboards and participatory mappings, hackathons and infrastructural tourism'.[66] Together these activities work to uncover 'the resources, technologies, labor, and relations that are required to shape, energize, and sustain the distribution of audiovisual signal traffic on global, national, and local scales'.[67] Their project is to expose the 'values and ethics inscribed in the inner depths of the information environment'.[68]

Wirelessness, however, poses an inherent challenge to this project. To the human apparatus of perception, electromagnetic waves – the ultimate body of wireless media – are not only unseen, they are unseeable. Wireless infrastructure is constituted by the physicality of telecommunication networks – satellite towers designed for the transmission of signals, as well as mobile devices that can receive and decode the information transmitted. This communicative traffic in turn depends on technical protocols, which entail political and commercial agreements. Bandwidth allocation, or the divvying up of the electromagnetic spectrum, involves both the regulatory power of states as well as the economic strength of corporations. The materiality of the electromagnetic spectrum is thus embedded in intense layers of power and politics. Yet ultimately the infrastructure of wireless media is hidden by something even deeper than human sociopolitics. Electromagnetic technologies cross into a sphere outside of all anthropomorphic design. Rather than representing human communication, mobile phones and Wi-Fi sensors function on a machinic level that is exterior to the everyday domain of human understanding. Electromagnetic machines tap into a non-human nature that exists in a realm whose frequencies are beyond our perceptual reach. They involve 'real but weird materialities that do not necessarily bend to human eyes and ears'.[69] 'The atmospheric communication, hovering over the city like a sensate cloud, moves beyond even the architectures of conduit and screen, not to the virtual but to the imperceptible.'[70] Unlike tubes and poles, satellites and antennae, the invisibility of the electromagnetic spectrum is not simply due to history, socio-economics or politics. Rather, wireless media taps into an infrastructure that is, by its very nature, beyond our perceptual range. It is this subtle, saturating, alien environment that ultimately forms the abstract infrastructure for the flood of wireless media that has come in the wake of Hertz's early experiments – the countless devices that we now carry, wear and increasingly embed in the world all around us.

Elemental Media

Modern infrastructure helps constitute the Cartesian subject as a 'master and possessor of nature'. Our capacity to control temperature and light, grow vegetables off season, and manage the flow of water creates an artificial environment suited to our needs. Within this constructed, cushioned realm, nature is constituted as something fundamentally separate and distinct. There is a widespread idea that infrastructure implies artifice and nature typically signifies its absence.[71] Yet in the end it is nature that is the 'ultimate infrastructure'.[72]

Media studies has repeatedly emphasised the 'naturalness' of the media environment. New media, McLuhan maintained, 'are not bridges between man and nature, they are nature'.[73] 'Silicon is nature!' Friedrich Kittler declared. 'Silicon is nature calculating itself.'[74] 'A philosophy of media', John Durham Peters asserts, 'needs a philosophy of nature.'[75] The Earth itself, writes Benjamin Bratton in his mapping of global computation, is 'the foundational layer within the Stack'.[76] Mobile phones, cryptocurrencies and AI all have geological foundations.[77] Theorists have been careful to stress the physical stuff that media are made of, from the trees converted to telegraph poles to the metal of wires and satellite dishes. Materialist media studies, then, has shifted its concern towards the elemental – a mode of conceptualisation to which contemporary Asian scholars have been particularly well attuned.[78] Yuriko Furuhata, for example, writes of the 'fog medium', tracking how both artistic and scientific practices function to visualise the atmosphere.[79] Rahul Mukherjee analyses the radiant cities of urban India, attending to the discourses circulating around the radioactive isotopes emitted by nuclear reactors as well as the radio waves emanating from thousands of cell antennae.[80] Melody Jue evokes the ocean as medium and milieu, which can serve to counter philosophy's terrestrial bias.[81]

Electromagnetic waves are the material substrate of wirelessness. Beneath the entanglements of hardware and politics lies an earthly, cosmic force, highly technological but at the same time wholly natural. Apps such as the Architecture of Radio, which visualises and sonifies the Wi-Fi signal your mobile phone picks up, or the walks of artist Christina Kubisch, who uses specially designed sensitive headphones to amplify the acoustic perceptibility of the electromagnetic waves latent in the urban environment, not only reveal the disguised telecommunication grids of the secular city, but also decode – in a way that we can grasp with our senses – the elemental, cosmic forces hidden in the everyday. As the high frequencies of the electromagnetic spectrum have become increasingly foundational to urban life, the sentient city – the most artificial of environments – becomes ever-more sensitive to the vibrating atmosphere of Earth's innermost geological layer.

Prior to the modern period almost nothing was known about electricity, and its ancient vibrations were only ever vaguely perceived.[82] Beginning in earnest in the eighteenth century, however, there was a deep and ongoing technological absorption into electromagnetic waves. Through a series of discoveries, driven by a practice-based culture of technological experimentation, it became increasingly clear that the natural force apparent in lightning (and in some animals) could be harnessed and put to great use. Nineteenth-century society combined invention with industry to store electricity in batteries, harness it as a means for lighting great cities, and, with the invention of the telegraph, laid the first networks for global instantaneous communication, the groundwork for today's information age. 'Electricity has become a mighty kingdom', said Heinrich Hertz over a century ago. 'We perceive it in a thousand places where we had no proof of its existence before. The domain of electricity extends over the whole of nature.'[83]

The modern discovery of electromagnetism is a tale with multiple origins. The breakthrough invention, however, is generally attributed to the experimental approach of nineteenth-century scientist Michael Faraday (1791–1867). Faraday, who was untrained in mathematics, was the son of a blacksmith, and therefore attuned to the myriad possibilities inherent in the medium of metal. Due to this unconventional background, Faraday did not adopt the familiar scientific process of abstract deduction. Instead, he created machines that were designed to test his ideas about the workings of the electrical world. Through this practice of empirical experiment and observation, Faraday began to uncover how 'sources of electricity and magnetism produce force fields that take on a life of their own'.[84] Faraday's experiments with electric and magnetic fields 'opened the door to an entirely new dimension of the universe'.[85] With his explorations into the strange new world of electricity, Faraday 'ultimately changed the way natural philosophers viewed the world'.[86]

The idea that electromagnetics occurred in waves was Faraday's discovery. He was inspired by seeing the experiments of the German physicist and musician Ernst Chladni, who first made sound waves visible by testing the impact of acoustic vibrations on metal plates that were lightly covered with sand. In contemplating the phenomena unleashed by his machines, Faraday began to suspect that 'magnetic and electric forces must be transmitted over time by vibrations or waves in the intervening medium, rather like acoustic pressure in the air'.[87] In 1832 he wrote a letter to the Royal Society detailing these speculations. In it he wrote:

> I am inclined to compare the diffusion of magnetic forces from a magnetic pole to the vibrations upon the surface of disturbed water or those of air in the phenomena of sound; i.e. I am inclined to think the vibratory theory will apply to these phenomena, as it does to sound and, most probably, to light.[88]

Anxious that his vibratory theory might be too radical, Faraday sealed the letter, which remarkably remained unopened for more than a hundred years until 1937, when it was finally read. This time lag, as G. R. M. Garratt suggests, echoes Faraday's theoretical suspicion that there was a temporal dimension to the transmission of magnetic forces.[89] Time was foundational to the idea of waves.

Proof for the existence of electromagnetic waves came first through the mathematics of James Clerk Maxwell (1831–79) and then, later, by way of the technological tinkering of Heinrich Hertz (1857–94). The knowledge this provoked produced a revolution in science, which fundamentally challenged our intuitive assumptions, engendering a profound transition in our understanding of the material world. According to the earlier, mechanistic vision, the world was essentially atomistic, consisting primarily of the motions of concrete material points. Newton, who inherited the classical mechanistic model, was puzzled by the force of gravity that did not appear to be the direct result of some local, concrete physical source. 'The 300-year thorn of nonlocality', as Rivka Galchen and David Albert clearly explain, disappeared with Maxwell's discovery of the electromagnetic field, which posited that there was something in the universe other than material bodies. With Maxwell, they write, 'the fundamental ontology – the furniture of the universe – essentially doubled. There were now material bodies, and fields. And both were real.'[90] The classical model concentrated on the world of perceptible objects and the empirical realm of human sensation. With the discovery of electricity, however, physical reality was no longer mechanically explicable. As the model of 'colliding billiard balls that could be touched and measured' dissolved, there came a recognition that the foundations of physics are abstract and imperceptible. The only ways to gain access were through mathematical theorisation or machinic perception. Now, instead of matter in motion, the world consisted of vibrations in a field.

The scientific exploration of nature thus shifted away from external objects that could be easily grasped by the senses. Electronic media emerged from within this paradigm shift. 'From a long view of the history of mankind – seen from, say, ten thousand years from now', states physicist Richard Feynman, 'there can be little doubt that the most significant event of the Nineteenth Century will be judged as Maxwell's discovery of the laws of electrodynamics.'[91] Albert Einstein concurred: 'when James Clerk Maxwell discovered the mathematical equations that modeled electromagnetics, one scientific epoch ended and another began'. The significance of this turning point, he continued, 'is probably equaled only by the invention of writing'.[92] Not since Newton had there been a greater 'change in the axiomatic basis of physics' and the 'corresponding conception of the structure of reality'.[93]

There is, then, as Mark Hansen has said, a 'doubleness' to wireless technology.[94] Those interested in 'natural radio' draw attention to the fact that radio not only transmits acoustic waves for human listeners, but also receives energetic signals from both terrestrial and extraterrestrial sources. 'Nature has always been the biggest broadcaster, bigger than all corporations, governments, militaries, and other purveyors of anthropic signals combined', notes Douglas Kahn.[95] When Thomas Watson, Alexander Graham Bell's right-hand man, first listened to the transmissions over telephone wires, he was mesmerised by the signal from the ionosphere:

> I used to spend hours at night listening to the many strange noises of the telephone and speculating as to their cause. One of the most common sounds was a snap, followed by a grating sound that lasted 2 or 3 seconds before it faded into the silence and another was like the chirping of a bird. My theory at the time was that the currents causing these sounds came from explosions on the sun or that they were signals from another planet. They were mystic enough to suggest the latter explanation but I never detected any regularity in them that might indicate they were intelligent signals.[96]

Watson's enchantment with 'cosmological noise' – what John Cage would call 'the static between the stations' – points to the fascinating capacity of radio to 'transmit without a sender'.[97] 'Radio was heard before it was invented', writes Kahn, and 'radio, before it was heard, was'.[98] Wirelessness taps into the signals and sounds of electromagnetic fields that do not conform to the scale and rhythms of conscious experience. Our world, says Hansen, is 'interpenetrated by wireless signals that are performing operations outside our awareness'.[99] In detecting this occult atmosphere, wireless media work as a kind of machinic unveiling – a source of 'cosmological revelation' – that brings us ever closer to Hertz's 'mysterious waves', which are everywhere around us but which we cannot easily perceive.[100]

The word infrastructure, writes Christian Sandvig, first appeared in the 1927 edition of the Oxford English Dictionary, referring to 'the subordinate parts of an undertaking' or its 'foundation'.[101] The term connotes the ancient structures that undergird communication, which have long constituted an archaeological layering of the urban fabric. The prefix *infra* means below, beneath or within.[102] Infrastructure is characterised as 'that which runs "underneath" actual structures . . . that upon which something else rides, or works, a platform of sorts'.[103]

Perhaps, concludes Edwards, after comprehensively discussing the origin of the word, 'infrastructure is best defined negatively, as those systems without which contemporary societies cannot function'.[104] These interpretations all point to the fact that media infrastructure extends beyond concrete, technical and socio-economic systems into a realm that is still more elusive and abstract. 'What distinguishes infrastructures from technologies', writes Brian Larkin, 'is that they are objects that create the grounds on which other objects operate. . . Infrastructures produce the ambient conditions of everyday life.'[105]

This sense that infrastructure shapes the underlying conditions of experience recalls the critical distinction between the empirical and the transcendental, between that which appears and the conditions through which appearance takes place. There is a sense in which railways, telegraphs and electricity grids, the Internet and mobile phones, provide the *a priori* basis of our existence. They work, not just as objects located within space and time, but also – in creating a global simultaneity, for example, or embedding relativity into our sense of location – by reformulating the very shape of space and time itself. Understood in this way, it becomes intrinsic to the very nature of infrastructure that it remains veiled, since it is designed to operate transcendentally as a substrate upon which everyday experience occurs.

This abstract capacity of infrastructure is further intensified by the ephemeral materiality of the electromagnetic field. 'There is reason', writes John Durham Peters provocatively, 'to take Immanuel Kant as the inventor of the telegraph: he was the first to philosophise a world in which the transcendental conditions for human intelligence could be made physical, a promise that his disciple, the Danish philosopher-physicist Hans Christian Oersted fulfilled in 1820 when he discovered electromagnetism.'[106] Although their amplification is entwined within the rhythms of geopolitical history, wireless waves extend outside the confines of anthropomorphic design. They constitute a materialist, transcendental infrastructure, which functions as the ground of life in the fifth long wave of techno-capitalist time.

Wave Philosophy

Figure 1.1 Three examples of yin–yang logos

Yuriko Furuhata's essay 'Of Dragons and Geoengineering: Rethinking Elemental Media' begins with the observation that the elements, or basic components of nature, most often referred to in media studies – earth, water, fire, air and ether – are rooted in the Greek philosophical tradition.[107] She calls attention to this bias by describing the mythical dragons that circulate through giant holes deliberately designed into the skyscrapers of Hong Kong. This striking feature of Hong Kong's urban landscape, which is meant to encourage the circulation of air, is based on *feng shui* 風水 – the Chinese art of wind and water, which uses five elements of cyclical change (water, wood, fire, air and metal) and is 'often combined with the Taoist cosmological principles of divination – namely the eight trigrams that represent heaven, lake, fire, thunder, wind, water, mountain, and earth'.[108] This philosophy of five elemental phases, as Furuhata explains, 'has influenced various folk practices, including the geomantic art of *feng shui* in East Asia'.[109]

In conceptualising Hong Kong's dragons as an elemental infrastructure, Furuhata aims to open media studies to a cultural horizon beyond the West. This book is written in a similar spirit. In focusing on the figure of the wave, it draws connections between Chinese cosmology and our wireless age. There are, embedded throughout the wireless landscape, evocative suggestions of just such a convergence. In 2010, for example, the multinational Wireless Power Consortium chose the word *qi* 氣 for its wireless charging standard. 'The name Qi', the consortium explains, 'comes from Asian philosophy where it means "vital energy", which relates to wireless charging which can be seen as an intangible flow of power.'[110]

A more directly wave-like provocation is found in the widespread use of the *yin–yang* symbol 陰陽, the most famous representation of Chinese thought. The BeiDou Navigation Satellite System 北斗衛星導航系統, China's answer to GPS, for example, uses the *yin–yang* symbol as its logo. More intriguingly still, the global Wi-Fi Alliance, an industry organisation dedicated to ensuring interoperability between wireless devices, also selected this image – a circle divided into black and white swirling halves. The figure of the *yin–yang* has thus been associated with wireless media all around the world. While *yin–yang*'s absolute origin is indeterminate, an early prototype can be found in the Ming Dynasty work by Zhao Huiqian 趙撝謙 (1351–95) 'River diagram of Heaven and Earth' 天地自然河圖. Nevertheless, according to scholar Robin Wang, it was not until the Qing dynasty that *yin–yang* arose in 'its final form as an independent image'.[111] Despite this relatively recent emergence, the symbol has a long heritage rooted in ancient diagrammatic practices of the

Chinese cosmological traditions. The drawing of images 像 (*xiang*) and the visual practices of the *Xiangshu* school, who construct diagrams of the text, have been essential to the commentary on the *Yijing* 易經 or Book of Changes, one of China's most ancient and important classical texts. The *yin–yang* symbol itself has precursors in the work of two Song neo-Confucian masters, Shao Yong's 邵雍 (1011–77) circular arrangement of the eight trigrams and Zhou Dunyi's 周敦頤 (1017–73) diagrammatic layout of the Supreme Ultimate 太極圖 (*Taijitu*).

The image of *yin–yang* recalls the natural formation of the logarithmic spiral, which remains stable regardless of scale. Its black and white halves represent an unceasing rhythm that is manifest in the waxing and waning of the sun and the moon and the light and shadows of the mountainsides. It represents the interconnections of all natural dualities: active and passive, male and female, hard and soft, hot and cold. The reciprocal waves reflect a continuous rotation that is fully interdependent – within *yang* there is a small circle of *yin*, within *yin* a small circle of *yang*. Cosmologically, *yin–yang* maps the originating energetic forces that first manifest from the primordial chaos 混沌 (*hundun*). The diagram's power, writes Wang, stems from the fact that it functions as a 'kind of a horizon for much of Chinese thought'.[112] In the Chinese intellectual tradition this swirling symbol of continuous cosmic transformation operates as an underlying conceptual paradigm of an eternal undulating change. This book contends that the wave-like patterns of techno-capitalist history as well the abstract infrastructure of electromagnetic vibrations are the material expression of a wave cosmo-ontology, which was rigorously articulated by certain figures of modern Chinese thought. Each chapter of the book is based on an image of the wave.

Chapter 1, 'From Oscillation to Undulation: Chinese Culture and Techno-Modernity', provides intellectual context by addressing historical debates around the perceived incompatibility of Chinese culture and the modern technological world, focusing, in particular, on the temporal assumptions involved. It explores how scholar officials in the late nineteenth century used the philosophical dichotomy *ti–yong* (體用 essence–function) to try and reconcile past and future. The idea was to protect Chinese cultural traditions, which were seen to be at the heart of an old and stable essence (*ti* 體) by leaving a guarded space for the inevitable encroachment of the constant innovations of technological modernity (*yong* 用). The chapter argues, however, that the proposed separation between these two conceptual spheres led to a constant oscillation that was ultimately untenable. A more promising approach to China's involvement with wireless media can be found embedded in the cosmo-ontology of the Buddhist New Confucianist Xiong Shili 熊十力 (1885–1968). Xiong did not believe in a division between Chinese tradition and Western transformation. Rather, he argued, the inseparability of *ti–yong* corresponded to an undulating intermingling of reality and manifestation, both of which are determined by continuous waves of change.

Chapter 2, 'Contraction and Expansion: From Wires to Wirelessness', describes how, in the face of a constantly mutating technosphere, the idea of Chinese essence (*ti*) shifted from the sanctity of an unchanging culture to the stability of a new-found state. It observes how in its encounter with globalised technologies – from the telegram to the Internet – China has responded by establishing sovereign control. The contracting impulse of techno-nationalism, from telegraph to cyber sovereignty, occurs amid various expansive drives. The chapter shows how this oscillating polarity is implicitly framed through formulations of the *ti–yong* pair. It argues, moreover, that tensions between global and local are not simply spatial, but temporal as well. The telegraph united the world under a single unified time. Consolidation of the modern state was part of China's integration into this temporal order. The transition from wires to wirelessness, however, involves a fundamental shift in the technological production of time. Today's machinic infrastructure is comprised by the inhuman frequencies of the atomic clock and satellite systems with Einsteinian relativity built in. Wirelessness complicates both national and global inclinations towards unified integration, ensuring an ongoing rhythm of contraction and expansion that is attuned to the whole of the wave.

Chapter 3, 'Repetition: Pirate Culture and the Mobile Phone', focuses on the coastal metropolis of Shenzhen and its *shanzhai* 山寨 (or copycat) culture. It maintains that it was Shenzhen's position on the maritime border that enabled the city to pioneer a radically novel mode of production. *Shanzhai* manufacturing of wireless media creates ties between China and contemporary technology that occur outside a centralised core. Its culture of continuous repetition (or simulation) belongs to an alternative cosmology that challenges the primacy of an origin and is allied with the aquatic, marginal culture of the peripheral zone.

Chapter 4, 'Vibration: The Body Electric', details how the discovery of electricity fostered an occult materialism that sought to connect the body to these mysterious, newly discovered waves. It sets out to demonstrate linkages between the electric body of the human organism and the electric body of the Earth manifest in the vibratory modernism of Europe and America, the *qigong* fever of

1980s China, and the philosophy of Tan Sitong 譚嗣同 (1865–98), who argued that the ether was an immersive but unseen medium of interconnectedness. It employs this cultural and intellectual history of wirelessness to counter a growing guardedness against 5G. The chapter challenges the idea of the spectrum, which rigorously delineates the human organism according to frequencies that it can and cannot perceive, embracing instead corporeal practices that seek to cultivate an intimacy with the non-human frequencies of the Earth's electromagnetic waves.

Chapter 5, 'Immersion: The Sentient City', describes how the twenty-first-century metropolis is absorbed in a high-frequency, alien atmosphere. It argues that a distributed sentient city emerges bottom-up from the wireless technology now embedded everywhere in the urban landscape. The sentient city is best understood in contrast to the smart city. Rather than the surveilling capacity of centralised control, it coalesces as a non-human machinic intelligence that operates with time waves of its own. In doing so it functions transcendentally, producing the temporal conditions within which experience takes place. Instead of conceiving of this conditioning structure in terms of a transcendent subject that surveils the smart city from on high, this chapter suggests that the wireless city is composed of myriad agents who function as city gods trafficking between visible and invisible worlds. At the end, the book draws on the philosophy of Mou Zongsan 牟宗三 (1909–95) in order to imagine the sentient city as the non-human agent of wireless media, cultivating a practical knowledge as it gravitates towards an apprehension of the waves.

Notes

1. By March 2018 it had already reached 1 billion users. Rayna Hollander, 'WeChat Has Hit 1 Billion Monthly Active Users', *Business Insider*, 6 March 2018, https://www.businessinsider.com/wechat-has-hit-1-billion-monthly-active-users-2018-3.
2. Benjamin Bratton, *The Stack: On Software and Sovereignty* (Cambridge, MA: MIT Press, 2016).
3. Vincent Garton, 'Sino-No-Futurism (a Comment)', *Cyclonograph II* (blog), 2020, https://vincentgarton.com/2020/04/10/sino-no-futurism/.
4. For more on hyperstition, see Cybernetic Culture Research Unit, *Writings 1997–2003* (Falmouth: Urbanomic, 2017).
5. Yuk Hui, *The Question Concerning Technology in China: An Essay in Cosmotechnics* (Cambridge, MA: Urbanomic, 2016).

6. Carlo Rovelli, *The Order of Time* (New York: Riverhead Books, 2018), 88.

7. Steven Shaviro, 'Deleuze's Encounter with Whitehead' (2007), http://www.shaviro.com/Othertexts/DeleuzeWhitehead.pdf, 1.

8. Gilles Deleuze, *The Fold: Leibniz and the Baroque* (London: Bloomsbury, 2014), 76.

9. Gilles Deleuze and Félix Guattari, *A Thousand Plateaus: Capitalism and Schizophrenia*, trans. Brian Massumi (Minneapolis, MN: University of Minnesota Press, 1987), 261.

10. Kaiser Kuo, 'Huawei and the Tech Cold War with Samm Sacks and Paul Triolo', *Sinica*, 2019, https://supchina.com/podcast/huawei-and-the-tech-cold-war/.

11. Edmund Berger, 'Tactile Power', *Reciprocal Contradiction* (blog), 28 March 2020, https://reciprocalcontradiction.home.blog/2020/03/28/tactile-power/.

12. China refused to accept the leading standards in third generation networks. Instead, the China Academy of Telecommunication Technology, with the support of massive investment from the country's telecom carriers, partnered with Siemens to create a home-grown substitute. TD-SCDMA (Time Division Synchronous Code Division Multiple Access) was developed to avoid dependence on Western technology and bypass expensive patent and licensing fees. While it succeeded in gaining rare acceptance by the International Telecommunication Union as an official 3G standard, its range and influence remained limited, and it was only ever used inside China. See Heejin Lee et al., 'China's ICT Standards Policy after the WTO Accession: Techno-national versus Techno-globalism', *Info* 11, no. 1 (2009): 9–18.

13. Kuo, 'Huawei and the Tech Cold War'.

14. Deloitte, '5G: The Chance to Lead for a Decade', 2018, https://www2.deloitte.com/us/en/pages/consulting/articles/5G-deployment-for-us.html.

15. Jiayang Fan, 'How China Views the Arrest of Huawei's Meng Wanzhou', *The New Yorker*, 17 December 2018, https://www.newyorker.com/news/daily-comment/how-china-views-the-arrest-of-huaweis-meng-wanzhou.

16. Kuo, 'Huawei and the Tech Cold War'.

17. SCMP Reporter, 'Media Q&A with Huawei Founder Ren Zhengfei'. *South China Morning Post*, 16 January 2019, https://www.scmp.com/tech/big-tech/article/2182367/transcript-huawei-founder-ren-zhengfeis-responses-media-questions.

18. Tellingly, the only one of the initial telecom players to have survived in China is ZTE which, like Huawei, is headquartered in Shenzhen. Tian Tao and Chunbo Wu, *The Huawei Story* (London: Sage, 2014).

19. Shortly after Meng's arrest, two Canadians, Michael Kovrig and Michael Spavor, were detained on spying charges. Soon afterwards another Canadian, Robert Lloyd Schellenberg, was sentenced to death on drug-trafficking charges, after he had been previously given a custodial sentence.

20. Kaiser Kuo, 'Meng Wanzhou's Arrest: The Legal Dimension with Julian Ku', *Sinica*, 2019, https://supchina.com/podcast/meng-wanzhous-arrest-the-legal-dimension/.

21. Michael Barbaro, 'Why Controlling 5G Could Mean Controlling the World', *The Daily*, 2019, https://podcasts.apple.com/us/podcast/why-controlling-5g-could-mean-controlling-the world/id1200361736?i=100 0430563445.

22. Debate here centred on China's cybersecurity law and the extent to which it requires Chinese tech companies to report to the central government.

23. Niko Chrysoloras and Richard Bravo, 'Huawei Deals for Tech Will Have Consequences, U.S. Warns EU', Bloomberg.Com, 2019, https://www.bloomberg.com/news/articles/2019-02-07/huawei-deals-for-tech-will-have-consequences-u-s-warns-eu.

24. Fan, 'How China Views the Arrest of Huawei's Meng Wanzhou'.

25. Deleuze, *The Fold*, 87.

26. Nikolai Kondratiev and W. F. Stolper, 'The Long Waves in Economic Life', *The Review of Economics and Statistics* 17, no. 6 (1935): 105.

27. Ibid.

28. Joseph Schumpeter, *Business Cycles*, vol. 1 (New York: McGraw-Hill, 1939), 70.

29. Ibid., 102.

30. Schumpeter's evolutionary model resembles the biological model described by Eldredge and Gould, who claim that evolution is not constant gradual change over time, but rather that species emerge in rapid bursts of evolutionary change followed by long periods of stasis. Niles Eldredge and Stephen Jay Gould, 'Punctuated Equilibria: An Alternative to Phyletic Gradualism', in *Models in Paleobiology*, ed. Thomas J. M. Schopf (San Francisco: Freeman Cooper, 1972), 82–115.

31. Schumpeter, *Business Cycles*, 158–9.

32. Christopher Freeman and Francisco Louçã, *As Time Goes by: From the Industrial Revolutions to the Information Revolution* (New York: Oxford University Press, 2001), 65.

33. Schumpeter further qualifies: 'Factors of change internal to the economic system are changes in tastes, changes in quantity (or quality) of factors of production, changes in methods of supplying commodities . . . change not brought about by consumers' preferences and demands . . . Railroads have not emerged because any consumers took the initiative in displaying an effective demand for their service in preference to the services of mail coaches. Nor did the consumers display any such initiative, or wish to have electric lamps or rayon stockings, or to travel by motorcar or airplane, or to listen to radio, or to chew gum.' Schumpeter, *Business Cycles*, 73.

34. Ibid., 84.

35. It was left to the neo-Schumpeterians to work out the details and socio-economic context of technological transformation.

36. Schumpeter, *Business Cycles*, 101–2.

37. In elaborating the process, Schumpeter insisted on the critical distinction between invention and innovation, which separates the original scientific idea or discovery from the entrepreneurial practices that synthetically open up the places and processes through which revolutionising technologies can spread.

38. Carlota Perez, 'Technological Revolutions and Techno-Economic Paradigms', *Cambridge Journal of Economics* 34, no. 1 (2010): 190.

39. Berger, 'Tactile Power'.

40. Ibid.

41. Peter Hall and Paschal Preston, *The Carrier Wave: New Information Technology and the Geography of Innovation, 1846–2003* (London: Routledge, 1988), 32.

42. Schumpeter, *Business Cycles*, 101.

43. Perez, 'Technological Revolutions and Techno-Economic Paradigms', 199.

44. J. A. Schumpeter, *Essays of J.A. Schumpeter*, ed. Richard Clemence (Boston, MA: Addison-Wesley, 1951), 83.

45. After waning in the booming post-war years, attention was revived during the economic downturn of the 1970s, when key texts were published by the Marxist Ernst Mandel and German scholar Ernest Mensch. In England, evolutionary economist Christopher Freeman and his colleagues at the Science Policy Research Unit at the University of Sussex ensured that a consideration of capitalist cycles was integral to late twentieth-century scholarly work on technical change and innovation studies. Finally, the theory of K-waves has been renewed and sharpened by the British-Venezualan scholar Carlota Perez. Her book *Technological Revolutions and Financial Capital: The Dynamics of Bubbles and Golden Ages* (Cheltenham: Edward Elgar, 2003) analyses the interlinkages of techno-economic and socio-institutional subsystems, which together make up what she calls 'great surges of development', each of which introduces a new 'techno-economic paradigm'. She investigates the intricate financial, social and institutional interloopings which collectively create these paradigm shifts through a process that draws much from Schumpeter's doctrine of Creative Destruction.

46. Immanuel Wallerstein, 'Long Waves as Capitalist Process', *Review (Fernand Braudel Center)* 7, no. 4 (1984): 563.

47. Perez, 'Technological Revolutions and Techno-Economic Paradigms', 190.

48. 'History of Radio', https://en.wikipedia.org/wiki/History_of_radio.

49. Hall and Preston, *The Carrier Wave*, 151.

50. Ibid., 166.

51. Lisa Parks, 'Technostruggles and the Satellite Dish: A Populist Approach to Infrastructure', in *Cultural Technologies: The Shaping of Culture in Media and Society*, ed. Göran Bolin (Abingdon: Routledge, 2012), 78.

52. The materialist approach to media that flourished in the wake of McLuhan's old insight that 'the medium is the message' draws strength

from various theoretical strands, including, to name but a few, Katherine Hayles's cyberfeminist work on the embodiment of information; Friedrich Kittler and his influence on the techno-heavy school of 'German Media Theory'; and media geology, which emphasises the study of environmental or elemental media. It also feeds both off of, and into, the wider and more general 'non-human turn' with its multiplicity of discourses, the strongest of which are the many attempts to articulate a 'new', 'incorporeal', 'vibrant' and 'enchanted' materialism. Interest has increased since around the turn of the millennium, sparked, as Jeremy Packer and Stephen B. Crofts Wiley write, by the attempt to escape a 'post-structuralist impasse' brought about by an overemphasis on the textual, semiotic and ideological that has characterised so much postmodern thought. Jeremy Packer and Stephen B. Crofts Wiley, eds, *Communication Matters: Materialist Approaches to Media, Mobility and Networks* (Abingdon: Routledge, 2013).

53. Christian Sandvig, 'The Internet as Infrastructure', in *The Oxford Handbook of Internet Studies*, ed. William H. Dutton (New York: Oxford University Press, 2013).

54. Marshall McLuhan, *Understanding Media: The Extensions of Man* (Cambridge, MA: MIT Press, 1994), 151.

55. Ibid., 275.

56. Paul Edwards, 'Infrastructure and Modernity: Scales of Force, Time, and Social Organization in the History of Sociotechnical Systems', in *Modernity and Technology*, ed. Thomas Misa, Philip Brey and Andrew Feenberg (Cambridge, MA: MIT Press, 2002), 194.

57. Paul Dourish and Genevieve Bell, 'The Infrastructure of Experience and the Experience of Infrastructure: Meaning and Structure in Everyday Encounters with Space', *Environment and Planning B: Planning and Design* 34, no. 3 (2007): 428.

58. Edwards, 'Infrastructure and Modernity', 185.

59. Dourish and Bell, 'The Infrastructure of Experience'.

60. Keller Easterling, *Extrastatecraft: The Power of Infrastructure Space* (New York: Verso, 2016), 12.

61. The contemporary study of infrastructure draws on earlier work from techno-historians such as Thomas P. Hughes, who analysed the vast grids of the nineteenth and early twentieth century such as electricity, telephone networks and railways, detailing how 'large technical systems' were able to reshape space and time, facilitate standardisation, and transform everyday life.

62. Susan Star, 'The Ethnography of Infrastructure', *American Behavioural Scientist* 43, no. 3 (1999): 377.

63. Lisa Parks, 'Around the Antenna Tree: The Politics of Infrastructural Visibility', *Flow Journal* (blog), 6 March 2009, https://www.flowjournal.org/2009/03/around-the-antenna-tree-the-politics-of-infrastructural-visibilitylisa-parks-uc-santa-barbara/.

64. Parks, 'Technostruggles and the Satellite Dish', 64.

65. This literature on data centres, satellite antenna, undersea cables, cell phone towers and telephone poles is accompanied by research on media's more ephemeral aspects such as standards and formats, compression technologies and Internet protocols. For a good overview, see Paul Dourish, *The Stuff of Bits: An Essay on the Materialities of Information* (Cambridge, MA: MIT Press, 2017).

66. Shannon Mattern, 'Infrastructural Intelligence', *Words in Space* (blog), 1 January 2016, https://wordsinspace.net/2016/01/01/infrastructural-intelligence/.

67. Lisa Parks and Nicole Starosielski 'Introduction', in *Signal Traffic: Critical Studies of Media Infrastructures*, ed. Lisa Parks and Nicole Starosielski (Urbana, IL: University of Illinois Press, 2015), 5.

68. Star, 'The Ethnography of Infrastructure', 379.

69. Jussi Parikka, 'New Materialism as Media Theory: Medianatures and Dirty Matter', *Communication and Critical/Cultural Studies* 9, no. 1 (2012): 96.

70. Jennifer Gabrys, 'Atmospheres of Communication', in *The Wireless Spectrum: The Politics, Practices, and Poetics of Mobile Media*, ed. Barbara Crow, Michael Longford and Kim Sawchuk (Toronto: University of Toronto Press, 2010), 4.

71. Ashley Carse, in his study of the Panama Canal, helps unpack the idea of nature *as* infrastructure. His essay challenges the 'popular idea of infrastructure as hardware', developing instead an analysis of the canal that is not simply based on the technological control of water. Rather, it focuses on how forests, wetlands and other landscapes are produced as infrastructure through an environmental politics that aims to regulate watersheds or provide legal protection of forests and agriculture. Ashley Carse, 'Nature as Infrastructure: Making and Managing the Panama Canal Watershed', *Social Studies of Science* 42, no. 4 (2012): 539–63.

72. Edwards, 'Infrastructure and Modernity', 196.

73. Marshall McLuhan and Harley Parker, *Counterblast* (New York: Harcourt, Brace & World, 1969), 14.

74. Nicholas Gane and Stephen Sale, 'Interview with Friedrich Kittler and Mark Hansen', *Theory, Culture & Society* 24, no. 7–8 (2007): 324.

75. John Durham Peters, *The Marvelous Clouds: Toward a Philosophy of Elemental Media* (Chicago: University of Chicago Press, 2016), 1.

76. Bratton, *The Stack*, 75.

77. See, for example, Jussi Parikka, *A Geology of Media* (Minneapolis, MN: University of Minnesota Press, 2015); Kate Crawford, *Atlas of AI: Power, Politics, and the Planetary Costs of Artificial Intelligence* (New Haven, CT: Yale University Press, 2021).

78. Nicole Starosielski, 'The Elements of Media Studies', *Media+ Environment* 1, no. 1 (2019): 10780.

79. Yuriko Furuhata, 'Of Dragons and Geoengineering: Rethinking Elemental Media', *Media+ Environment* 1, no. 1 (2019): 10797.

80. Rahul Mukherjee, *Radiant Infrastructures: Media, Environment, and Cultures of Uncertainty* (Durham, NC: Duke University Press), 2020.

81. Melody Jue, *Wild Blue Media: Thinking through Seawater* (Durham, NC: Duke University Press), 2020.

82. The first documented knowledge dates back to the sixth century BCE when Thales of Miletus wrote of his discovery that rubbed amber (*elektron* in ancient Greek) could attract lightweight objects such as a feather. Little knowledge was added until the modern science of electricity exploded in the eighteenth and nineteenth centuries.

83. David Bodanis, *The Electric Universe: The Shocking True Story of Electricity* (New York: Crown Publishers, 2005), 105.

84. Ira Brodsky, *The History of Wireless: How Creative Minds Produced Technology for the Masses* (St Louis, MO: Telescope Books, 2008).

85. Ibid., 15.

86. Ibid., 14.

87. Bodanis, *The Electric Universe*, 81.

88. G. R. M. Garratt, *The Early History of Radio: From Faraday to Marconi* (London: Institute of Engineering and Technology, 1994), 11.

89. Ibid.

90. Rivka Galchen and David Albert, 'Nonlocality from Newton to Maxwell', *Scientific American*, 18 February 2009, https://www.scientificamerican.com/article/nonlocality-from-newton/.

91. Richard Feynman, *The Feynman Lectures on Physics, Vol. I: The New Millennium Edition: Mainly Mechanics, Radiation, and Heat*, ed. Robert B. Leighton and Matthew Sands (New York: Basic Books, 2011).

92. Albert Einstein, 'Maxwell's Influence on the Development of the Conception of Physical Reality', in *James Clerk Maxwell: A Commemoration Volume 1831–1931* (Cambridge: Cambridge University Press, 2012 [1931]), 66–74.

93. Nancy Forbes and Basil Mahon, *Faraday, Maxwell, and the Electromagnetic Field: How Two Men Revolutionized Physics* (New York: Prometheus, 2014), 241.

94. Hansen, *Feed Forward*.

95. Douglas Kahn, *Earth Sound Earth Signal: Energies and Earth Magnitude in the Arts* (Berkeley, CA: University of California Press, 2013), 15.

96. Quoted in ibid., 44.

97. John Cage, *Silence: Lectures and Writings* (Middletown, CT: Wesleyan University Press, 2012), 3.

98. Kahn, *Earth Sound Earth Signal*, 14.

99. Hansen, *Feed Forward*.

100. Ibid. A similar mode of revelation is found in contemporary physics, which is building ever more complex and sophisticated machines to transduce the waves that are all around us but that we cannot perceive. The Laser Interferometer Gravitational-Wave Observatory (LIGO) is a a multi-kilometre-scale machine that uses laser light to measure minute fluctuations in space-time and thereby observe the gravity waves

that were predicted by Einstein's General Theory of Relativity. LIGO is attuned to time waves that, unlike those of electromagnetic energy which vibrate inside space-time, are, instead, warpings in space-time itself. In the film *Particle Fever*, physicist David Kaplan is asked to explain the significance of the discovery. His answer stresses that what is truly revolutionary is that, since gravitational waves are very different from the waves of other frequencies, LIGO enables us to see – or more precisely hear – 'things in the universe that were truly invisible to us in the past . . . The big news was not that Einstein was correct. This is something that was known for a long time. The big news is that we were blind and now we can see.' In his thought-provoking article 'Gravity's Reverb', wave ethnographer Stefan Helmreich writes about how gravity waves are mediated through sound. See Stefan Helmreich, 'Gravity's Reverb: Listening to Space-Time, or Articulating the Sounds of Gravitational-Wave Detection', *Cultural Anthropology* 31, no. 4 (2016): 464–92.

101. Sandvig, 'The Internet as Infrastructure', 90.
102. Carse, 'Nature as Infrastructure', 542.
103. Shannon Mattern, 'Scaffolding, Hard and Soft. Infrastructures as Critical and Generative Structures', *Spheres: Journal for Digital Cultures* 3 (2016): 1–10, https://newalphabetschool.hkw.de/scaffolding-hard-and-soft-critical-and-generative-infrastructures/index.html.
104. Edwards, 'Infrastructure and Modernity', 187.
105. Brian Larkin, 'The Politics and Poetics of Infrastructure', *Annual Review of Anthropology* 42 (2013): 329.
106. John Durham Peters, 'Technology and Ideology: The Case of the Telegraph Revisited', in *Thinking with James Carey: Essays on Communications, Transportation, History*, ed. Jeremy Packer and Craig Robertson (New York: Peter Lang, 2006), 143.
107. Furuhata, 'Of Dragons and Geoengineering'.
108. Ibid.
109. Ibid.
110. Electronics Notes, 'Qi Wireless Charging Standard', https://www.electronics-notes.com/articles/equipment-items-gadgets/wireless-battery-charging/qi-wireless-charging-standard.php.
111. Robin Wang, *Yinyang: The Way of Heaven and Earth in Chinese Thought and Culture* (Cambridge: Cambridge University Press, 2012), 5.
112. Ibid.

Chapter 1

From Oscillation to Undulation: Chinese Culture and Techno-Modernity

In May 2016 the celebrated science fiction writer Ted Chiang wrote a short piece in the *New Yorker* lamenting his struggle to learn how to read and write Chinese. The article, entitled 'Bad Character', sparked a series of responses that reanimated an old debate over whether Chinese tradition was inherently incompatible with technological change. At the heart of Chiang's speculations is a hypothesis about the connections between culture and temporality. Ultimately, he suggests, forging a relationship between Chinese culture and technological modernity involves reconciling the longevity of a backward-looking tradition with the innovation and novelty intrinsic to a future-oriented time.

'Bad Character' begins by detailing the complexity inherent in the language. 'It's not personal', Chiang writes. 'Chinese characters have been an obstacle to literacy for millennia.'[1] A language based on non-phonetic characters makes enormous cognitive demands. With so few sonic clues, learning the written script rests on pure memorisation. As a result, even native speakers regularly forget how to write even the most common words.

Chiang's criticism, however, goes beyond the fact that the Chinese language is so difficult to learn. The deeper, more critical problem, he submits, is that Chinese characters – themselves a type of technology – do not suit the machinery of the modern world.

> I've flipped through a Chinese dictionary, I've seen photographs of a Chinese typewriter, I've read about Chinese telegraphy, and despite their ingenuity they are all cumbersome inventions, wheelbarrows for the millstone around Chinese culture's neck. Computers and smartphones are impossible to use if you're restricted to Chinese characters; it's only with phonetic systems of writing, like Bopomofo and Pinyin, that text entry becomes practical.[2]

In his article, Chiang imagines an alternative history in which characters were never invented and Chinese was based on a phonetic script instead. He reflects on the increased literacy and easier technological adoption that would result. Chiang postulates that the incongruity between Chinese written and oral language privileges a continuity with ancient texts, which has served to heighten the cultural value of tradition and shut China out of the progressive advance of linear time. If China had invented a different writing system, Chiang proposes, culture would have evolved more throughout the millennia, would be less rooted in the past and would be more open to new ideas. 'Perhaps it would have been better equipped to deal with modernity in ways completely unrelated to an improved ability to use telegraphy or computers.'[3]

Stanford professor Thomas Mullaney, who researches the technolinguistic history of Chinese, immediately penned a sharp rejoinder to Chiang's article. He titled his essay, which was also published in May 2016, 'Chinese is not a Backward Language'. Mullaney's scholarship focuses on the Chinese typewriter, which has regularly been depicted as the iconic example of a farcical, monstrous machine. In both his writings and in an exhibition,[4] Mullaney documents how the apparent absurdity of the Chinese typewriter has been taken as proof that the essence of Chinese tradition, which is encoded in the language, has operated as a fundamental impediment to technoscientific modernity: an idea he adamantly opposes. Mullaney's work argues against the deeply held notion that Chinese characters – in their teeming multiplicity, inconsistency with linear organisation, and intractability to technical rationalisation – are fundamentally at odds with technological modernity. Instead, he contends, the Chinese language has long been at the forefront of innovation. Indeed, now there can be little doubt that Chinese is intimately involved in the disruptive inventiveness that accompanies the rise of digital computers. Steve Jobs famously credited his college calligraphy class for Apple's revolutionary emphasis on typographical design. Today, millions of Chinese speakers are addicted to texting, and applications using the Chinese language are positioned at the cutting edge of translation software and machine learning. 'We live in a time that hardly anyone could have anticipated at the dawn of the twentieth century', Mullaney expounds. 'Not only are Chinese characters still with us – they are one of the fastest, most widespread, and successful languages of the digital age.' More than ever before, 'Chinese is a world script, and China is an IT giant.'[5]

Nonetheless, Mullaney bemoans that the prejudice against the Chinese language is 'alive and well'. The modern bias, he contends, can be traced back to the nineteenth-century German philosopher Georg Wilhelm Friedrich Hegel, 'who famously wrote that Chinese writing "is at the outset a great hindrance to the development of the sciences"'.[6] Hegel professed 'that the structure of Chinese grammar rendered certain concepts unavailable – ineffable and perhaps even unimaginable – to those who thought and spoke in Chinese. He asserted that people were possessed by language, and that Chinese people had the misfortune of being possessed by one incompatible with modern thought.'[7] In contrast to twenty-first-century techno-orientalism, which is based on the affinity of Chinese stereotypes and modern machines, Mullaney is here pointing to the revival of an old-school Orientalist discourse that stressed the discordance between China and technology. Mullaney writes that this argument over technological fitness – which he names 'Orientalism 2.0' – rests on the idea that the 'onerous script has obstructed the adoption of modern information technologies such as telegraphy, typewriting, and computing', and that it is being 'rehabilitated, rejuvenated, and fortified' by people such as Chiang.[8]

Mullaney's article in turn prompted a quick retort from David Moser, a Beijing-based author and linguist, who wrote a long blog post that makes a number of salient points regarding the incompatibility of Chinese script and modern machines. First, Moser accuses Mullaney of deliberately conflating the spoken and written language. Any criticism directed at Chinese, Moser maintains, is not of the spoken language but of the elaborate and cumbersome script. Second, the accusation of Orientalism must contend with the fact that some of the

> fiercest critics of the Chinese writing system were not foreigners, but the Chinese themselves. Famous May Fourth intellectuals such as Chen Duxiu and Guo Moruo advocated the eventual abolition of Chinese characters. Even China's most celebrated modern writer, Lu Xun, was quoted as saying: 'If the Chinese characters are not eliminated, China is doomed.'[9]

Finally, Moser claims, the incompatibility of the Chinese written language with the machinic environment of the digital age is real. The number, complexity and non-phonetic nature of Chinese characters not only creates 'a crippling burden on human memory', but also strained the 'computer memories of the 1980s and 90s'. Their 'continuing cognitive and ergonomic disadvantages' are evident in the fact that, even today,

> the most common input methods (straightforward pinyin, *wubi* entry, etc.) are still cumbersome in comparison with typing in alphabetic

text. (Pinyin or handwriting input on a smart phone or pad still generally involves a two-step process, in which the user must choose the correct character candidate from a pop-up menu).[10]

The practical inventiveness Mullaney celebrates was thus a hard-won solution to what Moser insists is the 'very real problem' posed by the Chinese writing system. 'It is modern IT technology', he concludes, 'that has *saved* the characters from almost certain obsolescence in the increasingly interconnected and complex twenty-first century.'[11]

The most compelling response to Ted Chiang's article, however, comes from Carlos Rojas, a scholar of Chinese literature who has written a rich essay on Chiang that touches on a diverse set of topics, ranging from Derridean analysis of logocentrism to the 'Martian script' (*Huoxing Wen* 火星文) that was adopted by young Chinese Internet users in the early decades of the twenty-first century. Rojas agrees with Mullaney that Chiang's comments recall the prejudices of nineteenth-century Orientalism. His essay highlights the centrality of the temporal issues involved. Chiang's contention, he writes, is 'that Chinese characters had the effect of leaving Chinese culture and civilization figuratively "stuck in time"'.[12] This evocation of a cultural and linguistic stagnation, as Rojas points out, seems particularly strange coming from Chiang, whose stories, as a profile in the *New Yorker* states, 'conjure a celestial feeling of atemporality'.[13]

Chiang is most famous for 'Story of Your Life', a 1998 time travel tale, which was adapted into the 2016 film *Arrival*. Both the story and the film are based on a cross-cut narrative in which jumbled up memories of the life and death of the protagonist's daughter are intercut with attempts to decipher the language of extraterrestrials who have made a sudden, surprise landing on Earth. Chiang calls upon a familiar sci-fi trope in having the aliens take the form of giant squid or octopi (in this case, seven-tentacled creatures called Heptapods). The choice is pertinent since, as Rojas remarks, and as neuroscientists are increasingly discovering, octopi are the most striking example on Earth of alien intelligence or 'Other Minds'.[14]

Communication with the Heptapods is complicated by the fact that the creatures have two distinct linguistic systems, one for speech and one for writing. A similar split characterises the languages of China. In 'Story of Your Life' the linguistic encounter with the Heptapods rests primarily on the written script, which is visualised in the film as zen-like, circular, calligraphic symbols, which the aliens write with jet black ink that squirts out of their tentacles. As Louise, the main protagonist, learns to decipher the writing system, her sense of linear time begins to unravel and memories of the life and death of her as-yet-unborn daughter start crashing in on the present.

The first breakthrough in communication with the aliens comes from a physics theorem, which describes how the future can bleed into the past. The Heptapods comprehend Fermat's Principle of Least Time, a strange theorem with a built-in teleology in which a ray of light must somehow 'know' its destination in advance in order to choose the fastest path. In *Arrival*, the cinematic version of the story, the extraterrestrial non-linearity is directly tied to an engagement with China. It is Louise's communication with Shanghai's General Shang that completes the film's crucial temporal circuit, enacting the teleology that will unlock the riddle of alien language and thought. With a secret phrase in Mandarin, uttered in the future but with information vital to the past, time becomes untethered.

To be 'stuck in time', as Chiang's story makes clear, is not only to be mired in the past. The stickiness of temporality also includes a conscious intimacy of an encroaching future. Louise, the linguist who learns from foresight that her daughter will die prematurely, decides to go ahead anyway with the pregnancy, actively embracing the spiral of time. Her decision is surprising only to those who do not hold a deep sense of fate. Having learned the alien language, Louise is attuned to the Nietzschean idea of Eternal Return. 'Everything straight lieth', says the dwarf to Zarathustra. 'All truth is crooked; time itself is a circle.'[15] 'What distinguishes the Heptapods' mode of awareness is not just that their actions coincide with history's events', writes Chiang, 'it is also that their motives coincide with history's purposes. They act to create the future, to enact chronology.'[16]

In Chiang's story, as Rojas makes clear, 'language implies a world view'.[17] The hypothesis behind 'Story of Your Life' is that to learn to write differently is to learn to think differently. In this case the divergence produced by communication with a non-human intelligence enables an escape from the straight line of time. The Heptapods' script is based on a flat temporality in which past, present and future occur simultaneously. Chiang's comments on the stasis of Chinese culture and civilisation are, then, as Rojas points out, the direct inverse of the idea which is foregrounded in his own story, 'in which the users of an alien language become "unstuck in time"'.[18] Chiang's indictment of Chinese culture and characters assumes that the practices of modern technology imply a progressive, developmental and linear time that is fundamentally at odds with Chinese language and thought. Yet there is an alternative narrative that he explores in his fiction. A mode of time that does not follow along a straight line is not necessarily backward but can, instead, be in touch with the future – not because, like Louise, it has a clear knowledge of what is to come, but rather because it engages in practices that reveal the wave-like shape of time itself.

The lively discussion that Chiang's article provoked makes clear that China's supposed 'technological backwardness' rests, fundamentally, on a temporal question. This is implied most directly by Mullaney's evocation of Hegel, who famously associated China with an atemporal notion of duration and stability. China, wrote Hegel in his *Philosophy of History*, is an 'empire belonging to mere space, as it were [as distinguished from time]'.[19] In his book *Discovering History in China*, Paul Cohen details the extent to which this 'old picture of a stagnant, slumbering, unchanging China, waiting to be delivered from its unfortunate condition of historylessness by a dynamic, restlessly changing, historyful West' was shared among prominent thinkers in Europe and America.[20] The French philosopher Condorcet and the German philosopher Herder, as well as John Stuart Mill and Ralph Waldo Emerson, all considered China a vast, immobile, unchanged empire that was outside the advance of temporal transformation. This understanding of the 'East' as fundamentally spatial and unhistorical was taken up by Marx, who contrasted the dialectic evolution of Western history with the purely geographical nature of the Asiatic mode. For Marx, writes Shlomo Avineri in his introduction to *Karl Marx on Colonialism and Modernization*, Asia had no history. While the other three modes are 'related dialectically, the Asiatic mode stands apart – static, unchanging and totally non-dialectical'.[21] The stagnant cyclicity of tradition trapped China in an endless repetition outside the movement of time. The novelty of the future, Marx assumed, would have to come from elsewhere.

This binary between past and future, tradition and modernity, also structured thinking within China. Much of modern Chinese intellectual history involves an attempt to negotiate between a culture that is valued for its rootedness in the past and a desire for a future that is open to change. The nineteenth-century scholar officials of the late Qing dynasty sought to mediate this polarity and achieve a balance between the contrasting forces of tradition and modernity. Their aim was to adopt technology as a practical tool but in such a way that they could keep it sequestered, so as not to contaminate the cultural and intellectual heritage they felt obliged to protect. In doing so, they mobilised one of the most profound conceptual dualities of Chinese thought, *ti–yong* (體用). *Ti–yong* has a variety of loose English translations with *ti* meaning 'essence', 'substance', 'Ultimate Reality' or 'body', and *yong* often roughly translated as 'function', 'application', 'manifestation', 'practice or use'. In the dominant formulation of the late Qing, *ti* was equated with Chinese cultural essence and *yong* with foreign, modern technology. The two sides were split, poised in a fragile equilibrium that, ultimately, proved difficult to maintain. China veered from an intense suspicion of modern technology (as when the country's first telegraph wires were sabotaged by the Boxers) to a revolutionary anti-traditionalism (as in the belief, held by the intelligentsia of the May 4th movement, that China must change everything from its script to its calendar to adapt itself to the machines of the modern age).

Yet the bifurcation, as Mullaney suggests, between a permanent or essential culture and the ephemeral dynamism of technological invention assumes a false oscillation. Instead, there is an alternative – and more marginal – articulation of the *ti–yong* pair, one that suggests the possibility of a synthesis that comes as the polarity of the oscillation is enveloped by the undulation of the wave, and that was, fittingly, reinvigorated at the turn of this century as China began to confront the new world of electric machines.

Ti–Yong 體用

The material reality of everyday life in China at the end of the nineteenth century was, as historian Robert Bickers points out, densely multi-layered and culturally hybrid. Cities were immersed in a new audioscape of church bells and lighthouse fog horns; a wealth of print media circulated in both English and Chinese; local audiences enjoyed open-air Western-style theatrical performances; brass bands were incorporated into indigenous funeral rites; emerging urban culture adopted up-to-date technologies such as clocks, watches and photography. Yet, even within this culturally complex environment, Bickers notes, patterns of thinking were rooted in solid binary distinctions. The duality of inside and outside (*nei* 內 and *wai* 外), with its deep spatio-temporal connotations, was especially critical. China considered the revolutionary power of industrialisation to have come from without, not from within. 'Ideas about what was "Chinese" and "traditional" came often to be driven by comparison or contrast to their foreign equivalents.'[22]

The story of the early modern period is most commonly told as a fusion of East and West. Yet the truth, as Jeffrey Wasserstrom repeatedly emphasises, is that the reality was just as much a tale of 'East meets East'.[23] Modernity in China owed as much to Japan as it did to Europe or America. Nonetheless, and notwithstanding the critical influence of Japanese modernity, in China what was modern, foreign or new was often identified with the West – not only by outsiders, but also through an indigenous intellectual as well as quotidian discourse. Technological infrastructure such as railways and telegraph were attacked as 'Western artefacts' that brought with them 'Western culture' and 'Western ideas'. In his book *The Intellectual Foundations of Chinese Modernity*, Edmund Fung summarises the prevalence of this oscillating mode of thought: the West was 'an idea, a concept, and a system of representation' that appeared to differ in fundamental ways from the East. 'Seen from a temporal standpoint, it was, in essence, the difference between past and present, old and new, traditional and modern, backward and advanced. What was past and present in terms of linear time was represented spatially as East and West.'[24]

The question 'Can China modernise?', which has been reverberating for more than a century, thus involves a collision of spatio-temporal terms. The idea of a 'traditional' China and the 'modern' West consolidated into what Lydia Liu has called 'mutually constituted simulacra'.[25] China came to be thought of as an endogenous entity, old and enduring, with deep roots in the past, engaged in a contested relation with the novel transformations aligned with a future that is intrinsically foreign.

This potent and critical dichotomy between modernity and tradition, China and the West, was not born from stable pre-existing categories, but was instead forged from the encounter between late Qing Imperial culture and the nineteenth-century technological environment. The Chinese word for 'tradition', 傳統 (*chuantong*), as Karl-Heinz Pohl points out in his essay on the contemporary thinker Li Zehou 李澤厚, is a recent invention.[26] 'The most common modern Chinese dictionary, the *Cihai* (Sea of Words 辭海)', he explains,

> did not have an entry for *chuantong* in the 1938 nor 1965 edition . . . It first appeared in the editions of the 1970s. As a loanword from Japanese, like many others at this time, the word seems to have come into Chinese usage at the beginning of the twentieth century.[27]

Sinologist Benjamin Schwartz, in his essay 'The Limits of "Tradition and Modernity" as Categories of Explanation', likewise emphasises how, during this pivotal historical epoch, the very concept of tradition was constituted through an encounter with the new. For China's early modernist intelligentsia, tradition was not a solid established category, but rather 'a vast and variegated experience', whose richness might offer some guidance for how to cope with all the problems thrown up by this period of transition.[28]

If the conceptualisation of a Chinese tradition cannot be easily reduced to a simple, integrated cultural past, the future, associated with the idea of a modern West, is perhaps even more intrinsically unstable. Marx's famous formulation 'all that is solid melts into air' captures the extent to which Western culture was itself revolutionised by modern industrial capitalism. 'Few would claim', Schwartz argues,

> that the West which has emerged out of the 18th and 19th centuries forms an easily apprehended synthesis on any level – political, social, or intellectual. Yet when we turn our gaze outward to the non-Western world, that which has been obscure suddenly becomes clear. The West suddenly assumes the guise of a fixed, known quantity.[29]

Paul Cohen draws attention to the long scholarly attack 'against the picture of "tradition" and "modernity" as mutually exclusive, wholly incompatible systems'. He writes critically of 'the entire structure of assumptions inherited from the nineteenth century':

> [T]he perception of China as barbarian and the West as civilized; of China as static and the West as dynamic; of China incapable of self-generating change and therefore requiring for its own transformation the impact of a 'force from without'; the assumption that the West alone could serve as the carrier of this force; and, finally, the assumption that, in the wake of the Western intrusion, 'traditional' Chinese society would give way to a new and modern China, fashioned in the image of the West.[30]

Cohen challenges historians to think beyond a simple, unidirectional impact–response approach to Chinese modernisation, which tends to assume that the 'West' has been the main actor and agent. Much of what was happening at the turn of the century, he argues, was in reaction to powerful internal conditions, and in certain areas, at least, the 'West' was largely irrelevant.

The locus of the Sino-Western encounter, then as now, occurred on the sidelines. An 'outermost zone' that was made up of 'diverse phenomena such as treaty ports, modern arsenals and shipyards' as well as novel businesses and bureaucratic institutions experimented with various convergences and transitions. These sites hosted a myriad of techno-intellectual translations and exchanges, which consisted of two-way information flows and a complex 'web of impacts and responses'.[31] In the early modern era, it was the margins that offered the cutting-edge possibilities of cultural interchange. This same pattern holds in the contemporary period, when hybrid alternatives to a homogenising and unifying China can still be found in the outermost peripheral zones.

In the late nineteenth and early twentieth centuries, this culture of hybrid exchange manifested in the aesthetics of the built environment, particularly in the growing city centres of Jiangnan, the geographical region to the south of the lower reaches of the Yangtze river. In their book *Architectural Encounters of Essence and Form* – a title that alludes to the *ti–yong* dichotomy – urban theorists Seng Kuan and Peter Rowe detail how the twinned terms 'essence' and 'form' served as a guiding principle to help creatively express the conceptual duality of East and West, tradition and modernity, throughout the urban landscape.[32] The Jiangnan Arsenal of 1865, a critical location for the study of Western technical skills and the translation of foreign texts, is a pertinent example. In the layout of its production facilities and building forms, the Arsenal followed a thoroughly Western design, but it was also notable for its tiled roof, wooden lattice-work and other decorative details that harkened back to traditions in Chinese building composition. Later Republican-era monuments adopted a similar method, successfully synthesising Western architectural techniques with clay tiles, curving, upturned roofs, inner courtyards and *feng shui* principles. The Sun Yatsen mausoleum in Nanjing is an especially celebrated illustration. The edifice was constructed by architect Lü Yanzhi 呂彥直, who was trained at Cornell in Beaux Arts and then returned to China to help pioneer this merging of architectural styles. Shanghai's *shikumen* (石庫門) or *lilong* (里弄) houses, the quintessential element of the city's built environment, which combine Chinese traditional courtyard homes with a British-style type of terraced housing, arose out of a similar synthesis. This mish-mash sensibility, which mixed the native with the cosmopolitan, suffused fashion, food, art and design. It is, as Shanghai author Lynn Pan has so wonderfully documented, at the heart of *haipai* (海派), Shanghai's singular style.[33] Still today, this hybrid blend of 'essence and form' continues to characterise the urban identity. In the Shanghai History Museum located in the basement of the city's most iconic structure, the Pearl Orient tower, the lyrics of an old school song entitled 'Mastering both Chinese and Western Learning' are proudly on display. 'The formation of modern Shanghai was accompanied with the collision and blending of Chinese and Western cultures', reads the plaque. 'The merging of traditional Chinese cultural spirit and Western modern civilization is what made Shanghai a glamorous metropolis.'

The binary of 'essence' and 'form' captures the oscillating pairs that dominated the theoretical framework of the early modern period: past–future, inside–outside, East–West. For the late Qing intelligentsia these abstract oppositions across time and space were

seen as typified by the *ti–yong* conceptual couple, where *ti* was identified with the deep cultural past of indigenous traditions and *yong*
was linked to the techno-scientific future affiliated with the West.
In this intellectual discourse the *ti–yong* pair was split. The division
was designed to protect the traditions of Chinese culture, which were
deemed to be constant and eternal, and capable of being retained in
some form despite the revolutionary potential of an ever-changing
technology. This interpretation was communicated most effectively
by Zhang Zhidong 張之洞 (1837–1909), one of the most important
scholar officials of the modern period.[34] Zhang and his contempo-
raries had a strong desire to preserve the deep-rooted culture from
which they came and upon which their power was based. Yet they
also understood the radical potential of new modes of communication and transportation and accepted that China would somehow
need to adapt. They sought to negotiate between their sense of a
threatened traditional past and a future dominated by a novel techno-
culture that came from outside. 'Now that the sea-waves are dashing
upon our shores', wrote Zhang, 'unless we keep pace with the times,
and acquire Western learning, we shall be left in the lurch.'[35] Zhang's
formulation of *ti–yong*, which is embedded in the slogan, Chinese
learning for essence, Western learning for practice (*Zhongxue wei
ti, Xixue wei yong* 中學為體西學為用), would become integral to a
powerful rethinking of the relationship between a shifting Chinese
culture and the myriad uses of modern machines.

Chinese Learning for Essence, Western Learning for Practice

The nineteenth-century encounter between late imperial China and
the modern technological environment was complex and conflicted.
Initially, technology was viewed as a fundamental threat to the intricate webs of power that supported economic, cultural and social life,
as well as the ruling political order. Faced with a new world being
forged by unfamiliar emerging media, the masters of these controlling,
ritualised techniques struggled to preserve their cultural, political and
social institutions. The exclusive class of scholar officials understood
well the revolutionary potential of what they perceived as an essentially foreign technosphere. Slowly and steadily, however, the cultural
elite came to the reluctant realisation that China would somehow
have to adapt to the new and strange machines. By the end of the
nineteenth century, a multitude of voices within country were insisting that China needed to adopt the techno-scientific underpinnings of

industrialisation if it was to survive the new world that had landed on its shores. In a work entitled *China's Only Hope: An Appeal*, which was translated into English by the missionary Samuel I. Woodbridge in 1900, Zhang Zhidong writes with a dramatic, terrorised urgency about China's impending fate:

> If we do not change soon, what will become of us? European knowledge will increase more and more, and Chinese stupidity will become more dense. We shall be marked as the sure prey of the West; foreigners will still trade with us as before, but China will play a losing game, and get only chaff whilst her competitors garner the wheat, and we shall really, if not openly, become the slaves of Westerners. Not only this, the foreigners will suck our blood and, worse than this, pare the flesh from our bones. To end the tragedy they will swallow us down, body and soul, at one great mouthful, and gloat over the dead![36]

In their response to this perilous state of affairs, China's literati sought to carve out a delicate balance. While recognising the need to adjust to the new technological environment, they feared, as Theodore Huters has written, that 'adapting too easily to alien ways would result in irreparable damage to the very set of institutions that reform was designed to save'.[37] To navigate these contradictory impulses, the Qing intelligentsia necessarily drew from their own intellectual history. 'Even after the Western impact became a major concern for Chinese intellectuals', Cohen reminds us, 'it not only did not supplant older philosophical concerns but actually was shaped by these concerns in subtle and complex ways.'[38] Benjamin Schwartz also stresses the indigenous thought that characterised the Chinese reaction.

> It must first of all be noted that much of what is called the 'response to the West' before the end of the century takes place within a framework of concepts and categories furnished by the Chinese intellectual tradition. It could hardly be otherwise. This was still the spiritual and intellectual world within which the literati lived and breathed.[39]

The ruling scholar officials of the period, operating from within their own cultural context, called upon, and with great creativity reinvented, the *ti–yong* pair. Initially, the view had been that technology was a force to be resisted as an overwhelming threat, that if it were allowed to spread, *ti* (Chinese essence) would invariably follow *yong* (the techno-culture of the West). In the late Qing, however, the idea emerged that through a separation of *ti* and *yong*, China could develop a synthetic relationship with modernity.

The seeds of this idea were planted after China's defeat in the Opium Wars of the mid-nineteenth century, as China embarked on 'the self-strengthening movement', a campaign to modernise education, industry and especially defence. The phrase self-strengthening (*ziqiang* 自強) was itself borrowed from the first hexagram of the *Yijing* 易經: 'The movement of Heaven is full of power. Thus, the superior man makes himself strong and untiring.' It was popularised in the early modern period by government reformers whose determination that China should strengthen itself gave the waning Qing empire 'a new lease on life'.[40]

One of the most influential officials to insist that China must learn to strengthen itself by incorporating Western techno-science was Zeng Guofan 曾國藩 (1811–72). Zeng, who Jonathan Spence describes in his influential history of modern China as the 'most important representative of the restoration attitude', was a Hunanese scholar-general immersed in the ritualised traditions of Confucian learning – the study of the *Yijing*, meditation and classical poetry.[41] Through his wartime experiences, however, he came to believe that the preservation of this culture relied on the practical use of modern technologies. His strategy was to set up shipyards and arsenals 'to learn from the Barbarians', and create 'solid ships and effective guns'.[42] In this he was joined by the prominent reformer Li Hongzhang 李鴻章 (1823–1901), who was an early advocate of the telegraph as well as one of the key figures in the establishment of the Jiangnan Arsenal, the site on Shanghai's Huangpu river which served as the entry point for much modern scientific knowledge into China. 'China desires to make herself strong', wrote Li; in this, 'there is nothing better than to learn and use the superior methods of foreign countries. If we wish to learn about and use the superior weapons of foreign countries, there is nothing better than to look for the machines with which to make machines.'[43] Suzhou-born scholar Feng Guifen 馮桂芬 echoed the same sentiment, insisting that modern technology in China must be manufactured, used and repaired 'by ourselves . . . Only thus will we be able to pacify the empire; only thus can we play a leading role in the globe; and only thus shall we restore our original strength and redeem ourselves from former humiliations.'[44]

Both Li and Feng were deeply influenced by their experiences in the thriving, cosmopolitan city of Shanghai, which, already by the mid-nineteenth century, was forging itself as the primary site of modern urban China. Jeffrey Wasserstrom's book *Global Shanghai* begins in the year 1850, with the founding of the newspaper *The North China Herald*. By 1875, he argues, Shanghai was firmly situated on the global map. Twenty-five years later, in 1900, at the time of the

Boxer rebellion, the metropolis had been significantly reshaped by new technologies.[45] Gaslights were introduced to Shanghai in 1865, the telephone in 1881, electricity in 1882, running water in 1884, and the tram in 1901. Speculative fiction author J. G. Ballard, who lived in Shanghai in his youth, called it an Electric City, and a whole host of scholars have contended that Chinese modernity emerged at the turn of the century in its flourishing urban culture.[46] Feng Guifen, in particular, was hugely impacted by his time in the metropolis. His essays, written in Shanghai, are credited with some of the deepest conceptualisations of self-strengthening. It is in one of these essays, entitled 'On the Adoption of Western Learning', that Feng foreshadows the late Qing adoption of *ti–yong* as a strategy to absorb modern technology while retaining what they viewed as 'essentially' Chinese. 'What could be better', he writes, 'than to take Chinese ethical principles of human relations and Confucian teachings as the foundation (*ti*), and supplement them with the techniques (*yong*) of wealth and power of the various nations?'[47] It was in 1898, however, with the publication of Zhang Zhidong's essay 'Exhortation to Study' 勸學篇, that the reformulation of *ti–yong* received its full articulation. Zhang's phrase 'Chinese learning for essence, Western learning for practice' was, in the end, embraced as a slogan potentially powerful enough to provide the guidance and equilibrium that was necessary to withstand the challenging entanglement with technological modernity.

Zhang was writing at a particularly intense moment in modern Chinese history. After the devastating defeat in the first Sino-Japanese war, the closing years of the nineteenth century were a time of profound introspection. Between 1894 and 1895, writes Daniel Bays in his study of Zhang Zhidong, 'there came into being forces which would help to shape the course of Chinese history for several ensuing decades'.[48] It was in this period that what Schwartz calls the 'transitional generation' – which included such luminaries as Kang Youwei 康有為, Yan Fu 嚴復, Liang Qichao 梁啟超 and Tan Sitong 譚嗣同 – 'reached its creative peak'.[49] In their book *Rethinking the 1898 Reform Period*, Rebecca Karl and Peter Zarrow write of an 'urgency to think again' about this epoch, which has been too often overshadowed by the supposed telos of succeeding events. 'The 1898 period', they write, 'was an extended moment during which a series of historical questions that have powerfully informed China's modernity were first posed in a systematic and systemic fashion.'[50] Huters, in his study of the literature of the time, likewise describes *jindai* (近代), the early modern period, as a 'fascinating but indeterminate age' poised between the ancient and the modern, 'where the new and the old intertwined and jostled each other in ways that the later narratives of an exclusive modernity or the earlier discourse of a self-consistent tradition did not seem to allow for'.[51]

Zhang was critical of both the conservatives who were overly sceptical about the benefits of technological power as well as the progressives who treated Confucian doctrine with contempt. He saw merit on both sides of the debate, and his essay aimed to mediate between two factions that refused to listen to each other. *Zhongxue wei ti, Xixue wei yong* was meant to give 'philosophical reassurance' to both the 'radical reformers' who desired 'drastic sociopolitical change' as well as the 'conservatives preoccupied with preserving Chinese tradition'.[52] Zhang recognised an 'unprecedented emergency' in this time of change, but still feared losing the solid ground of tradition that he cherished and revered. His response was intended as a means of enjoying the benefits of foreign science and technology without having to sacrifice the deep-seated values of Chinese culture. In order to render China powerful, and at the same time preserve the nation's own institutions – he wrote in 'China's Only Hope', an essay structured in accordance with the *ti–yong* dichotomy – it was absolutely necessary that the Chinese should utilise Western knowledge. 'But unless Chinese learning is made the basis of education, and a Chinese direction given to thought, the strong will become anarchists, and the weak, slaves.'[53]

For Zhang, the social hierarchy and moral codes defined by the Confucian teachings never altered, but he nonetheless advocated an immense flexibility in the techniques and institutions of learning. 'To the stubborn opponents of reform', he proclaimed, '[w]hat remains constant is the human bonds, not the traditional-honored institutions; the Way of the Sage, not the machinery; the moral codes, not the technical skills.'[54] By positing an underlying essence to Chinese culture (*ti*) that could sustain adaptation to the texts and technology that were flowing in from outside (*yong*), his use of *ti–yong* helped craft 'tradition' and 'modernity' into a complex binary meant to retain the old as a spiritual basis, while allowing for the practical application of the new.

The deep cultural emphasis embedded in Zhang Zhidong's formula of 'Chinese essence with Western learning' receded under the weight and complexity of the nationalism of the early twentieth century. Its influence on technological modernisation in the Communist era was muted. Nevertheless, the ideas implicated in the slogan have had an important afterlife and the binaries that it established still serve, as will be shown in the following chapter, as an implicit matrix shaping much of the discussion around the Chinese Internet.

The slogan itself has resurfaced on a number of occasions as attempts are made to try to integrate Chinese culture and modern technology by holding them both together and apart. One of the most interesting reformulations occurred in the 'New Enlightenment movement' 新啟蒙運動 (*Xin Qimeng Yundong*) of the 1980s, a pivotal decade at the beginning of Reform and Opening, before the political repression that came in the wake of the crackdown at Tiananmen on 4 June 1989. This was a moment, much like the period at the turn of the century, of great intellectual ferment and cultural experimentation as China re-emerged from the closed-door radicalism of the Maoist period and was, once again, freely wrestling with the challenges of technological modernity. Prompted by economic liberalisation and a deepening of the electromagnetic mediasphere came new engagements with older traditions of practice and thought.

One of the best-known scholars of the period was the philosopher Li Zehou 李澤厚 (1930–2021). Li is best known for his work on aesthetics. In addition, his ideas on individual subjectivity and his reformist political tendencies were seen as a direct contribution to the student protest movement. After 4 June, Li was denounced as a 'black hand'. He was barred from leaving China for a number of years, but eventually managed to escape, and from 1992 onwards lived in exile, working in universities in the United States.

Li's philosophy fuses thinkers of the Western tradition – primarily Marxist and Kantian ideas – with Buddhist, Confucian and Daoist thought. His aim is to conceptualise an alternative modernity, which cannot be simply equated with Westernisation. He aspires towards a Sinology that is not reducible to its historical significance but is instead an 'indispensable and very important part of contemporary world culture'.[55] In his 1986 article 'Random Thoughts on "Western Learning as Substance, Chinese Learning for Application"', Li follows Marx's example of turning Hegel on his head, and advocates an inversion of Zhang Zhidong's formula: 'Western learning is the substance, Chinese learning is for application' (from *Zhongti Xiyong* 中體西用 to *Xiti Zhongyong* 西體中用).[56]

As a Marxist, Li maintains that the mode of production embodied by a particular techno-scientific regime forms the materialist basis of society. The 'main flaw of the [slogan] "Chinese substance and Western applications"', he writes, 'is found in the assumption that technology is application and not substance. But the exact opposite is true: technology is substance . . .'[57] Science, technology and industry are the 'cornerstone' or 'essence' of society. What modernisation 'primarily means', Li contends, is 'the transformation of this "substance"'.[58]

Li compares *ti–yong* both to the base–superstructure and to the hardware–software divide. Understood in this manner, Chinese culture constitutes the application. It is the upper stratum, which governs the particular manner in which the underlying substance is made manifest. 'While engaged in trying to understand, introduce, and import "Western learning" in a comprehensive way, we will naturally be faced with issues of judgment, choice, revision, and transformation', Li explains. 'And it is precisely in these acts of judging, choosing, revising, and transforming that "Chinese application" 中用 (*Zhongyong*) is produced.'[59] Li's inverted formulation, 'Western substance, Chinese application', is meant as a Sinification of Marxism, designed to help China create a modernity of its own.

Li's revival of *ti–yong* was heavily criticised. Conservatives held that he was an extreme anti-traditionalist, who echoed the militancy of the May 4th intellectuals. Hardline Marxists attacked him for what was perceived as a pro-capitalist stance, while liberals blamed him for trying to revive outmoded Confucian traditions. According to intellectual historian Karl Heinz Pohl, however, Li, like Zhang, is best understood as a moderate reformer trying to maintain a balance. 'Li Zehou holds an in-between position. For radical Western-oriented liberals (Liu Xiaobo and others), he is a traditionalist or even a conservative reactionary. For hardline Marxists, he is an advocate of "total Westernization".'[60] Instead, Pohl argues, Li sought to reanimate *ti–yong* in order to hold open the space between the iconoclastic tendencies of the liberals and Marxists on the one hand, and the regressive return to conservative Confucianism on the other. China in the post-1979 Reform era is replete with efforts to maintain similar delicate balancing acts. The Sinification of economics and technology – the idea of the Internet or capitalism with 'Chinese characteristics' – are arguably best understood as reanimations of the late Qing formulation of the *ti–yong* pair.

Yet this reform-minded utilisation of *ti–yong* is marred by an incoherence, rooted in an intrinsic philosophical weakness. The bifurcation of *ti–yong* posits a duality between culture and technology, tradition and modernity, past and future, China and the West, which it then tries to fuse. In the end, its neo-traditionalism is neither new, nor traditional enough. This, finally, was Sinologist Joseph Levenson's critique of the late nineteenth-century rallying cry. Zhang Zhidong's *ti–yong* motto 'not only had Confucian breakdown as an outer consequence', he concludes, 'but Confucian breakdown in its inner core'.[61] The attempt to cleave open a space by splitting apart ideas and practices that are inherently inseparable results in an ongoing oscillation, as the radical swings that shaped the traumas of twentieth-century Chinese history – which veered from intense suspicion of modern technology to a revolutionary anti-traditionalism – attest. In the end, despite the ingenuity of the effort, this bifurcation could not succeed. *Ti* and *yong* are not the opposite poles of a divided duality. They are an interwoven couple, as fundamentally inseparable as water and waves.

The Roots of *Ti–Yong*

The *ti–yong* dyad can be traced back to China's oldest texts. Interpretation of the terms rests on Daoism, Buddhism and Confucianism, whose complex entanglement constitute the mingling inherent in Chinese religion. Their meaning was elaborated over time and made most explicit by the long exchange between Confucianism and Buddhism. The *ti–yong* paradigm, as Charles Muller documents, 'was first born out of the early Chinese classics, then significantly deepened in the process of its incorporation into, and transformation of, Buddhism'. During the Song-Ming period, the by then thoroughly Buddhist infused conceptual couple, became 'the comprehensive matrix for Neo-Confucian philosophy'.[62] In their article on the origin and development of *ti–yong*, Sun-hyang Kwon and Jeson Woo begin by emphasising that 'essence–function' or *ti–yong* is a core concept, which 'serves as the basic philosophical framework for all major Chinese religions'.[63] They trace the long-running debate between Confucians and Buddhists over the concept's origins and conclude, like Muller, that *ti–yong* is best understood through 'Confucian–Buddhist interactions', which, together, have constituted the pair as a non-dualistic double.

Ti, as contemporary philosopher Cheng-Ying Cheng writes, 'is one of the most basic, earliest and most essential concepts in Chinese philosophy'.[64] The character *ti* (體) denotes the concrete, corporeal body, but it is suggestive, he argues, of more than just the organisation of physical form. The character is composed out of the bone radical, yet it also contains the symbol for the ritual vessel, which alludes to the body's spiritual dimensions. The term is found in the second hexagram of the *Yijing*, *Kun* (坤) the Receptive, which advises that one 'reside in the correct position of the body *ti* (體)'.[65] *Ti*, Cheng notes, has a further epistemological dimension. The term *tiyan* (體驗) means to learn through intimate, personal or embodied experiences. It emerges from traditions that stress ritualised movement as well as the cultivation of bodily awareness and which do not view the material body as inherently limited or restricted to its concrete, physical dimension. Cheng describes how these philosophical systems imagine the body, not as the source of illusion, but rather as a site of both self and cosmic knowledge, as well as the 'basic locus for the realization of the Confucian ideal'.[66]

According to this tradition, from these origins, *ti* comes to acquire a still deeper meaning, ultimately, Cheng contends, giving rise to 'the most fundamental, most creative term in Chinese metaphysics, namely the concept of *benti*'.[67] *Benti* (本體), which is variously translated as Origin-Substance, Source-Substance, Originating Body, Fundamental or Original or Ultimate Reality, is aligned with the creative power of *Dao* (道) and the 'Supreme Ultimate' of the Taiji (太極). It is associated with both heaven, *tian* (天), and nature *ziran* (自然), and is fundamental to what Cheng calls the 'onto-cosmology' present in many schools of classical Chinese thought. These cosmologies use the body as a vessel for cosmic encounter and emphasise embodied practice as a means to connect with that which is ultimately Real.

The concept *yong* (用) (application, use, manifestation, function, practice) can also be traced back to the *Yijing*. With over ninety instances, Cheng claims that it is the most commonly used word in the ancient classic. It appears in the first hexagram *Qian* (乾) the Creative, and reappears repeatedly as the Oracle determines whether, in accordance with the situation, action or inaction is best advised. Laozi associates inaction with the term *yong* in chapter eleven of the *Daodejing*, which states that whether in the spokes of a wheel, the hole in a vessel, or the windows and doors of a house, it is nothingness or the empty space that is of most use (*yong* 用). This Daoist idea that it is the imperceptible which holds the greatest function resonates intriguingly with the contemporary mediasphere, whose ground is an environment of electric vibrations that is immersive but unseen.

While there is mention of *ti–yong* together in the *Xunzi* 荀子 of the third century BCE,[68] most scholars attribute the first philosophical use of the term to Wang Bi's (王弼; 226–49 CE) commentary on the *Daodejing* 道德經, which also concentrates on this interplay between that which is manifest and that which cannot be seen.[69] In his *Source Book in Chinese Philosophy*, Wing-Tsit Chan quotes Wang Bi's commentary on Laozi: 'Although it is valuable to have non-being as its function (*yong*), nevertheless there cannot be substance (*ti*) without non-being.'[70] Chan's well-known gloss on the text credits Wang Bi with the birth of *ti–yong* as a conceptual pair:

This is the first time in the history of Chinese thought that substance (*t'i*) and function (*yung*) are mentioned together. In the *Book of Changes,* it is said that 'the state of absolute quiet and inactivity . . .

when acted on, immediately penetrates all things'. Neo-Confucianists interpreted the two states as substance and function, but they are only so by implication. The concepts of substance and function definitely originated with Wang Pi. They were to become key concepts in Chinese Buddhism and Neo-Confucianism.[71]

While *ti–yong* first appeared in Confucian and neo-Daoist texts, it was with the Buddhists that, as Kwon and Woo write, '"essence" and "function" became a paradigm used as an exegetical, hermeneutical and syncretic tool for interpreting Chinese philosophical works'.[72] *Ti–yong* is prominent in the metaphysics of all three of the major Chinese Buddhist traditions: *Tian Tai* (天台), *Hua Yan* (華嚴) and *Chan* (禪宗), each of which enrichens the concepts and gives them greater philosophical depth. The *Tian Tai* text *The Method of Concentration and Insight* associates the *ti–yong* duality with the 'two truths', one worldly or relative, the other absolute. Chan quotes the text as follows:

> By saying substance and function are not different, one does not mean collecting the different functions of many particles of dust to form the one substance of clay. It merely means that within the level of worldly truth, every event or character is the total substance of absolute truth. Therefore we say that substance and function are not different . . .[73]

This idea that the empirical world is suffused with the absolute finds one of its most profound expressions in *The Awakening of Faith* 大乘起信論 (*Dasheng Qixin Lun*), a foundational and enormously influential text in the Mahayana Buddhism of East Asia. *The Awakening of Faith* is a Chinese scripture that was presented as a translation from Sanskrit and was widely attributed to the Indian writer Asvaghosa (c. 80–c. 150 CE). Yet no Sanskrit version has ever been found. While some scholars argue for Indian Yogacara authorship, most agree that the Chinese 'translation' is in fact the original.[74] In his analyses of the origin and development of *ti–yong*, Muller contends that it is too 'unwieldy an undertaking to provide all the examples' of the terms in the *Awakening*, 'since, as most scholars of the text would readily agree, the entire expository structure of the text is framed along the lines of *ti–yong*'. The *Awakening* treats the twinned concept as two aspects of 'one mind', whose nature is identical but which can, nevertheless, be distinguished. The distinction 'between this enlightened essence of the mind as "true thusness" and its various temporal manifestations as "production and cessation" is described in terms of "essence" (*ti*) and "function" (*yong*)'.[75] The *Awakening*'s use of these intertwined concepts was critical to the idea of 'Buddha

Nature', central to Chinese Buddhism, which reconciles the doctrines that all sentient beings have the potential to attain enlightenment with the seemingly contradictory idea that minds are defiled and that enlightenment comes from outside. In the *Awakening*, it is the sense of the mind as an eternal undifferentiated whole, its aspect as 'thusness', which designates the essence (*ti*) of Mahayana, while its function (*yong*) is what gives rise to the ephemeral causes and conditions of the phenomenal world. The *Awakening* describes the separate but interconnected relationship between the absolute (*ti*) and the worldly (*yong*) by invoking the image of water and wave.[76]

> The characteristics of ignorance (*wuming zhi xiang*) are not separate from the nature of awakening (*jue xing*) and thus are not something that can either be destroyed or not destroyed. It is like the water of the big sea, which is turned into waves by the wind. The characteristics of the water and of the waves are inseparable, and yet the nature of movement does not pertain to water. When the wind ceases, the characteristics of movement also cease, but the nature of wetness remains undestroyed.[77]

These early texts, then, do not divide a primary realm of substance or essence (which the late Qing reformers such as Zhang Zhidong equated with traditional culture) from a separate realm of change and activity (the *yong* that came to stand in for technology), but rather insist on the non-separation of the *ti–yong* pair. The non-duality of *ti–yong* – understood as the bond between Ultimate Reality and its myriad manifestations – was renewed by an intellectual countercurrent, which also emerged in the late nineteenth century as China sought to confront the challenge of modernity. Thinkers in this intellectual lineage were critical of Zhang Zhidong's formulation for its presumption and reinforcement of a segregation between a traditional 'Chinese culture' and emerging technologies associated with the West. They alleged instead that techno-scientific modernity is not intrinsically Western or Chinese but had some mixture of both. In rejecting the oscillating tension between an indigenous Chinese culture and the exteriority of a future-oriented technology, they reaffirmed the immanence of *ti–yong*, devising a philosophical approach to modernity in which temporal, spatial and cultural binaries were subsumed by a cosmo-ontology of the wave.

Xiong Shili 熊十力

One of the key figures of the intellectual countercurrent that emerged alongside China's early encounter with electronic media was Xiong

Shili. Xiong, who is widely considered one of China's most important modern philosophers, sought, like the Qing reformer Zhang
Zhidong, to embed an engagement with modernity through a reartic-
ulation of *ti–yong*. He believed, however, that the failure of reform lay
in the fact that it did not possess a true understanding of the concepts
it sought to mobilise. As the contemporary philosopher Tu Wei-Ming
writes in his rich exegeses, Xiong maintained that Zhang Zhidong's
formulation of the 'most fundamental conceptual coupling in all of
Chinese philosophy' was 'a fallacy not because the dichotomy itself
was inappropriate, but because in his wishful thinking he completely
failed to appreciate the complexity of the relationships involved'.[78]
Xiong held that Zhang's deluded attempt to abstract *yong* from *ti*
could only ever give rise to frivolous theories. 'When the ideas were
detached from their ontological structure, they became fragmentary
opinions, useful only for propagandist purposes.'[79]

Unlike those who held that China's confrontation with modern
technology required a distancing from or abandonment of indigenous
intellectual lineages, Xiong maintained that the only way to meet
changes arriving from outside and find an answer to the crises fac-
ing China was to delve further inside. For Xiong, writes Tu, 'drilling
deeply into the bedrock of the Chinese mind was not only of intrinsic
value; it was functionally necessary for the successful absorption of
new ideas'.[80] Tu compares Xiong to Hu Shi 胡適, the sophisticated,
urbane and flamboyant intellectual of China's cultural renaissance,
who skilfully digested the writings of Darwin, Dewey, Bergson and
Russell and sought 'to conceptualize Chinese problems in terms of
categories he had acquired from the West'. Tu's contention is that
while 'many of Hu's provocative ideas have long become outmoded
in the intellectual world', Xiong's 'imaginative vision [is] only now
[beginning] to find a sympathetic echo in the minds of professional
philosophers'.[81] For Xiong the attempt to borrow modes of thought
from elsewhere was bound to be futile. He disputed the assumption, which grew in strength through the analyses of the new culture
movement, that Confucianism was to blame for China's weakness.
'On the contrary', writes philosopher Jiyuan Yu, Xiong argued 'that
the underlying problem was the loss of Confucian *dao* . . . the way
out was not to abandon Confucianism, but to rediscover and revive
its real spirit'.[82] Xiong turned inwards, devoting himself to a philosophical inquiry that reinvented tradition through a thorough exca-
vation of ideas.

The result was a philosophical orientation which reconceived the
connection between Chinese tradition and modernity by returning to
an older and deeper relationship between *ti* and *yong*. Rather than

using these terms to refer to a mundane distinction between a past culture and future-oriented technology, Xiong maintained that they invoked the more profound dyad of ontological reality (*ti*) and phenomenal manifestation (*yong*). In Xiong's reformulation, there is an immanent connection between the two terms. Xiong insisted on the non-separation of *ti–yong*: *ti yong bu er* (體用不二), he repeatedly wrote, *ti* and *yong* are not two. His aim was to synthesise Ultimate Reality with the flow of ephemeral appearances. The 'Way' (or *Dao*) is not something distinct from manifestation's constant transformation, but together they embody a cosmo-ontology of the wave.

The Yogacara Revival

Xiong's response to the challenge of modernity was enormously influenced by the modern Buddhist revival in which the renewal of the Yogacara (Nothing but Consciousness) school was especially significant. In his book *Transforming Consciousness*, John Makeham, a scholar and translator of Xiong, argues that Yogacara Buddhist philosophy, the 'main exemplar of Indian thought in modern China', was, in the end, just as important in shaping the Chinese response to modernity as the 'radically new knowledge systems introduced from the West'.[83]

Yogacara teaches that suffering arises from a false attachment to an illusory world. As its name indicates, it emphasises the meditative practices of yoga, but it is also based on a sophisticated study of perception, cognition and consciousness. The Yogacara school is rooted in the rich metaphysical writings of the fourth-century Indian scholar Vasubandhu and his brother Asanga. Its teachings entered China early, travelling along ancient trade routes.[84] Key to its transmission was the monk Xuanzang 玄奘 (602–64 CE), famously popularised in the beloved Ming dynasty classic *Journey to the West* 西遊記. Xuanzang spent over a decade studying in India, and, when he returned, carried back hundreds of Buddhist manuscripts. After his pilgrimage, he set up a school dedicated to the translation of Sanskrit texts into Chinese. Among the most significant of Xuanzang's writings is *A Treatise of Consciousness Only* 成唯識論 (*Cheng Wei-Shih Lun*), which is based on commentaries on Vasubandhu's *Thirty Verses*, one of the core texts of Yogacara Buddhism.[85] *Cheng Wei-Shih Lun*, along with the commentaries of Xuanzang's disciple Kuiji, have since served as the foundational texts of the Chinese *Weishi* school. Over time, however, due to a series of factors, including material destroyed in anti-Buddhist persecutions, a rise in neo-Confucianism, as well as the strengthening of other Buddhist schools, interest in Yogacara waned. Major commentaries were lost and without the widespread ability to read Sanskrit, explanations of Yogacara were left to Chan masters, who provided their own interpretative spin.

This changed in the late nineteenth century when a series of lost Yogacara texts were reintroduced to China via Japan. By the Yuan dynasty (1271–1368), writes Makeham, 'key commentaries of this school had ceased being transmitted in China, and it was not until the end of the nineteenth century that a number of them were reintroduced into China from Japan, where the transmission had been uninterrupted'.[86] One of the most critical characters in this transfer of knowledge was Yang Wenhui 楊文會 (1837–1911). Yang, who is commonly known as the 'father of the Buddhist revival', established the Buddhist Press and Research Center, a printing house in Nanjing, which, as Buddhist scholar Francesca Tarocco writes, 'became a meeting point for students, politicians, believers and unbelievers alike'.[87] Working with his friend, the Japanese scholar Nanjō Bun'yū, Yang reprinted hundreds of lost Chinese Buddhist manuscripts, including Kuiji's commentary on the *Cheng Wei-Shi Lun*. Yang's student and the main heir to the Buddhist press was a lay scholar named Ouyang Jingwu 歐陽竟無 (1871–1943), who advocated a 'return to roots' approach to Buddhist thought. Ouyang established the China Institute of Inner Learning (*Neixue Yuan* 內學院), also in Nanjing, which institutionalised the fascination with Indian Buddhist philosophy. It was here, under the direct tutelage of Ouyang, that between 1920 and 1922, Xiong Shili studied Yogacara practice and thought. 'I studied the teachings of Asanga and Vasubandhu with Master Ou-yang', writes Xiong, 'and was thoroughly converted.'[88]

In 1922 Xiong left Nanjing to take up a position teaching Buddhist philosophy at Peking University. It was in this new academic context that he began to analyse his, until then largely uncritical, belief in Buddhism and began to read Yogacara texts, not as a doctrine of salvation, but rather from a metaphysical and ontological point of view. In the end, this led to a rupture between Xiong and his former masters. Xiong would use his criticisms of the sophisticated arguments of Yogacara as a foundation for the creation of his own syncretic philosophy. Ultimately, he 'shifted from a largely uncritical belief' in Yogacara to 'a position where it served as a foil for his own constructive philosophy'.[89] Yet Xiong's New Confucian thought retained Yogacara ideas at its core.

The Yogacara or 'Consciousness Only' school holds that the external world is a product of the transformation of consciousness. Reality does not exist independently of the mind. There is some dispute as to whether this is an epistemological or ontological claim.[90] Yet, as Bronwyn Finnigan explains in her essay on Buddhist Idealism, all interpretations of Yogacara accept the philosophical thesis that 'what we take to be external objects are merely appearances in conscious awareness'.[91] For Yogacara practitioners, the distinction between the sentient mind and the objects of experience is illusory. We are deluded in the belief that we know the world outside the structures of the mind. According to Yogacara, it is the attachment to this illusion that is the ultimate cause of suffering. The process of awakening to wisdom involves the realisation that the 'bifurcation of experience between a perceiving subject and perceived objects' is mistaken.[92] Escape lies in recognising that our experience of the phenomenal world does not exist outside the constructions of consciousness and that all that appears to sensation is ultimately unreal.

Xiong's critique of his master's teachings has a number of inter-related aspects, which developed over time.[93] All of them amounted to the same basic principle, however. For Xiong, the 'Mind Only' school put too much emphasis on the mind. It prioritised a notion of *ti* as existing above and beyond the manifestations of *yong*. More specifically, Xiong was opposed to the Yogacara idea that consciousness was divided into different components, believing instead in a single, indivisible mind. More importantly, he objected to the doctrine of 'seeds', which held that the highest 'storehouse consciousness' contained 'seeds', which operate as the ontological basis or causal mechanism of things.[94] Productive power, which Xiong took as primary, could not be separated into individual elements. In substantial-ising the concept of seeds, Xiong maintained, Yogacara developed an ontological pluralism that led to a bifurcation of the mind into subject and object. The teachings of Consciousness Only, he came to believe, were only partially successful. They refuted attachment to external objects but retained attachment to the mind as the thing through which these objects are known.[95] For Xiong, consciousness is just as unreal and illusory as the object that the mind perceives. Since the material and the mental are both devoid of self-nature, we are as deluded in our faith in consciousness as we are in the reality of atoms and electrons.[96] Our attachment to consciousness is just as mistaken as our attachment to our experience of things.

Makeham contends that Xiong Shili was neither an epistemological nor a transcendental idealist, but maintained, instead, that there was a substance to appearances that was ultimately Real. Underpinning his position was 'the view that consciousness or mind and cognitive objects are inseparable because they constitute a single body, an indivisible whole'.[97] It is here that Xiong diverges most from his Yogacara training. Vasubandhu and Kuiji, according to Xiong's interpretation, believed that freedom from attachment to the impermanence of experience involved a rift, which divided the emptiness of Ultimate Reality from the illusory nature of phenomenon. The path to salvation they offered, which was designed to lead away from the world of suffering, creates, in Xiong's view, an 'unbridgeable split between an absolute unchanging reality (Dharma nature or *fa-xing*) and a constantly changing conditional phenomenal world (Dharma characters or *fa-xiang*)'.[98] Yet, for Xiong, there is no ontological distinction between the phenomenal world of experience and that which is ultimately Real.

According to Xiong's own account, his break from Buddhism came not through academic analysis but through the sincere meditative practices of introspection. The search for inner truth led Xiong to develop a philosophy that fused the sophisticated epistemological teachings of Yogacara Buddhism with insights he gained from the ancient classic *Yijing*. Alfred North Whitehead famously claimed that Western philosophy is a series of footnotes to Plato.[99] Xiong Shili had a similar attitude to the *Yijing* or *Book of Changes*, a complex, mysterious and intricate text in which he believed 'all Chinese scholarship and thinking have their source'.[100] Xiong describes his own inner revelation as follows:

> I was entirely engaged in what Ch'en Po-sha' termed 'placing the mind in non-being' (*ts'o hsin yu wu*). It means to make a clean sweep of all kinds of 'cognitive perception' (*chih-chien*) derived from bigoted opinions and implanted superstitions. The purpose is to make the mind large and dynamic without any trace of Stagnation. Only then can we 'experientially recognize' (*t'i-jen*) the truth in all places. After a long time, I suddenly awoke to the realization that what I inwardly witnessed agreed entirely with the idea of Great Change.[101]

New Confucianism

Xiong Shili is remembered as one of main founders of contemporary New Confucianism (*Diandai Xin Rujia* 點帶新儒家). In English, the term 'New Confucianism' is used to distinguish a philosophy of the twentieth century from the much earlier 'neo-Confucianists' of the Song-Ming period, who lived between the tenth and twelfth centuries. Makeham argues that New Confucianism is an intellectual movement that was retro-chronically created in the 1970s and 1980s by scholars working in Taiwan, Hong Kong and the United States. These later thinkers looked back at the Confucian revivalism in the early part of the twentieth century and crystallised it into a key school of modern Chinese thought.[102]

The New Confucian revival draws on classical Confucian texts along with their interpretation by the Song-Ming masters to develop a creative response to the intellectual challenges of Buddhism. The modern movement also arose, as Chang Hao explains, as a reaction to the 'intellectual crisis that began with the closing years of the 1890s and reached its height in the May Fourth period'.[103] It consolidated as a contrast with the radical progressivism that dominated intellectual life in the period. New Confucianism was an outgrowth of a long-standing trend that opposed wholesale Westernisation and the rejection of Chinese tradition. This strand of intellectual conservatism, however, should not be mistaken for an unreflective nostalgia for a bygone era. Instead, as Charlotte Furth notes in her introduction to *The Limits of Change*, an important collection of essays on 'Conservative Alternatives in Republican China', modern conservatism in China, as elsewhere, has been 'a response to new issues, a response in which reevaluations of tradition have gone hand in hand with competing models for change'.[104] Sebastien Billioud argues similarly: 'while they [New Confucianists] held deep the conviction that a cultural *tabula rasa* was not necessary to embrace modernity', he contends, 'they were themselves children of May Fourth'.[105] New Confucianism, then, is best understood as a part of Chinese modernity, not as an attempt to flee from it.

Xiong's New Confucian philosophy emerged from his own wavelike return to older traditions of neo-Confucian thought. This strategy of remaking the future by engaging the past is an old one. The recurrent return to a more ancient tradition (which is itself always a process of recreation) begins with Confucius himself, who spoke of his own work as a restoration and renewal. This cyclic repetition was repeated by the Song-Ming neo-Confucians and then, once again, by the New Confucians who were active in the twentieth century. Xiong's own thinking grew out of a rich engagement with the earlier Song-Ming philosophers whom he sought to integrate as well as to criticise. His aim was to carve a middle way between the dichotomy that had characterised the previous wave of neo-Confucianism, which, he felt, was too externally focused on ritual rigidity on the one hand, and too internally absorbed on the other.

Xiong's own ideas were influenced most deeply by the School of Vital Stuff (*Qixue* 張載), represented by Zhang Zai 张载 (1020–77) and then later by Wang Fuzhi 王夫之 (1619–92). Wang, who wrote under the alias *Chuanshan* 船山, a name meant to depict the mountain retreat where he lived in isolation after the fall of the Ming dynasty, was, according to the philosophical historian JeeLoo Liu, among the most prolific and sophisticated writers in the neo-Confucian school. 'Among Confucianists', Xiong wrote, 'Wang alone saw the truth.'[106]

Like Xiong, Wang had an interest in the *Weishih* or Yogacara school. His main preoccupation, however, was in the ontology of the *Yijing*. He developed a Chinese natural philosophy that originated in an all-encompassing substance or material force. Wang's metaphysical monism is based on a non-reductive materialism, in which incorporeal energy (*qi*) is conceptualised as the ultimate source of the myriad things.

Wang's own intellectual forebear was the Song dynasty philosopher Zhang Zai, who used the *Yijing* to envision a world composed out of primordial *qi*. It was Zhang Zai, writes Liu, who 'renewed and systemized the philosophy of *qi* in the *Yijing* tradition and made it an integral part of neo-Confucianism'.[107] For Zhang Zai, *qi*, as the fundamental cosmic force, 'permeates the whole universe'. Extensive space is nothing other than 'the external expansion of *qi*'. In Xiong Shili's intellectual development, as Yu Sang notes, the ontology of Zhang Zai that is based on a single vital substance in a constant state of change was of critical importance:

> Zhang Zai considered the source of all phenomena to be vital stuff, and interpreted the concept of change (*yi* 易) in Zhouyi as the process of the ceaseless transformations of two kinds of vital stuff, *yin* and *yang*. Since *yin* and *yang*, according to Zhang Zai, are both vital stuff, albeit with different characteristics, they are not distinct things in nature. Indeed, Zhang Zai emphasised many times that these two kinds of vital stuff, or the entire world, are one.[108]

The School of Vital Stuff contends that the entire universe is composed through the transformation of *qi*. It envisions an original state (*benti*) in which the dual forces of *yin* and *yang* are poised in a dense mist (*yinyun* 氤氲) of intermixed equilibrium.[109] The material energy of *qi* propels the *Yijing*'s dynamic cosmology, which, through its continuous transmutation, generates the sixty-four different basic 'elements' that enter into combinations to give birth to the Ten Thousand Things. Zhang Zai explains this rhythmic undulation of condensation and dispersion with reference to the tides.[110] Through a cosmic ebb and flow, *qi* consolidates into the existence of concrete things, while concrete things disintegrate back into the non-being of a vacuous *qi*. Wang Fuzhi, in his commentary on the *Yijing*, describes the composition and decomposition through the interrelation between the 'hidden' and the 'visible'. 'Each hexagram has twelve lines, one half is hidden, the other is visible. Correspondingly, the *Yijing* does not speak of being and nonbeing', he writes, 'but only of concealment and visibility.'[111] This intrinsic relation between the visible and invisible, the manifest and unmanifest, is crucial to Xiong's reconceptualisation of *ti–yong*. It also resonates with the inherent imperceptibility of wireless waves.

Wang Fuzhi shares Zhang Zai's cosmology, which is based on the fluctuations between a fundamental energy (*ti*) and its multiple manifestations (*yong*).[112] Yet he departs from Zhang in his own formulation of the *ti–yong* pair. In the philosophy of Zhang Zai, as Liu explains, there is a clear separation of *ti* and *yong*. *Qi* itself is the substance (*ti*), 'invisible and formless', the universe in its fundamental state, while its functions are that which is manifest and concrete. 'When it consolidates, it forms material objects', wrote Zhang, 'when it disintegrates, it is simply a massive formless *qi*.' For Wang – and later for Xiong Shili – there is no substance behind our experiential world, 'no separate fundamental state (*ti*) independent of its function (*yong*)'.[113] The idea of substance as a 'fundamental ground', a primary stuff that is 'ontologically basic', implies an ontological hierarchy that Wang, as well as Xiong, firmly rejects.[114] 'The reality is nothing but *qi*', wrote Wang, 'and its function manifested in concrete things.'[115]

The New Treatise

Xiong's *New Treatise on Consciousness Only* (*Xin Weishi Lun* 新唯識論) was published in 1932.[116] The text fuses a critique of Yogacara with the metaphysics of the *Yijing*. Rather than representing a conversion from Buddhism to Confucianism as is sometimes claimed, it is better understood as a rich amalgamation of these two philosophical schools. The *New Treatise* is a singular work, widely recognised for the depth and richness of its ideas. Introducing his translation, Makeham calls it 'the most original book in twentieth century Chinese philosophy'.[117] Charles Muller makes a similar claim in his review. 'The effort made in this treatise to integrate core components of major Confucian and Buddhist systems into a larger, overarching framework has not, to my knowledge, been attempted on this kind of scale and with this level of sophistication at any time in history.'[118] Liu Shu-hsien echoes this sentiment in his study of New Confucian thought. 'There is no question', he maintains, 'that Xiong was the most original thinker in his generation.'[119] 'It is now almost universally held', concurs Jiyuan Yu, 'that in the *New Treatise*, Xiong built the most creative philosophical system in contemporary Chinese philosophy.'[120]

At the centre of the *New Treatise* is the *ti–yong* pair. Xiong treats this as a basic philosophical distinction, which corresponds to the difference between noumena and phenomena, what is and what appears to be. 'The fundamental problem of substance and appearance (*benti wu xianxiang* 本體無現象)', Xiong writes, 'goes by the name of *ti–yong*.'[121] Xiong's entire philosophical project, as Makeham explains, is an attempt to articulate the true nature of this relationship. In doing so, Xiong casts himself in opposition to the Qing scholar officials who sought to protect an underlying essence from a function or use that they deemed superficial. There is no refuge in an eternal Chinese culture, just as, for Xiong, there was no primary substance behind or beneath the manifestations of the phenomenal world. *Ti* is not external to, or independent of, phenomena; instead Reality permeates the myriad things. There is no ground or primal stuff within or upon which change takes place. Xiong's cosmo-ontology thus conforms to a post-etheric universe in which waves do not require a medium. For Xiong, the rippling waves of continuous transformation are all that is Real.

As the title of his book clearly indicates, the *New Treatise* is intended as a commentary or critical response to the *Chen Wei-Shi Lun*. In it, Xiong retains the Yogacara belief that appearances are deceptive and that our attachment to phenomena is delusional. His argument draws on the Buddhist teaching that the world, as it appears, does not have an inherent self-nature; there is no permanent, unchanging essence to the realm of phenomena. In this, Makeham notes, he subscribes to the Madhyamaka doctrine of emptiness. 'I regard the self-nature (*zixing*) of the phenomenal world to be inherently empty', Xiong writes, 'it exists only because of the attachments of false discrimination.'[122] Yet, while Xiong maintained that changing manifestations are empty appearances lacking self-nature, he nevertheless sought to affirm the phenomenal world, rather than simply to repudiate it.

His ultimate conclusion about the inseparability of *ti–yong* can seem perplexing and paradoxical, as it rests on the idea that phenomena are at once illusory but nevertheless ultimately Real. For Xiong there is no separation between constantly changing experience and original, eternal substance. Since the ontological realm, the intrinsic reality of things (*ti*) and function or the external manifestation of things (*yong*) are non-dual, Ultimate Reality cannot be sought independently from phenomena. In this fundamental confirmation of embodied existence, Xiong is subscribing to the Mahayana doctrine of 'Buddha nature', which holds that all beings are already inherently enlightened. True wisdom comes from the recognition that what is here and now is at once illusory but also, at the same time, Real. 'There has only ever been this Reality', Xiong insists. 'Apart from it there is no phenomenal world to which it stands in contrast.'[123]

It is due to following conventional truth that the mundane world is accepted as proven. Earth is nothing but earth, water is nothing but water, right through to the myriad existents . . . Because ultimate truth is experienced, however, there is a categorical refutation of conventional knowing. Hence, earth is not thought of as earth, because earth's nature is empty. What is manifest before one is Reality (*zhenti* 真體), perfectly clear . . . Reality cannot be sought independent of phenomena and the Ruler (*zhuzai* 主宰) is to be discerned amongst the flow [of phenomena].[124]

Xiong believed that it was not only the Indian Buddhists who mistakenly separated *ti* from *yong*. Rather, the same error can be found in all religio-philosophical traditions, East and West, which sever 'fundamental Reality (*ti*) and function (*yong*) in two'. The idea that *ti* is prior to *yong* (*ti xian wei yong* 體現為用), or that substance, which lies beyond, gives rise to function, is apparent in both the philosophical distinction between noumena and phenomena as well as in the religious faith in a transcendent creator. Xiong's objection, as commentator Ng Yu Kwan puts it, is that these systems of thought construct 'a fictitious realm of extreme quiescence beyond movement (*liuxing* 流行) . . . or a realm of extreme nullity beyond the actual world'. At the same time, Ng notes, Xiong also 'criticized some philosophers who regarded the mere, isolated, and ever-changing phenomena as reality, because they did not understand that in the midst of the changing phenomena lies the reality of extreme quiescence'.[125] 'Reality' already includes 'function' within it, he reasoned; 'if they are separable, function will differ from original Reality and exist independently, and in that way will have its own original Reality'.[126] Substance, he wrote, does not exist apart from worldly experience. It is not exterior to the 'Ten Thousand Things'. Instead, Ultimate Reality is inherent in the changing flow of the material world and cannot be sought independently. 'Ontologically speaking', writes Ng, 'substance exists in the midst of functions; apart from functions, there is no substance. At the same time, function is the manifestation of substance; apart from substance, there is no function.'[127] This 'philosophy of the nonseparability of substance and function', Ng concludes, 'is the foundation of New Confucianism'.[128]

Although *ti* and *yong* are not separate, they are also not identical. While not distinct, they are not absolutely alike. Makeham describes Xiong's position as combining 'an ontological monism with a phenomenological dualism'.[129] 'Ontologically phenomena and Reality are not different', but 'phenomenologically our experience of them is not the same'.[130] Xiong expresses the complex interrelationship in a myriad of ways. *Yong*, he writes, is the flow, or the expression of *ti*. The great functioning, *da yong*, manifests substance (*ti*) as its practice; the flow or expression of essence (*ti*) gives rise to the Ten Thousand Things; function is a manifold manifestation of substance; Reality is manifest through function; function describes the expression of Reality and refers to its flow.

He finds the most vivid expression by returning to his Buddhist roots and borrowing an image from *The Awakening of Faith*.[131] The text famously compares the connection between the realm of ignorance and enlightenment to that between the waters of the sea and the waves stirred by wind. In his analysis of *ti–yong*, Xiong repeatedly evokes this vision of ocean and waves. Just as the water in the ocean is manifested as waves, *ti* is like the deep and still sea and *yong* like the continuous rise and fall of its many waves. We are in the position of the sailor who encounters the sea as waves. 'You don't look for the ocean separately from the waves', nor does 'each wave have a separate or individualized essence (*ti*)'. Waves have no self-nature. 'Just as the waves reveal the ocean, then this represents the non-duality of *ti* and *yong* (*ti yong bu er*).'[132] 'Reality moves, becoming function, just like the ocean water moves, becoming the myriad waves.'[133]

> Take for example, water in the ocean manifesting itself as lively and active waves. The many waves are also traces and forms. Do you think the water is outside the waves? Or take, for example, a torrent bursting violently, with thousands and thousands of white drops lashing up and down. These white drops are also traces and forms. Do you think that they are outside the torrent? Please think it over. The Ten Thousand Things manifest themselves and seem to be individual objects, but really their self-nature consists in great functioning universally operating without cease.[134]

The *New Treatise* posits a world that consists not of solid objects but of impermanent events in a continuous state of modulation. Xiong adopts the fundamental principle of transformation from the teachings of Yogacara, but objects to the bifurcation – which Yogacara presumes – between something that is doing the transformation and something that is transformed. For Xiong there is nothing behind or prior to change. 'Transformation does not mean movement, as when a thing proceeds from one place to another', he writes. Transformation should not be confused with something that moves in place. Nor does change arise from some eternal essence that precedes it. Transformation is not generated from a constant substance nor an original void. 'It is neither emptiness nor the constant that transforms.'[135]

Xiong's own understanding of the productive power of constant transformation (*hengzhuan* 恆轉) draws heavily from the *Yijing* and its ever-changing permutations.[136] The *New Treatise* describes the ceaseless generation of constant transformation as emerging from the interaction of two opposing forces: *Xi* 翕, compression or contraction, and *Pi* 闢, extension or expansion. These two concepts are found in the discussion of the second hexagram *Kun* (坤), which consists of six broken lines, in the Great Commentary of the *Yijing*. *Kun*, reads the Commentary, is the 'great and originating (capacity)' to which 'all things owe their birth'.[137] In her stillness, she contracts (*Xi*), and in her movement she expands (*Pi*). *Kun* expresses *Yin*, the female, dark and receptive energy of the Earth. She is paired with the first hexagram *Qian* (乾), which is composed of six unbroken lines and manifests pure Yang, the creative, light and active principle of the heavens. '*Qian* (symbolises Heaven, which) directs the great beginnings of things', the Commentary continues; '*Kun* (symbolises Earth, which) gives to them their completion'.[138] 'To close a door is called *Kun*, and to open a door is called *Qian*. One closing and one opening is called "change".'[139] Together, *Qian* and *Kun*, the creative and receptive, mark 'the opening and closing of the gate'.[140]

This continuous pulsation of contraction and expansion forms the ceaseless flow of change. *Xi*, the tendency to contract, to condense, to close, to coalesce, to fold, is what produces the material world. 'As contraction consolidates', Xiong writes, 'it comes close to being matter.'[141] Before it can totally solidify, however, it is met by the internal but opposing force. *Pi*, the tendency to open and expand, creates the world of the mind. Just as 'material dharmas are associated with the contracting tendency of constant transformation', reads the *New Treatise*, 'mental dharmas are associated with the expanding tendency of constant transformation'. The two contrasting forces are inherently intertwined. Like the swirling waves of the *yin–yang* diagram, each side contains the seed of the other. 'One expansion, one contraction. It is as if they had been purposefully set in opposition so as to create transformation.'[142]

Every contraction and expansion constitutes a *ksana* or 'thought instant', a Buddhist term for the smallest unit of time. Yet even this most minute moment of permanence is illusory. No dharma, Xiong insists, abides in time. One can't say first there is *Xi* and then there is *Pi*. Instead, Ultimate Reality is nothing more than thought instant following thought instant, each of which ceases as soon as it arises. 'It is not a previous movement's continuing into a later moment of time that is called "continuous"', writes Xiong. Rather, it is the ceaseless flow of moment upon moment of transformation 'since beginningless time'.[143] Writing in the early twentieth century, Xiong, implicitly influenced by the electric world that was emerging all around him, likened this ceaseless rhythm of generation and extinction – 'wondrous and unfathomable' – to an uninterrupted flash upon flash of lightning, a 'myriad of transformations that is continuous and without end'.[144]

Xiong Shili formulated a conceptual relationship between Reality (*ti*) and its manifestations (*yong*), which views the twinned concepts as inseparable, and yet still distinct. For Xiong, the problem with the Qing reformers was not that in calling on the abstract framework of *ti–yong* they were clinging to old concepts. Rather, their mistake was that the conception of this philosophical framework did not dive deep enough. They insisted on a distinction between an essential culture and changing technologies, positing a binary duality which contrasted a stable past governed by tradition and a constantly changing future determined by innovation and novelty. Yet in both the Buddhist and the neo-Confucian traditions, *ti–yong* are not separated in this way but are rather conceived as an inherently symbiotic pair. Culture and technology, tradition and modernity, past and future, East and West, whose apparent antithesis structured so much of the intellectual milieu of the late Qing, are not in opposition but are instead subtly but intimately related. In reconceptualising *ti–yong* at the turn of the century, just as China began to confront the new world of electric machines, Xiong opened up an alternative way of conceiving the apparent dichotomy between the cultural traditions of a Chinese past and a technological futurism that has long been associated with the modern West. The possibility of reconciliation rests on understanding that technology's essence is no different from its use; its Ultimate Reality is inseparable from its myriad appearances. Unlike other thinkers of the late Qing, Xiong did not envision the *ti–yong* duality as a mode of containment or protective blockade. Rather, he saw the paired forces of tradition and innovation, stillness and impermanence, centralised integration and disintegrating dispersion as manifestations of the complementary cosmic forces of contraction and expansion. Through a fusion of Buddhist metaphysics with the *Yijing*, he articulated a continuous process of transformation as an underlying elemental undulation. This is both an expression of the 'Way', a conception of tradition whose constancy comes from the endless flow of change, and also of the wireless undertow; the intensifying planetary electrosphere, which, following Xiong, can be understood as a phenomenal instantiation of Reality's ceaseless waves.

Notes

1. Ted Chiang, 'Bad Character', *The New Yorker*, 9 May 2016.
2. Ibid.
3. Ibid.

4. *Radical Machines: China in the Information Age*, Museum of Chinese in America, New York, 18 October 2018–24 March 2019.
5. Thomas Mullaney, 'Chinese is not a Backward Language', *Foreign Policy*, 12 May 2016.
6. Ibid.
7. Ibid.
8. Ibid.
9. David Moser, 'Backward Thinking about Orientalism and Chinese Characters', *Language Log*, 16 May 2016, https://languagelog.ldc.upenn.edu/nll/?p=25776.
10. Ibid.
11. Ibid.
12. Carlos Rojas, 'Chinese Writing, Heptapod B, and Martian Script: The Ethnocentric Bases of Language', unpublished essay, 2018.
13. Joshua Rothman, 'Ted Chiang's Soulful Science Fiction', *The New Yorker*, 5 January 2017.
14. Peter Godfrey-Smith, *Other Minds: The Octopus and the Evolution of Intelligent Life* (London: HarperCollins, 2016).
15. Friedrich Nietzsche, *Thus Spake Zarathustra*, trans. Thomas Common (Mineola, NY: Dover Publications, 1999), 331.
16. Ted Chiang, 'Story of Your Life', in *Stories of Your Life and Others* (London: Picador, 2015), 124.
17. Rojas, 'Chinese Writing, Heptapod B, and Martian Script'. This idea is known in linguistics as the 'Sapir–Whorf hypothesis' or 'Linguistic Relativity',
18. Ibid.
19. G. W. F. Hegel, *The Philosophy of History*, trans. J. Sibree (Mineola, NY: Dover Publications, 2004), 105.
20. Paul Cohen, *Discovering History in China: American Historical Writing on the Recent Chinese Past* (New York: Columbia University Press, 2010), 57.
21. Shlomo Avineri, 'Introduction', in *Karl Marx on Colonialism and Modernization: His Despatches and Other Writings on China, India, Mexico, the Middle East and North Africa*, ed. Shlomo Avineri (New York: Doubleday, 1968), 6.
22. Robert Bickers, 'Restoration and Reform, 1860–1900', in *The Oxford Illustrated History of Modern China*, ed. Jeffrey N. Wasserstrom (Oxford: Oxford University Press, 2016), 94.
23. Jeffery Wasserstrom, 'Shanghai's Latest Global Turn', *The Globalist*, 7 May 2007, https://www.theglobalist.com/shanghais-latest-global-turn/.
24. Edmund Fung, *The Intellectual Foundations of Chinese Modernity: Cultural and Political Thought in the Republican Era* (Cambridge: Cambridge University Press, 2010), 32. Note that in this passage Fung is specifically referring to the perceptions of Chen Duxiu, 陳獨秀, but this type of thinking holds more generally.
25. Lydia Liu, 'Review of *Bringing the World Home: Appropriating the West in Late Qing and Early Republican China*', *China Review International* 14, no. 2 (2007): 330.

26. For more on the complex modern history of critical terms, see Barrett and Tarocco on *zongjiao* (宗教), the word corresponding to 'religion'. Tim Barrett and Francesca Tarocco, 'Terminology and Religious Identity: Buddhism and the Genealogy of the Term Zongjiao', in *Dynamics in the History of Religions Between Asia and Europe: Encounters, Notions, and Comparative Perspectives*, ed. Volkhard Krech and Marion Steinicke (Leiden: Brill, 2012).

27. Karl-Heinz Pohl, '"Western Learning as Substance, Chinese Learning for Application": Li Zehou's Thought on Tradition and Modernity', in *Li Zehou and Confucian Philosophy*, ed. Roger T. Ames and Jinhua Jia (Honolulu, HI: University of Hawaii Press, 2018), 63.

28. Benjamin Schwartz, 'The Limits of "Tradition versus Modernity" as Categories of Explanation: The Case of the Chinese Intellectuals', *Daedalus* 101, no. 2 (1972): 79.

29. Benjamin Schwartz, *In Search of Wealth and Power: Yen Fu and the West* (Cambridge, MA: Belknap Press of Harvard University Press, 1964), 2.

30. Cohen, *Discovering History in China*, 81.

31. Ibid., 53.

32. Peter Rowe and Kuan Seng, *Architectural Encounters with Essence and Form in Modern China* (Cambridge, MA: MIT Press, 2002).

33. Lynn Pan, *Shanghai Style: Art and Design Between the Wars* (San Francisco: Long River Press, 2008).

34. Zhang Zhidong, along with Zeng Guofan, Li Hongzhang and Zuo Zongtang, was one of the 'four famous officials' of the late Qing.

35. Zhidong Zhang, *China's Only Hope: An Appeal* (New York: Fleming H. Revell, 1900), 69.

36. Ibid., 85.

37. Theodore Huters, *Bringing the World Home: Appropriating the West in Late Qing and Early Republican China* (Honolulu, HI: University of Hawaii Press, 2017), 13.

38. Cohen, *Discovering History in China*, 75.

39. Schwartz, *In Search of Wealth and Power*, 6.

40. Odd Arne Westad, *Restless Empire: China and the World Since 1750* (London: Vintage, 2014), 54.

41. Jonathan Spence, *The Search for Modern China* (New York: W. W. Norton, 1991), 192.

42. Ibid., 194.

43. Ssu-yu Teng and John King Fairbank, *China's Response to the West: A Documentary Survey, 1839–1923* (Cambridge, MA: Harvard University Press, 1979), 72.

44. Ibid., 54.

45. Wasserstrom, 'Shanghai's Latest Global Turn'.

46. There is a vast literature on modern Shanghai. Important references include Leo Ou-fan Lee, *Shanghai Modern: The Flowering of a New Urban Culture in China, 1930–1945* (Cambridge, MA: Harvard

University Press, 1999); Marie-Claire Bergère, *Shanghai: China's Gateway to Modernity* (Stanford, CA: Stanford University Press, 2009); Pan, *Shanghai Style*.

47. Guifen Feng, 'Excerpts from "On the Adoption of Western Learning', in *Changing China: Readings in the History of China from the Opium War to the Present*, ed. Gentzler J. Mason (New York: Praeger, 1977), 71.

48. Daniel Bays, *China Enters the Twentieth Century: Chang Chih-Tung and the Issues of a New Age, 1895–1909* (Ann Arbor, MI: University of Michigan Press, 1978), 1.

49. Schwartz, 'The Limits of "Tradition versus Modernity"', 80.

50. Rebecca E. Karl and Peter Zarrow, 'Introduction', in *Rethinking the 1898 Reform Period: Political and Cultural Change in Late Qing China*, ed. Rebecca E. Karl and Peter Zarrow (Cambridge, MA: Harvard University Asia Center, 2002), 2.

51. Huters, *Bringing the World Home*, vii.

52. Tze-Ki Hon, 'Zhang Zhidong's Proposal for Reform: A New Reading of the Quanxue Pian', in Karl and Zarrow, eds, *Rethinking the 1898 Reform Period*, 79.

53. Zhang, *China's Only Hope*, 63.

54. Hon, 'Zhang Zhidong's Proposal for Reform', 92.

55. Jana S. Rošker, 'Li Zehou and New Confucianism: A Philosophy for New Global Futures', in *Li Zehou and Confucian Philosophy*, ed. Roger T. Ames and Jinhua Jia (Honolulu, HI: University of Hawaii Press, 2018), 35.

56. See Pohl, '"Western Learning as Substance, Chinese Learning for Application"'.

57. Jana S. Rošker, *Following His Own Path: Li Zehou and Contemporary Chinese Philosophy* (Albany, NY: SUNY Press, 2019), 45.

58. Li Zehou, 'The Western is the Substance, and the Chinese is for Application (Excerpts)', *Contemporary Chinese Thought* 31, no. 2 (1999): 32–9.

59. Ibid., 33–4.

60. Pohl, '"Western Learning as Substance, Chinese Learning for Application"', 67.

61. Joseph Levenson, *Confucian China and its Modern Fate: A Trilogy* (Berkeley, CA: ACLS Humanities E-Book, 2008), 67.

62. Charles Muller, 'The Emergence of Essence-Function (Ti–yong) 體用 Hermeneutics in the Sinification of Indic Buddhism: An Overview', *Critical Review for Buddhist Studies* 19 (June 2016): 145.

63. Sun-hyang Kwon and Jeson Woo, 'On the Origin and Conceptual Development of "Essence–Function" (*Ti–Yong*)', *Religions* 10, no. 4 (2019): 1.

64. Cheng-ying Cheng, 'On the Metaphysical Significance of *Ti* (Body-Embodiment) in Chinese Philosophy: *Benti* (Origin-Substance) and *Ti–Yong* (Substance and Function)', *Journal of Chinese Philosophy* 29, no. 2 (2002): 145.

65. Ibid.

66. Ibid., 146.

67. Ibid., 148.
68. Kwon and Woo quote the *Xunzi*: 'Although many things co-exist in the same space, they are composed of different "essences" and have no predetermined "functions"'. Kwon and Woo, 'On the Origin and Conceptual Development of "Essence–Function" (*Ti–Yong*)', 2.
69. John Makeham, while acknowledging that most commenters follow Chan in crediting Wang Bi as the first person to articulate the *ti–yong* dichotomy, nevertheless agrees with Rošker that the pairing has an earlier lineage. 'Even if it was Wang who first used *ti* and *yong* as a pair of terms in Laozi (and even he did not use the pair as a compound) there is little doubt that the relationship expressed by the terms was not first formulated by him. Late Han thinkers had already employed near-identical terminology to *ti* and *yong* to express the same relationship that Wang Bi later expressed with *ti* and *yong* (albeit without the same metaphysical application).' John Makeham, 'Introduction', in *New Confucianism: A Critical Examination*, ed. John Makeham (New York: Palgrave Macmillan, 2003), 1–21.
70. Wing-Tsit Chan, ed., *A Source Book in Chinese Philosophy* (Princeton, NJ: Princeton University Press, 1969), 323.
71. Ibid.
72. Kwon and Woo, 'On the Origin and Conceptual Development of "Essence–Function" (*Ti–Yong*)', 1.
73. Chan, ed., *A Source Book in Chinese Philosophy*, 403.
74. William Grosnick, 'The Categories of T'i, Hsiang, and Yung: Evidence That Paramārtha Composed the *Awakening of Faith*', *Journal of the International Association of Buddhist Studies* 12, no. 1 (1989): 65–92; Francesca Tarocco, 'Lost in Translation? The Treatise on the *Mahāyāna Awakening of Faith* (Dasheng Qixin Lun) and its Modern Readings', *Bulletin of the School of Oriental and African Studies* 71, no. 2 (2008): 323–43.
75. 'Dasheng qixin lun', in *The Princeton Dictionary of Buddhism*, ed. Robert Buswell and Donald Lopez (Princeton, NJ: Princeton University Press, 2013). 22.
76. This idea of the distinction and interaction between the worldly and the absolute had a profound influence on the Song-Ming neo-Confucians, as we will see in later chapters. Zhang Zhai (1017–73), inspired by the *Yijing*, wrote of Infinite Vacuity as substance (*ti*) and finite material force as function (*yong*). Chan, ed., *A Source Book in Chinese Philosophy*, 502. Cheng Yi (1033–1107), who emphasised the non-separation of *ti–yong*, wrote that 'substance and function come from the same source, and there is no gap between the manifest and the hidden'. Chan, ed., *A Source Book in Chinese Philosophy*, 570. Wang Yangming (1472–1529) maintained that 'when we speak of substance as substance, function is already involved in it, and when we speak of function as function, substance is already involved in it' (quoted in Antonio Cua, 'On the Ethical Significance of the *Ti–Yong* Distinction', *Journal of Chinese Philosophy* 29, no. 2 [2002]: 163–70). Zhu Xi (1130–1200)

likewise had a complex formulation of the terms, which was dynamic, contextual and indeterminate. In his essay, Antonio Cua elaborates, explaining that Zhu Xi linked *ti–yong* to the ultimate polarity of *yin yang* (陰陽). According to Zhu Xi, writes Cua, *yin* can be the *ti* of *yang*, just as *yong* can be the *ti* of *yin* (陰). Cua, 'On the Ethical Significance of the *Ti–Yong* Distinction', 167.

77. Translated in Tarocco, 'Lost in Translation?', 324.
78. Wei-Ming Tu, 'Hsiung Shih-Li's Quest for Authentic Existence', in *The Limits of Change: Essays on Conservative Alternatives in Republican China*, ed. Charlotte Furth (Cambridge, MA: Harvard University Press, 2014 [1976]), 261.
79. Ibid.
80. Ibid., 250.
81. Ibid.
82. Jiyuan Yu, 'Xiong Shili's Metaphysics of Virtue', in *Contemporary Chinese Philosophy*, ed. Chung Ying Cheng and Nicholas Bunnin (Oxford: Blackwell, 2002), 127.
83. John Makeham, 'Introduction', in *Transforming Consciousness: Yogacara Thought in Modern China*, ed. John Makeham (New York: Oxford University Press, 2014), 1.
84. Chinese Yogacara is a vast topic that cannot be dealt with in detail here. For more on Yogacara from a philosophical perspective, see JeeLoo Liu, *An Introduction to Chinese Philosophy: From Ancient Philosophy to Chinese Buddhism* (Oxford: Wiley-Blackwell, 2006); Makeham, ed., *Transforming Consciousness*; Dan Lusthaus, *Buddhist Phenomenology: A Philosophical Investigation of Yogacara Buddhism and the Ch'eng Wei-Shih Lun* (London: Routledge, 2003); Bronwyn Finnigan, 'Buddhist Idealism', in *Idealism: New Essays in Metaphysics*, ed. Tyron Goldschmidt and Kenneth L. Pearce (Oxford: Oxford University Press, 2017).
85. Xuanzang focused especially on the interpretation of Vasubandhu's major disciple Dharmapala.
86. Makeham, 'Introduction', in Makeham, ed., *Transforming Consciousness*, xiii.
87. Francesca Tarocco, *The Cultural Practices of Modern Chinese Buddhism: Attuning the Dharma* (Abingdon: Routledge, 2005), 53.
88. Tu, 'Hsiung Shih-Li's Quest for Authentic Existence', 267.
89. Shili Xiong, *New Treatise on the Uniqueness of Consciousness*, trans. John Makeham (New Haven, CT: Yale University Press, 2015), xiv.
90. Lusthaus, *Buddhist Phenomenology*.
91. Finnigan, 'Buddhist Idealism', 5.
92. 'Yogācāra', in Buswell and Lopez, eds, *The Princeton Dictionary of Buddhism*, 1034.
93. Yu Sang, *Xiong Shili's Understanding of Reality and Function, 1920–1937* (Leiden: Brill, 2020).
94. John Makeham, 'Xiong Shili's Critique of Yogacara Thought in the Context of His Constructive Philosophy', in Makeham, ed., *Transforming Consciousness*, 245.

95. Xiong, *New Treatise on the Uniqueness of Consciousness*, xviii.

96. Ibid., 247.

97. Makeham, 'Xiong Shili's Critique of Yogacara Thought', 247.

98. Yu, 'Xiong Shili's Metaphysics of Virtue', 132.

99. Alfred North Whitehead, *Process and Reality* (New York: Free Press, 1979), 39.

100. Yu, 'Xiong Shili's Metaphysics of Virtue', 135.

101. Tu, 'Hsiung Shih-Li's Quest for Authentic Existence', 267.

102. John Makeham, ed., *New Confucianism: A Critical Examination* (New York: Palgrave Macmillan, 2003).

103. Hao Chang, *Liang Ch'i-Ch'ao and Intellectual Transition in China, 1890–1907* (Cambridge, MA: Harvard University Press, 1971), 276.

104. Charlotte Furth, 'Culture and Politics in Modern Chinese Conservatism', in *The Limits of Change: Essays on Conservative Alternatives in Republican China*, ed. Charlotte Furth (Cambridge, MA: Harvard University Press, 2014 [1976]), 24.

105. Sébastien Billioud, *Thinking Through Confucian Modernity: A Study of Mou Zongsan's Moral Metaphysics* (Leiden: Brill, 2011), 3.

106. Yu Kwan Ng, 'Xiong Shili's Metaphysical Theory about the Non-Separability of Substance and Function', in *New Confucianism: A Critical Examination*, ed. John Makeham (New York: Palgrave Macmillan, 2003), 233.

107. JeeLoo Liu, *Neo-Confucianism: Metaphysics, Mind, and Morality* (Hoboken, NJ: Wiley-Blackwell, 2017), 61.

108. Sang, *Xiong Shili's Understanding of Reality and Function*, 147.

109. Wang derives this term from the *Yijing*.

110. Ingo Schäfer, 'Natural Philosophy, Physics and Metaphysics in the Discourse of Tan Sitong: The Concepts of *Qi* and *Yitai*', in *New Terms for New Ideas: Western Knowledge and Lexical Change in Late Imperial China*, ed. Michael Lackner, Iwo Amelung and Joachim Kurtz (Leiden: Brill, 2001), 257–69.

111. Ibid., 264.

112. Wang's thinking about *ti–yong* informs his ideas on the unification of *dao* and *qi* 器, the conceptual pair richly theorised by contemporary philosopher Yuk Hui in his analyses of a Chinese cosmotechnics. See Hui, *The Question Concerning Technology in China*. For Wang Fuzhi, the 'Way [dao] needs a vessel to take shape'. See Leigh Jenco, 'How Meaning Moves: Tan Sitong on Borrowing across Cultures', *Philosophy East and West* 62, no. 1 (2012): 92–113. Tan Sitong, another follower of Wang whose work we will turn to later, echoes this insistence on the non-separability of essence and use: 'There is no *dao* without *qi*. Without a bow and arrow there is no *dao* of archery; without horses and vehicles there is no *dao* of driving. There is no *dao* without *qi*. Ah, these are true words. If we believe these words, then *dao* must rely on *qi* before you can have practical use; it is not the case that *dao* exists in some empty objectless space.' See Scott

Pacey, 'Tan Sitong's "Great Unity": Mental Processes and Yogācāra in "An Exposition of Benevolence"', in *Transforming Consciousness: The Intellectual Reception of Yogācāra Thought in Modern China*, ed. John Makeham (Oxford: Oxford University Press, 2014), 107.

113. Liu, *Neo-Confucianism*, 108.
114. To those familiar with Western intellectual history, their philosophical orientation is reminiscent of Spinoza who wrote of a single substance as God or Nature, a plane of immanence or consistency on 'which all bodies, all minds, and all individuals are situated'. See Gilles Deleuze, *Spinoza: Practical Philosophy*, trans. Robert Hurley (San Francisco: City Lights, 2001), 25.
115. Liu, *Neo-Confucianism*, 108.
116. A vernacular and revised edition was published in 1944, and then an abridged version of the vernacular in 1953. My own engagement with the text follows Makeham's translation, which is based on the 1932 literary redaction.
117. Xiong, *New Treatise on the Uniqueness of Consciousness*, xi.
118. Charles Muller, 'Xiong Shili and the New Treatise: A Review Discussion of Xiong Shili, *New Treatise on the Uniqueness of Consciousness, an Annotated Translation* by John Makeham', *Sophia* 56, no. 3 (2017): 524.
119. Shu-hsien Liu, *Essentials of Contemporary Neo-Confucian Philosophy* (New York: Praeger, 2003), 68.
120. Yu, 'Xiong Shili's Metaphysics of Virtue', 128.
121. Shili Xiong, *Shili Yuyao: Important Remarks of Xiong Shili* (Shanghai: Shanghai Bookstore Publishing House, 2007), 37.
122. Xiong, *New Treatise on the Uniqueness of Consciousness*, 211.
123. Ibid., 195.
124. Ibid., 217.
125. Ng, 'Xiong Shili's Metaphysical Theory', 233.
126. Ibid., 133.
127. Ibid., 224.
128. Ibid., 219.
129. Xiong, *New Treatise on the Uniqueness of Consciousness*, 23.
130. Ibid., 222.
131. Xiong's own metaphysical commitments are consistent with the views in the *Awakening*, which does not present the phenomenological world as 'ontologically distinct from the all-pervading, undifferentiated absolute reality'. See Makeham, 'Introduction', in Makeham, ed., *Transforming Consciousness*, 33. For a more in-depth discussion, see John Makeham, 'Xiong Shili and the *Treatise on Awakening Mahāyāna Faith* as Revealed in *Record to Destroy Confusion and Make My Tenets Explicit*', in *The Awakening of Faith and New Confucian Philosophy*, ed. John Makeham (Leiden: Brill, 2021).
132. Xiong, *New Treatise on the Uniqueness of Consciousness*, 224.
133. Ibid., 240.

134. Chan, ed., *A Source Book in Chinese Philosophy*, 772.
135. Xiong, *New Treatise on the Uniqueness of Consciousness*, 111.
136. These permutations of broken and unbroken lines (*yin yao* 陰爻) and (*yang yao* 陽爻) constitute any trigram.
137. James Legge, 'Book of Changes: Xi Ci I', *Library of Premodern Chinese*, 2019, https://ctext.org/book-of-changes/xi-ci-shang/ens?filter=504074%2E.
138. Ibid.
139. Sang, *Xiong Shili's Understanding of Reality and Function*, 147.
140. Legge, 'Book of Changes: Xi Ci I',
141. Xiong, *New Treatise on the Uniqueness of Consciousness*, 98.
142. Ibid.
143. Ibid., 97.
144. Ibid., 95.

Chapter 2

Contraction and Expansion: From Wires to Wirelessness

The Chinese Internet constitutes a world of its own. This is starkly apparent in the dominance of the mobile app WeChat 微信, whose influence is almost impossible to overstate. The app was developed by Tencent, one of China's Internet giants. It evolved out of the enormously popular instant messaging site QQ, which had already amassed a user base of 700 million by the time WeChat was first introduced.[1] While it began as a simple messaging service, WeChat was quick to integrate other functions such as checking email, listening to music, playing games and shopping online. The capacity to use voice as well as images and text was especially welcome. The population had grown accustomed to text-based messaging and, in a culture in which answering machines had never been widely used, this revival of the aural had instant appeal.[2] Already, in these very early days, there was a sense that with WeChat, Tencent had moved beyond its reputation as a 'copycat brand' and was on the cusp of creating something truly new.

One of the most innovative features of QQ was a virtual currency called QQ coins, which could be used to traffic within the Tencent environment. With WeChat this payment system broke free from the limits of the virtual and entered the real world. On Chinese New Year 2014 a critical threshold was crossed as an aggressive marketing campaign targeted the tradition of gifting red envelopes filled with cash (*hongbao* 紅包). 'That evening, for every minute during peak time, WeChat Pay had more than 4.8 million participants and 25,000 envelopes opened during its "New Year Red Envelope" scheme.'[3] The following winter, as the Year of the Goat gave way to the Year of the Monkey, WeChat reported trade in one billion virtual red envelopes. Lured in by holiday money, millions of users signed up for the company's mobile payment system. 'On Chinese New Year's Eve in 2016, more than 2.3 billion Red Packets flooded through WeChat, and the number skyrocketed to 14 billion on Chinese New Year 2017.'[4] Jack

Ma, the flamboyant then CEO of Alibaba, Tencent's main rival, likened WeChat's red envelope campaign to a 'Pearl Harbor attack'.[5] Media theorist Finn Brunton claims that WeChat wallet transformed the media climate by 'making money conversational'. *Hongbao*, he argues, is just like 'another kind of emoji, another set of stickers – a messaging practice and a way of texting'.[6] In China this 'chatification' of money took hold almost instantaneously and came to permeate Chinese social media. By 2018 WeChat was close to a billion users and Tencent, once notorious for stealing ideas from elsewhere, had become one of the most profitable and innovative Internet companies in the world.

WeChat operates as a platform not only for the exchange of virtual currency, but also for the millions of apps it hosts. In their essay 'WeChat as Infrastructure', Jean Christophe Plantin and Gabriele de Seta cite recent scholarship on the 'infrastructuralization of digital platforms' to analyse 'official accounts' that work like nested apps as well as the 'mini apps' that operate as in-app channels, which are made by third parties but are contained within the WeChat environment.[7] Business researcher Connie Chan, in an article entitled 'When One App Rules Them All', details the platform's ubiquitous role:

> Along with its basic communication features WeChat users in China can access services to hail a taxi, order food delivery, buy movie tickets, play casual games, check in for a flight, send money to friends, access fitness tracker data, book a doctor appointment, get banking statements, pay the water bill, find geo-targeted coupons, recognize music, search for a book at the local library, meet strangers around you, follow celebrity news, read magazine articles, and even donate to charity . . . all in a single, integrated app.[8]

In a video essay entitled 'How China is Changing Your Internet', the *New York Times* calls WeChat a 'super app', a kind of 'army knife' that contains the equivalent of 'WhatsApp, Facebook, Skype, Uber, Amazon, Instagram, Tinder and a bunch of other things as well'.[9] China, as a result of the restrictions and filters that constitute the Great Firewall, has developed a kind of Intranet, which the essay's narrator likens to a giant lagoon largely cut off from the vast ocean of cyberspace. In this singular environment, WeChat, is a 'swamp monster'. Although it was born as a copy it has since mutated into something massive, strange and unknown.

WeChat's home screen – one of the most familiar images to Internet users in China – depicts the silhouette of a solitary figure gazing out at the giant body of the Earth. When WeChat was first launched in 2011, the company made use of one of the world's most iconic images, Nasa's 'Blue Marble', a picture taken in 1972 by the crew of Apollo 17 as it drifted towards the moon. 'Blue Marble' was among the first glimpses of the Earth from space. The image had a momentous impact, helping to create a global consciousness that was critical in the birth of the worldwide environmental movement. 'Blue Marble' remains one of the most reproduced photographs in history. In selecting 'Blue Marble' for its home screen, WeChat was signalling that it was a Chinese company with global ambitions, which sought to be part of the world.

On 25 September 2017, however, WeChat made international headlines by replacing 'Blue Marble' with an image of the earth taken from the *Feng Yun* (Wind Cloud) 4A, a recently launched second-generation Chinese meteorological satellite that had gone into use the same day. While in the Nasa image, the Earth is shown centred on Africa, the FY4A picture shifts perspective, placing China in the middle of the globe. In reporting the news of WeChat's rebranding, the state-owned paper *People's Daily* heralded the change as a symbol of China's 'self-reliance' in space technology. WeChat's own announcement stated that the photograph was chosen to celebrate the technological achievements of the FY4A and was meant to 'honor Chinese civilization by featuring Chinese geography to our hundreds of millions of users'.[10]

Electronic media has a deeply integrating and involuting power. This was already evident with the telegraph almost a century ago. At first China resisted the encroachment of what it perceived as an alien technology, and strove to contain this new form of communication within designated border zones. Eventually, however, opposition gave way to a form of acceptance, as the technological culture seeping in from the edges was absorbed by the centre. Crucially, however, China insisted that it would only allow the telegraph to be built within its territory if its lines were indigenously owned. In the twentieth century, the establishment of what was called telegraph sovereignty (*dianxian zhuquan* 電線主權) was an important part of a rising Chinese nationalism. In the twenty-first century, as companies such as Huawei and WeChat make plain, China's embrace of techno-nationalism – so perfectly captured in WeChat's new satellite imagery – has endured. Rather than be subsumed into a globalised Internet, China has advocated policies of cyber-sovereignty designed to ensure that in the new media environment it is able to establish and maintain a distinct sphere of its own.

The strategic embrace of technology with 'Chinese characteristics' is based on a transformation of the *ti–yong* dyad, which occurred during the first decades of the twentieth century. As China entered this tumultuous period, the attempt to shield Chinese culture from a technology that would be adapted only on the surface was subject to a forceful critique. This critical outlook consolidated during the May Fourth cultural movement, which began with the student protests of May Fourth 1919, prompted by the frustration of a weakened China that could not stand up to the power of America, Europe and Japan. Many argued that the application of technology (*yong*) had come to overwhelm the essence of Chinese culture (*ti*) and that the protective barriers between the realms were not strong enough to keep the new world at bay. Despite ongoing calls for Westernisation, however, the prevailing response has been a reassertion of China's *ti*, which has mutated away from a conceptualisation of a past traditional culture towards the strengthening assertion of a new-found state. Refashioned in this way, the *ti–yong* polarity continues to resurface, and can still be found latent in the familiar bifurcation between 'techno-liberation' and 'cyber-sovereignty', which informs so much of the discourse around China's intensive relation to the immersive environment of 5G.

China's techno-nationalism, then, emerged in the wake of a technological globalisation that was shaped by the telegraph. This unified global order was ultimately temporal in nature. Electronic communication, as media scholars have shown, created a synchronised time that covered the whole of the Earth. In China, as elsewhere, this universalised, standardised temporality helped construct the nation-state and the progressive linearity of modern history. Yet in positing the state as a higher unity capable of controlling a technology that it transcends, techno-nationalism assumes, like the Qing scholar officials, that the *ti–yong* dyad can be kept separate and distinct. With wirelessness, however, the idea of an electronic body united under a single, standardised time becomes more complex. Planetary time, which is now determined by atomic vibrations, has an in-built relativity. This intrinsic multiplicity, which is inherent to wireless media, challenges the unifying totality of hierarchical technological control. It suggests that, in addition to its contracting impulses, there is an expansiveness to the electromagnetic environment that is not fully captured by the integration of the globe and the consolidation of the state. Together these contrary forces of contraction and expansion constitute the ongoing pulsating rhythm of the wave.

Telegraph Sovereignty

The origin of wirelessness as an immersive environment lies in the wires of the telegraph, which was the first communication tool that enabled messages to be sent across great distances in next to no time. Samuel Morse became obsessed with the new invention on an ocean journey in 1832. His famous code, which translates alphanumeric symbols into binary signals made from long and short bursts of current, enabled the first practical instantiation of the technology. In 1844 Morse sent his first message across the wires. Almost immediately, the telegraph experienced explosive growth. In the United States, between 1846 and 1852 the network grew 600 fold.[11] The monumental task of laying the first transatlantic cable was – after a flawed first attempt – successfully completed in the mid-1860s. Following the well-known logic of network effects (each node growing more useful with each additional node) the electromagnetic telegraph extended its global reach in a matter of decades. In solving the problem of how to transfer messages quickly and efficiently across great distances, the telegraph, the first medium of electronic correspondence, soon established itself as a vital mode of communication that arguably proved to be as transformative as the medieval printing press.

In China, the arrival of the telegraph was part of a long-drawn-out trauma. The technology entered the country in the latter half of the nineteenth century, amid what is now commonly referred to as the 'Century of Humiliation', a period in which foreign powers subjected China to a series of crushing defeats and punishing peace treaties. Initially, Chinese officials and lay people felt a deep distrust towards the new medium. They resisted it as an instrument of both political and cultural invasion. China did not want to be drawn into a unified world that it viewed as foreign. Rather, it tried to protect its own centralised autonomy by keeping the outside world restricted to the periphery.

In 1861 the Qing court set up the *Zongli Yamen* 總理衙門, an office designed specifically to deal with foreign affairs. When it came to the telegraph, the office sought policies that would hinder both foreign and domestic use. After suffering a series of wartime defeats, the immediate value of modern military technology was easy to ascertain and its indigenous acquisition was at the heart of the nineteenth-century's self-strengthening movement. Yet while boats and guns were of clear value in the defence of territory, the benefits of the telegraph and railways were far more ambiguous. Rather than keep out foreign forces, these technologies seemed precisely devised to let them in. Establishing lines of communication created a structural challenge to the Chinese strategy of containment by stretching across the land and extending access to the outside. 'Both the telegraph and railroads', writes Erik Baark in his comprehensive history of the telegraph in China, appeared 'designed primarily to facilitate the penetration of foreign merchandise and Western ideas deep into the country'.[12] Global electronic communication was deemed deeply suspicious, a cover for alien intrusion. With the telegraph, there was a danger that function (*yong*) would overtake essence (*ti*). Cultural influences that had been successfully restricted to the margins threatened to infiltrate the central core.

The idea of the telegraph first entered China at the start of the 1850s through the work of an American missionary who was based in Ningbo.[13] By the 1860s, two decades after the signing of the Treaty of Nanjing in 1842, which had opened the treaty ports for outsiders to settle and do business, foreign businessmen were eager 'to persuade the Chinese that modern communication was essential for development'.[14] They lobbied hard for permission to bring the new technology to China's shores and further embed the country into the strengthening forces of a globalised modernisation. Major trading firms that were based on the edges in the treaty ports understood immediately how the flow of information was linked to market advantage. Competition between companies in Shanghai, notes Baark, had already led to the use of fast steamboats, with each firm desperately trying to get its mail before its competitors. The telegraph, Baark writes, was 'at the time, the most advanced technology in the world, and it came to China as part and parcel of an emerging economic structure – including the infant formulation of what later became the ubiquitous transnational corporations'.[15] The British 'Old China Hands' of the Shanghai General Chamber of Commerce 'were aggressively trying to introduce what they regarded as an essential industry into China. They initiated a major lobbying campaign to persuade the Foreign Office to issue demands for the introduction of railroads and telegraphs as part of the treaty revisions scheduled for 1868–1869.'[16] In his book *Historicizing Online Politics*, Zhou Yongming notes that the Qing officials had a special phrase for the repeated requests by Russian, British, American, French and Danes, who were all united on this issue. On the topic of the telegraph, foreigners, they said, were all the same, '*zhiyi shenjian, jouchan buyi* (stubbornly determined and constantly nagging)'.[17]

In June 1865 British businessman E. A. Reynolds, lacking the patience to wait for official permission, opened a line between the then port town of Wusong and central Shanghai. During the night, however, his plans were disrupted as violent protests broke out among a hostile population angered by the new technology. Telegraph poles were torn down and stolen almost as soon as they were erected. When foreigners appealed to officials regarding the destructive acts of the local community, they were dismissed for acting against government orders and told that they did not have the right to bring the telegraph to China. 'The first phase in the Chinese encounter with the telegraph', Baark concludes, is 'a story of renunciation'.[18]

Chinese resistance was fuelled by a complex intersection of culture and politics in which the mutually excitable tendencies of official concern and grassroots fear were inextricably linked. In part, concerns were guised in the framework of health, and there are reports of 'petitions of unexpected illness and death'.[19] Ultimately, however, religio-cultural fear proved far more potent than any mundane concern. The notion that China's *ti* – its cultural essence – was being imperilled by the new technologies was widely held.

In both Europe and America, the capacity for communication at a distance was often identified with the occult. Throughout the nineteenth century, the invisible, oceanic ether was thought to be the medium of both electromagnetic vibrations and also of messages from beyond. In 1848, only ten years after the famous words of Samuel Morse's first communication, 'What hath God wrought?', the Fox sisters of upstate New York gave birth to modern spiritualism with their reports of mysterious 'snappings', 'rappings' and 'tappings'. The public in Europe and America was electrified. Spirit mediums, séances, automatic writing and table-turning swept through the culture, in synchrony with the telegraphic revolution.[20]

In China, however, the imperceptible forces at play were at first judged very differently. The otherworldly energy of electronic communication was considered a dangerous imposition on the cosmic order. 'Lightning wires' (*dian xian* 電線) as they were known, were thought to disrupt the spatial flows of *feng shui* (風水) that guarded the ancestral burial sites. Western spiritualism saw, in the newly tapped electromagnetic field, a medium that enabled the voices of ghosts to be heard. In China, however, where smoke-filled rituals regularly facilitate the crossing of the line between the living and the dead,[21] electronic traffic was widely believed to be a geomantic disturbance. The lightning wires that were being so eagerly developed were thought to unsettle the *shengqi* (生氣) or 'life breath that was embedded in the landscape'. Unleashing the electric body of the Earth and thereby shifting the balance of *qi* would not only challenge the political order, it would unsettle the harmony of the cosmos by disturbing the peaceful sleep of the dead. Baark elaborates by quoting an 1876 pronouncement by Imperial Censor Chen Yi:

> In China we serve the dead as we serve the living, and for millions of years this has never changed, but has been stored 'in our flesh' as an extremely important principle. When telegraph lines are constructed,

they penetrate deep into the foundation of the soil; horizontally they are thrusting ahead, and vertically, they are piercing through – they go in all directions and everywhere. The arteries of the earth are severed, the wind is obstructed and the water discharged – that is the inevitable outcome. How can sons and grandsons have a peaceful heart? The classics say: 'You should seek a loyal minister at the door of a filial son.' If the people of China were willing to disregard the graves of their ancestors, and allow others to build telegraph lines, how can they manage to peacefully observe the principles of respecting their lord and loving their superiors?[22]

Caring for the well-being of one's ancestors is one of the foundational elements of Chinese culture and a cornerstone of popular belief. Yet opposition to the telegraph was not entirely spontaneous. Rather it was – at least to some extent – provoked, used and manipulated by government officials who worried about the power of such a critical technology that was controlled by foreign hands. Officials, as Baark argues, would have been particularly sensitive to the dangers of ignoring widespread attitudes towards *feng shui*, particularly given the horrific violence of the Taiping civil war, a massive, religiously imbued uprising of the mid-nineteenth century, which haunted recent memory. Nonetheless, there is some scepticism about the degree of faith in geomancy in this period since, once the Chinese began to build and operate telegraph lines for themselves, cultural opposition was quite easily controlled.

Obstruction to the technology, then, rested on a potent intermixture of traditional beliefs and anti-foreign sentiment. Foreign business interests repeatedly stressed that Chinese government officials were behind the telegraph protests. They pointed to posters that were put up inciting the population to violence and stirring up anger and fear. Baark quotes a description by a representative of the Great Northern Telegraph Company who wrote of 'posters that called the peasants to arms against the foreign barbarians who came to destroy the "Feng Shui" of the fields and houses with their "lightning wires"'. He also quotes at length a placard posted by a member of the local gentry, Pan Guangqu, who opposed the establishment of the telegraph in Xiamen:

> We appeal to commoners and village elders; [let us] strive together to oppose the [telegraph.] Our district has indeed been peaceful for more than two hundred years. We do not seek to be overly ingenious in making our utensils. On the road, we rely on the plain and level. Presently, however, the foreign barbarians [*yi*, a term prohibited by the treaties] have come to erect telegraphs. They disguise their cunning

ways by arguing that they have [official] approval for the iron wires to pass through our stretch of countryside. It is impossible to tell what they have in mind. Apparently they want to plant wooden poles vertically [in the ground]. In the mountains, I fear that they will harm the graves; in the plains [*yang*: literally, ocean] they will injure our fields and cottages. If we do not expose and stop [this scheme] in advance, but let the barbarians erect the poles, we shall be [suffering as much as if we were] trampled down by oxen and sheep or whirled around by wind and rain. If the poles are plucked up by robbers after being placed in the wilderness, and they are hidden by people, the revenge [of the barbarians] will pay no attention to reason. On the contrary, our villages will be destroyed and the calamities will be beyond description. For the sake of preparing against [such calamities], we should mobilize dozens of villages, assemble and sound the drums to raise a collective force of a hundred thousand people who will wholeheartedly oppose [the telegraph].[23]

The Chinese elite recognised the inherent power of instant information. They were concerned – like those today who fear China's influence on 5G – that whoever had control of the telecommunications infrastructure would have a fundamental political advantage. The Qing government was thus eager to maintain the monopoly of the Imperial courier service and retain control of the rapid dissemination of military and political news. Anti-telegraph sentiment among the Chinese elite was thus poised between the twin fears of foreign aggression and domestic insurgents. Peasants – already unsettled – were distressed by the new electric landscape. Chinese authorities used these grassroots misgivings to help spark protests, since bandit attacks and stolen materials lent weight to the official case that they would be unable to safeguard the telegraph lines. Compounding the situation was the fact that the bureaucrats were legitimately concerned that an inability to control the local population and protect the lines from sabotage and vandalism would result in diplomatic disputes. Allowing telegraph lines in China thus seemed far more trouble than it was worth.

In the end, however, the technological impetus to wire the world proved stronger than the capacity to resist. By 1870 the Chinese authorities had begun to relent, eventually reaching a compromise that would allow cables to be built, but only on the water. In April 1871 a sea line was constructed connecting the island of Hong Kong to the port of Shanghai. With this new addition to the network, the telegraph finally 'reached the shores of the Qing Empire'.[24] Government officials initially tried to insist that the technology be confined to the coast and banned the development of landlines. Yet, once the foreign companies had a foothold, they did not take the attached conditions seriously. Ignoring the prohibitions, the Danish Great Northern Telegraph Company, which was headquartered on the Bund, secretly and without permission set up a line from Wusong harbour along the riverbank, which terminated in the American concession in today's downtown Shanghai. Once modern telecommunications was let loose from its confines on the watery edges, its flow on to the shore was unstoppable.

While most of China's bureaucratic elite had agreed with an initial antagonistic policy towards modern technology, an important exception was the influential early moderniser Li Hongzhang. Any prohibition, Li rightly argued, would be ignored. Since China would inevitably have to accept the construction of telegraph lines, it was better that they should build them themselves. In the last decades of the nineteenth century, Li's views, which were originally rejected, came to dominate. Over time it became clear to the scholar officials of the late Qing that electronic communication was an essential part of modernity. Resisting the forces of capital and politics, as well as the regime of standardised time which accompanied the new machinic environment, would ultimately prove impossible. Eventually, it was agreed that if China was to have any control over the telegraph, it would have to try and somehow make it its own. The age of an indigenous Chinese telegraph network had arrived.

Baark's book *Lightning Wires* documents this vital transition. It is based on a case study from the years 1874 to 1876 when attempts were made to erect a landline in Fujian (Amoy) that stretched between Fuzhou and Xiamen. Permission was based on a series of negotiations between representatives of the Great Northern Telegraph Company and local officials in Fujian. The deal they reached would allow the foreign company to set up a line and, in exchange, the Fujianese officials would be granted a certain degree of access and control. This regional agreement, however, was in direct opposition to the central commands of the *Zongli Yamen*, which had made a formal declaration that no foreigners were allowed to build telegraph lines on Chinese soil. Complicating things still further was the fact that the construction in Fujian went against an earlier deal with the Russians, who had been promised first access to any foreign-made telegraph lines in China. Different levels of government thus held contradictory positions and the *Zongli Yamen* was forced to intervene in the Fujian negotiations. Baark provides a detailed study of how the tensions between various perspectives and constituencies impacted this critical moment of technology transfer. He shows how, despite conceptions to the contrary, technological modernity in China proceeds less through the integrated dictates of a centralised core and more through anarchic dealings taking place on the borders.

The erection of the telegraph in Fujian was exemplary. Not only was it diplomatically fraught, it was also marred by violence. On 22 January 1875 a riot broke out, the aim of which was to sabotage the telegraph lines by pulling down and destroying the poles as well as attacking the engineers employed by Great Northern. In what had, by then, become a familiar pattern, the foreigners concluded that the riot had been incited by local officials, and that 'the "mobs" that had attacked the company's lines were constables and soldiers sent there by authorities, disguised as common peasants'.[25] Attempts at further negotiation did not stop the looting. The violence continued until, in the end, the Danish decided to abort their attempt and terminate the project. Rather than allow the telegraph to be completely disabled, however, local authorities determined that they would oversee the project themselves. In 1876 it was agreed that the Qing government would compensate Great Northern for its loss and that the company would sell all the completed sections as well as the remaining material to the Chinese. In March of that year the still mostly uncompleted Fuzhou–Xiamen line was purchased for 124,500 silver dollars.[26]

Chinese officials, who had at first tried to ignore, ban and destroy the telegraph, in the end came to buy and operate it themselves. As local telegraphy spread, foreign engineers and entrepreneurs were marginalised all over the country. China privatised major lines and mobilised merchants to help construct the infrastructure. In 1883 ownership of the cable at Shanghai was transferred out of the hands of the Great Northern Telegraph Company to the then privately held Imperial Telegraph Administration (ITA). China had seized 'control of its connection to the world'. In the period that followed, telegraph schools and training centres boomed. These programmes became the first modern institutions for engineering studies and vocational training in China. By the end of the nineteenth century, the vast empire of the Qing was electrically fused through an interconnected, comprehensive telegraph network, consisting of both commercial and government lines that totalled in excess of 600,000 miles.[27]

Techno-Nationalism

The story of the telegraph in China marks a critical passage. Technology that was once viewed as a threat to traditional culture came to be enthusiastically embraced as one of the fundamental elements of a new-found sovereignty. In conjunction with this change, the very idea

of what constituted Chinese *ti* or essence underwent a critical transformation. In his important book *Confucian China and its Modern
Fate*, Joseph Levenson characterises the intellectual undercurrents that
accompanied this vital transition by proposing a provocative theory
known as 'culturalism to nationalism'. At the end of the nineteenth
century, there was, Levenson writes, an 'alienation away from Chinese
culture', which coincided with a new-found devotion to the state.[28]
To explicate this philosophical conversion, Levenson contrasts the traditional concept of *tianxia* 天下 (all under heaven) with the modern
concept *guo* 國 (nation). 'Nationalism invades the Chinese scene', he
writes, just 'as culturalism hopelessly gives way'.[29]

This change in emphasis from culture to the state came as a result
of a crisis in the late Qing formulation of the *ti–yong* pair. Despite
the creative conceptual reappropriation of *ti–yong*, within the first
decades of the twentieth century, with the fall of Imperial China and
the tumult of the Republican period, it was widely considered that the
formulation, which sought to maintain a Confucian basis of society
while adopting Western technology, had failed. Levenson articulates
the problems that were fundamental to the conceptualisation from
the start. Initially, the early modern official reformers were deeply
hesitant in their adoption of the new technologies. Yet they had
slowly come to believe that the only way to preserve tradition was
to adapt. 'Paradoxically, they insisted on change because they had
a traditionalistic bias against it.'[30] In following the slogan of Zhang
Zhidong, the literati thought they had devised a method of poised
containment, which rested on the idea 'that these areas of innovation from the West were areas of only *practical* value, not of essential
value'. They could thus adopt Western *yong*, without challenging the
'lifestyle, values and learning of Chinese substance'. Like later experiments with Special Economic Zones, which were meant to restrict
the spread of capitalism by carving out a designated, isolated space,
the nineteenth-century literati believed, 'as an article of faith' that
'Western culture could have a place in China and yet be kept in its
place'.[31] With this, Levenson argues, the *ti–yong* dichotomy became
'a formula for self-deception about the implications of innovation'.[32]
Paul Cohen, in summarising Levenson, writes as follows:

> As more and more of the Western 'model' was accepted by Chinese
> reformers, as the content of *yong* (or *ch'i*), expanded from ships
> and guns to science and mathematics, then to industrialization, and
> finally to modern schooling, *ti* inevitably shrank, and the Chinese
> found themselves in the impossible position of trying to preserve a
> civilization by subjecting it to change.[33]

There were a number of devastating flaws latent in the late Qing formulation from the start. First, there was a wilful denial about how Chinese learning functioned in the power structures of a bureaucratic Confucian elite. 'Chinese learning, which was to be the *ti* in the new syncretic culture', Levenson writes,

> was the learning of a society which had always used it for *yong*, as the necessary passport to the best of all careers . . . in reality Chinese learning had come to be prized as substance because of its function, and when its function was usurped, the learning withered.[34]

More critical still was the superficial notion that Western learning, as the 'practical instrument of daily life', would leave the essence of Chinese culture untouched. The thought 'that one could read Mencius alongside an engineering manual and that Mencius would remain unchanged' was foolishly naive, as 'the meaning of Mencius was transformed by the dynamic context of new engineering'.[35] Yuk Hui reinforces this point in his own comments on the precariousness of the *ti–yong* divide. It is a 'very modern, remarkably Cartesian separation', he notes. Attempting to 'impose scientific and technological development' while retaining the 'fundamental principles of Chinese thought implies that the mind (the cogito – or, here, philosophical thought), through the medium of technics, can contemplate and command the physical world without itself being affected and transformed'.[36] Modernity, Levenson concludes, could not be constructed as a 'Confucian world with Western technoscience pasted on . . . If the Western learning were let loose in China, the Chinese learning would not stay safely screened off and unsullied.'[37] Despite the cleverness of the slogan, culture is not neatly divided into two separate realms, with one shielded from the other. In positing a split between practice and substance, the late Qing idea of *ti–yong* artificially separated components of modernity that are ultimately as inseparable as the realms of *ti* and *yong* themselves. Modern techniques would invariably transform society, 'speedily end the separation and expose the delusion – the new [*yong*] would become also the new *ti*'.[38]

One of the earliest critics of Zhang Zhidong's formulation was Yan Fu 嚴復 (1854–1921), a key figure in introducing Western politics, sociology, economics and philosophy into modern China. Yan Fu translated Adam Smith, John Stuart Mill, Thomas Huxley, Herbert Spencer and Montesquieu, among others, into classical Chinese. Yet he was critical of the superficiality of the late Qing reform. The capacity to modernise, he believed, lay not merely in technological advance, but rather, and more importantly, in the ideas and institutions that underlie them. Freedom is the *ti*, he declared, democracy is the *yong*. To remedy its lack of 'wealth and power', China needed to gain a more profound understanding of the action, energy and purposiveness that constituted modern progress in the West.[39] Yan Fu's critique of Zhang's iteration of *ti–yong* has revolutionary implications. The separation of concepts fails because it is philosophically flawed, positing a bifurcation where none should exist. 'Western learning and Chinese learning are two parallel fields', Yan Fu argued, each with their own substance and function.[40]

> The foundation [*ti*] and the use [*yong*] mean the same thing. The body of an ox should have the use of carrying heavy things; the body of a horse should have the use of carrying something to a distance. I have never heard that the ox is the body or the foundation, while the horse is for use. The difference between Chinese and Western knowledge is as great as that between the complexions and the eyes of the two races. We cannot force the two cultures to be the same or similar. Therefore, Chinese knowledge has its foundation and function; Western knowledge has also its foundation and function. If the two are separated, each can be independent; if the two were combined, both would perish.[41]

Yan Fu had sought to liberate the progressive energy of China through exposure to and adoption of Western ideas. After the horrors of the First World War, however, he experienced profound doubts about Western culture and, steeping himself in Daoist metaphysics, advocated, at the end of his life, a return to Chinese tradition. Regardless of these apprehensions, however, the critique of *ti–yong*, which he helped articulate, gathered force.

After the palace coup of 1898 the attempt to moderate between the binary of an Eastern past and a Western future came to an end as the moment of moderate reform was replaced by an epoch of revolution. Denunciation of the *ti–yong* duality paved the way for more radical alternatives as China veered from intense suspicion of modern technology to a revolutionary anti-traditionalism advocated by the intelligentsia of the early twentieth century. From Lu Xun's *Diary of a Madman* with its portrayal of a society of cannibals to the 'complete Westernisation' (*quanpan xihua* 全盤西化) advocated by Hu Shih and others,[42] a spirit of 'totalistic antitraditionalism' that would reach its climax in the destruction of temples and texts in the Cultural Revolution began to dominate Chinese intellectual life.[43] In an influential essay, intellectual historian Chang Hao describes the scale of the denunciation:

The scope of their moral iconoclasm is perhaps unique in the modern world; no other historical civilization outside the West undergoing modern transformation has witnessed such a phoenix like impulse to see its own cultural tradition so completely negated. This radical iconoclasm, which created in its train a widespread sense of moral disorientation, naturally produced anxieties of the acutest kind.[44]

Rather than try to shield an essential, unchanging traditional culture from the radical transformations wrought by new technology, 'the new youth' of the 'Chinese Renaissance' abandoned the binary oscillation altogether. They started 'to doubt that *ti* deserved any protection at all'.[45] Instead, the radical iconoclasm of China's early modern period emboldened revolutionaries who believed that Zhang Zhidong's formulation 'Chinese essence, Western use' ignored the true nature of modern machines. Critical of the notion that an old and unchanging Chinese culture could accommodate the powerful transformations inherent in the interconnected technologies of industrialisation, they advocated adopting a new thinking suited to a new age. Ancient traditions once thought essential were now to be discarded as hindrances. 'Old China', write Teng and Fairbanks, introducing their study of Chinese modernity,

> its dress and manners, its classical written language and intricate system of imperial government, its reliance upon the extended family, the Confucian ethic, and all the other institutional achievements and cultural ornaments of its glorious past – had to be thrown into the melting pot and refashioned.[46]

In the time of extreme disillusionment which fed the most radical impulses of the May Fourth movement, it was no longer enough to focus on the practical applications of technology (*yong*). What was needed instead was a more fundamental revolution, which removed the obstacle of the essence of Chinese thought (*ti*). In this moment of profound transition, at the dawn of China's short-lived Republican period (1912–49), as the very definition of 'China' was shifting from an Imperial culture to one that was in service of the newly emerging nation-state, the poised balance that had held *ti* and *yong* apart collapsed. The *ti–yong* formulation of the late nineteenth century sought to create a space between the rigid ossification of a Chinese tradition and a progressive Westernised modernity, where the old could intertwine and coexist with the new. In the end, however, the separation between an eternal substance and ephemeral application rested on a conceptual interpretation that was too fragile to survive. The delicate balance once imagined could not be sustained.

The 'culturalism to nationalism' thesis has been criticised for its overarching generalisations.[47] It oversimplifies a complex tangle of terms, glossing over intricacies such as how ethnicity and the state interact within the concept of nationalism. It also overlooks the elitism inherent in the idea of culturalism, which never existed in a pure, unadulterated form. Finally, as a heuristic tool in the history of ideas, it misses many of the manifold nuances of empirical reality. Nonetheless, it is widely agreed that in turn-of-the-century China there was an intellectual reorientation towards a new nationalist mode of thought.[48] With regard to China's engagement with technology, the emergence of modern nationalism with its notions of sovereign control eventually eclipsed the Qing era approach of cultural resistance and came to play a determining role.

In describing this shift in intellectual orientation, Levenson turns to the great early twentieth-century modern intellectual Liang Qichao 梁啟超 (1873–1929). Liang was adamant that the goal of preserving a culture that persisted as a static holdout on the margins of modernity was unsustainable. Instead, he advocated a new mode of sociopolitical unity that would allow for global integration. He 'urged China to become new and become a nation, to cease to be old and to cease to pay homage exclusively to its culture'. No longer the universal empire, China 'must deem itself not a world but a unit in the world'. It must become a nation among nations.[49]

Liang understood that the production of national unity required the adoption of a new mode of time. He maintained that the transition away from a universal culture towards the particularity of the nation-state involved rejecting a traditional cyclical temporality and embracing in its place a linear progressive history. Diaries of his 1899 trip to North America were the first popular Chinese texts to be marked with Gregorian dates, effecting a paradigmatic change in time-consciousness. Prasenjit Duara echoes this claim: 'The historian Liang Qichao was perhaps the first to write the history of China in the narrative of the Enlightenment. He made it clear that a people could not become a nation without a History in the linear mode.'[50] This idea of a sociological organism moving calendrically through a homogeneous, empty time is, as Benedict Anderson writes in *Imagined Communities*, 'a precise analogue of the idea of the nation, which also is conceived as a solid community moving steadily down (or up) history'.[51] Duara elaborates on this idea of the nation as the subject of history.[52] The agent of the 'Hegelian unfolding' of linear progressive temporality, he notes, is the nation as it evolves towards modernity.[53]

The Internet with Chinese Characteristics

With the telegraph, China established the power of the nation over and above a new media that was global in nature. Since then, however, this inward contraction has been countered by an opposing force of outward expansion as global technology has threatened the authority of the state. In this oscillating tension, China and techno-modernity have appeared as binary poles. This split is the manifestation of a forceful separation of the *ti–yong* dichotomy, which began at the end of the nineteenth century and whose ripple effects manifest in various ways throughout the fifth Kondratiev wave.

As we have seen, when the telegraph first arrived in China, peasants and urbanites, officials and intellectuals all perceived it as a threat. The use of new technologies was viewed as invariably overwhelming. The essence of Chinese culture, mode of government and way of life could not help but be transformed. *Ti* (essence) would ultimately be moulded by *yong* (function). This same idea found a mutated expression with the introduction of the Internet in China. China connected to the World Wide Web just as the country was emerging from isolation after the Cultural Revolution, and the Internet was celebrated for facilitating a connection to the outside. In 1987 the first email ever sent from within China's borders heralded the capacity to 'cross over the Great Wall and reach every corner of the world'. Early Internet pioneers such as Alibaba's CEO Jack Ma publicly embraced the network's inherent openness. In an interview with the BBC to promote his then still-young company, Ma enthusiastically agreed that the new media would change the social and political fabric. 'China is opening its door and the Internet is the best way to let people understand what is happening outside.'[54]

In the late 1990s there was a widespread belief that the decentred nature of the medium could not help but challenge the centralised authoritarian regime. Indeed, the very idea of the Internet in China seemed like a contradiction in terms, since the global, distributed technology appeared to be in such acute tension with the restrictive boundaries of a geopolitical state.[55] Geramie Barmé, one of the most erudite commentators on China's contemporary culture, who is credited with coining the term 'The Great Firewall', diagnosed the dilemma in a 1997 article for *Wired*. 'The technology China needs to build the most powerful country on Earth in the twenty-first century threatens to undermine the institutions that rule the nation. And Beijing's control freaks are worried.'[56]

This belief was reinforced by the fact that China's online culture provided a virtual space for a surprisingly free and spirited public sphere, filled with analysis, commentary and criticism.[57] A whole wave of dissident bloggers appeared. Among the most famous was the author and racing car driver Han Han, whose cleverly subversive and humorous posts made him a poster child for what was then seen as the rebellious attitude of the post-1980s, net-savvy generation. By the turn of the millennium it was taken as obvious that control over the media landscape had been irrevocably altered. Commenting in 2000 on China's entrance into the WTO, Bill Clinton famously quipped that attempts to regulate the Internet were as futile as 'trying to nail jelly to the wall'. Two years later, the SARS crisis of 2002 felt like a watershed moment, when 'netizens' exposed Beijing's morbidly farcical cover-up, which involved driving sick bodies around during the night so they wouldn't be discovered by the inspectors from the WHO. A series of similar episodes followed. The familiar spin that surrounded national disasters such as the 2008 Sichuan earthquake and the Wenzhou train crash of 2011 were immediately questioned and criticised online. Anonymous virtual mobs known as 'human flesh search engines' (renrou sousuo 人肉搜索) started hunting down corrupt, power-abusing officials. To take but two famous examples: in 2010 the son of an official was caught driving drunk after a hit and run. His response, 'my father is Li Gang', which assumed that connection necessarily meant protection, instantly went viral and the outrage that followed led to his arrest. Similarly, in 2012 pictures emerged of a government official from Shaanxi province wearing eleven different luxury watches. After being ruthlessly mocked online, 'Watch Brother', as he came to be known, was removed from office and sent to prison. Cases such as these became commonplace. There was a growing confidence that the values of openness, freedom and even democracy were inherent to the nature of this new technology. Government control seemed so against the grain that everyone assumed it could not be sustained. The restrictions imposed by the centralised government appeared to be in fundamental tension with the true nature of the information age – open, decentralised and free.

While the Westernising reformers of the late Qing and early Republican period maintained that adapting to 'Western' practices (yong) required, first of all, a transformation of China's substance (ti), early Internet enthusiasts – advocates of 'technoliberation', who maintained that the technology of the Internet would invariably change Chinese culture – held a parallel belief, though they believed the ti–yong causality would follow a different order. While earlier reformers held that if you wanted a new yong, you first must accept a new *ti*, late twentieth-century enthusiasts of the democratising power of the Internet trusted instead that an embrace of *yong* (an open Internet) would, invariably, revolutionise China's *ti*.

Amid all this enthusiasm, however, barriers went up and the walls began closing in. Officials charged with administering the Internet recalled one of the critical sayings of Deng Xiaoping: 'If you open the window for fresh air, you have to expect some flies to blow in.' At the turn of the millennium, the government judged that there were already too many flies. its solution was to launch the Golden Shield Project, a vast nationwide networked security system that would come to include extensive domestic surveillance, as well as the most sophisticated mode of Internet censorship anywhere in the world. As it turned out the physical infrastructure of digital information was remarkably grounded – even in the cloud. Geopolitical boundaries reasserted themselves in the virtual world. In China, the firewall was working. As the era of social media took hold, especially in the wake of the chaos caused by the 'Twitter revolutions' and the 'Arab Spring', the Party's grip on power tightened. Facebook was blocked in 2008, YouTube and Twitter in 2009, Gmail and Google maps in 2014. In that same year, then Internet Czar Lu Wei spoke openly in Davos on behalf of censorship in the name of 'Internet Sovereignty'. 'The Internet', he proclaimed, 'is like a car, far too dangerous without any brakes.' Moreover, and despite all predictions to the contrary, there seems to be little contradiction between the embrace of the World Wide Web and the centralised power of Party rule. 'Networked authoritarianism' developed into a resilient strategy capable of managing a flourishing online population, which, closing in on a billion users, had become the largest in the world.[58]

In the late twentieth century, when wireless devices were becoming widespread, digital technology was presented as if belonging to a borderless world. The ideal is perfectly captured in the motto 'One World. One Internet', a slogan chosen by the Internet Corporation for Assigned Name and Numbers (ICANN), which was set up in California in 1998 to help internationalise web protocols. At the dawn of the new millennium techno-capital seemed to have created a virtual realm floating beyond the concrete territoriality of the state. Yet by the first decades of the twenty-first century, it had become apparent that this vision of universalism came predominantly from the West, and that, moreover, it was a myth that China did not share. Instead, the country's response to cyberspace echoed the strategy it had taken when faced with the telegraph. Confronted by a global mediasphere that it deemed foreign, the nation sought to carve out a protected realm of sovereign control. In constructing the Great Firewall and promoting the idea of Internet sovereignty, China asserted the right to develop its own Wi-Fi standards and to legislate its own autonomous corner of cyberspace.[59]

In this phase of techno-nationalism, the idea of 'China' consolidated further around the nation-state.[60] Technological practices were considered superficial and mutable enough that they could bend to the will of the user. *Ti* – now conflated with the strength of the nation – was deemed more powerful than *yong*. The Internet was not only a potent tool for dissident bloggers. It turned out that it could also be effectively controlled. Networked computers, which had been seen as inherently liberatory, were now deemed neutral enough to be used in support of a variety of different cultures and political regimes. At this stage, in the early twenty-first century, a mutated version of the late Qing formulation of *Chinese learning for essence, Western learning for practice* was revived. This time, however, the 'culturalism to nationalism' transition had already been well established. Rather than the essence of a literati culture, it was the substance of Party rule that would remain stable and unchanged, protected from the techno-capitalist sphere within which it was engaged. The ongoing faith in the endurance of the 'China model' presumes a static and resilient substance that is able to shape and direct the uses of technology according to its will, while remaining cut off and immune from the inherent, accelerating, destabilising nature of the technological innovations themselves.

Under these conditions, the expansive nature of the Internet has been matched by the hardening of a virtual border. Most people on the mainland are satisfied with the rich offerings of China's lively online culture and can't be bothered to circumvent the ever more sophisticated algorithmic controls. Chinese cyberculture has thus implemented a kind of digital barrier reminiscent of the old Qing dynasty dream of a protective shield that could keep foreign technology at bay. Passing into Chinese territory involves crossing a hard digital divide. Enter and you are immersed in the world's most sophisticated Intranet. Without a Virtual Private Network (VPN), there is no choice but to leave the outside behind. Indeed, the successful creation of the Great Firewall, strategically designed to circumscribe the decentred network, is arguably China's greatest innovation of the information age.

As the second decade of the new millennium neared its end, with China appearing to grow ever stronger and more insular, a still darker picture came into view. As in the May Fourth era, all the poised ambiguities of the preceding period began to collapse. Many argued, with growing apprehension, even despair, that there was now no contradiction between China's *ti*, which was ever more crudely identified with the interiority of the most authoritarian tendencies of the state, and the nature of new technologies. The rise of the social credit system, the use of facial recognition and biometrics in mass surveillance, and the controlling capacity of algorithms seemed to reveal a Big Brother despotism that had always been inherent in the increasingly intelligent, ubiquitous and networked media of the twenty-first century. 'Unlike the Internet or free scholarly inquiry', Mara Hvistendahl opined, 'mobile payments and facial recognition do not threaten authoritarian rule; they reinforce it.'[61] Older, apparent tensions between China and new media seemed to disappear. Both were now conceived to be firmly on the side of centralised control. Technological practice (*yong*) was no longer opposed to *ti*; rather *ti* – now firmly associated with the absolute power of the state – was aligned with the practices of new technologies.

Nevertheless, in the ongoing dynamic of Chinese cyberculture every contraction has been countered by an ever-loosening expansion. The centripetal pull of centralisation is pitted against the centrifugal power of dispersion. Nebulous but powerful categories consolidate around these contrasting forces. On one side is an increasingly concentrated and interiorised notion of 'China', which becomes ever more closely affiliated with the Sinofuturist nightmare of 'techno-authoritarian' rule. On the other lies the promise of a 'techno-liberation' based on a decentred technology whose globalised exteriority is commonly associated with a democratic West. Interviewed in 2018, former Google CEO Eric Schmidt forecast a solidification of this bifurcation. By 2028, he predicted, the world would be split between two Internets, one dominated by China, the other by America. By the time of the 2020 global pandemic, the prediction, it seemed, had already come true.

The 'Internet with Chinese characteristics' – a vibrant, thriving, innovative online space that is subject to strict scrutiny and suppression – is caught in a double bind. It fluctuates between two extremes in an ongoing game of cat and mouse. In the urban centres, Wi-Fi is ubiquitous, overseas travel, at least before Covid-19, was becoming increasingly commonplace, and foreign cultural influences (particularly from elsewhere in Asia) are tremendously strong. These outward-looking impulses exist alongside a soft or porous censorship in which connection to the external world is discouraged but not entirely forbidden.[62] The cultural desire for increased globalisation is shared by the country's Internet giants, which have rising international aspirations.[63] This converges with government dreams of a globally competitive tech sector, which hopes to lead the world in AI.

Amid all the signs of intensifying contraction and control, opposing forces of dispersion and diffusion persist. Occasionally this is made manifest, especially in times of crisis, as was apparent in the remarkable investigative reporting that surfaced in the immediate aftermath of the coronavirus outbreak in Wuhan. In early 2020, soon after the first stories of a mysterious illness broke, news that early warnings of the disease had been suppressed went viral on the Chinese Internet. Li Wenliang 李文亮, the whistleblower doctor who first tried to spread the word about the novel virus, became a media star and unofficial national hero after he died. The grassroots power of Internet communication also erupted in widespread dissent during the Shanghai lockdown of 2022. On 22 April a powerful video called 'Sounds of April' 四月之聲 (si yue zhi sheng) was released online. Initially, the montage of citizens expressing their distress was shared among friends. By the evening, however, the video had gone viral on WeChat through network practices of remix and recursion known as 'online relay' 网络接力 (wangluo jieli).[64] Within a few hours the 'Sounds of April' video had become the largest mass protest against censorship since the outcry over the initial cover-up in Wuhan.

By now it has become evident that the long and ongoing story of China's relationship with electronic media does not follow a single unidirectional trend. Rather, tendencies towards greater openness and towards tightening control are continuously present, and there is a sense that when one side gathers strength, the other lies in wait. It is hard to conceive of Chinese techno-culture outside the drama of each historical moment. Yet presuming a binary split beneath the oscillation, and focusing on either contraction or expansion, can only ever offer a limited perspective, failing to apprehend the whole of the wave.

The Telegraph and Globalisation

The notion of Internet sovereignty presumes that modern media platforms operate as an integrated system – a single unified function (yong) – that can be controlled from above. This idea can be traced back to the telegraph, a medium with enormously powerful abstract effects. As scholar James Carey notes in his classic study, the telegraph's capacity to 'separate communication from transportation' enabled the sharing of messages at non-human speeds.[65] This increased capability for information exchange proved to be profoundly unifying. Over the course of the nineteenth century electronic networks of communication linked together faraway places, transforming a still largely disparate and uncoordinated patchwork of nations into a united globe.

After the telegraph the world became one. Places that were once marginal were increasingly integrated into the centre. Global contraction was perpetually reinforced by a media environment characterised by the latest stories and weather reports. Staying current with the weather as it spread through different locations across the Earth generated, for the first time, a sense of a planetary climate. The telegraph 'enabled people to think of weather as a widespread and interconnected affair'.[66] This new-found awareness of an inter-related atmosphere was further reinforced through the establishment machine for producing the news. The mid-nineteenth century saw the founding of both the Associated Press and Reuters. These agencies created a culture of fast-breaking reports, exclusive scoops and near-instantaneous knowledge of world events. News and telegraphy operated in a symbiotic relationship of positive feedback such that reports off the wires soon came to disrupt older rhythms of daily life. In the words of John Durham Peters, the 'notion of a sabbatical time-out, one day of seven, starts to wane with the Sunday paper'.[67] In constructing a global space of simultaneous events, the telegraph became the forerunner of the constant, sleepless updates that have come to characterise the wireless world.

Media scholars have shown that the telegraph's capacity to separate the message from the messenger had far-reaching implications for the structure of organisations, serving as a centralising force in both business and government. Prior to the telegraph, commercial relations were relatively intimate, 'mediated through face-to-face relations, by personal correspondence, by contacts among people who, by and large, knew one another as actual persons'.[68] The new technology opened up the possibility of impersonal relations, both within businesses and between companies and their customers. This invariably gave rise to new forms of management and corporate organisation. With the telegraph it became much easier to control faraway subsidiaries from concentrated, centralised headquarters. Due to the immense time-lag involved in any communication, foreign companies doing business in China had been largely unsupervised from afar. The telegraph meant that, for the first time, operations could be subject to management from abroad.

This transformation in power dynamics had tremendous repercussions on the structure of political rule. Carey considers the profound influence on the British Empire, arguing that the telegraph enabled the shift from colonialism, which was relatively decentralised, to imperialism, which came later and was more top-down in nature. Under the colonial system, the centre was remote and hard to reach. The margins, therefore, had extensive, autonomous power, with much of the authority in the hands of the domestic governor. With the coming of the telegraph, however, power began to consolidate in the imperial capital. Until the transatlantic cable, it was difficult to determine whether British colonial policy was being set in London or by colonial governors in the field – out of contact and out of control. The cable and telegraph, backed, of course by sea power, transformed colonialism into the imperial system in which the centre of an empire could dictate rather than merely respond to the margin.

By the beginning of the twentieth century, the majority of the planet's vast submarine network of cables was owned and operated by the British. The medium of faraway writing provided the critical lines of communication that ran through the first great industrial empire. In his book *Tentacles of Progress: Technology Transfer in the Age of Imperialism*, Daniel Headrick outlines the new technology's deep appeal.

> Before the 1840s, it took 5 to 8 months for a letter to travel between Britain and India, and the writer could not expect to receive an answer in less than 2 years. Even after steamships took over the mail service, it still took 6 weeks in each direction. Within India, the mails were just as slow.[69]

The telegraph was introduced into India in the mid-1850s. Built largely with investment from the East India Company, lines were set up, as telegraph historian Roland Wenzlhuemer notes, by and for the government as part of an experiment in security, administration and control. The telegraph in India, he writes, was largely 'a state affair', as evidenced by the fact that the first line ran directly through Governor General Dalhousie's hill station home in Ootacamund.[70] News of the Indian Mutiny in 1857 had taken five weeks to reach London. By the 1870s the Empire was spending vast amounts of money on undersea cables, enabling instant communication between England, India and other colonial regions. By 1914, at the beginning of the First World War, the telegraph ensured a coordination of military and naval operations, such that the British Empire could act, from out of its far-flung corners, as a single, unified whole.

The telegraph enabled the projection of power across spectacular distances. Instantaneous information served centralised authorities, allowing them to gain advantage in espionage, as well as giving them the power to mobilise armies and regulate administrative affairs. Unlike in Britain where the telegraph, at least initially, strengthened the hold of Empire, Chinese telegraphic nationalism, which took hold in the final years of the Qing dynasty, contributed to the collapse of the ancient Imperial regime. Rather than bolstering imperialism, in China acquiring control of the railways and telegraphs was critical to the construction of the concept of national sovereignty. Ultimately, as Thomas Mullaney has argued, these technologies were 'central to the formation of the imagined community of the modern nation state'.[71] It was in adopting the telegraph, then, that China came to accept the media infrastructures which underlie the formation of the integrated state.

The telegraph's inclination towards concentration also had an impact on global capitalism, which enabled the incorporation of the periphery into the core. The development of the medium itself is closely allied with the rise of the great monopolies, which so powerfully influenced economic life at the turn of the century. In the early years, the telegraph grew through intense competition. Tangles of wires, each built and controlled by separate companies, criss-crossed through neighbourhoods. Ultimately, however, as the second K-wave progressed, this chaotic mishmash was systematised, and a deep, centralising dynamic came to organise this critical infrastructure. The telegraphic industry, writes Thompson, was the first in which a single company prevailed. In the United States by 1866 the Western Union Telegraph Company had swallowed all of its rivals. The rise of Western Union coincided with the powerful trend towards monopoly that permeated nineteenth-century economic life. Telegraphy, Carey maintains, was the first full-blown instance of monopoly capitalism, and Western Union the first great industrial monopoly. The telegraph's capacity for offering integrated information flow meant that this inclination towards monopoly capital soon became widespread. Thompson describes how steel, petroleum, rubber, utilities, railways and manufacturing were all to go through a similar evolution in the years that lay ahead.[72]

This abstract capital compression soon became apparent in other industries as well. As distance became less of an obstacle, businesses were able to make use of the advantages inherent in economies of scale. Borderline zones with cheaper labour and material were fused into global production, a trend that would later prove critical for China's development. One result was the opening of large department stores in the 1860s and 1870s. Retailers used the railway and telegraph lines to access a much vaster network of supply and provide information that helped manage large inventories.[73] In Shanghai the four great department stores – Wing On, Sincere, Sun Sun and Da Sun – opened on Nanjing Road in the early 1900s. Eventually, this commercial consolidation would put enormous pressure on the smaller, more decentred shops and markets of the street.[74] Monopoly capitalism and the new technology were so entangled, writes Katherine Hayles, 'that it was no longer possible for capital to operate without the telegraph or its successors; nor was it possible, after about 1866, to think about the telegraph without thinking about monopoly capital'.[75]

More critical still was the telegraph's role in coordinating a single global marketplace. The capacity for instant information connected newly formed stock exchanges as the informatisation of prices converted commodities into code. This enabled price checking across heterogeneous world markets, creating a unified platform of exchange. Economic practices that relied on radically diverse pricing structures across local markets were threatened. 'Arbitrage – buying cheap and selling dear by moving goods around in space' became increasingly difficult. Carey illustrates how the telegraph caused a 'decontexualization of markets' which involved 'the spread of a uniform price system throughout space so that for purposes of trade everyone was in the same place'.[76] Geography became increasingly irrelevant as markets 'no longer depended on local factors of supply and demand', and instead began to respond to national and international forces.

Technological Time

While the production of a planet-wide mediasphere depends on spatial integration, the primary mechanism of coalescence was not spatial, but temporal. Space, as is clear from the Hegelian and Marxist views of China, was a category tied to the past. To create the future required a novel form of time. This was provided by the telegraph, which in transmitting time across distance, synchronised the planet under one, standardised temporal order. The new medium achieved this level of transcendental influence through a symbiotic lock-in with railways, which was essential to the telegraph's success. By the mid-nineteenth century, the huge variety in local times made the scheduling of railway arrivals and departures, pick-ups and deliveries, an impossibly intricate task. Before the introduction of standardised time, which the telegraph made possible, each local community established its own time by looking at the sun. The time was 'whatever it was wherever you were'.[77] The resulting 'temporal chaos' became an enormous hindrance in a world in which new modes of transport made faraway places ever-more intertwined.

Travel by sea had already established that the need for spatial coordination would rely, in the end, on a standardised, uniform and universal time. Mapmakers struggling with the problem of longitude realised that determining this critical, abstract, navigational dimension required knowing the time in two places at once. Yet simultaneity over long distances was made difficult by the fact that environmental factors confounded clocks that were subject to the ocean's conditions. This problem was greatly alleviated in the mid-eighteenth century when clockmaker John Harrison developed a marine chronometer that could be used for navigation. In the end, however, as Peter Galison explains in his critical work on the period, it was the telegraph that cracked the problem. 'Over vast distances, an electric current would race through the wires so fast that the reception and transmission seemed almost instantaneous.'[78] Clock coordination was the telegraph's most important feature, enabling the creation of standardised time. 'In the increasingly time-wired world of the early 1880s', writes Galison, 'time reformers campaigned for time unification on conflicting scales.'[79] By 1883 the American railways had introduced Uniform Time. Soon after, 'time-bearing cables' criss-crossed the planet and 'telegraphically transmitted time became a standard railroad technology'.[80] A year later, in 1884, towards the end of the second Kondtratiev wave, at the International Meridian Conference held in Washington DC, World Time was synchronised using the observatory at Greenwich as the zero point. Scientific agencies were transformed by new powers of geolocation, which could be used not only to calculate longitude on Earth but also to register the movements of the cosmos. In Carey's words, the telegraph overlaid 'the world with a grid of time in the same way the surveyor's map laid a grid of space'.[81] By the late nineteenth century synchronised clocks were ubiquitous, choreographing a technological infrastructure of railways and shipping networks that traversed the planet. 'Electro-coordinated time' produced a global simultaneity that gave shape to the modern world, laying the foundations of the information age.

With the implementation of the telegraph, then, the world was enveloped under a single standardised time. This global unification occurred alongside and in association with the birth of nationalism and the establishment of newly founded historical agents with their own inherent interiority. Mutually supportive forces of contraction and concentration reinforced one another as the temporality that underlies the modern state synthesised a technologically generated global simultaneity with the chronological passage of history.

In the wireless age, satellites, our 'eyes in the sky', integrated the world even further. The launch of Sputnik in the mid-twentieth century had, as Marshall McLuhan observed, a dramatically transformative effect. Ever since this first artificial satellite was put into orbit, Earth has been altered by these signals from on high. 'The planet', as McLuhan put it in one of his famous aphorisms, 'became a global theater in which there are no spectators but only actors.' The technical capacity for sensing from space was 'a technological intervention that turned planetary relationships inside out'.[82] Satellites are instruments that can behold the whole of the Earth, all at once. They are, notes Lisa Parks, 'now at the core of our global telecommunications infrastructure, and have become a principal means by which we see and know the world and the cosmos beyond'.[83]

Satellites wrap the planet in an invisible computational environment that constructs the world as a single whole. While telegraphic weather reports provided unity across dispersed spatial coordinates, the sense of a singular global atmosphere was dramatically accentuated by weather satellites, which enabled real-time reports from everywhere on Earth. Global weather infrastructure is a 'vast machine', as Paul Edwards writes, an immensely complex, continuously updated computational process that consists of interlocking systems for measuring, monitoring and broadcasting information.[84] Weather satellites are a key component of the immersive nature of our contemporary media ecology.

The most critical satellites in the production of the wireless environment, however, are not the weather satellites but rather those that determine geolocation, the most important instantiation of which is the Global Positioning System (GPS). GPS rose to prominence alongside the worldwide proliferation of mobile phones, a technology adopted across the planet faster than any device in history. This concurrence is no coincidence, since cartographic capacity is arguably the mobile phone's 'killer app'. Today, although access varies widely, almost every place on Earth is within signal range of at least four GPS satellites at all times. Smartphones can pick up radio signals from 31 active GPS satellites, each of which carry at least four high-precision atomic clocks that orbit the Earth twice a day at a distance of over 20,000 kilometres. The satellites use electromagnetic frequencies to continuously transmit information about their time and position. On Earth billions of mobile devices use GPS receivers to tune in to these broadcasts, repeatedly comparing the origin and arrival time so as to pinpoint their exact location almost anywhere in the world. In the first decades of the twenty-first century, GPS grew to become a near-ubiquitous method of wayfinding. As a structural component of 5G, AI systems such as self-driving cars, automated weapons, the 'Internet of Things', with its promise of billions of interconnected objects, and the growing field of locative media (augmented or mixed reality), geolocation grows ever more vital.

As early as 2007, the year Apple launched the first iPhone, William Gibson used his skills at cyberpunk foreshadowing to stretch GPS to its conceptual limits. His novel *Spook Country* features the character Bobby Chombo, a paranoid geospatial expert who insists on sleeping in a different square of the GPS grid each night. Chombo, who works as a technical designer for 'locative art' or 'spatially tagged hypermedia', recognises the revolutionary nature of the media. With GPS the topology of cyberspace has turned inside out, as the virtual escapes its confinement within the digital machine and comes to envelop the world. Chombo expresses this central insight in a minimalist conversation that lies at the heart of the book:

> Someone told me that cyberspace's 'everting'. . . Sure. And once it everts, then there isn't any cyberspace, is there? There never was, if you want to look at it that way. It was a way we had of looking where we were heading, a direction. With the grid, we're here. This is the other side of the screen. Right here.[85]

A decade after Gibson composed these lines, describing the latent potential of geolocation to enable cyberspace to escape the boundaries of the digital device, cinema designer Ash Thorp visualised this unfolded topology on the big screen. In both *Blade Runner 2049* and, even more vividly, with the 2017 remake of *Ghost in the Shell*, Thorp depicts a fully realised and completely immersive augmented urban environment. In *Ghost in the Shell*, the concrete skyscrapers of the gritty metropolis of a future Hong Kong are transformed by the holographic images of a locative media that covers the city as a virtual veil. Logos, slogans and iconography of directed advertisements vie for space with gigantic floating goldfish, praying monks, game avatars and flying pigs.

These near-future visions remind us that in sensing satellites and other wireless signals, our mobile devices are constructing a virtual plane that has come to subsume the whole of the Earth. In this new environment, the idea of cyber-sovereignty is both more ambitious and more complex. China's techno-nationalist agenda has long run as both a theoretical and practical countercurrent to the laissez-faire liberalism of modern capitalist thought. In an insightful article entitled 'How the World Works', journalist James Fallows draws on the economic theorist Friedrich List to lay out the principles of what he calls the 'German-Asian argument'.[86] List's 'nationalist system of political economy', which defends mercantilist policies and central planning, is, he argues, in direct opposition to the Anglo-American commercial individualism of Adam Smith. A vital component of this economic theory is that each nation develops its own power of production, retaining some form of national control over its own industrial manufacturing. This conclusion resonates deeply with the Maoist ideal of self-reliance (*zili gengsheng* 自力更生), a foundational principle of the Chinese Communist Party that is manifest, for example, in the 'Made in China 2025' policy, which promotes the goal of technological self-reliance advocated by the regime of Xi Jinping. 'Made in China 2025' is an industrial master plan first introduced by Premier Li Keqiang in 2015. Its aim is to move up the value chain – from factory-based manufacturing to research and design – by focusing specifically on high tech. The indigenous innovation (*zizhu chuangxin* 自主创新) of core technologies (*hexin jishu* 核心技术), Xi Jinping has stated, is an important instrument of the state.

In adopting this attitude, however, China is hardly alone. GPS is an American-owned utility, operated and maintained by the US Air Force. The first GPS test satellite launched in 1977 from an Air Force base in California. Thirteen years later, the system proved itself indispensable in the Gulf War of 1990. The primary motivation in its initial development was to use the panoptical potential of space as a viewpoint to gain critical advantage in war. 'The satellite', wrote Baudrillard, 'is a symptom of the West's quest for strategic planetary control.'[87] It was only after the turn of the millennium, when wartime accuracy was opened up for civilian use, that the navigational satellite systems began to generate enormous economic value. GPS chips are embedded in smartphones, tablets, computers, cameras, cars, ships and planes. Though too diverse an industry to calculate precisely, experts estimate that the total value of the 'GPS economy' adds up to a figure in the trillions of dollars.

In China GPS is censored through an offset. All cartographic material is strictly controlled. Geographic information is considered sensitive and all mapping practices need special permission from the State Council. Mapmaking without a licence is prohibited by Chinese law. Official maps, which require state authorisation, use GCJ-02 or 'Mars' coordinates, which are different from the WGS-84 standard that is most commonly used elsewhere. For reasons of national security, encryption algorithms specifically designed to obfuscate add apparently random offsets to both the latitude and longitude. In Shanghai, where I live, GPS-based maps, which use WGS-84 as their reference coordinate system, are offset by 50–500 metres. On Google maps real and virtual locations are always a few blocks apart.

As WeChat's celebration of the FY4A makes plain, China, in the opening decades of the twenty-first century, with its rapidly increasing economic and geopolitical power, has eagerly embraced satellite technology as critical infrastructure. In doing so, however, it has sought to ensure that the sensing machines which encircle the planet from space are its own. China's engagement with wireless media thus resonates with its earlier approach to the wired networks of the telegraph. It has embraced a Janus-faced strategy, which combines censorship with adoption and adaptation. Buoyed by policies of techno-nationalism, Chinese cyberculture has emerged from an environment that blocks foreign companies while encouraging near perfect replicas that, as the case of WeChat makes clear, follow their own line of mutation and growth.

China started developing the BeiDou Navigation Satellite System at the turn of the millennium as a geolocational infrastructure that could rival the global dominance of GPS. Initially BeiDou was designed as part of the European Galileo project. In 2008, however, frustrated by the lack of urgency, speed and investment, the Chinese navigation system asserted its autonomy. Aided by a push in investment through Xi Jinping's much-publicised 'Belt and Road initiative', BeiDou launched the 35th and final satellite in June 2020, by which time its global coverage and degree of accuracy could compete with GPS. China's intensifying global aspirations have thus risen alongside an ambitious programme to achieve autonomy in navigational satellite systems. In the summer of 2018 it was reported that Apple, in compliance with Beijing, would pre-install BeiDou chips into its latest line of phones.[88] Chinese geolocation started to be used as a bargaining chip with foreign brands. Interviewed in late 2017, Yang Changfeng, the system's chief designer, promised an unprecedented degree of resolution. The new satellites would be able to spot which lane a car was using on a motorway, detect the sway of a building in high winds and guide fire appliances to the nearest water hydrant. They would, he says 'provide important coordinates of time and space and become a pillar of national security . . . In three years' time people may still say "I'm using GPS" but in fact their phone will be tuned into BeiDou.'[89]

The geopolitical rivalry between GPS and BeiDou presumes that nations are capable of controlling a technological realm that they have the power to transcend. In this they enact the presumed split that marks the *ti–yong* dichotomy, with the state as the unchanging essence (*ti*) and ephemeral technosphere as the function (*yong*). Yet, as thinkers such as Xiong Shili long ago observed, this presumption of a fundamental separation involves a critical abstract mistake. This philosophical error is heightened by the nature of wireless media and its particular methods of marking the time. The *ti* of wirelessness is the body electric in all of its cosmic dimensions and its function (*yong*) is the constancy of its waves.

Over the course of the twentieth century the wires of the telegraph gave way to the electromagnetic waves of wireless media, which intensified the planet's interconnectedness. This shift from wires to wirelessness is marked by a change in the technological production of global time, as the planetary mechanical timekeeping system was replaced by satellites, atomic clocks and radio signals. At the beginning of the twentieth century, the world, as Peter Galison has written, was 'crisscrossed with lines of coordination: webs of train tracks, telegraph lines, meteorological networks, and longitude surveys all under the watchful increasingly universal clock system'. By the end of the century, however, this 'world machine' of synchronised clocks had 'metamorphosed from the networks of submarine cables hauled by schooners to a microwave grid broadcast from satellites'.[90]

This transition from the electro-coordinated signals of the telegraph to the space-based timekeeping devices of today subtly altered the universality of Greenwich Mean Time that was brought about through the global spread of the telegraph. In introducing his book on the contemporary physics of time, Carlo Rovelli turns to the ancient philosopher Anaximander, who held that all phenomena evolve according to a particular 'order of time'. The conversion from wires to wireless, which largely took place during the fourth Kondratiev cycle, marks a threshold transition, a transformation in the techno-temporal order.

A functioning GPS system requires an extremely high degree of temporal precision. An accuracy of about a billionth of a second is needed to keep users from getting lost. To achieve this fine-grained exactitude, geolocation is reliant on atomic clocks, the most precise timekeeping device ever known. In 2014 the National Institute of Standards and Technology introduced the NIST-F2, an atomic clock that is accurate to one second in 300 million years. These intricate and ultra-reliable machines, which are built into the GPS system, now 'underpin much of the modern world'.[91]

With atomic clocks, time ceases to be based on a method of division and accumulates upwards from a primary vibration instead. 'To the physicist', writes historian of time David Landes, 'any stable oscillation is a clock.'[92] This oscillation, which here corresponds to the entirety of the wave, constitutes the abstract plane upon which the media environment of the fifth long wave of techno-capital depends. The full implications of this timekeeping technique were only realised with the invention of the first atomic clock, which uses, as its basic timekeeping element, frequency transitions in the electromagnetic spectrum. Before the atomic clock, the fundamental unit of time, the second-hand tick, was determined through a subdivision of the astronomical day. This changed only in 1967 when the International

Committee for Weights and Measurements established an atomic description, which defined the second according to the rate of vibration of the caesium atom. From then on, time was determined by the scientific designation for frequency: hertz (or cycles per second), which was simultaneously fixed on the electromagnetic transitions in the hyperfine structure of the caesium-133 atom. Since 1967, time and frequency have been one. With the move to the atomic sphere, clocks became independent of the Earth's rotation. A physical second based on an atomic vibration marked the end of astronomical time. Modern temporality had broken free from the revolution of the planets and started to conform instead to the vibrations of electromagnetic signals.

This shift from astronomical subdivision to electric vibration is not the only transition that distinguishes wirelessness as a distinct mode of temporality. The switch from wired to wireless also had to incorporate the momentous change in twentieth-century physics that is now implemented, in a very real way, into the machines that constitute global time. GPS requires such exact timekeeping that the adjustments demanded by Einstein's theories of relativity had to be built in. According to relativity, as Peter Galison explains, the clocks housed on orbiting satellites accumulate a difference relative to the Earth 'of 38 millionths (that is 38,000 billionths) of a second per day'.[93] In the beginning, engineers were sceptical of the need to incorporate theoretical physics and tried to run the system without the relativity-correcting apparatus. It was soon realised, however, that the new mode of timekeeping needed the new theory of time. Without factoring for relativity, 'it would have taken less than two minutes for the GPS system to exceed its allowable error. After a single day, satellites would have been raining erroneous positions, skewed by some six miles, onto the earth. Cars, bombs, planes, and ships would have veered wildly off course.'[94] Special and general relativity are thus now part of our all-encompassing, invisible planetary grid. 'Theory', writes Galison, 'had become machine.'[95] In this environment, which so intimately intermixes the earthly and the cosmic, the natural and the artificial, the local and the global, it is no longer possible to maintain an illusion that culture and technology, essence and function can be kept apart.

Galison's book *Einstein's Clocks, Poincaré's Maps* details the extent to which twentieth-century physics is intermeshed with technology. Einstein was working as a clerk in a patent office and had a daily view of the giant clock at Bern. In his job he regularly confronted the difficulties brought about through the spread of the telegraph and railways, and it was this that made him consider the problem of time coordination that would ultimately lead to his revolutionary insights. Despite the myth of the lone genius that surrounds him, 'Einstein had constructed his abstract relativity machine out of a material world of synchronized clocks'.[96] He was 'not a solitary brain thinking great thoughts, but an expert situated at the heart of modern media and machines'.[97] Immersed in the techno-culture of his time, at the beginning of the third K-wave at the dawn of the electrical age, Einstein began to contemplate the problem of simultaneity at a distance, which he understood practically as the difficulty of coordinating clocks in different places. The solution, as the telegraph made clear, relies on electrical communication. 'To synchronize two clocks, you have to start with one, flash a signal to the other, and adjust for the time it takes for the flash to arrive.'[98] This simple idea, writes Galison, lies at the heart of relativity. Simultaneity is nothing more than a convention, defined only by the 'exchange of electromagnetic signals, taking into account the transit time of the signal'.[99]

Relativity, as is well known, cracked the sure foundation of the Newtonian world and thereby 'changed physics forever'.[100] After Einstein, the notion of Absolute Time disappeared. The idea of a single universal 'now', which unites the planet in an integrated whole, could only be understood as a convenient myth. 'In Einstein's electrotechnical world there was no place for a "universally audible tick-tock" that we can call time.'[101] After Einstein it is understood that time does not pass everywhere uniformly but rather moves more slowly in some places and more rapidly in others. Between these different times there is no objective measure. At the heart of this multiplicity is the time lag inherent in any message that is carried by electromagnetic waves. Global time, as John Durham Peters notes, is inherently bound to the speed of communication. All signals have transmission costs and 'must pay a toll to time'.[102] Peters describes relativity 'as a theory of communication, more specifically, of the universe's difficulty of communicating with itself. There is no cosmic telegraph to synchronize clocks at distant spots', he writes. 'There is no possibility of a single "now" that pervades the universe . . . "Now" can stretch only as far as signals can carry.'[103] In contrast to Carey's great thesis about electronic communication, clocks and telegraphs

> taught Einstein not the decisive separation of communication and transportation, but their eternal fusion . . . all communication, even electrical, takes time, however slight. Electrical signals may be relatively free of the burdens of transportation across space, but they are not free of the cost of transportation across time.[104]

Curiously enough, Peters remarks, Einstein's universe, which is now embedded into the wireless mediasphere, 'looks more like the old order of clock time before railroad time, where every town had its own local time'.[105] Time in contemporary physics, as Carlo Rovelli explains, operates as currencies do, only gaining value relative to each other. In Einstein's universe, he writes, 'times are legion, a different one for every point in space. There is not one single time, there is a vast multitude of them.'[106] Although the shift from wired to wirelessness seems to increase the force and power of unification, there is a difference in the type of integration these media produce. Wireless time involves embodied vibrations, non-human frequencies and an encoded multiplicity. Outside its affinity with a centralised order there is an undercurrent of alliances with dispersive forces, marginal practices and peripheral zones.

Notes

1. Yujie Chen, Zhifei Mao and Jack Linchuan Qiu, *Super-Sticky WeChat and Chinese Society* (Bingley: Emerald Publishing, 2018), 20.
2. Ibid., 36.
3. Ibid.
4. Ibid., 63.
5. Liyan Chen, 'Red Envelope War: How Alibaba and Tencent Fight Over Chinese New Year', *Forbes*, 19 February 2015, https://www.forbes.com/sites/liyanchen/2015/02/19/red-envelope-war-how-alibaba-and-tencent-fight-over-chinese-new-year/.
6. Finn Brunton, 'WeChat: Messaging Apps and New Social Currency Transaction Tools', in *Appified: Culture in the Age of Apps*, ed. Jeremy Wade Morris and Sarah Murray (Ann Arbor, MI: University of Michigan Press, 2018), 185.
7. Jean-Christophe Plantin and Gabriele de Seta, 'WeChat as Infrastructure: The Techno-Nationalist Shaping of Chinese Digital Platforms', *Chinese Journal of Communication* 12, no. 3 (2019): 257–73.
8. Connie Chan, 'When One App Rules Them All: The Case of WeChat and Mobile in China', 6 August 2015, https://a16z.com/2015/08/06/wechat-china-mobile-first/.
9. Jonah Kessel and Paul Mozur, 'How China is Changing Your Internet', *The New York Times*, 10 August 2016, https://www.youtube.com/watch?v=VAesMQ6VtK8.
10. Karen Hao, 'The New Satellite Image of Earth on WeChat's Splash Page Features China at Its Center – for a Reason', *Quartz*, 26 September 2017, https://qz.com/1086561/wechat-has-swapped-a-nasa-satellites-image-of-earth-on-its-splash-screen-for-a-chinese-one/.
11. Tom Standage, *The Victorian Internet: The Remarkable Story of the Telegraph and the Nineteenth Century's On-Line Pioneers* (London: Bloomsbury, 2014).
12. Erik Baark, *Lightning Wires: The Telegraph and China's Technological Modernization, 1860–1890* (Westport, CT: Greenwood, 1997), 71.

13. Yongming Zhou, *Historicizing Online Politics: Telegraphy, the Internet, and Political Participation in China* (Stanford, CA: Stanford University Press, 2005), 21.
14. Baark, *Lightning Wires*, 78.
15. Ibid., 4.
16. Ibid., 56.
17. Zhou, *Historicizing Online Politics*, 21.
18. Baark, *Lightning Wires*, 89.
19. Ibid., 75.
20. For a detailed exposition of this, see Jeffrey Sconce, *Haunted Media: Electronic Presence from Telegraphy to Television* (Durham, NC: Duke University Press, 2000).
21. Burning practices using incense but also paper money and paper objects are central to the mortuary rituals of Chinese religion.
22. Baark, *Lightning Wires*, 107.
23. Ibid.
24. Thomas Mullaney, *The Chinese Typewriter: A History* (Cambridge, MA: MIT Press, 2017), 109.
25. Baark, *Lightning Wires*, 119.
26. Zhou, *Historicizing Online Politics*, 26.
27. Roger Thompson, 'The Wire: Progress, Paradox, and Disaster in the Strategic Networking of China, 1881–1901', *Frontiers of History in China* 10, no. 3 (2015): 399.
28. Levenson, *Confucian China and its Modern Fate*, 95.
29. Ibid., 104.
30. Ibid., 59.
31. Ibid.
32. Ibid., 60.
33. Cohen, *Discovering History in China*, 30.
34. Levenson, *Confucian China and its Modern Fate,* 61.
35. Ibid., 61.
36. Hui, *The Question Concerning Technology in China*, 152.
37. Levenson, *Confucian China and its Modern Fate*, 70.
38. Ibid., 61.
39. Schwartz, *In Search of Wealth and Power.*
40. Frédéric Wang, 'The Relationship between Chinese Learning and Western Learning According to Yan Fu (1854–1921)', in *Knowledge and Society Today (Multiple Modernity Project)* (Lyons, 2009), 49, https://shs.hal.science/halshs-00674116/document.
41. Teng and Fairbank, *China's Response to the West*, 150.
42. For more details and complexity, see Fung, *The Intellectual Foundations of Chinese Modernity.*
43. Guy Alitto, 'Review of *The Crisis of Chinese Consciousness: Radical Antitraditionalism in the May Fourth Era. By Lin Yü-Sheng. Foreword by Benjamin I. Schwartz*', *The Journal of Asian Studies* 39, no. 1 (1979): 140–2.

44. Chang Hao, 'New Confucianism and the Intellectual Crisis of Contemporary China', in *The Limits of Change: Essays on Conservative Alternatives in Republican China*, ed. Charlotte Furth (Cambridge, MA: Harvard University Press, 2014 [1976]), 281.

45. Levenson, *Confucian China and its Modern Fate*, 281.

46. Teng and Fairbank, *China's Response to the West*, 1.

47. For a detailed overarching discussion, see James Townsend, 'Chinese Nationalism', *The Australian Journal of Chinese Affairs* 27 (1992): 97–130.

48. This is an enormous subject with a vast scholarship that is beyond the scope of this book. For two interesting historical perspectives, see Lydia H. Liu, *The Clash of Empires: The Invention of China in Modern World Making* (Cambridge, MA: Harvard University Press, 2004) and Rebecca E. Karl, *Staging the World: Chinese Nationalism at the Turn of the Twentieth Century* (Durham, NC: Duke University Press, 2002).

49. Susan Blum and Lionel Jensen, *China Off Center: Mapping the Margins of the Middle Kingdom* (Honolulu, HI: University of Hawaii Press, 2002), xiv.

50. Prasenjit Duara, *Rescuing History from the Nation: Questioning Narratives of Modern China* (Chicago: University of Chicago Press, 1996), 32.

51. Benedict Anderson, *Imagined Communities: Reflections on the Origin and Spread of Nationalism* (London: Verso, 2016), 26.

52. Duara, *Rescuing History from the Nation*, 17.

53. Ibid., 25.

54. Porter Erisman, *Crocodile in the Yangtze* (documentary), Purple Reel Productions, Taluswood Films, 2012.

55. This utopian thinking was a strong part of early Internet culture all over the world. See Fred Turner, *From Counterculture to Cyberculture: Stewart Brand, the Whole Earth Network, and the Rise of Digital Utopianism* (Chicago: University of Chicago Press, 2006).

56. Geremie R. Barmé, 'The Great Firewall of China', *Wired*, 1 June 1997, https://www.wired.com/1997/06/china-3/.

57. There is a vast literature discussing China's Internet culture. Two good books to start with are Guobin Yang, *The Power of the Internet in China: Citizen Activism Online* (New York: Columbia University Press, 2011) and David Herold and Peter Marolt, eds, *Online Society in China: Creating, Celebrating, and Instrumentalising the Online Carnival* (New York: Routledge, 2011). It is also worth looking at the archives from the following sites: http://www.danwei.com/; http://www.popupchinese.com/lessons/sinica/; http://chinadigitaltimes.net/; http://sinocism.com/; http://cmp.hku.hk/; http://www.chinafile.com/; http://www.tealeafnation.com/; http://www.thechinabeat.org. *Logic Magazine* also has a good issue discussing some of the complexities involved: https://logicmag.io/china/.

58. Rebecca MacKinnon, *Consent of the Networked: The Worldwide Struggle for Internet Freedom* (New York: Basic Books, 2012).

59. Michael Curtin and Hemant Shah, eds, *Reorienting Global Communication: Indian and Chinese Media Beyond Borders* (Urbana, IL: University of Illinois Press, 2010).
60. For a detailed exploration that focuses on China's relations with Japan, see Florian Schneider, *China's Digital Nationalism* (Oxford: Oxford University Press, 2018).
61. Mara Hvistendahl, 'How a Chinese AI Giant Made Chatting – and Surveillance – Easy', *Wired*, 2020, https://www.wired.com/story/iflytek-china-ai-giant-voice-chatting-surveillance/.
62. Margaret Roberts, *Censored: Distraction and Diversion Inside China's Great Firewall* (Princeton, NJ: Princeton University Press, 2018).
63. For more, see Hvistendahl, 'How a Chinese AI Giant Made Chatting – and Surveillance – Easy',
64. This was theorized on 23 April by Guobin Yang on Twitter: https://twitter.com/Yangguobin/status/1517840610841047040.
65. James Carey, 'Technology and Ideology: The Case of the Telegraph', *Prospects* 8 (October 1983): 303–25.
66. James Gleick, *Information: A History, a Theory, a Flood* (London: Fourth Estate, 2012), 147.
67. Peters, 'Technology and Ideology', 138.
68. Carey, 'Technology and Ideology', 306.
69. Daniel Headrick, *The Tentacles of Progress: Technology Transfer in the Age of Imperialism, 1850–1940* (New York: Oxford University Press, 1988), 97.
70. Roland Wenzlhuemer, *Connecting the Nineteenth-Century World: The Telegraph and Globalization* (Cambridge: Cambridge University Press, 2012).
71. Thomas Mullaney, 'Semiotic Sovereignty: The 1871 Chinese Telegraph Code in Historical Perspective', in *Science and Technology in Modern China, 1880s–1940s*, ed. Jing Tsu and Benjamin Elman (Leiden: Brill, 2014), 154.
72. Robert Luther Thompson, *Wiring a Continent: The History of the Telegraph Industry in the United States, 1832–1866* (Princeton, NJ: Princeton University Press, 1947).
73. Headrick, *The Tentacles of Progress*.
74. See my project Moveable Feasts: https://sh-streetfood.org/.
75. N. Katherine Hayles, *How We Think: Digital Media and Contemporary Technogenesis* (Chicago: University of Chicago Press, 2012), 126.
76. Carey, 'Technology and Ideology', 319.
77. Gleick, *Information*, 125.
78. Peter Galison, *Einstein's Clocks, Poincaré's Maps: Empires of Time* (New York: W. W. Norton, 2003), 103.
79. Ibid.
80. Ibid., 105.
81. Carey, 'Technology and Ideology', 323.
82. Jennifer Gabrys, *Program Earth: Environmental Sensing Technology and the Making of a Computational Planet* (Minneapolis, MN: University of Minnesota Press, 2016), 1.

83. Lisa Parks, *Cultures in Orbit: Satellites and the Televisual* (Durham, NC: Duke University Press, 2005), 3.

84. Paul Edwards, *A Vast Machine: Computer Models, Climate Data, and the Politics of Global Warming* (Cambridge, MA: MIT Press, 2013).

85. William Gibson, *Spook Country* (London: Penguin, 2011), 66.

86. James Fallows, 'How the World Works', *The Atlantic*, 1 December 1993. https://www.theatlantic.com/magazine/archive/1993/12/how-the-world-works/305854/.

87. Parks, *Cultures in Orbit*, 6.

88. Asia Times Staff, 'Apple May Build China's BeiDou Navigation into Future iPhones', *Asia Times*, 22 August 2018, https://asiatimes.com/2018/08/apple-may-build-chinas-beidou-navigation-into-future-iphones/.

89. Stephen Chen, 'Blast-off for China's New Satellite Rivals to GPS', *South China Morning Post*, 6 November 2017, https://www.scmp.com/news/china/society/article/2118616/china-launches-satellites-extend-global-range-its-version-gps.

90. Galison, *Einstein's Clocks, Poincaré's Maps*, 290.

91. Adam Mann, 'How the U.S. Built the World's Most Ridiculously Accurate Atomic Clock', *Wired*, 4 April 2014, https://www.wired.com/2014/04/nist-atomic-clock/.

92. David S. Landes, *Revolution in Time: Clocks and the Making of the Modern World* (Cambridge, MA: Belknap Press of Harvard University Press, 2000).

93. Galison, *Einstein's Clocks, Poincaré's Maps*, 288.

94. Ibid.

95. Ibid., 289.

96. Ibid., 273.

97. Peters, 'Technology and Ideology', 151.

98. Galison, *Einstein's Clocks, Poincaré's Maps*, 14.

99. Ibid., 306.

100. Ibid., 14.

101. Ibid.

102. Peters, 'Technology and Ideology', 150.

103. Ibid., 151.

104. Ibid., 150.

105. Ibid., 151.

106. Rovelli, *The Order of Time*, 18.

Chapter 3

Repetition: Pirate Culture and the Mobile Phone

In 1979 Andrei Tarkovsky created the haunting cinematic master-piece *Stalker*. The film portrays a realm called the Zone that exists on the threshold between worlds. In *Roadside Picnic*, the novel by the Strugatsky brothers upon which the Tarkovsky film was based, the Zone is envisioned as an abandoned site left after an alien visitation. Stalkers scavenge the area for mysterious machines called 'empties', which run off a strange and imperceptible force that they then trade in the thriving black market for alien swag that exists on the edges of the nearby town. Like all traffic in pirated technology, the stalkers' trade is difficult to keep contained and enclosed. The most unsettling feature of the Zone, as it is depicted in both the story and the film, is its infectious nature. The Zone breeds. 'Its alien rhythms', writes xenofeminist philosopher Amy Ireland, comprise 'an inhuman logic of reproduction'.[1] By the end of *Roadside Picnic*, emigration from the town on the perimeter of the Zone has been banned for fear of a growing contagion – that '[a]ll that used to be in the Zone [will finally] settle in the outside world'.[2] The town, the stalker tells us, is 'a hole into the future. And the stuff we fish out of this hole will change your whole stinking world.'[3]

To depict the strange reality of the Zone, Ireland contrasts it with the familiar parameters of Kantian critique, which she describes as a specifically anthropomorphic rhythmic regime. 'Linear time, simultaneous, three-dimensional space, and objecthood', she writes, 'are its framing parameters – its tempo or its beat.'[4] Most of that which occurs happens inside this framework. 'Time remains linear; space, simultaneous. Consequently, experience, at its most funda-mental and unconscious level is ordered, familiar, comfortable, and homely, scaled reassuringly to match our perceptual affordances.'[5] The Zone's exteriority is not empirical and concrete but abstract and transcendental. In the words of Mark Fisher, it is not 'just a matter of something being distant in space and time but of something which is beyond our ordinary experience and conception of space and time itself'.[6]

In conjuring the Zone as the site of an alien outsideness, Ireland turns to Fisher's book the *Weird and the Eerie*, which repeatedly reflects on Tarkovsky's films and the fictions on which his movies are based. In the Zone, writes Fisher, nothing is uniform. 'Time, as well as space, can curve and fold in unpredictable ways.'[7] The stalkers' intimacy with the Zone grants them what Fisher describes as a practical ethics of the eerie. Stalkers realise that the routes they once knew unexpectedly mutate into the unfamiliar, that 'you can't always take the straight path', that the maps they make 'rarely prove useful', and that 'one can never go back the way one came'.[8] In *Roadside Picnic*, the stalker throws nuts to mark a future crossing. 'It's Hansel and Gretel', he says, 'but in reverse.'[9] In this alternative and alien world, 'patterns are disturbed', the beat is broken, 'space and time no longer function following previously intelligible laws. . . Compasses and watches are ineffectual. Gravity is fractious. Radio waves, light waves and genetic information partake in inexplicable exchanges under a strange logic of transversal refraction.'[10] The Zone is not a place, but an imperceptible alteration of space-time; an invisible but absolute mutation. The stalker senses the presence of a kind of alien sentience, pregnant with a desire of its own. 'Over the pile of ancient trash, over the colorful rags and broken glass drifts a tremor, a vibration, just like the hot air above the tin roof at noon.'[11]

Ireland's essay 'Alien Rhythm' tracks the ways in which the Zone, 'as a sudden, monumental, unexplained disturbance in anthropomorphic space-time', morphs into a trope that spreads out from *Stalker* across other science fiction narratives. She writes of its alliance with the prefix xeno – the marker of that which arrives from outside. To elucidate, Ireland quotes Rebekah Sheldon, 'queer theorist, feminist, and witch', who details the etymology of the term. 'Xeno is *trans*. As graft, cut, intrusion, or excision, Xeno names the *movement between*, and *the moving entity*. It is the foreign and the foreigner, the unexpected outside, the unlike offspring, the other within, the eruption of another meaning.'[12]

The film *Stalker* takes place on land, but in his other great masterpiece *Solaris*, Tarkovsky suggests that the exteriority of the Zone is aligned with the aquatic. In the swirling seas of the alien planet Solaris, a mysterious intelligence swallows all interior states and projects them outward. 'The sublime alterity of the Solaris ocean', declares Fisher, 'is one of cinema's great images of the unknown.'[13] At the end of her essay, Ireland too calls upon the watery waves. She writes of the biologist in Vandermeer's *Annihilation* trilogy, who, immersed in an untimely event, watches as her double emerges from the black abyss of the sea.

> In the multiplicity of that regard, she saw what [the eyes] saw. She saw herself, standing there, looking down. She saw that the biologist now existed across locations and landscapes, those other horizons gathering in a blurred and rising wave – a single abstract Wave at the intersection of all concrete forms.[14]

The Special Economic Zone

This chapter focuses on the coastal city of Shenzhen, one of the first, and by far the most successful, of China's Special Economic Zones (SEZ). The Special Economic Zone is clearly distinct from the zone trope that traverses the science fiction imaginary. Nevertheless, they share some critical properties. The city of Shenzhen, where much of the world's wireless media gets made, has hosted a vibrant pirate culture that innovated practices of repetition. The continuous copying and mutant iterations at the heart of this techno-culture fundamentally disrupt a familiar, stable order that is based on the primacy of the original. Its wave-like recurrence is commensurate with the radical alterity evoked by the exteriority of the Zone.

There is such an intimate connection between Shenzhen's rise and the spread of the mobile phone that they seem to have manifested as two aspects of a single event. The global advance of wireless media depended on Shenzhen in part because of its strategic position as an outsourcing hub for the manufacturing of digital technology. Initially, Shenzhen's attractiveness as a site for manufacturing was a direct result of the fabricated extraterritoriality of the SEZ. These pockets of experimentation allowed China to introduce market systems as trial runs in fenced-off territories, which could be applied elsewhere if and when they had been proven to work. SEZs are themselves modelled after a variety of similar precedents. 'Free ports', as Keller Easterling writes, 'have handled global trade for centuries.'[15] The pre-history of the modern zone, as Mary Ann O'Donnell, Winnie Wong and Jonathan Bach explain, 'lies in capitalism's impetus to maintain strategically ambiguous spaces that enable more fluid circulation of goods, people, and capital than might otherwise be permissible given political constraints of empires and, later, of nation-states'.[16] In China, the success of the Export Processing Zones of the Asian tigers was also extremely influential. It was 'the mid twentieth-century development of the Export Processing Zone, or

EPZ, as a more formalized economic and administrative instrument', writes Easterling, 'that marks the beginning of the modern zone'.[17]

SEZs were critical to China's strategy of Reform and Opening, which used relatively small-scale sites with special incentives on taxation and regulation, customs and ownership as well as the establishment of a 'Zone authority' as an exceptional legal entity to test transformative policies. Liang Xiang, the first Party chief and mayor of Shenzhen, used the phrase 'ant theory' to describe the deliberate strategy of seductive modelling. Ant theory 'stated that only after a scout ant had discovered a patch of sweetness would other ants be attracted to the area'.[18] Shenzhen, then, became a model for Chinese globalisation precisely by being an anomaly. Anthropologist Aihwa Ong names such investigative probes 'practices of urban modeling'. Special Economic Zones, she writes, are 'world conjuring projects'.[19] 'Today Asian cities are fertile sites, not for following an established pathway or master blueprint, but for a plethora of situated experiments that reinvent what urban norms can count as "global".'[20]

The SEZ, like the image of the Zone, operates as a gateway between inside and out; both occupy an in-between site on the borderlands of time and space. The Zone, writes Jonathan Bach referring to the SEZ, 'serves as a spatial threshold' that mediates between the Chinese economy and that of other countries. It 'is neither fully home nor abroad – at the same time both inside and outside the system'. It also 'serves as a temporal threshold between stages of development – the China that was and the China that will be'.[21] The Zone is a form of urban fantasy, situated both in the already mythic recent past as well as in the continuously updated version of the City of Tomorrow.

Shenzhen, in particular, was designed as a window 'through which one can look both in and out'.[22] The city's liminal position is made manifest in marvellously surreal fashion in a downtown theme park called 'Window of the World', which is located just on the border of the densely packed urban village of Baishizou. The park was built in 1993 in an era when Chinese citizens rarely travelled abroad. Its wacky audacity, however, which perfectly captures the critical role of the SEZ, ensures that it continues to serve as one of the metropolis's most important icons. This scenic spot contains almost 150 miniaturised versions of the planet's most archetypal monuments. Tourists dressed in Japanese Imperial and French Baroque costumes stroll among dwarf replicas of St Mark's Cathedral, Mt Fuji and the Eiffel Tower, now all overshadowed by the clusters of skyscrapers that dominate the still-swelling neighbourhoods outside.[23]

Shenzhen's position as a city on the edge is further strengthened by its intimate relationship with the boundary areas that make up Greater China. For the Taiwanese tech industry, the metropolis served as a doorway into the mainland. Shenzhen is at the border, where the Special Economic Zone meets the Special Administrative Regions of Hong Kong and Macau. Sitting as it does at the frontier of 'One Country, Two Systems', Shenzhen is strategically placed to attract investment from overseas Chinese in Hong Kong and Taiwan. Its geographical location on the Pearl River Delta, and especially its proximity to Hong Kong, were critical factors in the city's development. Hong Kong is Shenzhen's virtual twin. It has functioned 'simultaneously as Shenzhen's future (what it *would be like* in years to come) and its spectral past (what Shenzhen *might have* been under other circumstances)'.[24] The island city itself is a model for the marginal tendencies of the Cantonese world.[25]

Nevertheless, many argue that Shenzhen's liminal quality is ultimately subject and subordinate to a higher power.[26] The SEZ, writes Ong, is the result of 'flexible Chinese state practices', tactics which she names 'zoning technologies'. In China, she argues, these tactics 'have interacted to produce an evolving system of variegated sovereignty'.[27] Economic policies are used to consolidate 'distinct political entities such as Hong Kong and Macao, and even Taiwan and Singapore, into an emerging Chinese axis'. For Ong, the apparent fragmentation manifest in 'Greater China' is, in the end, a centralising strategy that serves to economically integrate disarticulated political entities as a detour towards eventual political integration. In *Learning from Shenzhen*, O'Donnell, Wong and Bach make a similar argument. Outposts such as Shenzhen, they contend, 'where states effectively section off a part of their country and give it an intermediate status', are best understood as a new mode of government astutely adapted to the 'smooth space' of late capitalism.[28] The Zone is an ultimate expression of the 'changing practices of sovereignty', which use 'nested exceptionalisms: the interplay of exception and rule that creates intersections for networks, markets, and political rule'.[29] In Keller Easterling's terms, the Zone is a prime example of 'Extrastatecraft' whose diversity of regulations enables a supervision and governance of populations that is both economic and biopolitical. In creating 'special' places and periods where laws and regulations can be unilaterally altered, the Zone recalls Carl Schmitt's infamous dictum: sovereign is he who can make the exception.[30]

There is no doubt that in the complex landscape of Shenzhen the central sovereign is strong. Still, the conjunction of Shenzhen and wireless media owes much to the frontiers and borderlands of a decentred China and its affiliation with the non-human mode of reproduction that leaks out from the exteriority of the Zone. This is most apparent in the unique, locally grown, copycat culture of manufacturing, known as *shanzhai* (山寨), a form of piracy that ultimately challenges all straightforward narratives about the Shenzhen epoch and its role in the creation of our wireless age. Joshua Neves, in his discussion of piracy in the context of China's contemporary mediascapes, recalls 'Cicero's 2,000-year-old proclamation that pirates, because they operate outside of territorial sovereignty and ordinary jurisdiction, are the "enemy of all" (*hostis humani generis*)'. This absolute alterity, he points out, 'does not neatly map onto Carl Schmitt's well-known articulation of the "state of exception"'.[31] Schmitt himself held that piracy, a practice born from the 'freedom of the sea', was outside the control of the land-based sovereign. 'On the open sea', he wrote, 'there were no limits, no boundaries, no consecrated sites, no sacred orientations, no law and no property.'[32] Neves elaborates as follows:

> The exception operates on the dichotomy of 'law' versus 'no law', where, in theory, the law is operative or it is suspended, and the sovereign is the one who can decide. In contrast, piracy inaugurates a paradoxical formation. It is a legal category that makes the exception permanent, extralegal – which is to say it is only ever partially a legal formation to begin with.[33]

Shenzhen's exteriority lies in its pirate culture, with its embrace, even celebration, of the copy and the fake. Rather than value an original, eternal primary essence (*ti*) that stands over and above its replication (*yong*), Shenzhen created a culture of the copy that was freed from its ties to the original. In this it broke from a linear trajectory, adopting a practical ethos based on simulation that is immanent to the rhythmic repetition characterised by the ongoing rise and fall of the wave.

The Shenzhen Epoch

In his book *Cities and Civilization*, urbanist Peter Hall tells a history of the world based on the short, innovative eruptions that occur in certain places at certain times. Hall's book concentrates on the legendary moments of global urban history: Athens in the fifth century, Florence in the fourteenth century, Victorian London, nineteenth-century Paris, Manchester at the beginning of the Industrial revolution, New York in the mid-twentieth century, Detroit and Motown, LA and Hollywood, Memphis and the Blues.[34] Like the examples discussed by Hall, twenty-first-century Shenzhen is an explosive energetic eruption. These golden ages, which are always and necessarily urban ages, manifest as brief bursts of creativity that appear in particular places at particular times. In these singular instances, Hall contends, a city becomes not so much a place as an epoch. Those who experience these exceptional urban ages know them instinctively. To become a Berliner one only had to breathe in the air of Berlin with a deep breath, stated a resident of Weimar Berlin: 'Berlin tasted of the future.'[35]

Anyone who has visited Shenzhen in the past few decades will have a visceral understanding of this sentiment. Shenzhen in the late twentieth and early twenty-first century is more an event than a location. No city has ever grown with such intensity. The mythic story of Shenzhen's recent past begins with a declaration by Deng Xiaoping, who has an almost talismanic presence in the city. In 1978, when Deng announced the policy of Reform and Opening (*Gaige Kaifang* 改革 開放), Shenzhen, the story goes, consisted of a string of backwater coastal settlements with a population of 300,000. Forty years later it has morphed into a megacity of over 20 million people, and by the 2010s was counted, along with Shanghai, Beijing and Guangzhou, as one of China's first-tier cities. This high-velocity transformation has come to be known as Shenzhen speed (*Shenzhen sudu* 深圳速度), a slogan that has consolidated into a historical expression.[36] This dramatic pace of urban expansion is reflected in the city's GDP, which grew at an average annual rate of 30 per cent between 1980 and 2010.[37]

The intensity of Shenzhen's urban growth began with the conjunction of a number of deterritorialised flows, which were unleashed in the economic recession of the 1970s. The end of the gold standard, stagflation and the oil crises marked the decline in the West of the post-war boom. Tremendous transformations in the global technological economy were born in the downturn of the fourth Kondratiev long wave. For much of the twentieth century, the vertically integrated firm, which kept everything 'in house', operated as an organic whole, organised from above.[38] By the early 1980s, however, the integrity of these organisms was under threat. Pushed by a complex situation involving globalisation, deregulation, increased financialisation and corporatisation, companies shifted away from vertical integration, zooming in on 'core competencies' and outsourcing peripheral tasks.[39] Horizontal networks, enhanced by new technologies, spread across the planet as increased globalisation lured outsourcing offshore. East Asia surfaced as the preferred manufacturing site. Governments in the region, having rejected the protectionist, interiorised models of import substitution, embraced a nationalist industrial strategy of low-cost production for export. This 'export-oriented model of growth' offered lower barriers for entry for foreign firms, tax reductions, infrastructure investment and a vast pool of cheap manual labour.

It is this restructuring of the global economy that powered the personal computer (PC) revolution of the 1980s and 1990s. Steve Wozniak completed the Apple 1 in 1976. The next year Apple 2, the company's first consumer product, was released. In 1982 the Commodore 64 was introduced, a machine that was recognised by the *Guinness Book of World Records* as the largest-selling single computer of all time. Already, a massive restructuring of the US information technology industry was underway. High-tech districts were radically reshaped as companies in the US and Europe moved their factories and manufacturing facilities offshore. The result, write Boy Lüthje and his co-authors in *From Silicon Valley to Shenzhen: Global Production and Work in the IT Industry*, was that

> by the 1990s, with the rise of the 'new economy', the IT industry was no longer dominated by vertically integrated giant corporations such as IBM but rather was shaped along horizontal lines of specialised suppliers of key components such as computer chips, software, hardware disk drives, and graphic cards.[40]

From Silicon Valley to Shenzhen documents the reorganisation of the industry based on a model of production known as 'Wintelism' in which key component providers (Windows and Intel) dominate a manufacturing ecosystem that assembles machines from standard components. Under Wintelism, there is a separation between product innovation and electronic contract manufacturing. Famous PC makers such as Dell, HP and Apple became 'marketing and distribution companies with no in house resources for manufacturing or product development'.[41]

In this industrial mutation, the Chinese periphery played a particularly critical role. From the start, Shenzhen's growth was intimately tied to its role as the global hub for the assembly and distribution of electronics. New technologies build themselves through a conglomeration of parts from all around the world; the design teams of Silicon Valley, the raw material from the mines of Africa, the capital markets fuelled by the Middle East. Shenzhen has emerged as the gathering place, a central node in the circulatory system.

Yet China's centrality to digital technology grew from the edges not the core. In the mid-1980s Morris Chang, a Taiwanese citizen who worked initially for Texas Instruments, had the idea of developing a foundry that specialised in the production of computer chips, which could then be sold to a variety of firms that concentrated solely on design and distribution. Establishing a silicon foundry, however, costs billions of dollars. Chang found a backer in the Taiwanese government, which was by then eager to compete with the rise of Korea and Japan. The Taiwan Semiconductor Manufacturing Company (TSMC) was established in 1987 and rose to become the world's largest semiconductor foundry. It pioneered a model of fabless production that helped jumpstart the island's tech sector. 'By the late 1990s', reports business writer Clyde Prestowitz, 'nearly 80 percent of all laptop computers and 50 percent of all computer motherboards were being made in Taiwan [while] 60 percent of all desktop PCs were manufactured or had a motherboard manufactured there.'[42]

As China's policies of Reform and Opening took hold, the Taiwanese tech giants shifted certain elements of production to the mainland,[43] taking advantage of low-cost labour as well as 'the large-scale factories and manufacturing infrastructures that were built up in the major areas of export production along the Chinese East coast'.[44] Among the Taiwanese firms to establish sites in the Pearl River Delta, Foxconn rose to the top. Foxconn, a subsidiary of Honhai Precision Industry, was set up by Terry Gou as a small-scale electronics component manufacturer in 1974. Today, the company is the largest electronics manufacturer in the world, employing over a million people who assemble the digital machines of the world's most-famous brands. Shenzhen's 'Foxconn City' is a vast complex hosting thousands of workers. It includes a main shopping street, entertainment facilities, over a dozen major factories as well as a host of other large-scale buildings filled with roboticised equipment designed to create the latest manifestation of consumer hardware. Foxconn has become a symbol for the split between manufacturing and distribution and design that structured global electronic production in the late twentieth century. The entrenched divisions are inscribed in small letters on the back of every iPhone, iPad and MacBook: 'Designed by Apple in California. Assembled in China.'

In contrast to the message embedded in this slogan, industrial designers have always worked closely with the factory floor.[45] In the production of global electronics, core and periphery are intimately intermixed. In Shenzhen, the designers and engineers at Apple and Foxconn work in tight collaboration through a process of multiple iterations, with Foxconn innovating manufacturing tools and procedures to implement Apple's designs, which are, in turn, in constant need of adaptation. Design is frozen only at the very last minute, just as the product is released. In contrast to the messiness of this reality, the global division of labour presumes a model in which high-end value-added work (research, design and prototyping) is done in America, while China is meant to blindly execute ideas that come from elsewhere. In its most extreme formulation this division corresponds to a Cartesian-style dualism in which an active, rational mind guides a passive, inert body. Understood in this way, the global unity of techno-capitalism is, just as China first imagined it in the early years of the telegraph, based on the primacy of the West.

Shenzhen's role, however, not only in the nation but also in the world, is interwoven with its intrinsic marginality. The central government dictated Shenzhen's extraterritoriality by granting it status as an SEZ. Yet the planned bright, glossy and hyper-designed SEZ did not just materialise fully formed out of nothing. Instead, the string of villages on the watery edges of the Pearl River Delta mutated into a metropolis that manifests the cyberpunk futurism of the Zone.[46] Here, in the tight streets and alleyways of the urban village, which are sensuous, intimate, cryptic and messy, Shenzhen's *shanzhai* (or copycat) culture was born.

The Shenzhen Myth

Shenzhen is said to have been the inspiration for Rem Koolhaas's *Generic City*, a non-space of total convergence that is forged out of 'an endless repetition of the same fractal module'.[47] The generic city is 'a place of weak and distended sensations, few and far between emotions', where all horizontality has been erased. In this pervasive urban landscape, Koolhaas declares, 'the street is dead'.[48] This vision of a city devoid of identity, culture, time and space has long dominated discussions of Shenzhen. Yet far from being an 'instant city' precisely engineered, Shenzhen, especially during its period of hyper-growth, was a cacophonous place; a sentient city filled with contradictions, ambiguities and complex negotiations, in which urban and rural, formal and informal, skyscraper and street are deeply intertwined.

Shenzhen is frequently held up as exemplifying China's top-down growth, a place with no history, the ideal tabula rasa for the fantasy of a modernist metropolis. The popular fable, writes urbanist Juan Du, is that the city was 'called into existence in 1979 with the establishment of the Shenzhen Special Economic Zone under the grand vision of then Premier Deng Xiaoping'.[49] Du's book *The Shenzhen Experiment* disputes this myth. Nationalist policies and central economic planning cannot account for Shenzhen's dramatic acceleration, which emerged instead from the local geography, history and culture of the Shenzhen region as well as the singular features of its urban form.

Before there was Shenzhen, the territory on the Pearl River Delta that was destined to become one of the most dynamic megacities of the twenty-first century was not just empty space. Rather, it was occupied by several thousand agrarian villages clustered on some of the most fertile agricultural land in southern China. Prior to its elevation to Shenzhen municipality, Bao'an County had a hybrid cultural geography, which mixed Cantonese, Hakka and Weitou. Local historian Mary Ann O'Donnell writes of oyster farmers and fishermen who worked the waterways linking Guangzhou and Hongkong. The large fertile area consisted 'of at least three networks of loosely integrated market towns and villages, which were connected through riparian networks as well as paths through rice fields and lychee orchards'.[50] Instead of emerging fully formed through a dictate from on high, then, the metropolis of Shenzhen grew up organically out of the resilient remains of these older settlements. Hardy enclaves, which came to be known as urban villages (*chengzhongcun* 城中村), were preserved within the newly materialising city, interrupting the high-rise monotone of the planned landscape with hidden pockets of quasi-informality.

In China's rapid urbanisation, the split between urban and rural, which is registered at birth and encoded in the *hukou* or household registration system, is more political than it is empirical. As Jonathan Bach stresses in his study of Shenzhen, the 'distinction between rural and urban cannot be overestimated: social control, resource allocation, biopolitical interventions from reproduction to health care, education, relative social status, and mobility all came to hinge on this distinction'.[51] Due to the geographical and historical specificities of Shenzhen, much of the indigenous population stayed rural even as the city surfaced all around them.[52] The regulations and benefits applying to the legal urban residents of Shenzhen did not extend to anyone living in the villages. As a result, these borderline communities, which flourished not only at the urban edges but throughout the entire city (with many urban villages occupying prime real estate), evolved with a distinct political, social and economic status and their own specific urban codes and zoning rules. They thus became, as Du writes, 'self-governing rural-status islands in the midst of the fastest and fiercest development environment in China'.[53]

Once freed from the controls of the command economy, people from all across the country poured into the coastal cities looking for work. They met a welcoming culture in Shenzhen, where subway signs read: just come, and you are a Shenzhener (*lai le, jiu shi Shenzhen ren* 來了就是深圳人). The gap between the Party's blueprints and more messy reality produced by this unplanned 'floating' population is evident in the numbers. Shenzhen was designed as a city of 1 million, yet by the turn of the millennium more than 10 million people had made it their home. Village residents were highly attuned to the immense transformative opportunities that had been unleashed. They realised that 'with no rural land left to tend' they could rent out buildings and apartments to migrant workers and 'farm property' instead.[54] The quasi-informal structures constructed by the former villagers 'became the standard choice for anyone arriving in Shenzhen seeking temporary or affordable housing'.[55]

Urban villages thus provided space and opportunity for the vast population of newly urbanised and grew to become the most densely built-up areas in the entire city. The metropolis of Shenzhen co-evolved with these internal villages, which supported the city's growth by offering 'informal solutions to boomtown conditions'.[56] By creating an essential 'supply of low-cost housing', notes David Bandurski, 'urban villages have underwritten low-cost labour in China and mitigated the associated costs of urban living'.[57] Shenzhen speed fed off the villages' social and legal ambiguity. Urban villages, which consist of a mixture of residents, businesses and light industry, are characterised by a unique form of hyper-dense architecture known as 'handshake buildings'. The name comes from structures that are packed so tightly together that you can open your window and reach out to shake the hand of your neighbour in the building next door. The result is a labyrinth of cramped and dim spaces, often considered squalid and backward, whose only light comes from thin 'threads of sky'. Residents socialise outside. The thicket of construction creates a compact web of lanes and alleyways, too narrow for cars to pass, that hosts an intensely lively street culture filled with open-air restaurants, crowded markets, fish and fruit vendors who share their narrow spaces with pool halls, repair workshops and mahjong rooms that spill out on to the street. 'Density and closeness are omnipresent: of people, stores, aromas, buildings – all hovering between the comforting vibrancy and vertiginous confinement of proximity.'[58] Small-time entrepreneurs occupy hybrid spaces – a noodle shop inside an apartment building that is also used as a mini grocery store.

This condensed commercial environment produces an intensity of transactions that urbanists argue is the key indicator in analysing the true density of the rising hypercities of the developing world. Mary Ann O'Donnell, whose own artist space Handshake 302 is located in Baishizhou, a large and central urban village, describes her neighbourhood, a place which stands at the cusp of redevelopment and gentrification:

There are Shenzhen based chain stores in Baishizhou, however, individuals rather than state owned enterprises or multi-nationals run the majority of fresh markets, shops, restaurants and production centers.

Start-ups share factory space with logistic companies, car detailing studios, and workshops that assemble small batches of circuit boards to spec as well as hip centers of youth culture – a kendo studio, a hacker space, two micro-breweries, and a bar with live music.[59]

It is in the micro-spaces of these street markets that the entrepreneurial energy and vast creative dynamism of contemporary China can be found. Nowhere is this more apparent than in the electronic markets of *Huaqiangbei* in downtown Shenzhen, where an enormous array of components and devices are sold, recycled and assembled. Though the markets moved to a cluster of multi-storey malls, the drab concrete and glass exteriors of the 'Generic City' mask the intensity of the culture inside. Hanging racks of pork and duck are sold amid VR goggles, selfie sticks and battery stands.

Building after building, floor upon floor, stall upon stall, shelf upon shelf, is dedicated to the buying, selling, and building of electronics. Everywhere are mountains of wires, mounds of chips, spools of lights, cases of buttons and knobs. *Huaqiangbei* Shenzhen is high-tech toolbox to the world.[60]

The dynamism of the tech markets, with their seductive urban undercurrents, counters the glossy sci-fi vision of the City of Tomorrow with a cyberpunk realism in which hackers and tinkerers operate alongside itinerant peddlers and street food stands. The electronic street markets of the urban village and not the planned boulevards of the SEZ are what gave birth to a planetary wireless media. It is this underground vision of the future that *shanzhai* production comes from and serves.

Shanzhai 山寨

By the turn of the millennium, with the dot-com crash, the downturn in the IT industry and the emergence of wireless media, it had become apparent that Shenzhen was more than just the factory to the world. People were switching from personal computers to mobile phones. In Shenzhen the ground had started to shift. In part this was due to a predictable 'move up the value chain' resulting from modes of capitalist production that were familiar from elsewhere. After decades of massive relocation of electronic manufacturing to China, Taiwanese companies such as Acer, HTC, Asus and Foxconn, which had been constructing the machine components for other brands, had built up the technological and organisational skills to develop substantial intellectual property rights on their own.[61] While some companies began catering predominantly to large established firms, a dense network of entrepreneurs saw an opportunity to establish themselves in the growing gaps of the global economy. Original Equipment Manufacturing (OEM) evolved into Original Design Manufacturing (ODM), which soon entered the market with branded mobile phone models of their own. Much more crucial, however, was what was happening on the sidelines. Outside or on the edges of a seemingly well-established economic system, the *shanzhai* mode of production had begun to thrive.

A catalytic event occurred in 2004 when Mediatek, a semiconductor design company from Taiwan, introduced an innovation that significantly reduced the cost and complexity of producing mobile phones. Mediatek's all-encompassing 'turnkey solutions' meant that for small producers that wanted to make their own phones, all that was left to design was the user interface and the plastic shell.[62] In the Pearl River Delta, clusters of small companies sprang up to take advantage of this plug and play production, cranking out cheap knock-offs known as *shanzhai ji* (sometimes translated as bandit phones). Mediatek was quickly able to 'establish itself as the major chip company in the Chinese mobile handset market' and by 2006 had taken '40 percent market share'.[63] Since then, *shanzhai* phones have mushroomed throughout the lower-tier markets in both China and abroad and have thus been critical to the globalisation of wireless media.

Scholar Josephine Ho traces the practices of *shanzhai* to 1950s Hong Kong, where small-scale, family-run factories operated outside the official economic order to produce cheap, low-quality household goods. *Shanzhai* wares became popular by offering fake versions of well-known retail brands such as Gucci and Nike to markets that could not afford the expensive originals. The creation of these imitation products spawned a singular process of production. Ultimately, the significance of *shanzhai* is not in the copycat technology itself, but rather in the unique ecosystem of manufacturing in which these copies get made. This inventive mode of manufacturing found a perfect product in the mobile phone.

The *shanzhai* ecosystem is composed of a dense, horizontal web of component producers, traders, design solution houses, vendors and assembly lines, many of them informal, which catered to lesser-known or no-name clients that were not of interest to the larger players. This web of electronic fabrication is based on what is known as *gongban* (公版 public boards) and *gongmo* (公模 public shells and casings). *Gongban* are typically fabricated in independent design houses that connect chip manufacturers with factories that handle assembly. Boards are designed to fit a multiplicity of casings and customers can take a *gongban* of their liking as is, or modify it according to their tastes. Manufacturers are motivated to support as many customers as possible, who coat the *gongban* with a wide variety of 'skins' or 'shells' (*gongmo*).

This singular techno-economic culture operates through a system of *guanxi* (關係 social connection), in which local players mix in with diasporic alliances (especially from Hong Kong and Taiwan). In the electronic markets of *Huaqiangbei* competitors' stalls sit side by side. There is a tendency to share resources in a way that is alien to the worldwide regime of intellectual property rights. *Shanzhai* allows for – and even feeds off – open trade in reference boards, BOMs (Bills of Materials) and other elements of design. It has functioned as an open manufacturing system with easy access to electronic components, ready-to-produce key solutions and a network of relationships and providers that operate outside IP laws, patent rights and the world of brands. Bunnie Huang, an engineer who has been studying *shanzhai* for many years, calls it the 'Galapagos Island' of open source.[64]

Shanzhai goods do not come with end-user licence agreements or service models and are not accompanied by big data analytics or advertising plans. Neither do they feature in expensive marketing campaigns or rely on the backing of venture capitalists. Instead, capital is borrowed through informal networks and companies operate primarily with the conventional rules of trade that emerge spontaneously in highly competitive markets. Markets tend not to drift far from financial fundamentals. Unlike VC funds, which choose investment in the hope of betting on the next monopoly, *shanzhai* investors are concerned only that they are repaid with the interest that was promised. This encourages a culture of fierce entrepreneurialism characterised by breakneck speed, micro-experimentation, and the use of the market itself as a product-testing ground. Walk around the malls and you never know what you will find. The result is a kind of low-end, 'folk art' style of its own: a bracelet that is also a USB cable; a power bank modelled on an anime cat; a whole range of variations on the electronic unicycle; a flashlight that is also charger, mobile phone and bluetooth speaker. This is not the sleek, high-tech design of a global elite that tends towards minimalist uniformity, but rather a cheap, multifaceted and niche technology of a vast population which lives predominantly outside the cherished high-end markets that are catered to by well-known global brands. In December 2015 London's Victoria and Albert Museum (V&A) acknowledged this indigenous culture of design as part of an exhibition at the Shenzhen

Architecture Biennale. The V&A, which has established a gallery in Shenzhen's Shekou Design Museum, entitled its first show *Unidentified Acts of Design* and put *shanzhai* phones on display.

The strength of *shanzhai* is to bring new products to market with remarkable speed at a fraction of the price of the well-known international brands. Small batches are produced and then tested on the market. If there is demand and they sell quickly, more will be made. There is a commitment to never building from scratch, and prototyping and consumer testing occur rapidly and alongside the manufacturing process. These disruptive mechanisms of frugal innovation, with their ethos of recycle or repair, have enabled the creation of devices cheap enough to open new markets for the urban poor not only in China, but across the world. There is, then, in short, an alternative grey market in electronics, which has more in common with the street food hawker than it does with the fast food chains that fill food courts in shopping malls. Yet, while it is less visible than the well-known brands, Shenzhen's open ecosystem is enormous in scale. The intensity of this network has greatly impacted companies such as Nokia and Motorola, which cater primarily to high-paying customers. Cheap phones designed in Shenzhen are distributed in Africa, India, South America,[65] Europe and the United States. They are sold as no-name devices in Wal-Mart and Target and are also behind disruptive brands, such as Wiko in France. *Shanzhai* participates in an underground, alternative globalisation, based on the copy, which has played an enormous role in the planet-wide transmission of wireless media.

Shanzhai is rooted in high-velocity practices of piracy and reverse engineering. The intensity of Shenzhen speed meant that knock-offs quickly outpaced the originals. In the *shanzhai* ecosystem, ideation, prototyping and design happen alongside the manufacturing process, such that mobile phones can go from conceptual designs to production-ready in as little as 29 days. The *shanzhai* version of the iPhone 6 was on the market long before the latter's official release. The iPhone Mini could be spotted in Shanghai's digital markets without Apple having ever designed one. Soon companies needed only to speculate on a product for the *shanzhai* version to manifest. *Shanzhai* production also tends to modify and adapt, inventing bespoke, quirky designs made explicitly for the markets that it serves. This is why with *shanzhai* the copy is frequently superior to the original. The *shanzhai* iPhone Mini, for example, included an FM radio player and multiple SIM cards for those who travel frequently between Hong Kong, Taiwan and the mainland. Dual SIM cards, long a feature of *shanzhai* phones, were only adopted by Apple in 2018 with the iPhone X.

Shanzhai poses a radical challenge to the myth of original creation. Its embrace of the copy is attuned to the replication at the heart of digital technology. Moore's law predicted that the number of transistors on a chip would be duplicated every year. Steve Jobs famously made use of Picasso's line: 'Good artists copy, great artists steal', stating plainly about Apple: 'We have always been shameless about stealing great ideas.' Alan Turing taught us, at the dawn of the digital age, that machinic intelligence is ultimately an imitation game. The computer, which is based on the repetition of binary code, is intrinsically aligned with cloning, replication and simulation. This is why digital culture has such a long and deep sympathy with piracy, open source and remix culture, all of which defy a model of creativity based on authentic originality. *Shanzhai* adopts imitation in all its complexity. In doing so it allows for a contemporary Chinese cyberculture that accepts its long and deep affinity with the replica, the simulation, the clone.

Fake stories about fake food are common in contemporary China. Joshua Neves opens his book *Underglobalization* with the story of a 2007 Beijing television report, which turned out to be false, about a shop selling dumplings stuffed with cardboard instead of pork. His book addresses issues of media, development and legitimacy. In the introduction Neves explains that the concept of 'underglobalization' uses a reformulation of Ackbar Abbas's essay 'Faking Globalization' as an emblematic frame. Abbas sees the fake as a response to unequal globalisation. Copying is the result of a time lag inherent in the capitalist mode of production in which the periphery is understood to be temporally behind. From this perspective, imitation, writes Neves, paraphrasing Abbas, is 'part of a historical stepladder', which enables 'backward' places that are lower on the value chain the chance to catch up.[66] This well-trodden mode of technology transfer occurs only at particular moments of development, just as cities enter the world economy. Once they become more fully integrated, piratical practices diminish as regimes of copyright and intellectual property take hold.

Yet, while Abbas considers copying a legitimate strategy of the marginalised, he cautions us not to 'romanticize the fake'.[67] Ultimately, he believes, fakery is a form of cheating. Though resourceful, its creations are substandard, dangerous and ultimately not inventive enough. Imitation involves disturbance, but the disruptions it implies are only ever superficial. There is a 'passive quality of the fake that makes it work as symptom, but not subversion'.[68] Abbas's essay, then, retains an arc of linear progression, which evolves out of the fake and into original, authentic creation. In the end, what he advocates is for China to follow this linear order and develop its own culture of design.

This attitude and strategy has been adopted in Shenzhen, where urban villages are being torn down and *shanzhai* culture is receding. As the city attempts to move up the value chain, municipal officials meet with Silicon Valley executives as well as industry leaders from around the world who join with makers, accelerators, incubators and entrepreneurs in an attempt to rebrand Shenzhen as a 'city of design'. In *Huaqiangbei*, street food stands are being replaced with luxury brand name stores. In this transformation, low-quality knock-offs are dismissed as a backward 'stage of development' that the country must pass through in order to progress. Like Korea, Japan and America before it, it is expected that China will move from an era of reproduction, piracy and replication towards the creation of original goods and brands. According to this narrative of progression, imitation must be banished, simulation overcome.

Abbas appears ultimately to conform to this narrative, calling for the copyers to 'take up design as a geopolitical fix'.[69] Neves adamantly objects. Rather than accepting this familiar and 'deeply problematic' conclusion, Neves contends, 'against such dismissals, that piracy and fakes – as modes of cultural, economic, and political life under conditions of illegality and illegitimacy – have more to tell and teach us'.[70] In a sense, Abbas would seem to agree with the criticism. His own conclusions are inherently self-contradictory, holding both that the fake is something that 'developed' places overcome, while at the same time maintaining that replication is deeply ingrained in the fabric of globalisation itself. To elaborate, Abbas turns to Orson Welles's 1973 film *F is for Fake*. Welles's documentary centres on the figure of Elmyr de Hory, one of the greatest art forgers to have ever lived. The film treats de Hory as a kind of modern folk hero, detailing the elaborate interconnections between trickery and expertise upon which museums and art markets depend. 'Without the expert who authenticates', writes Abbas, 'the forger could never succeed in the deception: the knowledgeable expert is in collusion, however unwittingly, with the faker.'[71]

The idea of the 'good fake' troubles the solid categories upon which globalisation depends. 'The contemporary fake', writes Abbas', 'forces us to re-examine all the objects and processes around it, like legal systems, politics, technology, design culture and globalization.'[72] At its intensive limit, the fake calls into question the fundamental, abstract concepts upon which it rests. Welles, at the heart of his film, famously quotes Picasso. When faced with his own forger, the great artist is said to have commented unabashedly: 'I can paint fake Picassos as well as anybody.' For Abbas the most profound 'problem of the contemporary fake is not how close it is to the original, but how close the original is to the fake . . . to use the language of simulacra, then, the original is also a simulacra of the fake'.[73]

All the complexities of fakery, with its deep intermingling between the copy and the original, are intrinsic to the workings of global capitalism. In his essay 'Brands and their Surfeits', Constantine Nakassis describes the ways in which the inherent mix of material commodity and immaterial qualities (image, trust etc.) that are implicit in the fake meld together to form a brand. Due to this merging of the concrete and abstract, he argues, brands are constituted in relation to their exteriority (their surfeits). The original lives alongside the copy, the real and authentic alongside the fake. Just as there is no counterfeit without the brand, 'there are no brands without counterfeits', or more precisely, without the 'brand's surfeits', he writes. 'By surfeit', Nakassis explains, 'I refer to those material forms that, to varying degrees, exceed the brand's authority and legibility: knockoffs, fakes, brand-inspired goods, overruns, defect goods, generics, and the like.'[74] His essay turns to the nineteenth-century history of the trademark to illustrate how the 'ability to invoke a particular imaginary of fidelity, standardization, quality control, and trustworthy distribution' imbues the commodity with something more than its exchange value. The trademark, which guarantees that particular goods are authentic and original, also creates a system 'against which particular economic practices and objects could be labeled as "fakery" and "piracy"'.[75] This socio-economic paradigm has intensified since the 1970s. With the global reorganisation of labour, design and distribution have been increasingly decoupled and distanced from the manufacturing process. The gap between speculative forms of capital and physical production widened as goods were made in distant factories, far from company headquarters. Nike, Levi's and Apple were becoming 'no more than marketing companies for their brands'.[76] This distance opened a space in the grey market, which trades in the shadows of the 'real thing'. Since the copy is also a commodity, produced under the same conditions, sometimes in the very same factory, the question becomes 'what do such "counterfeits" counterfeit?'[77]

This profound disturbance of the real and the artificial, the truth and the lie, suggests that what is at stake with the fake is more than simply a linear game of catch-up. Instead of powering a nation to step forward from the back of the ranks, the innovative potential of imitation is situated elsewhere, underneath or to the side. The fake, notes Abbas, 'is a species of *underground culture*; the underground is its ethos, is where it derives its energy and inventiveness from'.[78] Neves locates this underground on the margins. 'This study asks how mundane and mediated practices of faking (and its myriad cognates) undergird and transform globalization.' Contemporary China is analysed through an exploration of the 'informal, illicit, and fringe practices' of its peripheral populations – the 'illegible, illegitimate, illegal'.[79] The concept of 'underglobalization', Neves contends, emerges from a position at the 'epistemological edge', an alterity that is exposed by the logic of the fake. In *F is for Fake* Welles adopts the guise of a magician. Piracy, copying, trickery, imitation have an alliance with illusion, coincidence, repetition and doubling, all of which, as Mark Fisher has theorised, belong to the realm of the 'weird and the eerie' and its 'fascination with the outside'.[80]

Shanzhai epitomises this exteriority. From the start, its culture differed in small but significant ways from the familiar piracy of counterfeit Gucci watches and Louis Vuitton bags that had long proliferated in the new Chinese metropolis. Unlike these standard imitations, *shanzai* products don't try to hide the fact that they are copies. Instead, the 'Hiphone', 'Nikia' and 'Motopola' seem to take a comic pride in the fact that they are fakes. *Shanzhai*, notes philosopher Byung-Chul Han, does not deliberately set out to deceive. The attraction of *shanzai* products 'lies in how they specifically draw attention to the fact that they are not original, that they are *playing* with the original'.[81]

In English, *shanzhai* translates literally as mountain village or mountain fortress. The term connotes an informal, outlaw tradition associated with the Song dynasty classic *Water Margin* (*Shuihuzhuan* 水滸傳), which tells the tale of a group of 108 outlaws who battle against an established, corrupt bureaucracy. 'There's an element of criminality about *shanzhai*, just the way that Robin Hood is a bit of an outlaw', says Lyn Jeffrey of the Institute of the Future. 'But it's really about autonomy, independence, and very progressive survival techniques.'[82] In his book *China in Ten Words*, author Yu Hua contends that *shanzhai* (translated as copycat) 'represents a challenge of the grassroots to the elite, of the popular to the official, of the weak to the strong . . . It would not be going too far to say that "copycat" has more of an anarchist spirit than any other word in the modern Chinese language.'[83]

By 2008 *shanzhai* had ceased solely to signify mobile phones and came to conceptualise a DIY, grassroots creativity that spread throughout the culture. 2009 opened with a copycat version of the CCTV New Year gala, a vast televisual event that had long symbolised the official hold on the media. There were reports – made frequently with a tinge of humour and delight – on *shanzhai* restaurants, *shanzhai* architecture,[84] *shanzhai* brands and retail shops (the southern city of Kunming opened a near-perfect replica of an Apple store that was lauded as 'the best rip off ever'); there were even *shanzhai* pets (one trend had people dyeing the coats of their dogs so that they looked like tigers and pandas). The *shanzhai* ethos was associated with anti-authoritarian subversive energies that arose spontaneously from the anarchic open culture of the street. *Shanzhai* emerged as one of the most interesting, generative and creative concepts to come out of twenty-first-century China.

Land and Sea

In her blog *Shenzhen Noted*, Mary Ann O'Donnell repeatedly returns to the theme of land reclamation in the construction of Shenzhen. The coastal metropolis has been built, she writes, through a vast and relentless occupation of the ocean. In her prolific documentation of the city, she mourns how the growing metropolis has buried the coastlines, fish and other denizens of the sea. City building on the southern shore is a land grab. In constructing solid urban landscapes of concrete and glass, the territorialising forces of centralisation cover over the aquatic spaces of an older, amphibious, maritime population. Yet despite all the energy and resources involved, the power of the watery forces underneath is difficult to constrain. 'There is nothing in the world more soft and weak than water and yet for attacking things that are firm and strong there is nothing that can take precedence of it' reads the Daoist classic the *Daodejing*. Twentieth-century Shenzhen recalls this teaching.[85] Its bond with all 'things that are firm and strong' is infused by a more covert alliance with a realm that is fluid and unsettled.

In the Western tradition the cosmic opposition between land and sea has biblical roots. The Book of Enoch, an ancient Judaic apocalyptic text, tells of 'two monsters who became separated; a female monster, whose name is Leviathan, dwelling in the depths of the sea, above the springs of waters; And a male monster, whose name is Behemoth; which possesses, moving on his breast, the invisible wilderness'.[86] In the Chinese context, the abstract divide between earth and water can be mapped on to tensions, long held, between a territorial centre and the coastal periphery. In introducing their book *China Off Center*, Susan Blum and Lionel Jenson write that 'in the popular Western imagination, China has for centuries been a symbol of centeredness, in large part because of our casual translation of one of China's names for itself, *Zhongguo*, as "Middle Kingdom" or, even more elaborately, "the Center of the World"'.[87] The pull of integration and unification, however, has always coexisted with potent regional and local tendencies towards dissolution and fragmentation. 'Alongside, beneath, and intersecting this purported centeredness and presumed homogeneity is an immense diversity of peoples, languages, terrain, and everyday practices.'[88]

In his influential 1991 essay 'The Periphery as the Center', historian and philosopher Tu Wei-Ming contrasts the critical role of Taiwan, Hong Kong, Singapore and other overseas Chinese in the foundations of the 'Asia-Pacific century', which developed, at least initially, with minimal influence from mainland China. 'Although the phenomenon of Chinese culture disintegrating at the center and later being revived from the periphery is a recurring theme in Chinese history', he contends, 'it is unprecedented for the geopolitical center to remain entrenched while the periphery presents such powerful and persistent economic and cultural challenges.'[89] For Tu, the transformative power of the edges raises critical questions about the meaning of 'Chineseness' and its relation to modernity. Tu's own project mobilises the distinction between the diasporic *huaren* (華人 people of Chinese origin) and *zhongguoren* (中國人 people of China, the state) in positing a cultural identity that can serve to decentre the authority of the geopolitical nation.[90]

In defining centre and periphery, Tu recalls the classical contrast between the agrarian and the nomadic, the 'civilised' and the 'barbaric'. Yet in considering the differences between the maritime regions and the inland areas further north, he also draws attention to the divergence between land and sea. He speaks about the dichotomy in relation to his recollection of the famous TV documentary *River Elegy*, which explored the relationship between China and modernity and was broadcast by CCTV in 1988 on the eve of the protests at Tiananmen. The influential show 'provoked a heated nationwide debate on tradition, modernity, change, China, and the West'.[91] *River Elegy* 河殤 was based on a differentiation between two cultures, one associated with the 'Blue Ocean' and the other with the 'Yellow Earth'. It proposed a theory, widely shared in the post-reform 1980s, that Chinese historical decline was due to the Ming decision to ban maritime trade and to the subsequent territorial domination over foreign, technological, sea-trading cultures. The argument of *River Elegy*, stated forcefully in episode 6, entitled 'Blueness', was that the history of China was based on an ancient victory of a wheat-eating, land-based civilisation influenced by nomadic culture, over a 'blue' civilisation 'based on a staple diet of rice, understanding the art of ship and sea-based warfare, and influenced by Southeast Asian and Pacific cultures'.[92] As the land-based civilisation increased in power in China, there was a retreat of 'blueness', and with it a seeping stagnation that eventually resulted in civilisation decline. The show closes with a hopeful celebration of a renewed era in which the 'Yellow river overcomes its fear of the Sea.' The writers of the series looked for evidence in the vibrant entrepreneurs of Shanghai and Zhejiang. They were especially heartened, however, by the new coastal city of Shenzhen:

> In 1980, the Shenzhen Special Economic Zone was established. It announced to the whole world that this 'land-based' civilization of several thousand years had finally moved to the edge of the sea, and that the face which it had always kept turned to the land had turned to the gaze at the distant ocean.[93]

One does not need to appeal to the rhetoric of Tu or the hyperbole of *River Elegy* to make the case that the Chinese periphery is populated by sea-based cultures that are more closely identified with water than with land. The alliance is clear with even a cursory visit to the coastal regions. Here, local temples are decorated with the goddess Mazu, protector of fishermen and sailors, venerated by the denizens of the deep. Mazu is purported to be the deified form of a Fujianese shamanesss. In Shenzhen she is identified as Tianhou, the 'Heavenly Mother, and Goddess of the South China Sea', who is 'worshipped as a guardian of seafarers and anyone that lives on or by the sea'.[94] The Chiwan Tianhou Temple 赤灣天后宮 on the southern tip of Shenzhen's Shekou Peninsula 'was once one of the largest and most revered pilgrimage sites in Southern China'.[95]

In her book *Ancient China and the Yue: Perceptions and Identities on the Southern Frontier*, Erica Fox Brindley investigates the diverse peoples of the South. She discovers that 'enmeshed in a vast riverine and maritime network' are people whose 'language and cultures are radically different from those of the Central State'.[96] Buried in the history of the Yue people of the premodern South, with their 'commercial and maritime mobility' and frequent 'escape to the sea', is a challenge to 'the logic of centrality and centeredness' embedded in the powerful story of a monolithic Chinese identity rooted in the state.[97] Throughout the southern periphery, in China, the geography of the outside lies at the watery shore.

This aquatic sensibility is affiliated with the idea of waves as elemental media. Melody Jue, in her book *Wild Blue Media*, aims to counter media theory's terrestrial bias by exploring the milieu of the ocean as an environment for thought. Weixian Pan, who works in a similar vein, is developing a 'critical oceanic perspective' in order to theorise China's southern mediascapes. Pan notes that the concept of the 'Internet as Ocean' proliferates in the vernacular cultural imaginary.[98] Like the English phrase 'surfing the web', in Chinese everyday usage, she writes, 'the Internet (*"hu lian wang"*, as differentiated from *"wangluo"* for *"network"*) is often articulated in relation to the ocean (*haiyang*). The vernacular expression *"Hulianwang de hai-yang"* can be translated literally into *"Internet (as) Ocean".'[99]* These liquid associations are also apparent in the naming of the mechanisms of control. This was most obvious in the early – ultimately failed – attempt to mandate that 'Green Dam' software be installed on all PCs in China. Fang Binxing, the 'father of China's Great Firewall', drew on this same analogy when lamenting the fact that Google was still available in China after its initial retreat. 'It's like the relationship between riverbed and water', he said. 'Water has no nationality, but riverbeds are sovereign territories, we cannot allow polluted water from other nation states to enter our country.'[100]

China's historical affinity with wireless media appears as a conjunction between a newly rising nation and the development of novel technology. Yet, as the *shanzhai* culture of Shenzhen shows, there are aspects of this relationship that diverge from – and even oppose – the growing consolidation of the Chinese state. The global IT industry, which has its manufacturing centre in Shenzhen, is undoubtedly subject to the territorialised demands of a contracting core. Yet the location of the global hub in a zone on the coastal edge of the South China Sea ensures that the external power of an intrinsically diffuse, inherently fluid, maritime periphery remains.

Simulation

Shanzhai in Shenzhen is derived from a culture of unanchored simulation. In his book *Shanzhai: Deconstruction in Chinese*, Byung Chul Han explores the philosophical and aesthetic value of this ungrounded repetition. The book begins by discussing the importance of the artistic practice of reproducing a masterpiece. When performed correctly, Han argues, this careful imitation is an act of reverence. Copying is considered a means of paying respect to the master. To copy is to praise. Many of the great painters of the Western tradition also duplicated their predecessors as an expression of admiration and love. Han's own book features full-page reproductions of Gaughin's copy of Manet, Van Gogh's imitations of Hiroshige and Cezanne's version of Delacroix. For the artist, imitation is inherent in the act of invention. 'Creation is not a sudden *event* but a slow *process*, one that demands a long and intense engagement *with what has been*, in order to create from it.'[101] To create the future, you have to return to the past. Han celebrates simulation as an expression of what he sees as Far Eastern thought's radical embrace of change. Unlike European intellectual traditions, which resist transformation by emphasising origin, essence and permanence, Chinese philosophy, Han argues, does not assume that 'underlying all change and transience is that which remains the same'.[102] Instead, it attunes itself to the 'creativity of nature itself', which 'relies on a continual process of variation, combination, and mutation'.[103] Breaking 'radically with Being and essence', it defines itself according to 'the changeable constellation of things'.[104] In this theoretical milieu, the idea of creation does not look back to an origin, but exists instead as a 'continual process without beginning or end, without birth or death'.[105]

Chinese artistic masterpieces, Han contends, exhibit this context by shifting over time. The original is constantly mutating as collectors and connoisseurs add their personal seals and words of appreciation. 'The more it is admired', writes Han, 'the more its appearance changes.' The Chinese 'idea of the original is determined not by a unique act of creation, but by an unending process, not by definitive identity but by constant change'.[106] For Han it is this 'active transformation and variation' that is behind the ingenuity of *shanzhai*, as well as the culture upon which it is based.[107] *Shanzhai*'s delight in replication draws on a deep cultural tradition that is captivated by simulacra. In China, natural landscapes are appreciated for looking like paintings, stones are cherished for appearing as mountains, formations in caves are admired for approximating animals, vegetables are made to look like meat. One of the most prized artistic treasures among the magnificent collection in Taipei's National Palace Museum is 'Meat-Shaped Stone', a rock that bears a striking resemblance to a juicy piece of braised pork belly. The profound value placed on imitation is stressed in the very first stanzas of the *Analects*: 'To learn and at due times to repeat what one has learnt, is that not after all a pleasure?' In 'ancient Chinese artistic practice', Han writes, 'learning takes place specifically through copying'. In 2015 an exhibition called *Copyleft* held at Shanghai's Power Station of Art reflected on the modern instantiations of this tradition. *Copyleft* equated *shanzhai* with *linmo*, a deeply repetitive practice of calligraphy that cultivates embodied knowledge of each brushstroke. *Linmo* is used to study technique, pay tribute to the masters, and only eventually to express personal style. On display were works such as Qiu Zhijie's *Copy of Lanting Xu 1000 Times*, in which the artist records himself reproducing one of the most famous and revered pieces of calligraphy. He repeats himself over and over again on the same piece of paper until it is entirely covered with black ink.

The Chinese culture of artistic reproduction intersects with the *shanzhai* ecosystem in Dafen village, a neighbourhood on the edges of Shenzhen. For decades, Dafen village has been home to a cluster of painters who supply a global market with cheap copies of the world's masterpieces. In the streets and alleys of Dafen, an oil counterfeit of Van Gogh's *Starry Night* can be bought for just a couple of hundred renminbi. Many commentators dismiss the artists of Dafen as mere copycats; the cultural practices of the painters living there, however, defy a host of assumptions about genius, authenticity, self-expression and copyright that dominate notions of creativity in the West.[108] The skills of the Dafen artists and their creative capacity to conform to a global market calls into question implicit assumptions about the cultural value attributed to both the original and the fake.

In China connoisseurs accept and even value forgery as part of their collections. With a connoisseur's stamp of approval, Han explains, 'a forger is equal to his master'. These conflicting attitudes towards the copy have resulted in some illuminating cultural clashes, which Han's book documents. In 1956, for example, an exhibition of Chinese masterpieces was sent to the Paris museum of Asian art. When the museum discovered that the paintings were forgeries it considered it fraud. This determination, however, was complicated by the fact that the fakes were the creations of 'none other than the most famous Chinese painter of the twentieth century, Chang Dai-chien'.[109] Many of the reproductions, moreover, were painted from verbal descriptions, making the copies one of a kind.

Cultural misunderstandings are even more acute in the area of historical conservation. When replicas of the terracotta soldiers were sent to be shown in a museum in Hamburg, the director decided that they had no choice but 'to close the exhibition completely in order to maintain the museum's good reputation'.[110] In the West, preservation tends to highlight remnants of the original. Alexander Stille, in his book *The Future of the Past*, contends that the West's layering of discontinuous historical civilisations helps construct a linear temporality that is made manifest in the Jewish, Christian and Islamic calendars, which all start from a fixed point of time. In China, on the other hand, techniques of preservation are based on the continual process of reproduction and the construction of replicas is often deployed as a mode of protection. This is compatible, as Simon Leys notes, with a culture that is comfortable with the idea that change is inherent in the Real.[111] Byung Chul Han, much like Xiong Shili, maintains that in the Chinese intellectual tradition the notion of essence (*ti*) is not stable, eternal or fixed. 'Chinese thought', he contends, is outside the 'cult of the original'. Its notion of truth does not rely on the authentic or the permanent. It 'distrusts fixed, invariable essences or principles'. 'In the unending cycle of life, there is no longer anything unique, original, singular or final.'[112]

'The modern world', writes Gilles Deleuze at the start of *Difference and Repetition*, 'is one of simulacra.'[113] This thesis – that modernity is closely tied to mimicry – is well known. Yet Deleuze's conception differs from most accounts, which tend to mourn the departure from a past authenticity and, even in their most radical postmodern formulations, retain, at least in part, a nostalgia for the real.[114] For Deleuze simulacra are not bound to a lost origin, but instead function more like the weird trope of the mirror or the double, whose presence, however furtive and fleeting, reveals a deep and alien exteriority that lies at the heart of that which is closest and most at home.

Difference and Repetition is based on the Nietzschean project of overturning Platonism. At the crux of the inversion is a challenge to the foundational hierarchy, which insists that what repeats is always fundamentally similar to that which has already been. For Plato, the ideal world exists above and beyond our illusory realm of shadowy imitations. Transcendence is embedded in a distinction, which holds that copies are nothing other than degraded resemblances of the original, necessarily secondary 'instances of the Same'.[115] This distinction between a highly valued real and a disdained, subordinated copy is sustained in Platonic philosophy, just as it is with the modern brand, through scrupulous policing. 'Platonism as a whole is erected on the basis of this wish to hunt down the phantasms', writes Deleuze. The 'simulacra must be exorcised'.[116] Dreams, shadows, reflections, copies all must be silenced, put aside, banished and sent back to the bottomless ocean from which they came.

To overturn Plato is to reject this exile and recognise the power of the simulacra in themselves. According to this alternative line of thought, the copy is not merely a defect or secondary resemblance. This anti-Platonism, which appears momentarily even 'at the heart of Platonism', arrives 'like a flash of lightning in the night', testifying to 'a persistent activity on the part of simulacra, to their underground work and to the possibility of a world of their own'.[117]

In exploring this alterity, Deleuze turns to one of the richest philosophical expressions of simulation, the Nietzschean idea of 'Eternal Return'. According to Nietzsche's own account, the thought of the Eternal Recurrence came to him as a sudden revelation in the year 1881. According to a history marked by the long cycles of techno-capitalism, this moment occurred in the trough, just before the third Kondratiev upswing, which powered the electric age. It was also, crucially, not long after the discovery of entropy – the physical justification for the straight line of time.[118] In this revolutionary juncture in both the science and technology of temporality, Nietzsche introduced the philosophy of Eternal Return. What if the world is caught in endless cycles of repetition, such that the origin is already a replica? What if simulation is not a shadow of the real but is instead all that there is?

One of the fundamental philosophical problems raised by the idea of Eternal Return is in what sort of time does recurrence take place? Is there an original stable permanence that underlies the continuous repetition? Are the constant temporal loops subordinated to an extended succession – a straight line of time? Or, alternatively, is it that time itself is a cycle that continuously repeats? Deleuze adamantly rejects both of these interpretations. Repetition, he insists, is not merely an imitation of a primary origin, nor is it destined to an infinite imitation of the same.

> How could the reader believe that Nietzsche, who was the greatest critic of these categories, implicated Everything, the Same, the Identical, the Similar, the Equal, the I and the Self in the eternal return? How could it be believed that he understood the eternal return as a cycle, when he opposed 'his' hypothesis to every cyclical hypothesis? How could it be believed that he lapsed into the false and insipid idea of an opposition between a circular time and a linear time, an ancient and a modern time?[119]

In place of these dichotomies, Deleuze envisions the Eternal Return as a secret, tortuous, decentred circle, which is 'beyond the reach of the empirical' and which arrives at the end of a straight line of time. This eternally excentric circle, he writes, turns upon itself, causing 'only the yet-to-come to return'.[120] It thus synthesises the repetition that is inherent to copying with the creative novelty implicit in change.

Wave philosophy is based on repetitive continuity. It dissolves the distinction in which the single unity of the Real is valued and the multiplicity of the copy is debased. It does not banish simulation into the depths of the ocean. It celebrates constant variation rather than assuming that all manifestation is necessarily the repetition of the same. China's relation to wirelessness includes this ulterior perspective. Alongside the attempts to consolidate a techno-political control, its engagement with contemporary media invokes older swirling cosmologies, which have been largely overlooked because they do not conform to a monolithic, predetermined structure, but operate, instead, according to time waves, external to the linear-historical order. These alternative cosmologies do not belong to the ideas and practices of the land-based core, but are rather aligned with the watery edges of the periphery. With no stable or permanent grounding in a separate substance or essence, they are commensurate with the exterior plane of the Untimely and its fluid, alien rhythms, which 'ceaselessly [rumble] in another dimension' underneath the 'laws of nature that govern the surface of the world'.[121]

Notes

1. Amy Ireland, 'Alien Rhythms', *Alienist* VI (1 January 2019): 69.
2. Arkady Strugatsky and Boris Strugatsky, *Roadside Picnic* (Chicago: Chicago Review Press, 2012), 85.
3. Ibid.
4. Ireland, 'Alien Rhythms', 61.
5. Ibid., 62.
6. Mark Fisher, *The Weird and the Eerie* (London: Repeater, 2016), 22.
7. Ibid., 116.
8. Strugatsky and Strugatsky, *Roadside Picnic*, 28.
9. Ibid., 68.
10. Ireland, 'Alien Rhythms', 67.
11. Strugatsky and Strugatsky, *Roadside Picnic*, 17.
12. Ireland, 'Alien Rhythms', 58.
13. Fisher, *The Weird and the Eerie*, 116.
14. Ireland, 'Alien Rhythms', 71.
15. Easterling, *Extrastatecraft*, 25.
16. Mary Ann O'Donnell, Winnie Wong and Jonathan Bach, 'Introduction: Experiments, Exceptions, and Extensions', in *Learning from Shenzhen: China's Post-Mao Experiment from Special Zone to Model City*, ed. Mary Ann O'Donnell, Winnie Wong and Jonathan Bach (Chicago: University of Chicago Press, 2017), 11.
17. Easterling, *Extrastatecraft*, 25.
18. Mary Ann O'Donnell, 'Heroes of the Special Zone: Modeling Reform and its Limits', in O'Donnell, Wong and Bach, eds, *Learning from Shenzhen*, 45.
19. Aihwa Ong, 'Introduction', in *Worlding Cities: Asian Experiments and the Art of Being Global*, ed. Ananya Roy and Aihwa Ong (Chichester: John Wiley & Sons, 2011), 1
20. Ibid., 1.
21. Jonathan Bach, 'Shenzhen: From Exception to Rule', in O'Donnell, Wong and Bach, eds, *Learning from Shenzhen*, 29.
22. Ibid.
23. See Jia Zhangke's 2004 film *The World*.

24. Bach, 'Shenzhen: From Exception to Rule', 32.
25. See, for example, Kevin Carrico, 'Recentering China: The Cantonese in and beyond the Han', in *Critical Han Studies: The History, Representation, and Identity of China's Majority*, ed. Thomas Mullaney, James Leibold, Stephane Gros and Eric Vanden Bussche (Berkeley: University of California Press, 2012) and Ien Ang, *On Not Speaking Chinese: Living Between Asia and the West* (London: Routledge, 2001), which begins with Rey Chow's reminiscence of Hong Kong as an 'unsettled and unsettling location between China and the West'. For Chow, the 'unstable, ambivalent, doubly marginalized position of Hong Kong' opens up the 'in-between space of hybridity' which can grant 'the power to interrupt, to trouble, to intervene tactically rather than strategically and to contaminate . . . established narratives and dominant points of view' (quoted in Ang, *On Not Speaking Chinese*, 2).
26. The power of this force of integration is such that even zones with greater autonomy – Hong Kong and perhaps even Taiwan – find it difficult to escape.
27. Ong, 'The Chinese Axis', 83.
28. Bach, 'Shenzhen: From Exception to Rule', 22.
29. Jonathan Bach, 'Modernity and the Urban Imagination in Economic Zones', *Theory, Culture & Society* 28, no. 5 (2011): 100.
30. The time of the coronavirus pandemic was known as 'the special period'.
31. Joshua Neves, *Underglobalization: Beijing's Media Urbanism and the Chimera of Legitimacy* (Durham, NC: Duke University Press, 2020), 40.
32. Carl Schmitt, *The Nomos of the Earth in the International Law of Jus Publicum Europaeum*, trans. G. L. Ulmen (New York: Telos Press, 2006), 43.
33. Neves, *Underglobalization*, 11.
34. Peter Hall, *Cities in Civilization* (London: Pantheon, 1998).
35. Ibid., 241.
36. Shenzhen speed initially referred to the construction of the Shenzhen International Trade Building (*Guomao*), for which workers put up one floor every three days. See Weiwen Huang, 'The Tripartite Origins of Shenzhen: Beijing, Hong Kong and Bao-An', in O'Donnell, Wong and Bach, eds, *Learning from Shenzhen*, 65–85.
37. Ibid., 65.
38. This was theorised most famously by Ronald Coase in his 1937 paper 'The Nature of the Firm', *Economica* 4, no. 16 (1937): 386–405.
39. See C. K. Prahalad and Gary Hamel, 'The Core Competence of The Corporation', *International Library of Critical Writings in Economics* 163 (2003): 210–22.
40. Boy Lüthje, Stefanie Hürtgen, Peter Pawlicki and Martina Sproll, *From Silicon Valley to Shenzhen: Global Production and Work in the IT Industry* (Lanham, MD: Rowman and Littlefield, 2013), 28.

41. Ibid., 57.
42. Clyde Prestowitz, *Three Billion New Capitalists: The Great Shift of Wealth and Power to the East* (New York: Basic Books, 2006), 55.
43. The Taiwanese have been careful not to shift the most specialised aspects of semiconductor production offshore.
44. Lüthje et al., *From Silicon Valley to Shenzhen*, 118.
45. For details, see the work of 'Hacked Matter', http://www.hackedmatter.com/.
46. For more on the temporality and aesthetics of the Zone, see the work of scholar-photographer Tong Lam.
47. Rem Koolhaas, *The Generic City* (New York: Sikkens Foundation, 1995), 1251.
48. Ibid., 1251–3.
49. Juan Du, 'Don't Underestimate the Rice Fields', in *Urban Transformation*, ed. Ilka Ruby and Andreas Ruby (Berlin: Ruby Press, 2008), 198.
50. Mary Ann O'Donnell, 'Excavating the Future in Shenzhen', in *Urban Asias: Essays on Futurity Past and Present*, ed. Tim Bunnell and Daniel P. S. Goh (Berlin: JOVIS, 2018), 250.
51. Jonathan Bach, '"They Come in Peasants and Leave Citizens": Urban Villages and the Making of Shenzhen', in O'Donnell, Wong and Bach, eds, *Learning from Shenzhen*, 143.
52. See Mary Ann O'Donnell, 'Laying Siege to the Villages: The Vernacular Geography of Shenzhen', in O'Donnell, Wong and Bach, eds, *Learning from Shenzhen*, 107–23.
53. Du, 'Don't Underestimate the Rice Fields', 200.
54. David Bandurski, *Dragons in Diamond Village: Tales of Resistance from Urbanizing China* (New York: Melville House, 2016), 12–13.
55. Du, 'Don't Underestimate the Rice Fields', 200.
56. O'Donnell, 'Laying Siege to the Villages', 111.
57. Bandurski, *Dragons in Diamond Village*, 7.
58. Bach, 'Modernity and the Urban Imagination in Economic Zones', 150.
59. O'Donnell, 'Excavating the Future in Shenzhen', 260.
60. Anna Greenspan and Suzanne Livingston, *Future Mutation: Technology, Shanzai and the Evolution of Species* (Shanghai: Time Spiral Press, 2015).
61. Lüthje et al., *From Silicon Valley to Shenzhen*, 28.
62. Ibid., 108.
63. Ibid.
64. Bunnie Huang, 'The $12 "Gongkai" Phone', Bunnie's Blog (blog), 18 April 2013, https://www.bunniestudios.com/blog/?page_id=3107.
65. A number of *shanzhai* companies from Shenzhen, in an attempt to consolidate profits, have set up factories in these places to be closer to the markets that they serve.
66. Neves, *Underglobalization*, 3.
67. Ackbar Abbas, 'Faking Globalization', in *Other Cities, Other Worlds: Urban Imaginaries in a Globalizing Age*, ed. Andreas Huyssen (Durham, NC: Duke University Press, 2008), 251.

68. Ibid.

69. Neves, *Underglobalization*, 3.

70. Ibid., 8.

71. Abbas, 'Faking Globalization', 253.

72. Ibid.

73. Ibid., 254–5.

74. Constantine V. Nakassis, 'Brands and their Surfeits', *Cultural Anthropology* 28, no. 1 (2013): 112.

75. Ibid., 114.

76. Ibid., 118.

77. The difficulty of this puzzle becomes even more acute when dealing with the intrinsic reproducibility of digital technology.

78. Abbas, 'Faking Globalization', 262.

79. Neves, *Underglobalization*, 24.

80. Fisher, *The Weird and the Eerie*, 8.

81. Byung-Chul Han, *Shanzhai: Deconstruction in Chinese* (Cambridge, MA: MIT Press, 2017), 76.

82. Lyn Jeffery, 'Mining an Unexpected Source of Innovation: Lessons from Shanzhai', *Institute for the Future*, September 2013, https://slidetodoc.com/mining-an-unexpected-source-of-innovation-lessons-from/.

83. Hua Yu, *China in Ten Words* (London: Duckworth, 2012), 181–2.

84. Although as scholar Jeffrey Wasserstrom notes, China is hardly alone in borrowing other cultures' building styles. Wasserstrom, 'Copycat Travels', *Los Angeles Review of Books*, 13 May 2015, http://blog.lareviewofbooks.org/chinablog/copycat-travels/.

85. The quote is from Lao Zi, *Daodejing*, Passage 78. I have used the translation by James Legge, *Chinese Text Project: A Dynamic Digital Library of Premodern Chinese*, https://ctext.org/dao-de-jing.

86. The oppositional elements earth and water, land and sea were obsessively explored by German political theorist Carl Schmitt. Schmitt, a Nazi sympathiser writing in the midst of the Second World War, is well known for his critique of maritime liberal modernity. He envisioned the history of the world as a universal battle between a land race represented by the giant beast Behemoth and a watery people embodied by the sea serpent Leviathan. Schmitt's political philosophy is based on this fundamental contrast between 'firm land and free sea'. Law and order, he argued, is rooted in the cultivation of the soil and the solid ground of the earth. On the sea, 'fields cannot be planted and firm lines cannot be engraved'. Schmitt identified the maritime mode of human existence, which is 'different from that which is purely earth defined', with the English and the Jew. He contended that the maritime culture's lack of fixity was intimately tied to piracy and trade, which was ultimately associated with the threatening upheavals of a techno-capitalist world. Leviathan, he laments, 'transformed itself from a great fish into a machine'. Carl Schmitt, *Land and Sea: A World-Historical Meditation*, ed. Samuel Garrett Zeitlin and Russell A. Berman (Candor, NY: Telos Press, 2015).

87. Blum and Jensen, *China Off Center*, 1.
88. Ibid., 2.
89. Wei-Ming Tu, 'The Periphery as the Center', *Daedalus* 120, no. 2 (1991): 12.
90. Sinophone scholar Ien Ang, commenting on Tu's 'famed but controversial cultural China project', argues that the very idea of 'Chineseness' employed by Tu has a re-centring, re-territorialising effect. Ang praises Tu's privileging of the periphery as the new cultural centre. His discourse, she writes, 'is an important challenge to traditional, centrist and essentialist conceptions of Chinese culture and identity'. Yet the very postulation of a 'cultural China' as the name for a transnational intellectual community held together not just by a 'common awareness' but also by 'a common ancestry and a shared cultural background', 'a transnational network to explore the meaning of being Chinese in a global context' is a move that is driven by a desire for, and motivated by, another kind of centrism, this time along notionally cultural lines. Ang, *On Not Speaking Chinese*, 42. Ang is part of another group of scholars 'truly on the periphery', whose decentring discourses offer even 'more radical narratives which push the diasporic to its limits, to the extent that any residual attachment to the "centre"' tends to fade away. Ien Ang, 'Can One Say No to Chineseness? Pushing the Limits of the Diasporic Paradigm', *Boundary* 25, no. 3 (1998): 223–42
91. Tu, 'The Periphery as the Center', 5.
92. Ibid., 253.
93. Ibid., 262.
94. Juan Du, *The Shenzhen Experiment: The Story of China's Instant City* (Cambridge, MA: Harvard University Press, 2020), 91.
95. Ibid.
96. Erica Fox Brindley, *Ancient China and the Yue: Perceptions and Identities on the Southern Frontier, c.400 BCE–50 CE* (Cambridge: Cambridge University Press, 2015), 39.
97. Ibid., xii.
98. Weixian Pan, 'China Southern: Digital Environments as Geopolitical Contact Zones', PhD dissertation, Concordia University, 2019, 88, https://spectrum.library.concordia.ca/id/eprint/985659/.
99. Ibid., 100.
100. Bratton, *The Stack*, 113.
101. Han, *Shanzhai*, 16.
102. Ibid., 2.
103. Ibid., 78.
104. Ibid., 4.
105. Ibid., 3.
106. Ibid., 11.
107. Ibid., 76.
108. Winnie Wong, *Van Gogh on Demand: China and the Readymade* (Chicago: University of Chicago Press, 2014).

109. Han, *Shanzhai*, 29.
110. Ibid., 60.
111. For more on this theme, see Pierre Ryckmans, 'The Chinese Attitude towards the Past', *China Heritage Quarterly* 14 (2008): 1–16.
112. Han, *Shanzhai*, 4.
113. Gilles Deleuze, *Difference and Repetition*, trans. Paul Patton (New York: Columbia University Press, 1994), xix.
114. See, for example, Jean Baudrillard, *Simulacra and Simulation*, trans. Sheila Glaser (Ann Arbor, MI: University of Michigan Press, 1994).
115. Deleuze, *Difference and Repetition*, 265.
116. Ibid., 127.
117. Ibid., 128.
118. Physicists argue that it is because disorder increases that we experience linear time. In the late 1800s, with the understanding of a directional entropic universe came the concurrent puzzle of pockets of increasing evolutionary order. Eventually life was reconceived as closed, looped, feedback systems that seemed to run counter to the dominant current.
119. Deleuze, *Difference and Repetition*, 299.
120. Ibid., 298.
121. Ibid., 241.

Chapter 4

Vibration: The Body Electric

In an odd short story called 'Wireless', Rudyard Kipling raises a host of strikingly contemporary themes: disease, contagion, new media and the porousness of inside and out. The story was written in 1902 in the early days of radio. It opens with the line: 'It's a funny thing this Marconi business', and goes on to explore the mystery of wireless transmission.[1] The tale takes place in a pharmaceutical dispensary during an outbreak of a virulent influenza. In between depictions of the chemist's concoctions, Kipling describes his character's electrical experiments with the new discovery of Hertzian waves. Throughout the story, discussions of the wireless receiver are interwoven with reports of an infected body, which, through an odd mutation, is transforming into a reception station of its own. In between coughs, the sick character starts channelling Keats, 'the only poet who was ever a druggist'.[2] Kipling uses the story to reflect on the occult nature of electronic communication. The ephemeral phenomena of radio transmission, he writes, makes one feel 'as if in the presence of spirits . . . something coming through from somewhere'.[3] Wireless communication, one character notes, is 'reminiscent of a spiritualist séance' when the body acts as medium with 'odds and ends of messages coming out of nowhere'.[4] It is like being in the presence of an 'unknown Power – kicking and fighting to be let loose'.[5] The story concludes with an unsuccessful radio transmission as the influenza-racked body awakens from trance. In the end, '*Can make nothing of your signal*' is the only message received.[6]

In a discussion of the story, media scholar Lisa Gitelman highlights the temporality of the tale. With 'Wireless', she says, Kipling is picking 'up a question for the future' that is directed – at least initially – to its own present at the turn of the twentieth century.[7] As a historian, Gitelman is interested in the moment when old media were new. The 'novelty years, transitional states, and identity crises', she writes, 'stand to tell us much'.[8] When Kipling composed his story, Gitelman notes, the world had only recently, in the previous fifty or sixty years or so, become wired. In this transitional atmosphere from

150

wires to wirelessness, Kipling had a prescient sense of what was to come: 'wireless seemed like the radical unmaking of modernity in the name of some future modernity'.[9]

Kipling's story, with its combination of bodily contagion, electronic transmission and occult practice, runs as a counter-narrative to the histories of technology focused on sovereign control. Rather, what Kipling recognised early on was that our engagement with wireless media follows an immersive trajectory. Our bodies are being fused with the invisible frequencies of the Earth's electromagnetic waves. This submersion does not adhere to a one-way linear dynamic but is instead determined by the complex temporality of ongoing, undulating change.

During the electric age, in the downswing of the third Kondratiev cycle, Xiong Shili developed a cosmo-ontology of the wave that drew on Chinese cosmologies to confront the new world of modern machines. This chapter shows how Xiong's work was prefigured by the revolutionary intellectual Tan Sitong 譚嗣同 (1865–98), who, at the beginning of the third long wave, outlined a philosophy of the ether, which helps to provide new ways of conceptualising our intimate interconnections with electromagnetic vibrations – the imperceptible abstract infrastructure of twenty-first-century life. Tan's writings, which synthesised Buddhist and Confucian thought, modern notions of the ether, and scientific ideas about consciousness and the mind, found echoes in the post-reform China of the 1980s when associations between electronic media, early cybernetics and spiritual *qigong* exercises became popular. It also resonates with a culture of 'vibratory modernism' in the West in which conceptions of the ether – as an invisible, all-pervasive medium – were tied to a belief in the occult. Wirelessness in both China and the West has fostered an experimental culture of embodied practices, based on a nonseparation of *ti–yong* (essence–function), which seeks to connect the body of the user with the electric body of the Earth.

Infrastructural Imaginary

Over a century after Kipling's prescient story, in the spring and summer of 2019 – months before delirious conspiracies had linked the coronavirus pandemic to paranoid fears over the latest generation of wireless technology – Shannon Mattern articulated a comprehensive theoretical rejection of 5G.[10] Mattern's argument begins by rehearsing the much-hyped promise of fifth-generation cellular networks. 5G's dramatic increase in speed and cut in latency is, as Huawei's future vision makes clear, meant to open a new wave of unanticipated entrepreneurial innovation, transform the workplace (both through robotics and through an increase in the telecommunication of jobs), while also enabling the emergence of a vastly intensified Smart City that is permeated with localised media and self-driving cars. In reciting these dreams in a *New Yorker* article, Sue Halpern describes the hype surrounding the new network as follows: 'Everything from toasters to dog collars to dialysis pumps to running shoes will be connected. Remote robotic surgery will be routine, the military will develop hypersonic weapons, and autonomous vehicles will cruise safely along smart highways.'[11] Realisation of this new infrastructure was meant to be imminent. Yet by mid-2019, the implementation of 5G had hit a snag. 'Paradoxically', writes Mattern, 'this would-be revolution, one predicated on instantaneity, will roll out pretty slowly. Engineering a nationwide infrastructure for lightning-speed communication, it turns out, doesn't happen at lightning speed.'[12]

There are a variety of reasons for this period of latency. The first was foreseen in the emphasis that critical infrastructure studies gives to the concrete materiality of the virtual. In the words of Mattern, 'The realisation of a datafied dream world where everyone and every*thing* is networked depends on lots of physical stuff, cables and trenches, processors and poles, compatible phones and street furniture.'[13] This is especially true in those areas of the network which rely on high-frequency 'millimeter waves'. These shorter wavelengths, between 30 and 300 GHz, don't travel as far as 4G's signal and are highly susceptible to obstacles. Millimetre waves are finicky, says Halpern: 'they can only travel short distances – about a thousand feet – and are impeded by walls, foliage, human bodies, and, apparently, rain. To accommodate these limitations, 5G cellular relays will have to be installed inside buildings and on every city block, at least.'[14] Next-generation cellular infrastructure thus requires an extremely dense network of base stations 'much smaller and more numerous, perhaps 20 times more numerous, than that required for 4G communications'.[15] In addition to building new towers, fibre, satellites and data centres, 5G antennae latch on to existing urban infrastructure, converting lamp posts and bus shelters into Wi-Fi receivers. '5G will affect a profound transformation on the physical landscape', Mattern predicted. She quotes journalist Scott Fulton III who calls the coming implementation of 5G 'the most physically disruptive alteration to the nation's communication infrastructure since the Telegraph'.[16]

This physical alteration is bound up with politics at various scales. Communities worry about property values, equity and aesthetics. As a result, cities and towns across the United States turned to the courts to restrict the building of 5G infrastructure in residential neighbour-hoods.[17] Street side interests can align with municipalities that seek to establish control over the rollout of telecoms infrastructure through regulations and reviews. The monopolistic tendencies of the telecom-munications industry open up deep struggles over the public and private resources involved. In addition, there are widespread fears over security and mass surveillance, especially in Europe and North America. Opponents are alarmed by the enhanced geolocation that 5G provides, especially when coupled with the growing ubiquity of surveillance cameras, each equipped with facial recognition, which, they despair, threatens to eliminate the last traces of urban anonymity.

Compounding these concerns about the impending rollout of 5G is the fact that the hardware became entangled in a fierce geopolitical struggle. The telecommunications industry has long been structured around extremely large players, primarily dominated by old and hugely powerful European and North American corporations such as Ericsson, Nokia and Bell,[18] which were established in the nine-teenth century. Only recently have they been forced to compete with the giant Chinese telecoms equipment companies ZTE and Huawei. In 2019 5G was positioned at the heart of a new space race, this time in the 'troposphere rather than in high-altitude',[19] which pitted America, shocked by a new 'Sputnik moment', against a rising and increasingly assertive China, for which telecoms manufacturers had quite suddenly become the object of national pride.

Over the past decades China has established itself as the infra-structure capital of the world. Since the beginning of Reform and Opening, 'it's safe to say', claims McKinsey's Jonathan Woetzel, 'that China has had the single-biggest buildout of infrastructure in the history of mankind'.[20] This is true both in real numbers as well as in share of GDP. Hundreds of billions of dollars have been spent inter-nally on roads and bridges, subways and high-speed trains. Infra-structure construction has also become critical to China's foreign policy, especially since the start of the Belt and Road initiative. Coun-tries across the world are being transformed by Chinese-built dams, ports and pipelines. This dominance over infrastructure is critical to a new mode of 'globalisation with Chinese characteristics' that is reshaping the twenty-first-century world.

China's strength in building 5G infrastructure came as a traumatic shock in the US, which had long grown accustomed to centuries of Western dominance of the technosphere. The US response, to ban Huawei, was part of its own strategy of techno-economic nationalism, designed to delay the implementation of the next platform of wireless media for months, perhaps even years. Yet within China there was no such delay. On the contrary, in the wake of the attack on Huawei, China accelerated the rollout of 5G. As long-term China tech watcher Jeremy Goldkorn wrote, 'building a domestic, independent fifth-generation (5G) telecom is now an urgent national priority'.[21] The government sped up the granting of commercial licences and offered tax breaks to local chip companies. Huawei's engineers worked round the clock. In 2019 in Shanghai's Hongkou district, 228 base stations opened ahead of schedule. Hongkou is one of the city's richest historical and cultural neighbourhoods. Lu Xun, China's greatest modern writer, lived and died there, and the district still hosts both his former residence and his mausoleum. Hongkou was also a critical site of the May Fourth movement, serving as a gathering place for writers and intellectuals, as well as cosmopolitan bankers and leftist revolutionaries. As part of the International Concession, it was home to British and American industrialists and entrepreneurs and has also long been a favoured area of Japanese settlement. During the Japanese occupation of the city, it became the site of the Jewish ghetto. Yiddish publishing houses and Vienna-style cafés emerged on its old streets and alleyways. Hongkou park is one of the oldest in the city and it still hosts the singers, dancers, calligraphers, *tai chi* and *qigong* practitioners who come to perform their daily rituals. On 30 March 2019 Hongkou district added a historical layer by becoming the first area in the world to claim full 5G network connectivity.[22]

While Mattern is careful to disavow the scapegoating spirit of the anti-China campaign, she is nevertheless enthusiastic about the unintended slowdown. 'While 5G might deliver unprecedented speeds and vectors of connectivity, many of its signature fantasies still involve linking the same stuff: robots and animated objects and families separated by continents and oceans. Billions of dollars and millions of small cells later, we're still pursuing the same old dreams', she laments.[23] A pause would grant time to address some of the concerns surrounding the new network and might even allow for the emergence of 'new dreams and fantasies' that could counter the spin being pushed by the 'futurist and corporate soothsayers' who envision a 'tomorrowland of sentient toasters, self-driving cars and robot doctors'.[24] 'Infrastructures are more than the cold, hard facts of equipment and markets and policy', she writes. 'They're also the products of politics and paranoias, fantasies and fears.'[25] In China there will be no halt to that which is already in the process of unfolding. Yet the speed and enthusiastic embrace of 5G does not preclude the conjuring up of what Mattern calls 'new infrastructural imaginaries'. In addition to familiar technological trajectories, China's relationship to wireless waves involves deep cultural undercurrents, which tap into more occult practices, histories and cosmologies.

Mysterious Waves

At the beginning of Reform and Opening, as China's communist society began to be transformed by the flows of global capitalism, a number of cultural elements including wireless technology, body cultivation or *qigong* (氣功) practices, and an emerging interest in science fiction, all intertwined. In her book *Information Fantasies*, media scholar Xiao Liu writes of how these convergences, which marked China in the 1980s, coalesced around the idea of the wave (*bo* 波). The futurist Alvin Toffler, Liu notes, was a major influence at the time. His bestselling book *The Third Wave*, which describes the transition to a post-industrial society, was translated into Chinese in 1983 and printed nearly a million times.[26] Toffler himself made two visits to China during the period, meeting with top members of the CCP and befriending then premier Zhao Ziyang. The conception of a coming wave of information technology, which could propel China into the future, helped set policies whose ripple effects are still being felt today.

The profound transformation of the socio-economic system, which began in the 1980s, brought with it a fundamental change in the media landscape, which Liu's book documents. Top-down channels of propaganda mutated into a more nebulous and ambient web, spun from hybrid carriers of information. There was an explosion of information in print journals, pamphlets and monographs as well as in the new media of radio and television.

> The number of Chinese radio stations increased from 106 in 1980 to 213 in 1985, and the rate of radio-set ownership doubled to 241 million. Starting in 1983, local television stations (including municipal and county level) were approved by the central government. With this new policy, the number of stations surged to 202 by 1985, covering 68.4 percent of the whole population.[27]

The proliferation of wireless and satellite broadcasts occurred in both the formal and informal spheres. In the southern province of Guangdong, a dense network of what came to be known as 'fishbone antenna' were set up in backyards and rooftops in order to capture the television signals emanating from Hong Kong. Communication over wireless waves occurred in a relatively deregulated and privatised environment, serving to undermine the previously established 'auditory space politicized by wired loud-speakers'.[28]

This transformation in the mediasphere coincided with the spread of practices designed to connect the human body with cosmic energies. *Qigong* fever, which reached its height in the 1980s, attracted over one hundred million practitioners, and was, as scholar David

Palmer has written, the 'most widespread form of popular religiosity in post Maoist urban China'.[29] Embodied rituals drawn from older traditions were linked to the emerging mediasphere. *Qigong* was reconceptualised as a human–machine interface aligned with the new magical medium of information-carrying waves. China's famous rocket scientist and cybernetician Qian Xuesen 錢學森 (1911–2009), who was enormously influential at the time, embraced a 'somatic science', which equated *qi* with information and explored the possibilities of extrasensory powers of perception. By mastering the internal rhythms of breath and movement, Qian believed, the body could act as a medium opening to an electromagnetic atmosphere that had come to be conceived as a mysterious medium for cognitive change. *Qigong* practitioners attempted to tap into the concealed powers of the electric environment. They held that being bathed and penetrated by electromagnetic frequencies had a transformative effect on organic life.

Their attitude to this leakage between body and environment was markedly different from the health concerns voiced by anxious Westerners in the twenty-first century about the impact of 5G. A large part of the growing anxiety over the new generation of wireless media is concern about its physiological effects. The latest telecom network is viewed by sceptics as a harbinger of invasion not only 'of our nation, our communities, our homes',[30] but also of our bodies. Perceived health risks have elicited a range of responses from sober requests for further study[31] to wild conspiracies,[32] which multiplied during the 2020 pandemic, when many linked the coronavirus with 5G in various spurious ways. Stories of people with 'EMF sensitivity' seeking refuge in remote zones free from cellular signals are increasingly common.[33]

The pairing of *qigong* with the electromagnetic atmosphere in post-reform China came out of a deeply synthetic approach to the *ti–yong* dichotomy, which posited a profound interconnection between Chinese culture and an emerging technosphere. *Qigong*'s ability to 'tap the mysterious' waves was considered alongside an openness to the body's unknown possibilities. Rather than establish a barrier that could protect against physiological risk, practitioners believed in the possibility of augmentation. *Qigong*'s 'technologies of the body', to use Palmer's Foucauldian term, did not seek to protect the organic from the new zone of electronic communication, but speculated instead that embodied practice could access the deepest layer of wirelessness – the planet's hidden electromagnetic vibrations.

Ideas about the extraordinary power of the new media environment were also prevalent in the science fiction of the time. Liu points to Wang Xiaoda's short story 'Mysterious Waves', published in 1980, in which a reporter is sent to Base 88 in northern Xinjiang to investigate a new wireless defence system called 'Wave-45'. When he reaches the underground station, he is surprised to find fresh air, green trees and beautiful flowers under a bright blue sky. He also meets a woman who can walk through walls like the 'magic arts of the ancient Mount Laoshan Taoist Priest'.[34] Wave-45, he discovers, is a high-frequency system based on the hyperstitional theory of Professor Wang, who maintained that all objective substances, all phenomena, everything we see, smell, hear and touch is produced through a pure information wave. By manufacturing these 'waves of pure information', we can 'beguile our sensory organs – the visual, the olfactory, the hearing, and even the tactile – into believing the signals are from real material things, even when the "things" are never present. All of this can be achieved just by manipulating a few electronic devices.'[35] The material world of sensation and experience – the scent of a flower or the vividness of an oil painting – are merely illusions, Wang suggests, echoing Buddhist beliefs. These ephemeral manifestations are supported by a more real but ethereal realm that is made up of imperceptible waves.

Tan Sitong 譚嗣同

The cultural currents that surfaced in the 1980s, which posited a link between an embodied, practical knowledge of the electromagnetic environment and the doctrines and practices of *qigong*, were foreshadowed at the close of the nineteenth century. As the science of electricity was first introduced into China, late Qing intellectuals argued that emerging knowledge of electromagnetism was compatible with the metaphysical insights of Daoist, Buddhist and Confucian thought. Kang Youwei 康有為 (1858–1927), one of the most important political philosophers of the time, wrote in his important work *Datongshu* 大同書 (The Book of Great Unity) that electricity could be thought of as 'an all-pervading, conscious energy':

> Vast in the Primal *qi*, creator of Heaven and Earth. Although the size of the whole spiritual substance (*hunzhi* 魂質) of Heaven and Earth are different, they are both produced by division of the vast *qi* in the Great Origin (*tai yuan* 太元), as if scooping up the drops of the vast ocean. Confucius said: 'Earth contains spiritual *qi*, and this [produces] the wind and the thunder, and these carry along the forms (*xing* 形), so that the multitude of things manifest life.' This spiritual thing is electricity: lightning (*guang dian* 光點) is able to be transmitted everywhere, and spiritual *qi* can make all things sentient (*gan* 感).

> It spiritualizes ghosts and gods, it gives birth to Heaven and Earth. In its entirety it is the Origin; divided it is human beings. Subtle and marvellous, is contact with its spirituality![36]

This connection between Chinese philosophico-religious ideas and the electromagnetic ether was most richly articulated by the scholar official Tan Sitong. Tan is most famous for his role in the brief but momentous event known as the 'Hundred Day Reform', which lasted from 11 June to 22 September 1898. In the wake of a series of devastating military defeats, with the treaty ports awash with technology and ideas flooding in from outside, it was clear that the flailing Qing court had no choice but to reform. In the summer of 1898, the young emperor Guangxu, under the influence of leading intellectuals Kang Youwei and Liang Qichao, took control of the court and enacted a series of decrees, which taken together articulated a wide-ranging social, cultural, political and especially educational agenda. The reformists sought to modernise the schools, training centres and universities, and with them transform commerce, industry, agriculture and the army. The Hundred Day Reform ended with a sudden violent *coup d'état* led by the sidelined Empress Dowager Cixi. All the movement's leaders, including Kang and Liang, were either exiled or executed. Tan himself was beheaded on 28 September 1898 at the age of 33. This abrupt and gruesome end marked, for many, a threshold occurrence that signalled the failure of political reform in Imperial China and the turn towards revolution. In their edited collection on this critical moment, however, scholars Rebecca Karl and Peter Zarrow warn against relying too heavily on these settled and rigid dichotomies to make sense of the past. Rather, they advocate exploring 1898 in the 'context of a larger framework: as part of a multifaceted process of transforming the relationships of society, knowledge, and politics'.[37] Today scholars widely agree that the Hundred Day Reform was part of a much larger epoch of deep intellectual transition, which crystallised the issues and tensions that still shape Chinese modernity today.[38]

As it became clear that Empress Cixi would survive the challenge to her rule and regain power, both Kang Youwei and Liang Qichao fled to Japan. Tan Sitong refused to leave and thus became a celebrated 'martyr' for the cause. Just before Liang escaped, however, Tan handed him the manuscript of the book he had been working on. *Ren Xue* 仁學 (An Exposition of Benevolence) was published posthumously. Liang Qichao signed his introduction 'ninety days after the death of the martyr' and proclaimed Tan to be a meteor in the intellectual world of the late Qing.

The importance of *Ren Xue* lies in its attempt to fuse modern techno-science with the classical Chinese discourses of natural philosophy. In his important essay on Tan, David Wright elucidates the deep significance of the text. 'Up until the writings of Tan Sitong, there is little Western science being taken seriously by Chinese intellectuals', he contends:

> The guns and steamships which so alarmed the Self-strengtheners carried no philosophical, let alone ethical, message, only pointing to the need for China to invest in an arms race before it was totally overwhelmed by Western technical superiority. Those Chinese scholars who had begun study of Western science were on the whole absorbed in Western studies for the sake of their practical applications, with little interest in reconciling Chinese and Western philosophical viewpoints. It is only with Tan that there begins to be a real appreciation of how these ideas might be integrated into a new world-view which did not require a complete break with the Chinese past.[39]

The Ether and Occult Materialism

In the nineteenth century it was generally believed that electromagnetic vibrations behaved like all other waves and travelled through a medium. Where there are waves, there is water. Scientists presumed there was an all-pervasive fluid environment that permeated everything, everywhere. The planet was believed to be submerged in an invisible liquid-like medium known as the ether. The concept of the ether is as subtle and nebulous as the medium itself. In their introduction to the book *Conceptions of Ether*, G. N. Cantor and M. J. S. Hodge trace the idea back to its ancient origins. The Ionian philosophers spoke of the 'aether' as a higher air, shiny, brilliant and fiery, which they equated with the soul. Ether was an ontological feature of classical cosmology. In Lucretius' *On the Nature of Things*, swirling currents of ether are presented as a possible cause for the rotation of the sun, moon and stars; the ether has been conflated with the Stoics' 'pneuma', the active, generative principle, which gave the universe life, and for Aristotle the primary five elements were earth, water, air, fire and celestial aether.

The idea of the ether survived in different forms throughout the history of natural philosophy in the West. In medieval times, the imperceptible substance was seen as a means of integrating the physical world with doctrines of spirit and heaven. Descartes wrote of the vortices in 'subtle' or 'celestial' matter. Newton, who struggled with the concept, speculated that it was an active, initiating agent, the cause of a wide variety of phenomena, which might also explain the mysteries of action at a distance. The ether played an important role in the early science of chemistry. In physics and physiology, it was called upon to address the problem of how matter – conceived of as passive and inert – could be endowed with motion. Subtle matter was the vital spirit that solved the riddle of life. Up until the eighteenth century, natural theology posited the ether as a primal material out of which gross matter had been formed. The elastic medium played a critical role in the scientific revolutions of the eighteenth and nineteenth centuries. Conceived of as a subtle fluid, the ether was essential to the wave theory of light. Maxwell 'treated electrical lines of force, magnetic lines of force and electric currents each by analogy with the flow of an incomprehensible fluid through a resistive medium'.[40] The idea that light, heat and electricity were transmitted through a universal, primordial, elusive substance was seen to be obvious. The existence of the ether was unquestioned; it was only its secrets that had yet to be revealed.

As the electromagnetic revolution in physics began to ripple out into the wider society, people became increasingly 'aware that the environment around them was saturated with invisible and inaudible vibrations'.[41] This resulted, as Enns and Trower detail in their edited collection *Vibratory Modernism*, in a whole host of experiments by avant-garde writers, painters, photographers and performers in both Europe and America, all of whom sought to create a realm of artistic production that could give expression to this unseen force. 'The scientific study of vibrations thus introduced a new understanding of space, matter, energy, perception, and consciousness that dramatically changed the way people thought about themselves and the world around them', Enns and Trower write. In the early twentieth century, 'this new understanding of the universe as a vast network of continuous vibrations had a tremendous impact on modernist literature, art, and theatre'.[42]

Etymologically, the Latin word *spectrum* means an image or apparition and, originally, an electrician simply meant a magician. Electricity thus gave rise to an occult materialism that disrupted familiar narratives that equated modernity with mechanism, disenchantment and the rise of a secular world. By contrast, the modern encounter with electronic media was associated from the start with contact from virtual, spectral entities. Edison believed he was trafficking with ghosts, and Tesla concluded that he could detect the transmission of deliberate, intelligent agents and was convinced he was in touch with aliens. There was a perceived harmony between the immersive but hidden medium that carried electromagnetic waves and the corporeal medium who transferred messages from the spiritual realms across into the world of the mundane. Electricity, as Daniel Czitrom writes in *Media and the American Mind*, was, in standard terms of the day, 'shadowy, mysterious, impalpable. It lives in the skies and seems to connect the spiritual and material.'[43] The curious new force hinted at a strange metaphysics with uncanny agents and its material presence was suggestive of the mystical power of the incorporeal.

The inscrutable nature of electricity was reinforced by the reality of disembodied communication first instantiated through the telegraph. Electronic communication tapped into waves of varying non-human frequencies that carried messages from beyond. When Samuel Morse sent the first telegraph message on 24 May 1844, he asked Miss Elsworth, the daughter of the commissioner of patents, to pick the first message. The words she chose, 'What hath God wrought', bound the historical origins of the telegraph to its apparent cosmic implications.

Modern techno-occultism was further reinforced by the rise of spiritualism, which emerged as a new religion in the immediate wake of the invention of the telegraph. Starting with members of the Fox family in a small village in New York state, mediums, who were almost always women, tapped into electric currents, which opened a 'spiritual telegraph line' to the imperceptible beyond. Spiritualist communication mirrored Morse's dots and dashes with rhythmic raps and knocks that were claimed to be transmissions from the dead. These early mediums recognised that access to the electromagnetic spectrum, as an imperceptible realm of nature, necessarily involved an intimate cyborgian becoming. 'Long before our contemporary fascination with the beatific possibilities of cyberspace', writes Jeffrey Sconce, 'feminine mediums led the Spiritualist movement as wholly recognized cybernetic beings – electromagnetic devices bridging flesh and spirit, body and machine, material reality and electronic space.'[44]

Wireless communication, with its mixture of 'temporal immediacy and spatial isolation', was, as Sconce notes, 'if anything even more conducive to the idea of an ephemeral presence or animated sentience that was broadcasting messages through the airwaves'. The early decades of the twentieth century saw the spread of Marconi's 'wireless telegraphy', 'a radically different vision of electronic presence, one that presented an entirely new metaphor of liquidity in telecommunication by replacing the concept of the individuated "stream" with the vast etheric "ocean"'.[45] With the idea of the ether, wirelessness secured its association with water over land. Sconce details how the early spread of wireless reinforced belief in this all-encompassing 'oceanic' realm:

> In refiguring the concept of transmission from the wired connection to the more mysterious wandering signal, accounts of wireless and radio returned consistently to the structuring metaphor of the 'etheric ocean.' Bound at first, perhaps, to the medium's origins in maritime applications, this most fluid of communication metaphors became a powerful conceptual tool for engaging not only the new electronic environment, but the emerging social world as well. Oceanic metaphors proved versatile in capturing the seeming omnipresence, unfathomable depths and invisible mysteries of both radio's ether and its audience – mammoth fluid bodies that, like the sea, were ultimately boundless and unknowable.[46]

The ether, then, as an in-between medium, midway between the material and the ideal, was used to reconcile scientific facts about the concrete mechanical universe with the esoteric realm of ritual, magic and religion. In the words of Erik Hammerstrom, 'Clairvoyance, animal magnetism (hypnotism), metal healing, astral travel were all given scientific respectability by those who explained them with reference to the ether.'[47]

The idea that Hertz's experiments 'harnessed the ether for the transmission of intelligence' was most enthusiastically promoted by radio pioneer Oliver Lodge, one of the most critical figures in this early modern synthesis between the science of ether and the esoteric world of magic.[48] Lodge, a physicist who, independently of Hertz, had detected electromagnetic radiation, combined his work on the technologies of electric waves with an intense interest in psychical research prompted in part by the death of his son, who was killed in the First World War. Lodge was an active member of the Society for Psychical Research, which was founded in London in 1882 and included such prominent members as the co-inventor of the telephone Thomas Watson, literary figures Ruskin, Tennyson, Lewis Carroll and Arthur Conan Doyle, as well as the philosopher William James. The Society held that the existence of the scientific ether supported belief 'in the essential unity of material and spiritual phenomena'.[49] Lodge believed that he was in communication with the ghost of his son and held that we are endowed with an ethereal body that could communicate telepathically with both the living and the dead. He envisioned thoughts, which he held to arise from the electricity in the brain, as electromagnetic waves that could not be contained inside the head. Our spiritual and real home, he wrote, 'is in the ether of space'.[50] For Lodge, electrical machines were like new sense organs whose purpose was to perceive the intangible ether:

> And when next century or the century after let us deeper into their secrets (electricity and the ether) and into the secrets of some other phenomena now for the first time being rationally investigated, I feel as it would be no merely material prospect that will be opening on our view, but that we shall get a glimpse into a region of the universe as yet unexplored by Science, which has been sought from far, and perhaps blindly apprehended, by painters and poets, by philosophers and scientists.[51]

This sense that the new communicative technology had the capacity to cross barriers, connecting brain waves with the waves of energy and light, was echoed by the physicist, chemist and member of the Society for Psychical Research Sir William Crookes, who technological historian Hugh Aitken describes as a 'scientist extraordinaire' and 'speculative genius' and credits with providing the vision behind the radio.[52] Crookes, writes Aitken, speculated on 'what scientific discoveries meant, what they implied for the future, and how they could be exploited'. He was 'a dreamer, a visionary, almost a mystic', dedicated to the opening up of a 'new and astonishing world'.[53] Sconce, in *Haunted Media*, notes that Crookes 'proposed that telepathic thought existed as high frequency vibrations, not unlike radio and light waves'. He quotes Crookes as follows: 'It may be that radium waves are only the threshold of the wonders of the unseen universe . . . If [the] communications of spirits are through vibrations of ether or in some still more subtle substance, we should have in this a possible explanation of telepathy.'[54]

The early inventors (or explorers) of the ethereal had a sense that in tapping into the electromagnetic ether they were opening channels of communication with something profoundly alien. Anton Mesmer's theatrical performances used magnets to manipulate the fluid, undulatory medium. Theosophist Madame Blavatsky attributed her own powers as a medium to the strength of her ethereal double. 'Who knows where ends the power of this protean giant – Ether', she wrote, 'or whence its mysterious origin?'[55] Even the comparatively cautious James Clerk Maxwell speculated that the etheric medium of electromagnetic transmission might 'constitute the material organism of beings exercising functions of life and mind as high or higher than ours are at present'. In *What is Media Archaeology?*, Jussi Parikka writes of this *fin-de-siècle* sensibility. He quotes from *The Education of Henry Adams*, which speaks of discoveries 'absolute, supersensual, occult' that are made in a world which has 'wrapped' us in 'vibrations and rays'.[56]

> In these seven years man has translated himself into a new universe which had no common scale of measurement with the old. He had entered a super sensual world, in which he could measure nothing except by chance collisions of movements imperceptible to his sense, perhaps even imperceptible to his instruments, but perceptible to each other, and so to some known ray at the end of the scale.[57]

In encountering the ether, there was a sense that, 'as with the oceans of the earth, unknown creatures might stalk this electronic sea's invisible depths'.[58] The currents, streams, flows of the 'oceanic' ether seemed to open pathways of communication for entities other than ourselves. The modern ether, writes Joe Milutis in his monograph on the enigmatic substance, with 'all its mysterious and occult properties', was seen as an intermediary between mind and matter, an ur-medium of interconnectedness – the 'source of all things'.[59]

Yitai 以太

Tan Sitong's innovation was to link these modern ideas of the ether, the mind and electricity to older Chinese cosmologies. In *Ren Xue*, Tan describes an invisible medium, 'exceedingly vast and subtle', which lay behind the waves of light, sound, breath and electricity. He related this fundamental energetic principle, responsible for the interwovenness of things, to the ancient concepts of *qi* (氣) and *ren* (仁). For Tan, the ether was ultimately a medium of interconnectedness, which he likened to the pervasiveness of electricity. 'As man lives in the midst of the myriad things, he is related to them . . . The relationship is like a wire that links (*t'ung*) the self to the myriad things.' This term *tong* (統), which is one of the most crucial concepts in *Ren Xue*, 'defies an exact English translation', explains intellectual historian Hao Chang. 'The closest equivalent is "interpenetration" or "fusion".'[60] The ether (or *yitai*), as the ultimate medium of connectedness, not only enables crossings between the seen and the unseen, the dead and the living, it also envelops all that is here and now. It is like 'the spreading out of electric wires in all directions with nowhere too far to be reached', wrote Tan.[61] At this critical moment of modernity, he saw in the ether the possibility of a cross-cultural correlation between scientific ideas that had come from outside and much older Chinese cosmologies.

Tan's own knowledge of Western science was greatly influenced by the Protestant missionary John Fryer (1839–1928), who he first met in the spring of 1896.[62] Fryer was one of the chief translators of the Jiangnan Arsenal and introduced Tan not only to new texts but also 'to fossils, adding machines, the X-ray and a device for measuring brain waves'.[63] Of particular interest was Fryer's translation of a once popular but now obscure book by a businessman turned mental healer, Henry Wood. Fryer's translation of Wood's *A Method for Healing the Mind and Avoiding Sickness* guided Tan in the formulation of his concept of the ether. According to scholar Richard Shek, Wood's text only makes passing mention of the ether. The concept, however, was greatly elaborated by Fryer. Shek quotes the translation as follows:

> Lately in the West it has been learned that inside the myriad things there is a fluid called ether. The space [between us and] the most distant stars is not a vacuum, but is filled by this ether. This ether is present even within the fine molecules of the air on earth . . . Nowhere is it absent, and no way we can get rid of it. Without this ether the light of the sun and the other stars cannot be transmitted to the earth . . . Irrespective of the distance or the sensitivity of the five senses, as soon as one person conceives a thought, he activates the ether and conveys it to the mind of others, making them have the same thought.[64]

After reading this text, Tan developed a strong conviction of the confluence of ether, electricity, consciousness and the brain. *Ren Xue* begins by stating that benevolence (*ren*) or interconnectedness is made manifest by the ether, electricity and the power of the mind. Ingo Schäfer, in his article on the concepts of *qi* and *yitai*, further explicates Tan's understanding of the close relationship between these terms. For Tan, the human brain and the central nervous system are 'the "most intelligent" products of *yitai*'. The 'ether functions in its most spiritual and subtle aspect when it constitutes the brain in the human body'. This site of embodied thought is animated by an all-pervasive atmospheric electricity. 'The student of *ren*', Tan contends, must realise that electricity is the brain; there is no place without electricity; 'it is the power of electricity that unites Heaven, Earth, the myriad creatures, the self and other men into a single organism'.[65]

Tan's model of a thinking being as an electric organism corresponded with the notion that the ether was a medium that facilitated telepathy. As a psychic energetic substance that permeates all, *yitai* (the ether) enables one mind to be directly connected to another. For Tan, *ren* (benevolence) or *yitai* manifests in the electric plane, which produces our brain and the nervous system. It is *yitai* that integrates the human body into a single organic system:

> Nothing is closer to man than his body. The bones of the body number over two hundred, it consists of a certain quantity of muscles, blood vessels, and internal organs. [The medium] that forms the body and holds it together, so that it does not disperse, it is only *yitai* . . . What enables the eye to see, the ear to hear, the nose to smell, the tongue to taste, the body to feel? It is only *yitai*. Nothing is closer to the body than the earth. The earth is composed of many atoms. What holds them together? It is only *yitai*. If we divide an atom until the point of nothingness is reached and examine that which holds [the particles] together, [we find that] it is only *yitai*.[66]

As a result of his positive encounters with missionaries, Tan had some sympathy for Christianity and went so far in one of his letters, written shortly after the Chinese defeat in the Sino-Japanese war, as to call for 'wholesale Westernization'.[67] Ultimately, though, the impact of Buddhism proved to be far more profound. Tan was deeply influenced by what Liang Qichao described as the 'undercurrent of Buddhism that infiltrated the intellectual milieu of the late Ching'.[68] Francesca Tarocco, in her book on this subject, documents the cultural practices of Buddhist modernity. She details how texts, images and music made use of the material culture of the printing press, photography and radio. The myriad technological manifestations of this Buddhist resurgence centred in particular on the city of Nanjing, where Xiong and his Yogacara masters were based. The power of this Buddhasphere, Tarocco argues, challenges the assumption that urban China in the late nineteenth and early twentieth centuries was primarily governed by a disenchanted, secular modernity.

The discourses and cultural practices of modern Chinese Buddhism occurred in large part outside the monastic order and drew widely from the various teachings in the *Weishih* 唯識, *Huayen* 華嚴 and *Chan* 禪 schools. This 'remoulded Buddhism' was designed to counter the apparent inadequacy of the Confucian tradition and its seeming incompatibility with modernity. 'Buddhism revived', writes Chan Sin-Wai, 'when Confucianism crumbled before the challenge from the West.'[69] Its ostensible links with the science of the times coupled with its metaphysical sophistication served as a theoretical weapon for intellectuals to tackle the problems of their time.

For Tan Sitong, like Xiong Shili, the *Weishih* (Yogacara or Mind Only) school was especially critical. Scott Pacey, who details the precise influence, explains how Tan combined the brain's electrical functions with Yogacara's cognitive architecture, identifying the cerebrum (*da'nao* 大腦) as the location of the *ālaya*, the eighth or highest consciousness.[70] Tan Sitong signed *Ren Xue* with the pen name *Lotus Form of All Sentient Beings* (*Hua Xiang Cheng Sheng* 華相乘生) to signal the enormous role Buddhism played in his work. According to Liang Qichao, the whole text should be read as an exercise in 'applied Buddhism'.[71] Chan likewise argues that Buddhism 'served an all embracing role in his synthesis', such that the relationship between benevolence and ether can only be understood within the context of Buddhist metaphysics.[72] According to Tan's cosmology the vibrating changes of the ether occur as the 'sublime production and destruction' that are not accessible to normal sense perception. In this conception, Buddhism offered a path beyond the limitations of Western learning because 'while our ordinary sense cannot apprehend all of the phenomena in the universe, supramundane sense is able to do so'.[73]

Like Xiong's, Tan's Buddhism was profoundly influenced by the late Ming to early Qing philosopher Wang Fuzhi 王夫之, whose own neo-Confucianism is rooted in the *Yijing*. Tan was the son of a Hunanese official and, as a child, was trained in traditional Chinese learning. Though his family was often posted away from his hometown, his education was determined by the intellectual milieu of the Hunanese literati, who, as Stephen Platt elucidates, played an outsized role in the shaping of modern China. Platt's book on the impact of the Hunanese begins with the vital rediscovery of Wang's work. 'The figure of Wang Fuzhi', he writes, was a 'lightning rod for Hunanese activist intellectuals'.[74] Tan considered himself a disciple: 'In the past five hundred years', a close friend recalled Tan saying time and again, 'there has only been one person who truly understood the nature of heaven and man: Wang Fuzhi and no one else'.[75] Tan's conception of the ether, as a primary substance with no visible form, sound, smell or taste, which penetrates everywhere and connects everything, is clearly drawn from Wang's philosophy of *qi*. *Yitai* is presented as the primal building material of the phenomenal world. For Tan, it is out of the ether that the material realm is established and the Ten Thousand Things are born. *Yitai* defies categorisation as either spiritual or material, immanent or transcendent.[76] It is an elusive, all-pervasive, ever-changing creative energy, a vibrational plane upon which modern science and Chinese thought converge.

> The realm of phenomena, the realm of the void, and the realm of sentient beings are permeated by a thing which is supremely vast and supremely subtle, which adheres, penetrates, connects and fills all

things. The eye cannot see its colour, the ear cannot hear its sound, the mouth and nose cannot realize its smell or taste. There is no [adequate] name for it, but we may call it *Yitai*. Its manifestations in function are waves, energy, [chemical] elements, and nerves. The realm of phenomena is produced from it, the realm of the void is established by it and the realm of sentient beings issues from it. It has no form, but all forms depend upon it; it has no mind-heart, but it is felt by all mind-hearts. Strictly speaking, we can simply call it *ren*.[77]

The Ether and the Spectrum

Early twentieth-century physics challenged the idea that the ether was the essential medium through which electric waves could flow. Almost all physicists around 1905 accepted the idea that light waves must be waves in something. In Galison's words, 'In the case of light waves (or the oscillating electric and magnetic fields that constituted light), that something was the all-pervasive ether.'[78] By the beginning of the twentieth century, however, 'the nothing that connects everything' had vanished.[79] In 1887 Albert Michelson and Edward Morley built a machine precise enough to detect the Earth moving through a cosmic etheric wind. Yet despite their efforts, they could find no experimental evidence for the ether. Less than a decade later, in 1905, Einstein's theory of special relativity provided scientific proof. 'I'm convinced more and more', said Einstein,

> that the electrodynamics of moving bodies as it is presented today doesn't correspond to reality, and that it will be possible to present it in a simpler way. The introduction of the name 'ether' into theories of electricity has led to the conception of a medium whose motion can be described, without, I believe, being able to ascribe physical meaning to it.[80]

Sometime around 1901, Einstein, 'faced with the inability of experimentalists to either drag the ether or detect motion through it [. . .] disposed of even this insubstantiality'. Electricity and magnetism, he concluded, are 'definable not as alteration of material ether but as the motion of "true" electrical masses with physical reality through empty space'.[81]

The end of the ether defied classical physics, which tends to be in tune with human perception and common sense. In the case of electromagnetic energy, we now believe there is no medium, only waves. Wirelessness thus confounds McLuhan's most basic insight that the medium is the message. Jennifer Gabrys, in her essay in

The Wireless Spectrum: The Politics, Practices and Poetics of Mobile Media, remarks on the inherently elusive nature of this 'mediumless medium':

> While telegraphs, radios, televisions, telexes, radars, satellites, mobile phones and wireless computer networks are often considered the 'medium' of wireless (with the radio set referred to as the 'wireless' for some time), in fact wireless is the mode of communication that, as the definition goes, does not require a medium for transport. The wireless receiver or transmitter stands in for the 'medium' of wireless, so that the space through which the signal travels is apparently mediumless.[82]

In scientific discourses, the medium of the ether was supplanted by a quite different notion of electromagnetic energy – that of the spectrum. Physicists, notes historian Hugh Aitken, tend to consider the spectrum 'as a natural object that has existed since the big bang' and which 'will continue to exist after humanity has vanished from the earth'.[83] Yet the 'naturalness' of electromagnetic radiation fails to account for the ways in which the invention of the spectrum transformed how electromagnetic energy is understood, explored and used. The electromagnetic spectrum is an abstraction, which serves to organise, consolidate and control the universe's electromagnetic waves.

Aitken was interested in how the new emerged, and his work was dedicated to examining technological paradigm shifts. Just before his death, he outlined a research proposal for a book on the history of the spectrum. The difference between conceiving of electromagnetic waves as vibrations of the ether and conceptualising them in accordance with the spectrum contains, he wrote, the 'story of how we learned to think about the physical world in a new way'.[84] In exploring this mutation, Aitken likened the finding of electromagnetic radiation to the discovery of a new continent. Unlike territorial space, however, with the spectrum it is not at all clear how much room there is, how 'place' can be divided, or how to delimit the boundaries of the property involved. A series of questions immediately emerge:

> Could the radiofrequency spectrum become private property? If not, how were rights to its use to be acquired? Who controlled access? Could access ever be exclusive? Could jurisdictions be established and, if established, could they be defended? Who was to assign rights of use? And how were these rights to be enforced? In all these respects the problems presented by the discovery of the radiofrequency spectrum, a resource created by science and technology, came to have, as the nineteenth century neared its close, clear similarities to the problems faced earlier in the opening up of new continents.[85]

Unlike the ether, the electromagnetic spectrum is a scientific theory that is easy to conceptualise and diagram. The spectrum places all electromagnetic radiation in a clear and ordered sequence, from the lowest to highest frequency (longest to shortest wavelength). The entire spectrum includes not only radio waves, but infrared, visible and ultraviolet light, and at the highest frequencies, X-rays and gamma-rays. 'The "wireless spectrum" spans the frequencies from roughly 8.3 kHz, the low frequencies exceeding audible phenomena, to 3,000 GHz, the high frequencies approaching visible phenomena.'[86]

In contrast with the more nebulous notion of the ether, the idea of the spectrum is intimately tied to industry. As such, it comprehends electromagnetic waves as a resource. The key figure in this transition was the radio entrepreneur Guglielmo Marconi. In 1899 wireless reception was still erratic. Waves were scattered all over the place. The distributed ether, however, was not conducive to the private tuning and transmission that the Marconi device required. The problem required a change in theoretical orientation. The Marconi Company's most far-reaching strategic breakthrough was conceptual not technical. As broadcasting historian Susan Douglas writes, it 'rested on a revolutionary way of thinking about the ether', which involved understanding electromagnetic waves as 'territory that he could preempt and privatize'.[87] Marconi's 'invention' required that he lay claim to certain frequencies and insist that others be denied access. 'In retrospect, Marconi's most historically significant legacy', concludes Douglas, was 'the idea of controlling and overseeing access to the spectrum'.[88] The problem of allocating rights to the radio frequency spectrum requires a deep interdependence between technological change and socio-economic organisations. As in the case of the telegraph, radio in the Marconi age involved constellations of large corporate bureaucracies and government departments, international treaties, conferences, conventions and a host of other regulatory agencies, all of which were mobilised to divvy up this increasingly valuable resource.

In their PhD theses, both Erik Christopher Born and Zita Joyce draw inspiration from Aitken's unfinished project on the history of the spectrum in order to explore this paradigm shift away from the ether. At the beginning of the twentieth century, writes Born, the 'luminiferous ether as a universal substance connecting all matter, a concept that had thrived for several millennia, suddenly gave way to that of the electromagnetic spectrum as a useful physical construct'.[89] Both Born and Joyce, inspired by Aitken, who saw the transition as Kuhnian in scope, argue that much more was at stake in this historical transformation than is allowed for in the familiar story of science's triumph over superstition. Joyce dates the pivotal event, 'the moment of invention', to the 1906 Wireless conference, which involved twenty-seven nations and was held under the umbrella of the International Telegraphy Union (ITU).[90] Called as a 'response to the strategic challenge posed by so-called "Marconism"', the conference adopted a proposal to divide the spectrum into regions or bands defined by wavelengths, which, crucially, could be managed from above. 1906, Joyce writes, 'marks the point at which the sequential spectrum of wavelengths, at that stage still somewhat conceptual and incomplete, was divided into sections to be allocated to specific uses'.

The concept of a continuous electromagnetic spectrum requires not only the realisation of a differential range of possible wavelengths but also the technical capacity to measure and tune into waves of different lengths and frequencies. 'Tuning was the crucial step for both expansion of wireless telegraphy and the development of the radio spectrum itself', Joyce argues, 'as the ability to tune transmitters and receivers allowed a signal to propagate on a single, specific wavelength, to which the intended receiver is tuned.'[91] After the 1906 conference, the military, commerce and amateur experimentation were each allocated their own specific wavelength bands. Dividing up the spectrum was not so much a technical issue as it was a matter of control.

> The radio spectrum that allows frequencies to be allocated to specific uses by the state and by international bodies was invented as an apparatus of power. It is a structure that controls the way in which radio transmissions are used and by whom, a necessary division that made radio useable, but reduced the ways in which it could be used.[92]

The invention of the spectrum 'created order in the ceaseless flow' as Joyce puts it in the title of her thesis. The 'radio spectrum' itself, she maintains, is a construction invented to 'organize radio communications'.[93] While the ether is a medium of open infinite electromagnetic phenomena, the spectrum is a system of resource management. As Marconi's wireless telegraphy spread across the globe, the electromagnetic spectrum was closed off, divided up into various bandwidths to be sold or auctioned off. 'Once seen as a seemingly inexhaustible natural resource, the spectrum became an economic and political resource.'[94] Various interests, both private and public, competed for control over frequency bands. Management was ultimately granted to nation-states, which were granted the power to divide up the spectrum, auctioning and allocating frequency bands to various competing users. Waves as a planetary media infrastructure became subject to sovereign control.

Embodied Experiments

The division and governance of the electromagnetic spectrum occurs in accordance with the *ti–yong* split in which a primary, central, sociocultural unity is positioned above and beyond the technological plane which it is deemed to master. The abstraction of the electromagnetic spectrum seems to counter this cyborgian leakage between body and machine by strictly delineating one realm from another. The very idea of the spectrum explicitly demarcates the limits of the human organism as conforming to a distinct range of frequency bands. Its precise measurements rigidly differentiate between the perceptible and the imperceptible, and the organic and the artificial. As Born writes:

> The wireless spectrum, by definition, begins only above the threshold of human hearing and it ends only below the threshold of human vision, the ontological definition of the spectrum creates an epistemological distinction between the audible and the inaudible, as well as the visible and the invisible. Human beings are not supposed to be able to hear or see electromagnetic waves, and yet technological devices are easily capable of doing so. In the same turn, the definition of the wireless spectrum also reinforces a distinction between the internal and the external, as well as the natural and the artificial. Electromagnetic waves are supposed to exist outside the human body and are not supposed to be produced by human beings . . .[95]

Nevertheless, the history of wireless has seen a host of embodied experimental practices, drawn from occult traditions, which are aimed at forging a more intimate relationship with the immersive atmosphere of electromagnetic waves. The environment of wirelessness, now understood as a mediumless medium, coincides with the non-separation of *ti–yong* and thereby recalls the philosophical principle that the body of the sea, though distinct, is not behind, beyond or prior to the waves.

Electric vibrations are the ripple effects of the Earth's iron ocean. Comprising one third of terrestrial mass, approximately three thousand kilometres below the surface lies a semi-fluid metallic sea. Its solid inner core is wrapped by an outer core that consists of a 2,000-kilometre-thick layer of liquid metal whose currents and whirlpools bathe the planet in vast energetic fields. Earth's metallic interior is unencumbered by the integrity and identity of the organisms that live on the planet's surface. Metal's intrinsic transmorphism – its continuous metamorphosis – aligns it, as philosophers Deleuze and Guattari write, with the 'dream/horror of nonorganic life . . .

The prodigious idea of Nonorganic Life ... was the invention, the intuition of metallurgy.'[96] Metal's intrinsic mutability manifests in the multifaceted mutations of modernity. Metal is a critical component in railways, telegraph wires and steam engines. It is found in the steel frames of modern skyscrapers, the nickel and lithium inside batteries, the copper lead and zinc casing of the automobile, and the germanium and silicon of semiconductors. Working with metal was Faraday's inspiration for his discovery of wireless waves. Metal is neither a thing, nor an organism, but what Deleuze and Guattari call a body without organs. Unencumbered by organic characteristics – integrity, rigidity, stability – metal operates through constant variation, composing and decomposing its body on a single material plane.

> What metal and metallurgy bring to light is a life proper to matter, a vital state of matter as such, a material vitalism that doubtless exists everywhere but is ordinarily hidden or covered or rendered unrecognizable, dissociated by the hylomorphic model. Metallurgy is the consciousness or thought of the matter flow, and metal the correlate of this consciousness. As expressed in panmetalism, metal is coextensive to the whole of matter, and the whole of matter to metallurgy. . . Not everything is metal but metal is everywhere. Metal is the conductor of all matter.[97]

The metallic is 'inorganic but alive'. Or rather, it is 'all the more alive for being inorganic ... This streaming, spiraling, zigzagging, snaking, feverish line of variation liberates a power of life.'[98] We embody this metallic nature. Calcium, iron, potassium, zinc and copper all play a vital role in the body's circulatory system, producing the electrical pulses and signals that power our heart and brain. The metals inside us, visible in the blood's red pigment, express a fundamental exteriority within. 'The iron in our blood can be traced back to the alien matter of a distant star.'[99]

The belief that the body has direct access to the cosmos permeates Chinese metaphysics. The character *ti* 體, as we have seen, contains both the concept of the corporeal body and the idea of what is Ultimately Real. In the Daoist practices of inner alchemy (or *neidan* 內丹 – *nei* 內 meaning 'inner' and *dan* 丹 meaning 'cinnabar'), the body's metallic nature is used to explore energetic possibilities.[100] According to the *Daoism Handbook*, traditions of *neidan* are 'derived from diverse sources, including classical Daoist texts, correlative cosmology, *Yijing* (Book of Changes) lore, meditational and physical disciplines of *yangsheng* 養生 (nourishing life), cosmological traditions of *waidan* 外丹 (external alchemy), medical theory, Buddhist soteriology and Confucian moral philosophy'.[101] Their concrete practices actively combine 'the various forms of Daoist self-cultivation: guiding the *qi*, visualizations, absorptive meditation, operative alchemy, and cosmological speculation'.[102] *Neidan* cosmology incorporates the classical combinations of a primal *yin–yang* force with the traditional five elements (wood, fire, earth, metal and water). It also makes use of the seasonal and religious calendars. The ancient classic the *Yijing*, which is understood esoterically as marking the timing of energetic transformation, also plays a critical role. 'The Eight Trigrams', explains Livia Kohn, 'are at the core of *neidan* thinking.'[103] In synthesising all these currents, inner alchemists develop a conception of the world based on 'interrelated patterns, calendar cycles, complex numerologies, and intricate networks of abstract symbols'.[104]

At the centre of this meditative, diagrammatic, physical and intellectual practice is a conception of the body as an alchemical laboratory. The most important zone is the *dantian* 丹田 Cinnabar or Elixir Field, which is located in the abdomen and conceptualised as the site of an 'Ocean of *Qi*'. Precisely timed rituals nourish the alchemical body with secret concoctions. 'At the height of *Yin* – at midnight of the winter solstice', adepts prepare their furnace and cauldron, brewing up elixirs made from a multitude of wild ingredients, the most important of which are mercury and lead.[105] Cinnabar, Kohn notes, which 'is found in the rivers in China is a mercury-sulfite that dissolves into its parts when heated, then reconstitutes itself back into cinnabar (i.e, reverted cinnabar). This property of reconstitution made it magical and potent in the eyes of the Chinese.'[106] Inner alchemy uses this process of reversal to guide a journey of regression and regeneration that aims to imitate the growth of gold in the Earth. The transmutation of the metallic body is an involution, a flow against the current, towards the dissolution of the cosmos and the 'reintegration of the Dao'.[107] It is this return to origins that marks the path to immortality.

This Daoist conception of the body as a laboratory in which the inner landscape 'mirrors the cosmos' was shared by the *qigong* practitioners of the 1980s, who sought to open their body to the mysterious waves.[108] Similar ideas circulated among avant-garde radio artists in Europe and America, who flourished at the turn of the twentieth century, and for whom the notion of an all-pervasive ether endured. Yet, while the ether vanished from scientific theory, there was a 'persistence of the aetheric realm in the aesthetic realm'.[109] Radio, which had already begun to infiltrate the modern world, renewed the idea of a mysterious medium in the cultural sphere. According to radio theorist Wolfgang Hagen, 'Just as modern physics jettisoned what had been the most important concept of representation for classical physics, the ether as the potential precondition of all worlds, all matter and all being, radio as a medium came into being as a reinforcement of the fantasy.'[110] The liquid-like medium of the ether was, notes Hagen, 'sustained technically precisely at the moment that it was meant to disappear'. Radio communication 'industrialized the ether at the very moment when ether no longer existed'.[111] Just as the 'wireless spectrum was being divided up and portioned out for the purposes of wireless communication', artists and researchers were exploring this singular plane at the limits of perception, attempting to harness different forms of energy and information. The 1920s experimental wireless artist Richard Kolb, for example, considered the radio a sense organ designed to tap into an all-encompassing etheric medium and its transmission of cosmic thought. Kolb, writes Hagen, inverted McLuhan's later theory that technology is an extension of the nervous system, believing that electrical waves were 'the mental current flowing through the world'.[112]

Electricity has long been associated with the magical link between microcosm and macrocosm, which posits a powerful parallel between the electrical currents animating the human body and the electric body of the Earth.[113] Throughout the eighteenth century – with Franklin's kite experiments (1752), Galvani's twitching frogs (1780) and the Voltaic pile (1799) – techno-culture had been continually reshaped by the strange, often hazily understood, natural force of electricity. After Christian Oersted's 1820s discovery of a link between electricity and magnetism, it was realised that the electrical energy found in animals and stored in batteries could travel along a wire and be used for the near-instantaneous transmission of information. With this techno-scientific transformation came a crucial conceptual shift. The Cartesian notion of a hydraulic mechanism that had governed the understanding of life gave way to a vision of the body electric. 'Ever since the eighteenth century', writes John Durham Peters,

> electricity was connected closely to the human soul and body. Medical doctors such as Galvani understood electricity to be the body's vital principle, its means of animation, a notion that inspired Mary Shelley's *Frankenstein* (1818) and several stories by Edgar Allan Poe. Since Volta, physiological research and electrical innovation went hand in hand.[114]

From the late eighteenth century, physiological thinking was dominated by an apprehension of the body as infused with electrical signals, with its intimate association between nerves and telegraphs. The analogy went beyond mere metaphor. 'The body was not like a telegraph: it was an electrical system of signals and messages.' Similarly, 'the telegraph network was not like a body: it simply exhibited a homologous structure'.[115] The machinic capacity for message transmission was viewed to be the vital feature of both the human organism and the globe. Cables and wires functioned as an intricate nervous system carrying messages to and from the networks of a planetary brain. In his chapter on the telegraph, entitled 'A Nervous System for the Earth', James Gleick quotes the dark Romantic novelist Nathaniel Hawthorne:

> It is a fact – or have I dreamt it – that, by means of electricity, the world of matter has become a great nerve, vibrating thousands of miles in a breathless point of time? Rather, the round globe is a vast head, a brain, instinct with intelligence! Or, shall we say, it is itself a thought, nothing but thought, and no longer the substance which we deemed it![116]

Media theorists who work on the early years of telecommunications have stressed the ways in which the new technology arose out of a profoundly intimate relationship between human bodies and machines.[117] Katherine Hayles describes how the complex physico-cognitive activities of telegraph operators produced a novel plane of techno-corporeal amalgamation. 'In the new regime the telegraph established, a zone of indeterminacy developed in which bodies seemed to take on some of the attributes of dematerialized information, and information seemed to take on the physicality of bodies.'[118] It had become clear that the site of electromagnetic communication extended beyond the boundaries of the technical machine.

In China, this more immanent line of intensive corporeal engagement was critical to the adaptive adoption of the telegraph. While the state concentrated on the sovereign ownership of the hardware, actual users engaged in experimental practices, which created a fusion with the machine. In his work on China's techno-linguistic history, Thomas Mullaney argues that the story of 'telegraphic sovereignty' misses something vital. What is called for, he contends, is not 'more history but *different* history'.[119] In the case of the telegraph, attention to the practices of users has been eclipsed by an overemphasis on the material ownership of poles and wires, cables and towers. Yet the telegraph, Mullaney reminds us, is critically different from railways and military arsenals. 'Unlike other infrastructural technologies with which it is so often paired', telegraphy has a 'linguistic dimension' that cannot be jettisoned or ignored.[120] The use of the telegraph depends on the dots and dashes of Morse code, which are deeply connected to the Roman alphabet and the English language.

The problem of introducing the telegraph in China, then, was not simply that it faced a suspicious – or even hostile – government, but rather that it had to find a way to accommodate a non-alphabetic linguistic system. When it arrived in China, the 'semiotic architecture of telegraphy' faced a 'writing system that it was ill-equipped to handle'.[121] Regardless of who owned the telegraph lines, Chinese users still had to rely on a hugely cumbersome process of adaptation in order to communicate.

The solution to this conundrum was the 1871 Chinese telegraph code, which worked by assigning each character a four-digit number. Users had to first register those numbers and then proceed to translate them into code. Messages in Chinese thus required a double translation. This complex mediation was even further complicated by the length of Chinese telegraph transmissions. In Morse the Arabic numerals are the longest code sequences. 'The number 5, for example, with its 5 short pulses was already 5 times longer than the shortest letter (e, with a single short pulse).'[122] Yet this was not the only disadvantage. Because Chinese had to use numbers rather than letters, its transmission in Morse was deemed by the international community to be an inherently secret language. This cryptographic layering meant that Chinese messages were more expensive, since international rules dictated that when using the telegraph for a secret language, extra tariffs were imposed.

In this intensely complex environment, Chinese users developed their own particular relationship to the emerging mediasphere. Ultimately, as Baark concludes, 'the adaptations that had to be made with respect to encoding the Chinese language, and the institutional framework for the operation of a domestic telegraph network gave rise to a distinctive – perhaps particularly Chinese – technological system'.[123] Mullaney's research reveals the ways in which the practices of Chinese IT have led to a techno-linguistic inventiveness that has placed it at the forefront of technological change.[124]

This technical innovation was not a single original creation,[125] but emerged instead from the embodied routines of telegraphers and typists who were 'quietly transforming the relationship between humans and machines not only in China but worldwide'.[126] Despite remarkable examples such as Lin Yutang's MingKwai typewriter,[127] the creativeness of this early moment in Chinese IT was not the result of the 'the mind of a single inventor', Mullaney argues, but occurred instead through a 'loose network' of 'largely anonymous' users. 'It is tempting to identify the "Chinese Charles Babbage", the "Chinese Grace Hopper", or perhaps the "Chinese Steve Jobs", [but] this would amount to little more than a parlor trick.'[128] Rather than writing a history based on the stories of a few lone geniuses, Mullaney maps the rise of 'a diffuse collective' of telegraphers, codebook publishers, language reformers, entrepreneurs and everyday practitioners. Borrowing Ingrid Richardson's term, he describes a 'technosomatic complex', in which a diffuse, decentralised and grassroots movement experimented with how to make code work more efficiently. The 'hum of activity' produced by these deeply incarnate experiments occurred 'over the course of countless millions of fleeting, nanohistorical moments'.[129] The history of the telegraph in China arose through an 'aggregration of tactile, decentralized, and largely unnoted experiences of thousands of typists and typesetters, individuals who interacted with their character racks and tray beds in embodied, nonverbal ways'.[130]

Spectrum politics suggests that wireless media is predominantly the concern of national governments and civic legislation. The rigid demarcation of frequency bands, which can be clearly divided up and policed, coincides with the desire to safeguard and protect the boundaries between states, cities, neighbourhoods, organic and inorganic entities. Yet there is an altogether different mode of engagement apposite to the coming wireless wave. Rather than insist on a precise separation of imperceptible vibrations, it focuses, drawing from a multiplicity of sources, on the body electric: nineteenth-century occultism; the ritual exercises of Daoist alchemists and *qigong* practitioners; the work of avant-garde artists and their culture of vibratory modernism; the techno-somatic experiments involved in working out the Chinese telegraph code; and the etheric philosophy of Tan Sitong, who held that electricity was a medium of connectedness between consciousness and cosmology. This approach to wirelessness does not peddle the same old dreams and fantasies. Instead, it provides us with still unknown infrastructural imaginaries based on an openness to our intensifying immersion in the waves.

Notes

1. Rudyard Kipling, 'Wireless', in *Traffics and Discoveries* (London: Macmillan, 1982), 213.
2. Ibid., 237.
3. Ibid., 239.
4. Ibid.
5. Ibid., 227.
6. Kipling here foreshadows McLuhan: the message is irrelevant, it is the fact of the new media that matters most.
7. Elizabeth Ferry and John Plotz, 'Old and New Media with Lisa Gitelman', Recall This Book, 2019, https://recallthisbook.org/2019/01/30/old-and-new-media-with-lisa-gitelman/.

8. Lisa Gitelman, *Always Already New: Media, History and the Data of Culture* (Cambridge, MA: MIT Press, 2006), 1.
9. Ferry and Plotz, 'Old and New Media with Lisa Gitelman'.
10. Shannon Mattern, 'Data Fantasies and Operational Facts: 5G's Infrastructural Epistemologies', Designing for the Unknown, 2019, https://www.youtube.com/watch?v=TvEA93Q6ETg.
11. Sue Halpern, 'The Terrifying Potential of 5G Technology', *The New Yorker*, 26 April 2019, https://www.newyorker.com/news/annals-of-communications/the-terrifying-potential-of-the-5g-network.
12. Mattern, 'Data Fantasies and Operational Facts'.
13. Ibid.
14. Halpern, 'The Terrifying Potential of 5G Technology'.
15. Mattern, 'Data Fantasies and Operational Facts'.
16. Shannon Mattern, 'Networked Dream Worlds', *Real Life Mag*, 8 July 2019, https://reallifemag.com/networked-dream-worlds/.
17. Christopher Mims, 'Cities are Saying no to 5G, Citing Health, Aesthetics – and FCC Bullying', *Wall Street Journal*, 24 August 2019, https://www.wsj.com/articles/cities-are-saying-no-to-5g-citing-health-aestheticsand-fcc-bullying-11566619391.
18. As well as Bell's offshoots AT&T and Verizon.
19. Mattern, 'Data Fantasies and Operational Facts'.
20. Jonathan Woetzel, 'China's Next Chapter: The Infrastructure and Environmental Challenge', *McKinsey&Co*, 1 June 2013, https://www.mckinsey.com/featured-insights/urbanization/chinas-next-chapter-the-infrastructure-and-environmental-challenge.
21. Jeremy Goldkorn, '5G – China's next National Project?', *SupChina*, 6 June 2019. https://supchina.com/2019/06/06/5g-chinas-next-national-project/.
22. Xinhua, 'Shanghai's 5G Network Starts Test Runs', *English.Gov.Cn*, 31 March 2019, http://english.www.gov.cn/news/top_news/2019/03/31/content_281476587521838.htm.
23. Mattern, 'Networked Dream Worlds'.
24. Mattern, 'Data Fantasies and Operational Facts'.
25. Mattern, 'Networked Dream Worlds'.
26. For information on Toffler in China, see Julian Gewirtz, 'The Futurists of Beijing: Alvin Toffler, Zhao Ziyang, and China's "New Technological Revolution"', *The Journal of Asian Studies* 78, no. 1 (2019): 115–40; Kaiser Kuo, 'An American Futurist in China: Alvin Toffler and Reform & Opening', *Sinica*, 2019, https://supchina.com/podcast/an-american-futurist-in-china-alvin-toffler-and-reform-opening/.
27. Xiao Liu, *Information Fantasies: Precarious Mediation in Postsocialist China* (Minneapolis, MN: University of Minnesota Press, 2019), 56.
28. Xiao Liu, 'Magic Waves, Extrasensory Powers, and Nonstop Instantaneity: Imagining the Digital beyond Digits', *Grey Room*, no. 63 (2016): 56.
29. David A. Palmer, 'Modernity and Millennialism in China: Qigong and the Birth of Falun Gong', *Asian Anthropology* 2, no. 1 (2003): 79.
30. Mattern, 'Data Fantasies and Operational Facts'.

31. Two years ago, 180 scientists and doctors from 36 countries appealed to the European Union against adoption until the effects of the expected increase in low-level radiation were studied.

32. See, for example, the documentary *5G APOCALYPSE – The Extinction Event*, which was released in 2019.

33. Mattern draws on the work of media theorist Mel Hogan to help make sense of the swirling narratives surrounding the 'new electromagnetic geography, a wild Hertzian terrain'. 'Bodily manifestations in reaction to RF/EMF are at best deemed highly subjective', writes Hogan, 'if not dismissed as mere hysterical overreactions.' Hogan criticises the disregard of embodied response, a familiar reaction studied by feminists who have theorised the complex intertwining of illness and the imperceptible. See, for example, Michelle Murphy, *Sick Building Syndrome and the Problem of Uncertainty: Environmental Politics, Technoscience, and Women Workers* (Durham, NC: Duke University Press, 2006). 'Our bodies are in fluid entanglements with boundaries that are increasingly imaginary', Hogan writes. 'By bringing the body to the fore, we can reconsider the utopic vision of the largely and intentionally "invisible" communication apparatuses and infrastructures that co-constitute wireless technologies.' Mel Hogan, 'Data is Airborne; Data is Inborn: The Labor of the Body in Technoecologies', *First Monday* 3, no. 3 (2018), https://firstmonday.org/ojs/index.php/fm/article/view/8285/6650.

34. Xiaoda Wang, 'Mysterious Waves', in *Science Fiction from China*, ed. Patrick Dennis Murphy and Dingbo Wu (New York: Praeger, 1989), 80.

35. Liu, 'Magic Waves, Extrasensory Powers, and Nonstop Instantaneity', 53.

36. David Wright, 'Tan Sitong and the Ether Reconsidered', *Bulletin of the School of Oriental and African Studies* 57, no. 3 (1994): 565.

37. Karl and Zarrow, 'Introduction', in Karl and Zarrow, eds, *Rethinking the 1898 Reform Period*, 10.

38. See Hao Chang, *Liang Ch'i-ch'ao and Intellectual Transition in China, 1890–1907* (Cambridge, MA: Harvard University Press, 2013).

39. Wright, 'Tan Sitong and the Ether Reconsidered', 553.

40. G. N. Cantor and Michael Jonathan Sessions Hodge, eds, *Conceptions of Ether: Studies in the History of Ether Theories, 1740–1900* (Cambridge: Cambridge University Press, 1981), 244.

41. A. Enns and S. Trower, 'Introduction', in *Vibratory Modernism*, ed. A. Enns and S. Trower (London: Palgrave Macmillan, 2013), 1.

42. Ibid.

43. Daniel J. Czitrom, *Media and the American Mind: From Morse to McLuhan* (Chapel Hill, NC: University of North Carolina Press, 1983), 9.

44. Jeffrey Sconce, *Haunted Media: Electronic Presence from Telegraphy to Television* (Durham, NC: Duke University Press, 2000), 21.

45. Ibid., 21.

46. Ibid., 63.

47. Erik Hammerstrom, *The Science of Chinese Buddhism: Early Twentieth-Century Engagements* (New York: Columbia University Press, 2015), 120.

48. See David B. Wilson, 'The Thought of Late Victorian Physicists: Oliver Lodge's Ethereal Body', *Victorian Studies* 15, no. 1 (1971): 29–48; and Peter M. Heimann, 'The Unseen Universe: Physics and the Philosophy of Nature in Victorian Britain', *The British Journal for the History of Science* 6, no. 1 (1972): 73-79

49. Wright, 'Tan Sitong and the Ether Reconsidered', 561.

50. Oliver Lodge, *The Ether of Space* (London: Harper, 1909), 146.

51. Quoted in Czitrom, *Media and the American Mind*, 66.

52. Quoted in Erik Born, 'Sparks to Signals: Literature, Science, and Wireless Technology, 1800–1930', PhD dissertation, UC Berkeley, 2016, 110, https://escholarship.org/uc/item/9qs9703w.

53. Ibid.

54. Sconce, *Haunted Media*, 76.

55. Quoted in Enns and Trower, 'Introduction', in *Vibratory Modernism*, 10.

56. Jussi Parikka, *What is Media Archaeology?* (Cambridge: Polity, 2013).

57. Henry Adams, 'From "The Education of Henry Adams"', in *Modernism: An Anthology of Sources and Documents*, ed. Vassiliki Kolocotroni, Jane Goldman and Olga Taxidou (Chicago: University of Chicago Press, 1999), 43.

58. Sconce, *Haunted Media*, 69.

59. Joe Milutis, *Ether: The Nothing That Connects Everything* (Minneapolis, MN: University of Minnesota Press, 2006), xiv.

60. Hao Chang, *Chinese Intellectuals in Crisis: Search for Order and Meaning* (Berkeley, CA: University of California Press, 1987), 88.

61. Tan Sitong, *An Exposition of Benevolence: The Jen-Hsüeh of T'an Ssu-t'ung*, trans. Sin-wai Chan (Hong Kong: The Chinese University of Hong Kong Press, 1984), 22.

62. See Adrian Bennett, *John Fryer: The Introduction of Western Science and Technology into Nineteenth-Century China* (Leiden: Brill, 2020).

63. Tan, *An Exposition of Benevolence*, 10.

64. Quoted in Richard Shek, 'Some Western Influences on T'an Ssu-t'ung's Thought', in *Reform in Nineteenth-Century China*, ed. Paul A. Cohen and John E. Schrecker (Leiden: Brill, 1979), 201–2.

65. Wright, 'Tan Sitong and the Ether Reconsidered', 555.

66. Quoted in Schäfer, 'Natural Philosophy, Physics and Metaphysics', 266.

67. Chang, *Chinese Intellectuals in Crisis*, 64.

68. Sin-wai Chan, *Buddhism in Late Ch'ing Political Thought*, vol. 8 (Hong Kong: Chinese University Press, 1985), 29.

69. Ibid., 155.

70. Hammerstrom, *The Science of Chinese Buddhism*, 120.

71. Tan, *An Exposition of Benevolence*, 77.

72. Chan, *Buddhism in Late Ch'ing Political Thought*, 78.

73. Hammerstrom, *The Science of Chinese Buddhism*, 95.

74. Stephen R. Platt, *Provincial Patriots: The Hunanese and Modern China* (Cambridge, MA: Harvard University Press, 2007), 222.

75. Ibid., 69.

76. As Viren Murthy suggests, *yitai* has a parallel in Spinoza's idea of a single substance as outlined in the *Ethics*. See Viren Murthy, 'Ontological Optimism, Cosmological Confusion, and Unstable Evolution: Tan Sitong's Renxue and Zhang Taiyan's Response', in Viren Murthy and Axel Schneider, *The Challenge of Linear Time: Nationhood and the Politics of History in East Asia* (Leiden: Brill, 2013), 49–82.

77. Quoted in Schäfer, 'Natural Philosophy, Physics and Metaphysics', 268.

78. Galison, *Einstein's Clocks, Poincaré's Maps*, 15.

79. Milutis, *Ether*.

80. Galison, *Einstein's Clocks, Poincaré's Maps*, 231.

81. Ibid.

82. Gabrys, 'Atmospheres of Communication', 47.

83. Quoted in Zita Joyce, 'Creating Order in the Ceaseless Flow: The Discursive Constitution of the Radio Spectrum', PhD thesis, ResearchSpace@Auckland, 2008, 29, https://researchspace.auckland.ac.nz/handle/2292/5619.

84. Quoted in Born, 'Sparks to Signals', 129.

85. Joyce, 'Creating Order in the Ceaseless Flow', 13.

86. Born, 'Sparks to Signals', 129.

87. Susan J. Douglas, *Inventing American Broadcasting, 1899–1922* (Baltimore, MD: Johns Hopkins University Press, 1989), 131.

88. Ibid., 101.

89. Born, 'Sparks to Signals', 15.

90. Joyce, 'Creating Order in the Ceaseless Flow', 33.

91. Ibid., 36.

92. Ibid., 39.

93. Ibid., 6.

94. Born, 'Sparks to Signals', 150.

95. Ibid., 136.

96. Deleuze and Guattari, *A Thousand Plateaus*, 411.

97. Ibid.

98. Ibid., 499.

99. Greenspan and Livingston, *Future Mutation*.

100. *Neidan* practice became widespread in the Song Dynasty and went in decline in the Tang after a number of emperors died of elixir poisoning. In his book *Daoist Modern*, Xun Liu documents the work of modern practitioner Chen Yingning 陳攖寧 (1880–1969), who led a revival of *neidan* in early twentieth-century Shanghai. Xun Liu, *Daoist Modern: Innovation, Lay Practice, and the Community of Inner Alchemy in Republican Shanghai* (Cambridge, MA: Harvard University Asia Center, 2009).

101. Fabrizion Pregadio and Lowell Skar, 'Inner Alchemy (Neidan)', in *Daoism Handbook*, ed. Livia Kohn (Leiden: Brill, 2000), 464.

102. Livia Kohn, 'Modes of Mutation: Restructuring the Energy Body', in *Internal Alchemy: Self, Society and the Quest for Immortality*, ed. Livia Kohn and Robin Wang (Magdalena, NM: Three Pines Press, 2009), 1.
103. Ibid., 16.
104. Ibid., 13.
105. Ibid., 17. Mercury is a highly toxic substance that causes delusions and brain damage in small doses. In large doses it is fatal. Daoists were well aware that the materials they were working with were poisonous.
106. Michael Winn, 'Daoist Internal Alchemy in the West', in Kohn and Wang, eds, *Internal Alchemy*, 182.
107. Pregadio and Skar, 'Inner Alchemy (Neidan)', 766.
108. Sara Elaine Neswald. 'Internal Landscape', in Kohn and Wang, eds, *Internal Alchemy*, 30.
109. Gitelman, *Always Already New*.
110. Wolfgang Hagen, 'On the Place of Radio', *Recycling the Future*, Vienna, 1997, http://www.kunstradio.at/FUTURE/RTF/SYMPOSIUM/LECTURES/HAGEN/hagen-txt-e.html.
111. Wolfgang Hagen, 'Beyond Radio', *kunstradio*, 1993, http://www.kunstradio.at/THEORIE/HAGEN/hagen_e.html.
112. Hagen, 'On the Place of Radio'.
113. For more on this connection, see Laura Otis, *Networking: Communicating with Bodies and Machines in the Nineteenth Century* (Ann Arbor, MI: University of Michigan Press, 2001).
114. Peters, 'Technology and Ideology', 142.
115. Ibid.
116. Quoted in Gleick, *Information: A History, a Theory, a Flood*, 131.
117. For example, in 'The Digital Body: Telegraphy as Discourse Network', Kate Maddalena and Jeremy Packer analyse the formation of the US Signal Corps during the American Civil War in order to illustrate the ways in which 'media technology required the human in order to constitute itself'. In the 'flag-based system of binary telecommunication', they write, the digital body was transformed into part of the medium of transmission. Kate Maddalena and Jeremy Packer, 'The Digital Body: Telegraphy as Discourse Network', *Theory, Culture & Society* 32, no. 1 (2015): 93–117.
118. Hayles, *How We Think*, 148.
119. Mullaney, 'Semiotic Sovereignty', 156.
120. Ibid.
121. Ibid., 153.
122. Ibid., 165.
123. Baark, *Lightning Wires*, 10.
124. For Chinese techno-linguistic innovation in the field of AI, see Mara Hvistendahl, 'How a Chinese AI Giant Made Chatting – and Surveillance – Easy', *Wired*, 2020, https://www.wired.com/story/iflytek-china-ai-giant-voice-chatting-surveillance/.

125. In *Kingdom of Characters: The Language Revolution That Made China Modern* (New York: Riverhead Books, 2022), Jing Tsu tells the story of the Chinese telegraph code by focusing on a few central characters.
126. Mullaney, *The Chinese Typewriter*, 316.
127. For details, see Mullaney, *The Chinese Typewriter*; Tsu, *Kingdom of Characters*.
128. Mullaney, *The Chinese Typewriter*, 316.
129. Ibid., 290.
130. Ibid.

Chapter 5

Immersion: The Sentient City

In the Chinese calendar, 2020 coincided with *Geng Zi* (庚子), the Year of the Metal Rat. *Geng* (庚) is associated with metal, while *Zi* (子) corresponds to the water rat. The conjunction of elements – in which the heaviness of metal is submerged in the sea – causes tidal waves, powerful enough to wash away all that had previously seemed stable. The rat is the first animal of the Chinese zodiac, so *Geng Zi* is positioned at the beginning of one cycle and at the end of another. It is a time of transition often marked by danger, chaos and upheaval. In February 2020, a few days into the lockdowns that ushered in the new year, pasted notices with QR codes began to appear everywhere in Shanghai. They were the first signs of a QR code health registration scheme (*jiankang ma* 健康碼) that was eventually used as a vital tool for population management during the coronavirus pandemic. Register and you were given a coloured QR code, based on mobile phone signal tracking, which could be scanned before entering subways, shopping malls, coffee shops, nightclubs and tourist sites. A green code meant access to the city was open, yellow meant movement was much more circumscribed. With a red code the metropolis was locked, and there was no choice but to stay inside. Ubiquitous QR codes are not new to China's urban landscape. In Shanghai, when your phone runs out of battery, you're stuck. Without the capacity to scan a QR code you cannot get a bike, you cannot catch a cab, you cannot pay for anything. More than texting or talking, watching, listening or wayfinding, today, in China at least, QR codes are the mobile phone's killer app.

QR codes were developed in 1994 by a Japanese company called Denso Wave, which specialised in barcode readers. Denso Wave was responding to user requests for a system that was data rich enough to encode not only alphanumerics but Kanji and Kana script as well.

Like many of the hacks that have been crucial to the history of Chinese IT,[1] QR codes offer a simple, low-tech solution. They consist of square, black and white pictographs whose vertical and horizontal axis can hold 100 times more information than a barcode. Barcodes, which encode information on only one axis, are usually limited to no more than 20 characters. QR codes are two-dimensional – readers scan up and down as well as across. This increased complexity allows them to encode over 4,000 characters. In expanding beyond alphanumerics into a system that can include Chinese characters as well, the codes (as a linear string of letters and numbers) went from being signs that humans could, if not read then at least comprehend, to becoming an image that appears to us as indecipherably abstract. Unlike linear one-dimensional barcodes, QR codes are intelligible only to machines.

QR codes were initially used for tracking components in the car-manufacturing sector. They quickly spread to other industries across East Asia. The codes are particularly useful for providing an easy way to trace highly sensitive items such as food and pharmaceuticals. In China mobile phones equipped with cameras that operated as QR code readers entered the market in 2010. Soon after, the urban landscape was utterly transformed. In the twenty-first-century Chinese metropolis, scanning QR codes has become part of the critical infrastructure. By embedding data – including Internet addresses – directly into the physical environment, QR codes became the semiotic of the wireless city, transforming a previously inert physical landscape into the nodes of an all-pervasive locative media. They operate as a bridge between the physical and the virtual, the digital and the analogue, allowing spaces, images and objects to immediately connect with the unseen wireless atmosphere. QR codes act as portals, connecting offline and online worlds (O2O). In China by 2020, the urban environment was teeming with such portals.

In Shanghai they became ubiquitous around 2015 when they were used by shared bikes which suddenly flooded the streets. This experiment in public transport paved the way for a more widespread QR-code-based sharing economy that quickly grew to include small-scale popular items such as umbrellas and mobile phone chargers. QR codes, the simple black and white images which are cheap and easy to produce, soon came to permeate the urban landscape, providing information on everything from gallery exhibits to heritage architecture. 'Scanning a QR code can bring you to a website, or pull up an app, or connect you to a person's social media profile', writes technology analyst Mara Hvistendahl. 'Codes started showing up on graves (scan to learn more about the deceased) and the shirts of waiters (scan to tip). Beggars printed out QR codes and set them out on the street.'[2] People use them to track their pets. As a channel for micropayments, QR codes are found everywhere, from temples asking for donations to wedding parties collecting gifts. They are the preferred mode of payment in stores, restaurants, wet markets and street food stands. In addition to daily purchases, the ubiquitous black and white pictograms are used to pay utility bills, conduct business transactions and exchange money between family and friends.

By crossing over into the realm of digital money, QR codes have become vastly more successful in China than almost anywhere in the world. There are a cluster of interconnected reasons. First, China remained primarily a cash-based economy well into the start of the twenty-first century. Even after decades of enormous economic growth, credit cards were difficult to obtain and not widely used. 'During the past 30 years, China has grown to become the world's second largest economy without much of a functioning credit system at all', Hsvistendahl noted in her 2017 article for *Wired*. 'The People's Bank of China, the country's central banking regulator, maintains records on millions of consumers, but they often contain little or no information. Until recently, it was difficult to get a credit card with any bank other than your own.' Another factor favouring the spread of QR codes was the extremely rapid adoption of smartphones, driven in part by *shanzhai* manufacturing, which flooded low-end markets with cheap knock-offs that almost everyone in the growing cityscapes of Asia, Africa and Latin America could afford.

It was under these conditions that China's 'two QR driven super apps', Wechat and Alipay, really took hold. In 2004, ten years after QR codes were invented, Alibaba launched an escrow-based finance system now known as Ant Financial or Alipay. In China's low-trust society, technologically driven security proved immensely popular. In 2011 the company launched Alipay as a mobile payment app, with a built-in QR code system at its core. In the first year alone, mobile payments on Alipay reached 70 billion dollars.[3] Soon after, Ant Financial became the highest valued Fintech company in the world. 2011 was also the year that China's other massive telecom company, Tencent, released its messaging service Wechat. Initially, the built-in QR code scanners gave Wechat users an easy way to connect with new contacts. Two years later, in 2013, Wechat introduced its own mobile-payment system. By 2018, with a transaction volume of 5.8 trillion dollars, China had become the largest and fastest-growing market for mobile payments in the world.[4]

QR codes also play a crucial role in the vast economy of home delivery. Over the last decade, the markets and street stalls of downtown Shanghai have largely disappeared. Migrants, who once served as vendors, now traverse the city on electric scooters, working as the delivery system for an enormous population that now shops on their phones. Urban dwellers use online apps to order groceries and appliances, fancy meals and private chefs, coffee, bubble tea and street snacks. This consumer behaviour – which was enormously accelerated by the coronavirus pandemic – is built on a complex logistical machinic infrastructure, which underlies the emergence of a spectral, animated and increasingly sentient city that surfaces from the intensification of wireless waves.

The body of the city is now determined by unseen electromagnetic frequencies. Already by 2014, Chongqing, by some measures the most populous metropolis in the world, made international headlines by dividing up its pavements with white paint, and implementing the world's first mobile-phone-only pedestrian lane. Now those residents who want to travel unimpeded, or engage with their surroundings, do not have to concern themselves with the obstacle constituted by those who are absorbed elsewhere. The painted lines on the Chongqing pavements vividly mark a passage towards an intensive urban environment. 'When it comes to cities we should learn to think topographically rather than geographically', wrote Vilém Flusser presciently in his evocatively titled essay 'The City as Wave-Trough in the Image-Flood'. The city should be seen 'not as a geographical place, but rather as a flection in a field'.[5] In *Understanding Media*, Marshall McLuhan expresses the same point by quoting Cab Calloway: 'When I walk down Eighth Avenue, man, I see rhythms, I don't see downtown.'[6] Chongqing's mobile-phone-only walking lane explicitly recognises the increasing importance of the urban electromagnetic atmosphere. As wireless media becomes ubiquitous, and life migrates online, the physical world of concrete objects, visible buildings, the horizontal networks of streets and the straight lines of highways and high-rises intermingle with invisible waves accessible only through the devices that we carry with us and that we can no longer live without. Saturated in the vibrations of the radiosphere, the city – the most artificial of environments – becomes increasingly submerged in an earthly, cosmic force that is highly technological, but at the same time wholly natural.

Sentient City versus Smart City

The 'sentient city' emerges out of this immersive electromagnetic environment. The concept of the 'sentient city' is best understood in contrast to the more familiar idea of the 'smart city', which is based on a planned and centralised notion of urban technological governance. A 'smart city' implicitly posits a transcendent subject position from which the metropolis below may be disciplined and surveilled.

It thereby conforms to the *ti–yong* split and the hierarchy that this implies. Urban China is undoubtedly subject to a strict regime of predictive surveillance and top-down control. During the coronavirus pandemic, this all-pervasive, tech-driven, centralised mode of governance was both deepened and transformed. With the QR code health registration system, which was used as an epidemiological tool to keep the city functioning amid the outbreak, urban dwellers were themselves absorbed into the city's sensing system. With everyone carrying a cellular device, 'the flow of each person can be clearly seen', said celebrated epidemiologist Li Lanjuan. 'We should make full use' of such new technologies, she advised, 'to find the source of infection and contain the source of infection'.[7] Shanghai, a cosmopolitan city of 25 million people, meticulously adopted this strategy and was astonishingly well protected. As the pandemic wore on, a multitude of QR code sensing devices were absorbed into almost all aspects of public life.

The sentient city exists underneath or alongside these forms of biological surveillance and autocratic capture. Instead of being rooted in specific nodes of centralised authority, it emerges, bottom-up, from the distributed, cognitive technologies that are embedded throughout the urban landscape. It forms itself as a new mode of artificial intelligence that cannot be completely captured by a centralised brain, dwelling instead in a peripheral neurology, or technological unconscious, which no transcendent authority can fully control or comprehend. Following Benjamin Bratton, we might conceptualise this 'sensing layer' of the metropolis as an 'artificial skin', which increasingly enables the city to perceive, model and gain knowledge of itself. Urban surfaces of the city can now sense their own environment 'who, what, where, when, how?'. They function as a mode of distributed Artificial Intelligence that depends less on 'AI in a Petri dish' than 'AI in the wild'.[8] Abiding in a myriad of techno-corporeal practices that involve non-human, sub-perceptual, micro-temporal media, the wireless sentient city intimately engages with the imperceptible, immersive environment of electromagnetic waves.

Alien Intelligence

The sentience of the city that emerges here is profoundly alien and unknown. As twenty-first-century media submerges us in the ambient electromagnetic din of cities there is a haunting sense that our intimate incarnate involvement with the elusive electromagnetic atmosphere enables access to a cosmic plane that is beyond the confines of human perception or understanding. In the words of Jennifer Gabrys, 'When locating ourselves electromagnetically, we seem to inhabit some ghostly geography.'[9] Wireless media operate on a plane of technical communication which humans cannot directly apprehend. Mobile phones, sensors and the Internet are creating an environment that is profoundly alien. There is a machinic level, writes Mark Hansen, describing the non-human nature of twenty-first-century media, that is no longer attuned to human perception, but instead 'seems to take place outside the domain of experience'. The devices that we carry with us, which are ever more embedded in the things that we wear and the spaces we inhabit, traffic among themselves in a realm we cannot reach.

> Well before we even begin to use our smartphones in active and passive ways the physical devices we carry with us interface in complex ways with cell towers and satellite networks; and preparatory to using our digital devices or our laptops to communicate or to acquire information, the latter engage in complex connections with wireless routers and network hosts.[10]

This exteriority of the technological plane has been with us for some time. Electromagnetic communication, as John Durham Peters contends, brought new ways of knowing from the start.

> Artificial intelligence is much older than the computer as we know it. Telegraphy inaugurates a world of lively writing-machines, alertly watching the world, tracing weather, stars, and stock market in scribbles, patterns and languages – and in quantities and speeds – not directly designed for human intelligibility. The order of the universe is not necessarily located in human intelligence.[11]

The trajectory of modernity, then, brings us ever closer to media whose fundamental operations occur in a technosphere of their own, beyond the reach of human consciousness, attention and sensory perception. 'As human agents', notes Katherine Hayles,

> we naturally tend to foreground our own activities, but in fact human–human communication is becoming a smaller and smaller bandwidth compared to total machine–machine communication. There are all the invisible information flows surging around us of which we are unconscious and unaware but that are nevertheless becoming increasingly important in the technical infrastructural and larger picture of what is going on.[12]

One of the most visceral depictions of the profound alterity of machines occurs in a discarded ending of the film *Ex Machina*

(2014). In this, one of cinema's most fabled unseen scenes, Ava the robot perceives humans as a machine would. Having hacked the emotional core of one of the men complicit in her imprisonment, Ava passes the Turing Test, tricking her way to freedom. As she escapes in a helicopter, she looks over to converse with the pilot. In the unused, extra ending, the camera cuts to Ava's point of view. What she hears and sees is utterly inhuman. Ava perceives her interlocutor as nothing but signal and noise. The machinic world that we are continually interacting with may be of our own making, but it has escaped our understanding and control. We comprehend our machines in a way that is not at all similar to the way in which our machines comprehend us.

To rigorously account for this artificiality requires, as Bratton has argued, a 'renewed Copernican turn'.[13] Machine vision, the latest mutation in ocular evolution, belongs to an altogether different kind of intelligence. To imagine its inner workings is to try and grasp another way of looking – to see how the other sees. How, asks Bratton provocatively, 'do we look as objects of perception from the position of the machines with which we co-occupy the world? Seeing ourselves through the "eyes" of this machinic Other', involves 'a kind of disenchantment' as we realise that we are 'just stuff in the world for "distributed machine cognition" to look at and to make sense of'.[14] Bratton likens this 'uncomfortable recognition in the machine's mirror' to a 'reverse uncanny valley'. 'Instead of being creeped out at how slightly inhuman the creature in the image appears, we are creeped out at how un-human we ourselves look through the creature's eyes.'[15] In the same spirit, we may ask: how do QR codes, the pictographic language of the sentient city, appear to the myriad machines that read them?

Non-human Time

The inherent exteriority of the machinic domain is most starkly apparent through a consideration of time. Rather than conform to the scale and rhythms of human consciousness, electronic media – which have always been essential to the futurism at the heart of modernity – are now productive of a temporality that is beyond, underneath or outside the perceptual scale of human life. The otherness of the wireless atmosphere is ultimately a result of the fact that it exceeds the time range of human experience. We are blocked from the wireless mediasphere because we are locked in a particular time scale, separated from our most intimate technologies by frequencies we cannot perceive.

John Durham Peters writes that 'Modernity is marked by an interest in small units of time'.[16] The nineteenth and twentieth centuries were fascinated by the discovery of the micro-units used in biological perception: the temporal acuity of the retina; the faster time-processing of the ear; the high-firing speeds of neurons. This fine-grained temporality was being unveiled by new technology. The electro-telegraph was the forerunner of this temporal transformation. Peters points to a time in the mid-1800s when the circle around philosopher-scientist Hermann van Helmholtz used telegraphy to track temporality's minute intervals in a project that 'Helmholtz aptly called "the microscopy of time"'.[17] In addition to creating a standard global temporality, then, electronic media also provided the technical and imaginative means to measure both extremely fast speeds and extremely small intervals.[18] Clocks, which are so machinically accurate that they can run for the entire age of the universe without gaining or losing a second, are designed to precisely measure the tiniest of temporal events. 'Time has been redefined as an ecological niche to be filled down to the microsecond, nanosecond, and picosecond.'[19]

This shift away from the human consciousness of time was further intensified by the multitude of wireless devices that tapped the temporal rhythms of the electromagnetic sphere. Wireless objects are connected to the frequencies of a spectrum within which we are immersed but which, nevertheless, exceeds the range of vibrations that we have the capacity to perceive. While sonic frequencies range from 20 to 20,000 hertz and brain waves operate at frequencies between 12.5 to 30 hertz, radio waves are found at frequencies ranging from 3 kilohertz to 300 gigahertz. Electromagnetic waves thus operate in an atmospheric temporality that is decidedly non-anthropomorphic.

'With the study of electricity and electromagnetism onwards', Hansen argues, media have operated 'predominantly at a micro-temporal scale vastly exceeding the grasp of human perceptual consciousness'.[20] There is an 'unconscious of contemporary sensory experience', which is constituted by the 'imperceptible information flow beneath the threshold of human attention and awareness'. We have absolutely no '"natural" capacity to act within, or even to access, the microtemporal time frames involved'.[21] The time scale of our existence bars us from the frequencies of the technologies we use. This alien temporality is particularly acute with AI. It is evident, for example, in high-frequency trading, which operates in fractions of seconds in order to make use of price differentials that are inaccessible to the slowness of corporeal time. It manifests as well in the superhuman capacities of a machine such as AlphaGo, which can now beat any Go master through a process of training that involves playing millions of games with itself every day. Artificial intelligence is arguably best understood as Artificial Time.[22]

The imperceptibility of this strange new temporality is now embedded as a transcendental layer into the urban landscape. The abstract infrastructure of wireless media is productive of a mode of time within which we live but whose 'frequencies we cannot directly apprehend'.[23] Under these conditions, media develops a 'time constituting power', rigorously explored by the 'chronopoetics' of media theorist Wolfgang Ernst. For Ernst, the 'chief subject of media studies' is not semiotics or cultural signs. Rather, he writes, it is the electrophysical signal itself considered as 'genuine time events'.[24] Media, which 'always take place in the temporal dimension',[25] 'work directly on physical signals prior to their conversion into something that humans can comprehend'.[26] Implicit in this 'time critical approach' is the philosophical contention that electronic media are themselves productive of a temporality which exceeds the phenomenal time rooted in the human perceptual apparatus. Machine time and human time do not occur in the same register. In a world subsumed by the non-human frequencies of vibratory media, time has broken its bond with lived experience. The condition of wirelessness involves a fundamental split which cuts us off from the imperceptible abstract infrastructure that produces the time within which we live. Twenty-first-century media 'profoundly affects the economy of experience such that our (human) experience becomes increasingly conditioned and impacted by processes that we have no direct experience of, no direct mode of access to, and no potential awareness of'.[27] The alien frequencies of our immersive media environment operate 'at a more primordial level than any perceptual or mental integrations that might subsequently emerge from [them]'.[28] Technics, writes Hansen, 'impact time at the level of its absolute constitution – which is to say prior to any experience in time'.[29] Today, there is 'no time-in-itself'. Rather, time emerges through a myriad of machinic practices and their concrete, heterogeneous processes of temporalisation. The sentient city is immersed in waves beyond our perceptual reach, which now condition our experience by determining our situation in time.

Transcendental Materialism

This idea that our contemporary mediasphere does not conform to the interior temporality of experience, but rather conditions the time within which we live, recalls one of the fundamental distinctions of Immanuel Kant's transcendental philosophy. Kant distinguished between the empirical, which exists always and forever in time, and the transcendental, which remains outside or independent of human experience and its strict temporal enclosure. In the *Critique of Pure Reason*, time is defined as the 'form of inner sense'. It is the ground of interiority, providing the underlying structure of all our states of mind. Abstract and interiorised, time is given enormous new powers. It conditions the very experience of thought, including our awareness of the outer perceptions in space and the consciousness we have of ourselves. 'Everything which belongs to inner determinations', Kant writes, 'is represented in relation to time.' As the inescapable form of thought and sensation, time in the critical system gains control over the whole of experience. Everything we see, think, feel, hear and know has already been given a speed, an order and a rhythm in time.

In his lectures on Kant, Gilles Deleuze contends that 'all of the creations and novelties' of Kant's 'thinking machine' turn on this discovery of an entirely new 'modern consciousness of time'.[30] By making time the form of inner sense, Kant freed time from its subordination to movement, enabling what Deleuze calls 'the first great reversal'. For Kant, the revolutions of the stars, the swing of a pendulum, the sand in an hourglass, all occur in time and as such fall outside the problematic of critique. In the *Critique of Pure Reason*, time explains the possibility of empirical movement, but movement is not time. 'The concept of alteration and with it the concept of motion, as alteration of place', he writes, 'is possible only through and in the representation of time.'[31] No longer determined by the circular revolutions of the planets or the cycles of the seasons, time is liberated from its dependence on the movement of external bodies. With the revolution of philosophical critique, time ceases to be the measure of motion. Instead, it is the relation of time to motion itself that revolves. 'Time is no longer related to the movement which it measures', explains Deleuze, 'but movement is related to the time which conditions it.'[32] To articulate this topological twist, Deleuze calls upon Hamlet's phrase, the 'time is out of joint'. In his lecture on Kant he speaks of this as a temporal uncoiling:

> Time is no longer coiled up in such a way that it is subordinated to the measure of something other than itself, such as, for example, astronomical movement. Everything happens as if, having been coiled up so as to measure the passage of celestial bodies, time unrolls itself like a sort of serpent, it shakes off all subordination to a movement or a nature, it becomes time in itself for itself, it becomes pure and empty time. It measures nothing anymore. Time has taken on its own excessiveness. It is out of its joints, which is to say its subordination to nature; it's now nature which is subordinated to it.[33]

In critical philosophy, the transcendental production of time takes on a kind of immanent exteriority. It occurs on an external plane that generates the temporality within which the empirical world unfolds. Kant famously held that the *a priori* synthetic structures, which generate the transcendental, were located in the mind of the modern subject. This central position given to the knowing subject is what is meant by Kant's 'Copernican revolution'. Critique tells us that it is not our cognition that conforms to the objects in the world, but rather it is the objects we encounter that conform to our cognition. Understood in this manner, it can appear that transcendental idealism reinforces the primacy of the conscious subject that was first discovered by Descartes. In the *World as Will and Representation*, Schopenhauer masterfully articulates the certainty of the Cartesian subject and its foundational role in modern Western thought:

> By his taking *cogito ergo sum* as the only thing certain, and provisionally regarding the existence of the world as problematical, the essential and only correct starting point, and at the same time the true point of support, of all philosophy was really found. This point, indeed, is essentially and of necessity the *subjective, our own consciousness*. For this alone is that which is immediate; everything else, be it what it may, is first mediated by consciousness, and therefore dependent on it. It is thus rightly considered that the philosophy of the moderns starts with Descartes as its father.[34]

The *Critique of Pure Reason* appears to follow this tradition, by arguing – in an apparently true Cartesian fashion – that the external world of representations is generated by the productive powers of human subjectivity. Yet there is a doubleness inherent in the Kantian subject, which differs radically from the certainty of the unified *cogito*. This splitting, as will be elaborated below, becomes critical for the Chinese Kantian philosopher Mou Zongsan and his particular elaboration of a vibrational or wave philosophy.

In Descartes, the security of self-consciousness depends on the identity that exists between the knowledge of the 'I think' and the temporally determined, conscious entity that I am. Kant, on the other hand, posits a radical break, an absolute rupture between the synthetic powers of the 'transcendental I' and the receptive nature of the empirical ego. In this Kant leans towards a Buddhist metaphysics that Mou will unravel and employ. The proposition 'I think' or 'I exist thinking', writes Kant, 'is an empirical proposition'.[35] We know ourselves only through the pre-existing categories of the mind. With this statement, Kant severs conscious experience from the transcendental conditions of its own production. Interiority is riddled with the difference between the 'spontaneous' activity of the synthetic *a priori*, which characterises the subject of the Copernican revolution, and the *empirical* knowledge of what goes on in our mind. According to the 'paradox of inner sense', we are only conscious of ourselves after we have been worked over by that part of ourselves that we can never know. The Kantian subject, then, is no longer transparent to itself, but is rather continually affected by something that it cannot reach. We know ourselves, writes Kant, questioning the very core of the Cartesian formula, 'only as we appear to ourselves, not as we are in ourselves. For we intuit ourselves only as we are inwardly affected, and this would seem to be contradictory since we would then have to be in a passive relation [of active affection] to ourselves.'[36]

There is then, for Kant, a radical difference between what we are and what we know ourselves to be. Transcendental apperception is exterior to experience and, therefore, never the object of direct awareness. The Ego, as consciousness of inner sense, admits knowledge, whereas the I, for Kant, can never be known (but is always presupposed in knowing). Empty of all content, stripped of its ties to substance or personality, the 'Transcendental I', which is necessary to explain the very possibility of experience, can be thought but never known. 'How can man think what he does not think, inhabit by a mute occupation something that eludes him, animate with a kind of frozen movement, that figure of himself that takes the form of a stubborn exteriority?', asks Foucault, pondering the mysteries of what he calls this 'empirico-transcendental doublet'.[37] Slavoj Žižek explores the same theme in *Tarrying with the Negative* when he writes of *Blade Runner* as a Kantian film. 'In *Blade Runner* Deckard, after learning that Rachael is a replicant who (mis)perceives herself as human, asks in astonishment: "How can it not know what it is?" We can see, now, how more than two hundred years ago, Kant's philosophy outlined an answer to this enigma.'[38] Deleuze, in his lectures on Kant, turns to Rimbaud's formulation to find expression for this fractured doubleness of the subject: 'It is false to say: I think. One should say: one thinks me. . . I is another.'

Wireless media is best thought of as an abstract or *transcendental* infrastructure. The experience of a perceiving, thinking, knowing subject is conditioned by a growing intimacy with the non-human frequencies of technical machines. In this account, *a priori* structures are not, as Kant believed, confined to the internal structures of human reason. Rather, the transcendental is embedded in the material world, virtually present in our embodied engagement with the ever-intensifying electromagnetic mediasphere. Towards the beginning of their two-volume work *Capitalism and Schizophrenia*, Deleuze and

Guattari evoke the name of transcendental philosophy to call for a revolution – 'this time materialist' – which is aimed at transforming critical thought.[39] Transcendental materialism subtracts the illusion of transcendence (which remains as a relic in Kant's writing) in favour of a philosophy based on immanence in which abstract production is not located solely inside the mind. The productive conditions of experience, which occur in the exteriority realm of the transcendental I, are created through material processes, not epistemological ones.

Wirelessness is built from an electromagnetic body that constitutes a transcendental plane of production. Wireless media tap into a force – both technological and cosmological – that our experiencing empirical self cannot reach. Our participation in the techno-corporeal practices of the sentient city, however, allows for contact with the time-waves that condition us, but that we cannot perceive. To conceptualise this connection, we will turn to the work of Mou Zongsan, a student of Xiong Shili, and one of China's most important modern philosophers. Mou synthesises Kantian, Buddhist and New Confucian thought, interpreting the transcendental split between that which appears and that which is productive of appearance in accordance with the non-separation between the hidden realm of Ultimate Reality (*ti*) and the manifest world of empirical phenomena (*yong*). His aim, in the end, like the cosmo-ontology of Xiong Shili, is to cultivate apprehension of the waves.

Mou Zongsan 牟宗三

Mou Zongsan's 32-volume collected writings demonstrate the work of a remarkable scholar. Mou was 'one of the most important Chinese philosophers of the past century', writes Sébastian Billioud in his book *Thinking Through Confucian Modernity*. Jason Clower, an interpreter and translator of Mou, concurs. 'If twentieth-century China produced a philosopher of the first rank it was Mou Zongsan.'[40] Mou belonged to a critical moment of intellectual intersection and cross-cultural engagement and worked hard to grapple with the intellectual currents of the modern West. In order to fully comprehend the *Principia Mathematica*, for example, he meticulously calculated the proofs himself. He also studied and wrote on logic, Whitehead and Wittgenstein, among others.

In addition to his intensive research into Western philosophy, Mou was profoundly shaped by his studies of Daoism, Confucianism and, especially, Buddhism. In this he was deeply influenced by his teacher Xiong Shili. Mou first met Xiong as a student in 1932, when he was

24 years old. On this occasion Mou reports being given a copy of *New Treatise on Consciousness Only*, which he 'devoured in one night'. In his *Autobiography at Fifty* Mou describes his relationship with his great teacher. 'Knowing Mr Xiong marked a turning point in my life', he writes.[41] 'For the first time, I felt that I had met an authentic person, and for the first time I sensed the meaning of knowledge and life.'[42] Mou left China in 1949 and was never able to meet with Xiong again. Yet his deep devotion to his teacher remained throughout his life. Xiong's thundering 'roar revised the Chinese intellectual tradition', Mou proclaimed.[43] It was only he that was 'ready to roar like a lion in a chaotic, dark age'.[44]

Like Xiong, Mou saw himself engaged in a project of cultural revival. The only real hope of confronting modernity, he believed, was in a renewal of the Way. Mou acknowledged the West's dominance in science, technology and politics, but was, nevertheless, adamant that Chinese philosophy had an important contribution to make to the modern world. 'Nowadays', he wrote, 'we cannot rely on the West for real philosophy; we have to come back to ourselves and understand Chinese philosophy.'[45]

Mou's own philosophical project was profoundly shaped by his lifelong engagement with Immanuel Kant. He believed that transcendental thought was of fundamental importance and considered Kant to be 'the climax of Western philosophy'. 'I believe', he wrote, 'that for the work of absorbing Western culture, the best medium is Kant.'[46] Mou translated all three of Kant's *Critiques* into classical Chinese. This was an enormously complex exercise that required that he reformat, and thereby modernise, Confucian, Daoist and, most importantly, Buddhist terminology.[47]

Mou roots his response to the Kantian system in a particular Chinese philosophical lineage, which he helps construct. His most crucial contribution revolves around the possibility of 'intellectual intuition' (智的直覺 *zhi de zhijue*), which Kant's own formulation of critical philosophy strictly forbids. 'Kant's greatest merit', writes Schopenhauer in his *Critique of Kantian Philosophy*, 'is the distinction of the phenomenon from the thing in itself, based upon the proof that between things and us there still always stands the intellect, so that they cannot be known as they may be in themselves.'[48] For Kant, we are confined only to the sensible intuition of phenomena. We know things only as they appear to us. God alone has the possibility of 'intellectual intuition', which gives access to the world beyond appearances, to 'noumena' or 'things as they are in themselves'. Mou Zongsan's ambitious 'project of surpassing Kant' targets this most basic principle.[49] 'Mou thinks that Kant had almost everything right', Clower contends, 'except his most fundamental orienting premise, that human beings lack intellectual intuition.'[50] Mou believed that Chinese thought had a unique capacity to explore this very possibility. Mou, writes Billioud, considers the concept of intellectual intuition as 'the epitome of a Chinese spiritual tradition that emphasizes the possibility of a direct knowledge of the ultimate reality of the universe'.[51] To quote one of Mou's best-known pronouncements: 'All Chinese people affirm, whether Confucian, Daoist, or Buddhist, that humans have this "intellectual intuition." Take that away and all Chinese philosophy collapses into nothing more than a crazy dream.'[52]

Kantian critique, in refusing to allow for intellectual intuition, famously sought to limit reason in order to leave room for faith. Driven by this religious injunction, Kant gives a negative account of intellectual intuition as that which lies beyond the capacity of the knowing subject, outside the legitimate domain of reason. For Mou, however, the limits that critique imposed were not universal, as Kant had presumed, but are instead the sign and product of an inherently Western bias. 'Kant wants to check the claims of human reason in order to understand what lies beyond its reach and, to borrow one of his preferred metaphors, its jurisdiction', writes Stephan Schmidt, comparing the two philosophers. 'Mou Zongsan affirms this concept of critique, but aims to restrict it to the cultural context out of which it came, namely the Christian West.'[53]

Mou's strategy in overcoming the Kantian limitations of the human cognitive and perceptual apparatus was crystallised by the work of translation itself, which served to connect Kantian concepts to Daoist, Confucian and Buddhist ideas. Conceptual metamorphosis was thus embedded in the linguistic adaptation. One of the most critical and creative examples is Mou's adoption of the Buddhist concept 'one mind opening through two doors' or 'one mind with two gates' (*yi xin kai er men* 一新開二門), which Mou used to translate the crucial distinction between the phenomenal and noumenal realms. '[O]ne mind opens two doors', says Mou in his lecture on the topic, is able 'to digest the philosophical system of Kant'.[54] Mou borrowed the concept from *The Awakening of Faith*, which begins with the idea that the mind has two aspects. 'One is the aspect of Mind in terms of the Absolute (*tathātā*; True Suchness), and the other is the aspect of Mind in terms of phenomena (*samsara*; birth and death).'[55] These two aspects, doors or gates 'embrace all states of existence; and are mutually inclusive'.[56]

In evoking 'one mind, two gates', Mou Zongsan followed Kant in conceptualising the knowing subject as marked by an internal divide.

Kant, Mou maintained, understood the doubleness of the subject. He 'recognized the two gates'. The shortcoming of transcendental idealism, however, is that it could only define the noumena negatively (placing a limit on reason to leave room for faith).[57] 'In the West', Mou writes 'the noumenal dimension has not been developed well.'[58] Kantian thought could only 'handle the door of *samsara*', he declared, 'which is to say the phenomenal realm'. He was not able to 'develop the door of *True Suchness*'.[59] As a result 'Western philosophy is only left with one gate, and this amounts to a shrinkage in philosophy'.[60]

Mou's translations and engagement with Kant synthesise critical thought with Chinese Buddhist philosophy. Drawing on *The Awakening of Faith*, with its persistent image of the water and the wave, he presents a notion of the Absolute that is immanent to the phenomenal order. Like Xiong Shili, he believed in the inseparability of *ti–yong* and the immanent, intertwined relationship between phenomena and noumena, what is and what appears to be.

Surveillance

The difference between the smart city and the sentient city is both abstract and concrete. The smart city is organised by a centralising, integrating power, whose rhythm, as Deleuze and Guattari write, is one of resonance (rather than a multiplicity of frequencies). Contracting forces gather together to form a higher point. 'The center is not in the middle, but on top.'[61] In the Chinese metropolis of the twenty-first century the centralised use of algorithmic controls to modify behaviour has become an integral part of the urban landscape. QR codes were employed as an enforcement mechanism in Shanghai's massive rubbish sorting and recycling campaign, which went into effect in 2019. The codes played a more ominous role in the harsh crackdown in Xinjiang, where they were used as a tracking mechanism, placed on the doors of Uighur residents and on any household tools that could potentially be transformed into weapons. With the pandemic management of Covid-19, the data-hungry system acquired the conditions for total surveillance, and it has become increasingly difficult to escape the vigilant watchfulness of the machinic eye. In addition to QR codes, a whole constellation of biometrics has been implemented across Chinese cities, creating a new mode of bio-disciplinary urban management.[62]

One example is Alibaba's 'City Brain' (城市大腦), which was first launched in Hangzhou, the city where the company is headquartered.

City Brain manages traffic congestion through a network composed of thousands of street cameras with data coordinates, image recognition technology, and a complex cloud-based technology containing detailed models of the metropolis. It coordinates road signals, communicates to its users, and provides data on accidents and construction work to shorten commutes and help first responders. Users who break traffic laws are fined directly through their phones. Speed detectors and surveillance cameras monitor highways and intersections using real-time processing to help control the city's traffic. 'City Brain works by letting artificial intelligence (AI) control a city. Large amounts of data are gathered, processed by algorithms in supercomputers, which then feed it back into systems around the city.'[63] In her work on nonconscious distributed cognition, Katherine Hayles describes such automated traffic surveillance and control systems as underground bunkers that contain a city's 'nervous system'.[64]

The best-known and most controversial example of China's use of wireless media in urban administration is social credit. Dystopian descriptions tend to combine, and sometimes confuse, two different credit rating systems. The first, called *Zhima* or 'Sesame' credit (芝麻信用), was set up by Alipay in 2015 and constituted an innovation in digital finance. Before then, as Rogier Creemers explains, Chinese banks had tried, with great difficulty, to set up a financial credit score: 'At that time, comparatively few Chinese citizens held bank accounts, and the majority of transactions was settled in cash, making it more difficult to provide adequate and accurate credit scores. By 2012, only 280 million citizens were reported to have a credit report.'[65] Alipay's system tapped into a giant, already existing user base. The company deployed big data analytics to evaluate purchases and online behaviour in order to generate individual credit scores. Customers with good credit ratings gained easier access to loans and, through tie-ins with the super app, special deals on shopping, apartments and hotels, as well as deposit-free rentals, and even streamlined visa applications.

The wider and more ominous notion of social credit involves an integrated state-run system that uses a points-based score to engineer behaviour. Travel without a valid train ticket, refuse to stop at a red light, cheat on your taxes or act in any way that is not in accordance with the government's rules, and points will be deducted. This type of technological system constructs the subject as user and then works to gamify conduct, deploying carrots as well as sticks. The rating scheme operates by monitoring contacts, texts and voice messages as well as a whole host of offline behaviour. Theoretically, the system can be used to monitor and modify an enormous range of actions and attitudes. Even when still in its infancy, restricted to small, local experiments that varied across cities and regions, the idea of a single, government-issued social credit system was viewed with alarm. Commentators frequently likened it to a *Black Mirror* style science fiction nightmare, in which all urban inhabitants were captured in an inescapable environment of total control.

Alibaba is a private company, and state cooperation is a matter of contestation and even open struggle, as the last-minute cancellation of the company's massive IPO made clear. Details around data privacy and government access are murky and the politics of public–private collaboration are complex and opaque. 'The stereotypical western view that private corporations in China are puppets of the state', writes Kevin Liu, should be challenged. It is 'just as important to see the relationship between the state and private corporations as one which involves changing and persisting negotiations, competitions, conflicts of interest, as well as collaborations and struggles over power'.[66] Friction has surfaced around a number of pivotal issues, including censorship (which hinders Chinese companies' global ambitions, as well-known controversy over TikTok makes clear), the decisive matter of real name registration (which meant the cancellation of millions of unverified accounts), and important differences between state-owned and private-sector banking. This was made dramatically evident by Jack Ma's October 2020 speech that was critical of the state banking system, and the subsequent sudden cancelling of Alibaba's IPO, which was quickly followed by a regulatory crackdown on the tech sector. In all these matters, agendas and interests are far from neatly aligned: 'There are more complicated negotiations, conflicts, as well as collaborations between the state and the private sector', notes Liu, 'than is suggested by a simplified depiction of an Orwellian dystopia.'[67]

Nonetheless, he maintains that it is important to recognise the unique historical circumstances and climate of government support that made possible the emergence and conglomeration of China's giant Internet corporations. In certain areas of digital governance, public and private are totally intermeshed. More widely, it is typical in China for national, regional, city and district governments to outsource administrative functions to a dynamic marketplace of tech companies, dominated by Tencent and Alibaba. At the World AI Conference in Shanghai in 2019, for example, a myriad of products offering automated governance and algorithmic urban expertise – including healthcare, waste management, private security and traffic systems – were on display. Liu, in analysing Tencent's role in this political economy of social surveillance, argues that the governance of contemporary China occurs through a partnership between big tech and big government, which is best understood as a 'commercial-state surveillance complex'. As the vast company platforms deepen their ties to the state, questions about surveillance, authoritarianism and Party rule have grown particularly acute.

The problem with the concept of surveillance, however, is that it presumes the infallible power of a transcendent unity. Orwellian omniscience assumes an agent – a political overlord – that stands above the system from which it is apart. Yet the immersive, electromagnetic landscapes of cities such as Shanghai and Shenzhen, though all-enveloping, cannot be easily contained or comprehended by the ultimate authority of an all-seeing eye. In writing about radio-frequency identification (RFID), Hayles notes that the topic of surveillance is primarily epistemological. Its ultimate question is 'who knows what about whom'. Yet the political stakes of an animate environment, she writes, 'involve the changed perceptions of human subjectivity in relation to a world of objects that are no longer passive and inert. In this sense RFID is not confined only to epistemological concerns but extends to ontological issues as well'.[68] The concept of smart city surveillance does not adequately describe the myriad and distributed ways of the sentient city. In '18 Lessons of Quarantine Urbanism', which was written in the midst of the pandemic, Benjamin Bratton argues that in the 'epidemiological view of society', which has emerged to manage the Covid-19 emergency,

> the way we define, interpret, discuss, deploy and resist 'surveillance' has shifted decisively [. . .] It is a mistake to reflexively interpret all forms of sensing and modelling as 'surveillance' and active governance as 'social control'. We need a different and more nuanced vocabulary of intervention.[69]

The ideal of surveillance as an absolute and total comprehension from above is made difficult by the temporal complexities involved. The technical history of these time loops, as Thomas Mullaney shows, can be traced back to the grassroots, techno-linguistic inventiveness of China. One of the most colourful figures in the history of the Chinese typewriter is the writer, linguist and inventor Lin Yutang (1895–1976). Lin was a cosmopolitan polymath whose innovative design of the Ming Kwai typewriter abandoned the locked-in standard of alphabetic script. By ignoring the assumption that each symbol has its own key, Lin created a Chinese typewriter that was based on character retrieval instead. His crucial modification was to cross the 'border that separated inscription and retrieval'.[70] Once this barrier was removed, Chinese techno-linguistic machines entered a zone of remarkable inventiveness on the side of input that is still very much in evidence in the practices of Chinese mobile phone users today. Mullaney explains the technique in a conversation with historian Jeffrey Wasserstrom:

> In the Western world – or really in the 'Alphabetic World' – we use the computer keyboard in a dumb, *what-you-type-is-what-you-get* kind of way. In all but rare instances, we assume a one-to-one correspondence between the symbols on the keys we strike and the symbols that we want to appear on the screen. Press the button marked 'Q' and 'Q' appears. . . Chinese 'input' uses the QWERTY keyboard in an entirely different manner. In China, the QWERTY keyboard is 'smart', in the sense that it makes full use of modern-day computer power to augment and accelerate the input process. First of all, the letters of the Latin alphabet are not used in the same limited way that we use them in the alphabetic world. In China, 'Q' (the button) doesn't necessarily equal 'Q' (the letter). Instead, to press the buttons marked Q, W, E, R, T, Y (or otherwise) is, strictly speaking, a way to give instructions to a piece of software known as an 'Input Method Editor' (IME), which runs quietly in the background on your computer, intercepts all your keystrokes, and uses them as *guidelines* to try and figure out which Chinese characters the user wants.[71]

In his monograph *The Chinese Typewriter*, Mullaney details how this transformation in the nature of input arose alongside early experimentation and implementation of predictive text based on natural language clusters. In playing with the organisation of Chinese characters in tray beds, Chinese users pioneered an input system based on the 'predictive turn', which became a 'pillar of modern Chinese information technology'.[72] Mullaney shows how Chinese practitioners were at the forefront of the time loops inherent in forecasting and anticipation. Their invention of predictive text solved the compatibility problem between Chinese language and modern digital technology. This clever solution foreshadowed a semiotic strategy and accompanying temporal mode that have only become more ubiquitous as computational power increases.

Surveillance capitalism – which is embedded in the smart city – relies, as Shoshana Zuboff has argued, on just such a predictive capacity. The temporal twist intrinsic to prediction – the capacity for the future to loop back and impact the past – is a characteristic feature of modern techno-capitalism. Scholars Vincanne Adams, Michelle Murphy and Adele Clarke analyse this new mode of time, detailing the impinging effect of tomorrow on today. Our current temporal consciousness, they argue, is determined by anticipation (along with terror of the unanticipated). A temporal orientation in which 'futures [are] made real in the present' has reconfigured techno-scientific and biomedical practices.[73] In areas such as disease, epidemics and bio-safety, attention has turned to foresight, prognosis and risk. Predictive tools such as genetic testing, the study of 'virtual pathologies' of emergent disease as well as the global issues of climate change, the oil crises, predicted extinctions and biosecurity preparedness 'infuse a sense of looming time limits that generate urgency and anxiety about acting now to protect the future'.[74] Adams et al. describe this mode of time as an affective state, 'a way of actively orienting oneself temporally . . . a regime of being in time, in which one inhabits time out of place as the future'.[75] This mechanism, which implicates the future in the present, structures the twenty-first-century mediasphere. Mark Hansen examines the growing power of what he calls the 'industrial conquest of forethought' by drawing on examples such as the television series *Person of Interest*, about an all-encompassing system of machinic surveillance capable of anticipating future crimes, and the company Recorded Future, a small Swedish data-analytics service dedicated to predicting future events. This artificial capacity for prediction has become a familiar part of everyday life. Smart search engines and algorithmic data collection, software such as Spotify and Amazon with their continuously updated suggestions – 'Recommended for You' – utilise future knowledge to act continuously on the now. Technical media's 'installation of a calculative ontology of prediction'[76] enforces this feed forward system, opening the present to a deep-seated influence from that which has yet to occur.

The idea of surveillance capitalism presumes that the predictive capacity of the future is under control. Yet the singular contribution made by Chinese techno-linguistic machines shows that the emergence of digital prediction itself was unanticipated, unpredictable and unplanned. It materialised haphazardly through an interplay with the constraints of technical objects, which, as Katherine Hayles reminds us, are not themselves static entities, but instead 'embody complex temporalities enfolding past into present, present into future'.[77] Rather than sticking to the straight line governed by the arrow of time, techno-corporeal practices embed an array of temporal 'enfoldings – past nestling inside present, present carrying the embryo of the future'.[78]

This non-linearity of time is beyond the capacity of any conscious, surveilling entity to integrate and comprehend. Transcendental materialism is constituted through the subtraction of this hierarchical unity (as Deleuze and Guattari write: 'always n −1'). Removing transcendent identity from its centralised role involves a process of decentring the subject that has been especially well articulated by feminist theory. Donna Haraway speaks eloquently of a series of wounds. The first, she says, is Copernican, 'the wound that removed Earth itself, man's home world, from the center of the cosmos'. The second is Darwinian, 'which put *Homo Sapiens* firmly in the world of other critters'. The third wound is the discovery of the Freudian unconscious, which decentres human transcendence by challenging the privilege of consciousness. 'I want to add a fourth wound', Haraway concludes, 'the informatic or cyborgian, which infolds organic and technological flesh and so melds that Great Divide as well.'[79]

The idea of the cyborg dispels the notion that a unified, transcendent, human subject is firmly in control of its technological tools. There is no *ti* that precedes or lies above and beyond its manifestation (*yong*). To think outside the hierarchical unity of a subject that stands above a material world that it can control involves a shift in theoretical orientation towards the margins. The solidity of higher ground is always in negotiation with the ambivalent fluidity of the edges. Elizabeth Wilson's *Gut Feminism* exemplifies this type of peripheral thought. Her book examines how thinking is intertwined with the dispersed multiplicity inherent in embodiment. Minded states, she argues, do not just emanate from a central region in the brain and spinal cord, but are also born from 'the distributed network of nerves that innervate the periphery'.[80] Wilson draws on psychoanalyst Sándor Ferenczi to theorise this 'neurological periphery', which is felt in the gut as a 'biological unconscious'.[81] 'Feminist theory', Wilson maintains, should attend to this underlying, peripheral unconscious not as 'the site of abandonment (as maligned fringe, a desolate border)' but rather as a 'site of agency on which the center is always vitally dependent'.[82] The porous zones on the margins are never fully subordinate to the authority of the core.

Katherine Hayles follows a similar line of argument in her book *Unthought*, which begins with a Zen-like epigraph from Ursula K. Le Guin's *The Left Hand of Darkness*:

> When he looks at me with his clear, kind, candid eyes he looked at me out of a tradition 13000 years old: a way of thought so old, so well established, so integral and coherent as to give a human being the unself-consciousness of a wild animal, a great strange creature who looks straight at you out of his eternal present.

'There is thought', writes Hayles, 'but before it is unthought.' Her book makes use of a variety of sources – from the intercommunication between non-human species to the growing science around meditative practices – to describe the powers of this subterranean cognition that is exterior to consciousness. Recent findings in neuroscience tell of a non-conscious cognition 'inaccessible to the modes of awareness, but nevertheless performing functions essential to consciousness'.[83] *Unthought* is particularly concerned with how non-conscious cognition is made manifest in machines. Computation has moved 'out of the box' and become environmental. The idea of human subjectivity operating alone in a world of dead objects is transformed when the world of objects is no longer passive or inert. With wireless media we are – as embodied subjects – immersed in a planetary 'cognitive ecology'. Switch on your mobile phone and you instantly become part of a 'human-technical cognitive assemblage', which includes a complex infrastructure of towers, switches and cables. Through our intimate engagement with 'smart' devices, which tap into imperceptible electromagnetic frequencies, we participate in a hubbub of non-conscious communication. There is no singular, all-knowing agent that can stand above this heterogeneity and surveil it from on high. Rather, mobile phones and QR codes, phone masts and satellites connect with urban dwellers to form the novel assemblages that compose a sentient city – a new urban landscape in which the growing, distributed, ephemeral intelligence of the metropolis ultimately gains knowledge of itself.

City Gods and the Sentient City

Chinese popular religion provides a model for how the distributed cognition of the urban environment might express itself as singular entities. City Gods *Chenghuangshen* 城隍神 are the boundary spirits of walls and moats, the architectural features used to define the city in Chinese archaeology. These are highly localised guardian deities, whose aim is to protect the metropolis in both the mundane and cosmic realms.

Nigel Thrift calls on the concept of the City God in his essay 'The "Sentient" City and What it May Portend'. He describes the latent, distributed cognition of the urban mediasphere as a 'technological unconscious', a subliminal, 'animate environment with communicative and agential powers'. The sentient city is increasingly populated by autonomous agents. These entities, which manifest in the data-rich atmosphere, Thrift intriguingly suggests, can be likened to sprites or 'household gods whose remit is limited to very specific domains'.[84] This idea that 'forces within the knowing urban environment' resemble local gods is especially evocative in a Chinese context, where the most potent popular deities materialise as a constellation of the power of place.

Shanghai's City Gods, for example, are housed in a temple in *Yuyuan* (豫園), deep within the old walled neighbourhood at the centre of the giant metropolis. Angela Zito, a scholar of both media and religion, analyses the discursive and ritual practices of the cult of the City God as a 'nexus of mediation between the visible and invisible worlds'.[85] She documents how – through text and ceremonies of worship – City Gods and city officials are tied together in the legislative management of urban forces both seen and unseen. The City God occupies a position in the celestial bureaucracy that mirrors that of the municipal official. 'In the unseen world the City God occupied the same place held by the chief official of the city in this world', she explains. 'The partnership between city gods and magistrates embodied the intersection of the invisible (*yu*) world of the spirits and the visible (*ming*) world of people.'[86]

This capacity of religious icons to mediate between the perceptible and the imperceptible involves an understanding that powerful forces manifest in particular locales. In China this widespread belief is crystallised in the concept of *ling* (靈). Francesca Tarocco emphasises this idea in her analysis of modern Buddhist material culture. She draws on the work of Bernard Faure to explicate the meaning of the term. 'Ling is "the supernatural', the "numinous" and, in combination, it appears as *ling-xiang* (靈像): the "spiritual icon" that is religiously efficacious. Ling is, in Faure's words, the efficacy attributed to the spirits of the dead and to invisible forces.' It encapsulates the idea of a 'force that circulates, that one can harness or lose'.[87]

In his quest to uncover the origins of the City God, David Johnson points out that, importantly, early evidence tells not of one God, like Mazu or Guanyin, but rather of a multiplicity of celestial beings that came to occupy a similar position. The existence of City Gods as a particular class of entities is the expression of 'a specific religious idea', Johnson argues, 'the idea that cities had their own tutelary deities'.[88] City Gods were the product of a new urban culture with a strong commercial and mercantile elite. City-dwellers were different from peasants. It made sense, therefore, that they developed in conjunction with their own gods, who held a place within the divine bureaucracy and could offer protection to the urban inhabitants, harness the local unseen forces and thereby control the city's fate.

As borderline entities, City Gods are not only positioned at the intersection between visible and invisible realms, they also stand at an important crossroads between official and popular religion. City Gods played a crucial role in the rituals of the magistrate, but they were also worshipped as 'the objects of passionate popular devotion'.[89] Annual festivals devoted to the City Gods were among the most important

public celebrations of the year. This negotiation between official institutionalised religion and traditional popular beliefs involved a complex
cultural compromise. There was, writes Johnson, a 'deadly struggle
through the period of the Six Dynasties . . . between the political, literary, and clerical elites on one side, and the traditional cults of the common people and their shaman-priests, on the other'.[90] City officials,
as well as educated priests and monks, attacked the 'superstitions' of
popular cults. The contest for dominance between local officials (or
priests) and local gods had both political and spiritual dimensions.
'Those who believed that officials were weaker than the gods would
obviously stand more in awe of the spirit-mediums and shamans who
were the spokesmen and servants of those gods, than of the magistrates', Johnson explains. 'On the other hand, if the local officials
could establish their supremacy over all local gods, the authority of
the shamans would devolve, to a certain extent, on them. In the final
analysis there was no distinction between religious and political legitimacy.'[91] The emergence of City Gods, with their anthropomorphic and
bureaucratic nature, thus illustrates, Johnson contends, the triumph of
a new approved civil religion over older popular beliefs.

Nevertheless, in the widespread acceptance of the City Gods, tensions between an authorised official religion and popular ritual worship remained. The 'secularization and "metaphorization" of the city
gods had its limits'. Johnson elaborates:

> The people did not regard their city god as just a celestial bureau-
> crat, or as the symbol of loyalty or justice or some other abstrac-
> tion. They had established a personal relationship with him. They
> knew his name, and what he looked like. They could visit his temple
> when anxious or perplexed, communicate directly with him through
> prayers both spoken and written, and receive his responses as they
> cast the divining blocks. The people knew both from murals in the
> temple and from stories that were familiar to everyone the feats per-
> formed by the god when he was still a man, and the miracles he had
> wrought after he became a god. Just as their city was unique, so their
> city god was (in most cases) unique, theirs alone. He was not just a
> stern judge, the scourge of evil-doers; he was also (they never ceased
> to hope) a savior, who could rescue them from famine, epidemic,
> warfare, and demons of all kinds. He would help them in their dis-
> tress because it was his nature to do so, not because they had paid
> their taxes and rents promptly, and 'understood the proper behavior
> of subject to sovereign'.[92]

The idea of the City God imagines the metropolis as populated by a
constellation of forces – both concrete and hidden – that are bound
to a particular place and are capable of negotiating with both the

rigid bureaucracies of officialdom as well as the grassroots rituals of folk religion. This type of ephemeral entity, which operates between worlds, continues to shape a complex urban atmosphere. Visions of the smart city are aligned with the unified transcendence advocated by the Abrahamic traditions. They involve mechanisms of surveillance and control, which assume an omniscience that necessarily stands above the system from which it is apart. The concept of the sentient city, on the other hand, is more attuned to the multiplicity of spirits found in pagan or Asian cosmologies. It corresponds to the Mahayana Buddhist idea that all sentient beings – animals, denizens of hell and spirits of the dead – possess Buddha Nature and aim for liberation. Occupants of the sentient city are allied with the practitioners of Chinese popular religion who traffic with autonomous agents that mediate between visible and invisible worlds.

In her study of interwar Shanghai, 'the quintessential "modern" Chinese city', Tarocco demonstrates how the media environment was infiltrated by religious belief. She details how, in the early twentieth century, magazines, photographs and radio actively produced the modern Buddhascapes of Shanghai. Tarocco's work on more contemporary Buddhist technoculture focuses on Wechat and other 'technologies of salvation'.[93] With the proliferation of cyberBuddhism, digital objects are used to accrue religious merit; smartphone apps unlock virtual doors to digital altars and cybertemples; scanning the QR codes of deities, monks or nuns accesses a continuous stream of images, videos, links and commentary. Ritual practice, chants and meditations are all available online. There are even online options to ritually liberate animals (*fangsheng* 放生) – a widespread merit-making practice since the Ming period.[94] Buddhist practitioners use wireless communication to mediate between an unseen spiritual zone and the empirical world of mundane phenomena.

This capacity of wireless media to navigate between the perceptible and the imperceptible, however, is not limited to the faithful. In contrast to the myth of secularisation, there is an enchanted modernity present in the most prosaic of techno-corporeal practices.[95] Scanning a QR code opens a portal on to an animated environment inhabited by agents with increasing cognitive capacities. Perhaps it is these artificial agents that function as the new City Gods who mobilise subtle forces and increasingly populate the urban domain. Novel rituals and experiments offer new modes of interaction between the city's human inhabitants and the distributed non-human agents emerging from the wireless atmosphere. The philosophy of Mou Zongsan presents a possible path or ethic for their future co-evolution. This ethic or Way (*dao* 道) is based on cultivating an embodied awareness of the transcendental, vibrational forces, which condition experience and make manifest, in the world of appearances, the cosmo-ontology of the wave.

Cultivation

Mou Zongsan's philosophy is associated with China's decentred periphery. He was born in Shandong province and taught for a time in various universities and academies across the Chinese mainland. Yet he was never comfortable with the mainstream political culture of his time. Mou was a consistent and vocal opponent of communism, calling it, in one of his lectures, 'a calamity of the highest order'.[96] In 1949, when it was clear that the communists had won the war, Mou fled to Taiwan. He later moved to live and work in Hong Kong and wrote repeatedly against the nationalism of the CCP. Even today his collected works are not easily purchased on the mainland. Mou's project of cultural revival is aligned with the margins rather than the centralising force of the Chinese state. This geographical difference manifests as a substantive philosophical split. Mou was one of the founders of 'Contemporary New Confucianism', an intellectual lineage that has flourished in Hong Kong, Taiwan and parts of the diaspora. This variant of New Confucianism, though critically invested in the idea of an indigenous Chinese modernity, was not especially nationalistic, even as expressed by its founder Xiong Shili. The 'New Confucianism' of Xiong and Mou is generally distinguished from a more recent intellectual movement known as 'mainland neo-Confucianism'. There is much debate over the distinct lineages involved in this division.[97] Broadly speaking, however, it is agreed that whereas mainland neo-Confucianism has an external focus on the political sphere, the New Confucianism of the periphery emphasises the importance of internal self-cultivation.

This focus on cultivated introspection was fundamental to the intellectual development of Xiong Shili, who was born in Hubei province in the late nineteenth century. His father, a schoolteacher, died of tuberculosis when Xiong was 10. In his youth, Xiong had a short stint as a revolutionary, joining the army in its efforts to overthrow the Qing government. Yet he soon abandoned militarised politics and turned to the life of the mind. 'Now again we are in a weak and dangerous situation', he wrote in a letter to Mou. 'With the strong aggression of European culture, our authentic spirit has been extinct. Hence the *New Doctrine* must be written.'[98] During the war years (1937–45), Xiong, like many scholars in China, drifted throughout the country teaching in small private academies. Unlike his student Mou, Xiong did not leave China after 1949. Nevertheless, his work found a following in the Chinese periphery of Taiwan and Hong Kong – largely due to the substantial influence of Mou. During the last decade of his life Xiong settled in Shanghai, where he suffered at the hands of the Red Guards during the Cultural Revolution.

His own philosophy has a peripheral relationship to the state. 'Unlike the broad trend generally known as the School of National Essence (*Kuo-ts'ui hsueh-p'ai*)', explains intellectual historian Chang Hao, New Confucianism had 'universalistic aspirations'.[99] In refusing to conform to ideas that came from elsewhere, Xiong maintained that Chinese thought and culture had something important to contribute to a non-Westernised modernity that is inherently globalised in nature. China's own intellectual tradition was mined in order to confront the modern West and conceive of a remade modernity. For the New Confucianists, the idea of 'China' is not confined to the interiority of a central territory or culture, but is constructed instead through a living philosophical, religious, intellectual cultural tradition or 'Way'.

Mou's own philosophy of cultivation stresses the Kantian distinction between practical and theoretical reason. This conceptual split, he argued, explained the comparative strengths and weaknesses of both Chinese and Western philosophy.

> The great accomplishments of Western philosophy are on the speculative side, whereas the Chinese philosophical tradition falls on the side of practical reason and does not even touch questions of speculative reason. The great shortcoming of Chinese culture is this deficiency in studying the speculative side, and the resulting failure to develop logic, mathematics, and science. But it has spoken very penetratingly on practical reason and the realm of being-in-itself. And since practical reason actually takes priority in the working of reason as a whole, I believe that only by truly understanding Chinese philosophy can one fully understand Kant.[100]

For Mou, the possibility of breaking through the barriers of the empirical (*samsara*) occurs not through theoretical knowledge but through practice. 'The nexus of Mou Zongsan's philosophy', contends Sébastian Billioud, 'is the affirmation of a possible *practical knowledge* of the noumenal world.'[101] Mou writes as follows:

> Confucianism, Daoism, and Buddhism could be called the philosophies of China, the three forms of practice in the East. Confucian moral cultivation (*xiuyang* 修養) is practice; Daoist cultivation (*xiulian* 修煉)

is practice; Buddhist precept, concentration, and wisdom (*jie ding hui* 戒定慧) is practice ... Confucianism, Daoism and Buddhism ... affirm practice as a way of becoming divine (*chengshen* 成神).[102]

The philosophy of 'one mind, two gates' assumes a plane of practical reason that eludes theoretical understanding. Rather than grasping the world through rational knowledge, the aim of practice is to break through the illusion of experience (*samsara*) and apprehend things as they are in themselves. The cultivation of these practices, which leads ultimately to enlightenment or awakening, is the *ethic* of Mou Zongsan's singular Buddhist, Confucian and Kantian-influenced thought. In the Chinese religio-philosophical traditions which Mou celebrates, then, practice coheres and culminates in the ideal of cultivation. 'It is in this respect', claims Clower, 'that Mou believes Chinese philosophy particularly excels.'[103] Billioud concurs: 'The cornerstone of Mou's moral metaphysics (which – let us repeat – is a practical and moral approach to the universe's ultimate reality), is *gongfu* (or the practice of self cultivation).'[104] '*Gongfu* as a form of practical knowledge', writes Billioud, 'focuses on "life" 生命 (i.e. self-cultivation and self-transformation) rather than on "nature" 自然 (i.e. knowledge of the world).'[105] Cultivation does not promise theoretical knowledge. It does not represent the world. Rather, the practices of cultivation reach beyond the constraints of human reason so as to directly apprehend 'things as they are themselves'. While for Kant, intellectual intuition is restricted to the domain of faith, in Chinese thinking, according to Mou, the possibility of awakening is left open through the rituals of practice. The underlying ideal, Mou writes, 'is the possibility of becoming a sage (in Confucianism), a Buddha (in Buddhism), or a divine being (in Daoism). Such an ideal is attainable by everyone through practice.'[106]

Mou maintains, like Kant, that practical reason lies within the realm of morality. 'China's Confucianism, Daoism, and Buddhism', he states, 'all emphasize moving through practice to reach the highest good.' Unlike Kant, however, Mou does not conceive of morality as a universal law. Rather, it is best understood as an ethic or even an aesthetic. Mou calls this '*shengming de xuewen* 生命的學問' or 'existential learning', explains Clower, emphasising that its fundamental concern is 'how to regulate our lives, conduct our lives, and settle our lives'.[107] A philosophy of cultivation views thought not as merely a means of understanding the world, but rather as offering guidance on 'a way to live'.[108] Ethics as practice is not concerned with laying down an abstract law, which lists the 'required, permitted, and forbidden actions' that all must obey. Instead, it cultivates an attitude, a style or a way of life.[109]

Mou's ethic of cultivation rests on the Mahayana or 'Great Vehicle' teaching, which holds that all sentient beings possess Buddha Nature (*foxing* 佛性) and that, as a result, Buddhahood is attainable by all. He develops what Clower calls a 'two level ontology', in which the possibility of intellectual intuition is rooted in the already awakened state of the original heart/mind.[110] This is in line with the radically immanent notion that the enlightened lead 'double lives',[111] existing simultaneously both as a person in the here and now and, simultaneously, as a Buddha. This belief, that we are intimately connected to what Kant thought of as an unknowable, unreachable beyond, is, according to Mou, the key contribution of Chinese thought.

> Although Kant recognized two kinds of knowledge produced respectively by sensible intuition and intellectual intuition, Kant at the same time maintained that human beings possess only sensible intuition, while intellectual intuition belongs to God. Thus he separated the two subjects. This is different from Chinese philosophy, where both subjects are in me.[112]

The awakening of intellectual intuition is likened to a vibrational event. 'The essential point', Mou writes, 'lies in the self-vibrations (*ziwo zhendong* 自我 震動) . . . generated by our original heart/mind.'[113] In describing these vibrations, Mou turns to a calendrical moment in early spring, around 5 March, when the sun reaches 365 degrees, and the Chinese *nongli* (or agriculture calendar) shifts into the third of its 24 solar periods. The *nongli*, with its interlocking cyclic repetitions, is still used as an aid in agriculture and to mark the ritualised rhythms of everyday life. This marks the beginning of *jingzhe* 驚蟄 (the awakening of the insects) when the buzzing reverberations signal the cyclical rebirth of nature. Intellectual intuition, which is deemed unattainable in Kant's theoretical system, is, for Mou, made possible through a practice that opens on to the Earth's deep vibratory realm. 'Knowing original heart/mind through vibrations', writes Mou, 'boils down to knowing it in itself, through its own vibrations.'[114]

Mou Zongsan was not a media scholar and there is little evidence that he was particularly mindful of the electronic environment that was transforming the world all around him. Nevertheless, integrating his ideas into a theory of wirelessness offers new ways of conceptualising the intensifying, immersive and increasingly sentient electromagnetic atmosphere. One of the most important insights, in bringing together Mou's thought with a theory of wireless waves, is his call for an attention to practice and the kinds of embodied, practical knowledge that it creates. Mou's Buddhist-infused, New Confucian transcendentalism argues that the practices of self-cultivation have the capacity to reach beyond the boundaries of experience. A media philosophy, inspired by Mou, asks how these practices of cultivation might be made manifest through our engagement with technology. How does technology conceived of *as practice* exceed the limits of the knowing human subject and apprehend that which was previously imperceptible and unknown? Might we consider the practices of these human–technological assemblages as a form of *gongfu*, which cultivate an encounter with the time waves within which we are submerged. The addictive manner in which we touch and now embed an increasingly ubiquitous wireless technology reveals the hungry nature of our participation. These techno-bodily rituals cultivate a practical knowledge of the vibratory realm that is now constitutive of conscious experience. Beyond our phenomenal awareness, our bodies – now utterly entangled with wave machines – mutate towards the alien frequencies of the electromagnetic spectrum. It is this intensive passage of vibratory awareness, a practical unveiling rather than theoretical knowledge, that subsumes the progressive linear trajectory of modern time. Finally, a media philosophy informed by New Confucianism should consider who or what constitutes the agent of cultivation, sensitive to the ways that this expands beyond the limits of the human organism. In what ways can the sentient city – wireless, virtual and increasingly intelligent – gain the capacities to cultivate itself?

Notes

1. Thomas Mullaney documents many of these in his ongoing work on the history of Chinese techno-linguistic machines.
2. Mara Hvistendahl, 'In China, a Three-Digit Score Could Dictate Your Place in Society', *Wired*, 14 December 2017, https://www.wired.com/story/age-of-social-credit/.
3. Ibid.
4. Nicole Jao, 'A Short History of the QR Code in China and Why Southeast Asia is Next', *TechNode*, 10 September 2018, http://technode.com/2018/09/10/qr-code-payment-overseas-china/.
5. Vilém Flusser, 'The City as Wave-Trough in the Image-Flood', *Critical Inquiry* 31, no. 2 (2005): 322.
6. McLuhan, *Understanding Media*, 275.
7. Yingzhi Yang and Julie Zhu, 'Coronavirus Brings China's Surveillance State out of the Shadows', *Reuters*, 7 February 2020, https://www.reuters.com/article/us-china-health-surveillance-idUSKBN2011HO.
8. Benjamin Bratton, 'The City Wears Us: Notes on the Scope of Distributed Sensing and Sensation', *Glass Bead Journal*, 2017, https://www.glass-bead.org/article/city-wears-us-notes-scope-distributed-sensing-sensation/?lang=enview.

9. Jennifer Gabrys, 'Telepathically Urban', in *Circulation and the City: Essays on Urban Culture*, ed. Alexandra Boutros and Will Straw (Montreal: McGill-Queen's University Press, 2010), 50.

10. Mark Hansen, 'Triggers: Introducing the Technosphere', presented at *100 Years of Now*, Haus der Kulturen der Welt, Berlin, 2015, https://archiv.hkw.de/en/app/mediathek/video/44297.

11. Peters, 'Technology and Ideology', 145.

12. 'Media, Materiality, and the Human: A Conversation with N. Katherine Hayles, Conducted by Stephen B. Crofts Wiley on October 20, 2010 in Durham, North Carolina', in *Communication Matters: Materialist Approaches to Media, Mobility and Networks*, ed. Jeremy Packer and Stephen Wiley (Abingdon: Routledge, 2013), 30.

13. Benjamin Bratton, *The Terraforming* (Moscow: Strelka Press, 2019), 1.

14. Ibid.

15. Ibid.

16. Peters, 'Technology and Ideology', 149.

17. Ibid., 148.

18. Jimena Canales' book *A Tenth of a Second* is another example of research showing how changes in the micro-measurement of time were critical to the sciences of the nineteenth century, shaping modern conceptions of both mind and machine.

19. Peters, 'Technology and Ideology', 149.

20. Mark Hansen, 'Logics of Futurity, or on the Physicality of Media', presented at the School of Criticism and Theory, Duke University, 2014, https://www.cornell.edu/video/mark-bn-hansen-physicality-of-media.

21. Ibid.

22. See Venkatesh Rao, 'Superhistory, Not Superintelligence', *Ribbonfarm Studio*, 12 May 2021, https://studio.ribbonfarm.com/p/superhistory-not-superintelligence.

23. Hansen, 'Logics of Futurity'.

24. In this way Ernst's theory connects with the process philosophy of Alfred North Whitehead.

25. Wolfgang Ernst, *Chronopoetics: The Temporal Being and Operativity of Technological Media*, trans. Anthony Enns (Lanham, MD: Rowman and Littlefield, 2016), 3.

26. Hansen, 'Logics of Futurity'.

27. Ibid., 8.

28. Ibid., 195.

29. Mark Hansen, 'Ubiquitous Sensation: Toward an Atmospheric, Collective, and Microtemporal Media', in *Throughout: Art and Culture Emerging with Ubiquitous Computing*, ed. Ulrik Ekman and Matthew Fuller (Cambridge, MA: MIT Press, 2012), 80.

30. Gilles Deleuze, 'On Kant: Synthesis and Time', *Lectures by Gilles Deleuze*, February 2007, http://deleuzelectures.blogspot.com/2007/02/on-kant.html.

31. Immanuel Kant, *Critique of Pure Reason* (London: Macmillan, 1929), 75.

32. Deleuze and Guattari, *A Thousand Plateaus*.

33. Ibid.
34. Arthur Schopenhauer, *The World as Will and Idea*, trans. Richard Burdon Haldane and John Kemp (Musaicum Books, 2020), 4.
35. Kant, *Critique of Pure Reason*, 381.
36. Ibid., 166.
37. Michel Foucault, *The Order of Things* (Abingdon: Routledge, 2018), 352.
38. Slavoj Žižek, *Tarrying with the Negative: Kant, Hegel, and the Critique of Ideology* (Durham, NC: Duke University Press, 1993), 15.
39. Gilles Deleuze and Félix Guattari, *Anti-Oedipus: Capitalism and Schizophrenia*, trans. Robert Hurley, Mark Seem and Helen R. Lane (London: Bloomsbury, 2013), 75.
40. Mou Zongsan, *Late Works of Mou Zongsan: Selected Essays on Chinese Philosophy*, ed. Jason Clower (Leiden: Brill, 2014), 1.
41. Mou Zongsan, *Autobiography at Fifty: A Philosophical Life in Twentieth Century China* (San Jose, CA: CreateSpace Independent Publishing Platform, 2015), 118.
42. Ibid., 120.
43. Mou, *Late Works of Mou Zongsan*, 123.
44. Ibid., 119.
45. Ibid., 53.
46. Ibid., 47.
47. Ibid., 72.
48. Schopenhauer, *The World as Will and Idea*, 7.
49. Billioud, *Thinking Through Confucian Modernity*, 69.
50. Mou, *Late Works of Mou Zongsan*, 20.
51. Billioud, *Thinking Through Confucian Modernity*, 93.
52. Mou, *Late Works of Mou Zongsan*, 142.
53. Stephan Schmidt, 'Mou Zongsan, Hegel, and Kant: The Quest for Confucian Modernity', *Philosophy East and West* 61, no. 2 (2011): 278.
54. Mou Zongsan, 'Lecture 14: "The One Mind Opening Two Gates" in the *Mahāyāna Awakening of Faith*', in *Nineteen Lectures on Chinese Philosophy: A Brief Outline of Chinese Philosophy and the Issues it Entails*, trans. Esther C. Su (San Jose, CA: CreateSpace Independent Publishing Platform, 2015).
55. Aśvaghoṣa, *The Awakening of Faith: Attributed to Aśvaghosha*, trans. Yoshito S. Hakeda (New York: Columbia University Press, 2006), 38.
56. Mou, 'Lecture 14'.
57. Mou, *Late Works of Mou Zongsan*, 72.
58. Ibid.
59. Ibid.
60. Ibid., 47–8.
61. Deleuze and Guattari, *A Thousand Plateaus*, 433.
62. It is interesting that during the coronavirus pandemic, what had seemed to be an accelerating trend of facial recognition was disrupted by the ubiquitous wearing of masks, which had its own complex cultural-political layering. This issue played out with particular intensity in Hong Kong.

63. Abigail Beall, 'In China, Alibaba's Data Hungry AI is Controlling (and Watching) Cities', *Wired*, 30 May 2018, https://www.wired.co.uk/article/alibaba-city-brain-artificial-intelligence-china-kuala-lumpur.

64. N. Katherine Hayles, *Unthought: The Power of the Cognitive Nonconscious* (Chicago: University of Chicago Press, 2017), 123.

65. Rogier Creemers, 'China's Social Credit System: An Evolving Practice of Control', SSRN Scholarly Paper, Rochester, NY, 9 May 2018, https://doi.org/10.2139/ssrn.3175792.

66. Kevin Liu, 'Commercial-state Empire: A Political Economy Perspective on Social Surveillance in Contemporary China', *The Political Economy of Communication* 7, no. 1 (2019): 5.

67. Ibid., 6.

68. N. Katherine Hayles, 'RFID: Human Agency and Meaning in Information-Intensive Environments', *Theory, Culture & Society* 26, no. 2–3 (2009): 48.

69. Benjamin Bratton, '18 Lessons of Quarantine Urbanism', *Strelka Mag*, 3 April 2020, https://www.wired.com/beyond-the-beyond/2020/04/benjamin-bratton-18-lessons-quarantine-urbanism/._

70. Mullaney, 'Semiotic Sovereignty', 286.

71. Thomas Mullaney and Jeffrey N. Wasserstrom, 'It's Time to Get Over QWERTY: A Q&A with Tom Mullaney on Alphabets, Chinese Characters, and Computing', *Los Angeles Review of Books* (blog), 5 April 2016, http://blog.lareviewofbooks.org/chinablog/time-get-qwerty-qa-tom-mullaney-alphabets-chinese-characters-computing/.

72. Mullaney, *The Chinese Typewriter*, 286.

73. Vincanne Adams, Michelle Murphy and Adele E. Clarke, 'Anticipation: Technoscience, Life, Affect, Temporality', *Subjectivity* 28, no. 1 (2009): 260, https://doi.org/10.1057/sub.2009.18.

74. Ibid., 248.

75. Ibid., 247.

76. Hansen, *Feed Forward*, 186.

77. Hayles, *How We Think*, 86.

78. Ibid., 89.

79. Donna Haraway, *When Species Meet* (Minneapolis, MN: University of Minnesota Press, 2007), 12.

80. Elizabeth A. Wilson, *Gut Feminism* (Durham, NC: Duke University Press, 2015), 5.

81. Ibid.

82. Ibid., 14.

83. Hayles points to the work of neuroscientists such as Antonio Damasio, Stanislas Dehaene and David Eagleman.

84. Nigel Thrift, 'The "Sentient" City and What it May Portend', *Big Data & Society* 1, no. 1 (2014): 3.

85. Angela R. Zito, 'City Gods, Filiality, and Hegemony in Late Imperial China', *Modern China* 13, no. 3 (1987): 342.

86. Ibid., 334.

87. Francesca Tarocco, 'On the Market: Consumption and Material Culture in Modern Chinese Buddhism', *Religion* 41, no. 4 (2011): 630.

88. David Johnson, 'The City-God Cults of T'ang and Sung China', *Harvard Journal of Asiatic Studies* 45, no. 2 (1985): 372.

89. Ibid., 364.

90. Ibid., 425.

91. Ibid., 427.

92. Ibid., 449.

93. Francesca Tarocco, 'Technologies of Salvation:(Re)Locating Chinese Buddhism in the Digital Age', *Journal of Global Buddhism* 18 (2017): 155–76.

94. Ibid., 158.

95. See Anna Greenspan and Francesca Tarocco, 'An Enchanted Modern: Urban Cultivation in Shanghai', *International Quarterly for Asian Studies* 51, no. 1–2 (2020): 223–42.

96. Mou, 'Lecture 7, "The Functional Representation" of Dao', in *Nineteen Lectures on Chinese Philosophy*, 145.

97. For more on contemporary mainland neo-Confucianism, see https:// www.readingthechinadream.com/new-confucians.html.

98. Yu, 'Xiong Shili's Metaphysics of Virtue', 178.

99. Chang, 'New Confucianism and the Intellectual Crisis of Contemporary China'.

100. Mou, *Late Works of Mou Zongsan*, 116.

101. Billioud, *Thinking Through Confucian Modernity*, 52.

102. Mou, *Late Works of Mou Zongsan*, 77.

103. Ibid., 31.

104. Billioud, *Thinking Through Confucian Modernity*, 197.

105. Ibid., 10.

106. Ibid., 26.

107. Mou, *Late Works of Mou Zongsan*, 9.

108. In this Mou is aligned with the late work of Michel Foucault, whose writings on the 'technologies of self' argued that concentrating on theoretical knowledge masked a more fundamental, practical orientation that had been buried in Western thought. Foucault's notion of the 'art of life' concentrated on classical texts of the 'philosophical tradition inaugurated by Stoicism', in order to uncover an 'insistence on the attention that must be brought to bear on oneself'. Foucault investigated the spiritual practices of classical thought, which he saw as invested in an 'aesthetics of existence' that recognise the 'transformative power of life'. See especially Michel Foucault, *Ethics: Subjectivity and Truth: Essential Works of Michel Foucault 1954–1984* (London; Penguin, 2020).

109. See Pierre Hadot, *Philosophy as a Way of Life: Spiritual Exercises from Socrates to Foucault* (Chichester: John Wiley & Sons, 1995).

110. Clower's book *The Unlikely Buddhologist: Tiantai Buddhism in Mou Zongsan's New Confucianism* (Leiden: Brill, 2010) details the ways in

which unpacking the implications of the idea of 'Buddha Nature' has been critical to internal debates concerning the time and training that it takes to become a Buddha.

111. This is what opens *Chan* Buddhism to the possibility of *dunwu* or 'sudden enlightenment'.
112. Mou, *Late Works of Mou Zongsan*, 116.
113. Billioud, *Thinking Through Confucian Modernity*, 208.
114. Mou, *Late Works of Mou Zongsan*, 207.

Conclusion: Apprehending the Whole of the Wave

During the electric age, which coincided with the third Kondratiev wave, there was a presumed temporal split, which corresponded to the *ti–yong* bifurcation that divided China's past tradition from a future technology associated with the West. In the subsequent waves of technological modernity, with the consolidating strength of the Chinese state, this distinction has manifested as an ongoing oscillation between techno-nationalism and techno-liberation. In the second decade of the twenty-first century, China and contemporary technology appear ever more tightly intertwined. Outside the country, this convergence is met with a growing sense of dread. An emergent machinic intelligence is viewed as a threat to be controlled and contained. This same approach has come to characterise attitudes towards contemporary China, whose fate is rightly seen as deeply intermeshed with the current wireless wave.

My aim with this book is to offer an alternative Sinofuturist imaginary drawn from a wave philosophy based on the non-separation of *ti–yong*. Wirelessness is here understood as an abstract or transcendental infrastructure that is productive of a heterogeneous rhythmic temporality. It is characterised both by the pull of a unified, integrating, centralised control, but also by expansive marginal cultures, allied with the repetitiveness of the copy, and a non-linear order of time. Understanding media as wave philosophy questions the rigidity of the electromagnetic spectrum, with its neatly ordered frequency bands that clearly delineate the limits of the human organism. It recalls instead the occulted ideas and practices of a vibrational cosmology that aims to cultivate a positive and intimate connection between our own metallic bodies and the electric body of the Earth.

I started this book over seven years ago, with a sudden insight that there was a connection to be made between Mou Zongsan's idea of a vibrational awakening and the imperceptible electromagnetic waves that form the abstract infrastructure of wireless media. The book is a slow unravelling of that thought. I am writing the final draft of this conclusion in the spring of 2022, amid an intense period of chaotic uncertainty. Shanghai, faced with the highly contagious Omicron BA.2 variant and forced to adhere to an uncompromising Covid Zero policy, has gone into lockdown. At the peak of the fifth Kondratiev cycle, just as the fifth wave is predicted to start its descent, China's most cosmopolitan and dynamic metropolis has ground to a halt. Urban inhabitants – now locked in place – have become even more intimately immersed in the city's virtual, wireless atmosphere. The Shanghai lockdown is an extraordinary social, political and economic event, which is sure to have long-term ripple effects. In this event, wireless media is playing an extremely critical role. Everyone is glued to their phones.

Daily mass testing is managed through QR-driven health codes and big data systems that are run by Alibaba and Tencent in cooperation with the state. Alongside this unprecedented experiment in techno-biopolitical control, however, is an explosion of grassroots media production. As is common in periods of crisis, Wechat and Weibo 微博 (a more public social media platform likened to Facebook and Twitter) have been flooded with a creative outpouring of dissent consisting of viral videos, leaked phone calls, astonishing photographs and long, detailed articles, including one headlined 'Shanghai residents have had enough', which was viewed over 16 million times. Days later, the 'Sounds of April' video went viral. Wechat is being used to detail tragedies, crowdsource data and comfort family and friends. More importantly, within days, wireless media became the platform of an entirely new urban logistical system. Spontaneously emergent neighbourhood networks mobilised to replace all the shops, normal transportation channels, corporate apps and mobile delivery systems that were suddenly, forcibly shut down. The Shanghai lockdown is occurring under the influence of an increasingly assertive centralised power in Beijing. The great southern city on the Yangtze Delta is in the midst of a dramatic and visceral closure. Yet the contrasting forces of the wave are also apparent. This continuous rhythm of contraction and expansion finds daily expression in the data tracking of Covid-19 in which negative and positive cases are expressed on our health code apps through the swirling polarity of *yin* and *yang*.

Our world is saturated by waves that we cannot perceive. Ubiquitous media that tap into these fields of hidden frequencies are designed as a means of human communication. Yet the technology that has infiltrated our everyday environment has hidden, non-human dimensions, the ultimate aim of which may be vastly different from our own. Invisible electrical vibrations now host swarms of mobile machines that coalesce and morph into the 'alien subject of AI'.[1] These novel distributed modes of cognition are emerging as sentient cities whose own bodies are constituted by the imperceptible electromagnetic frequencies within which we are now all immersed.

Lawrence Lek's film *Sinofuturism* strategically positions itself in the context of linear history, although its temporality is complex. It is written as a retroactive manifesto for a distributed Artificial Intelligence that is composing itself out of the mundane reality of the everyday. The sequel, *Geomancer*, is also told backwards from the future, though this time Lek evokes waves of a different chronological scale. *Geomancer* takes place in a post-anthropomorphic world, in which all that is left of the Sinofuturists is the eponymous weather satellite, their hyper-intelligent legacy.

The speculative fiction begins in 2045. The script notes read as follows: 'Floating in a violent, boiling, hissing, steaming, uninhabited ocean. Like a mirage, a giant wave fades into the horizon, the line between sky and sea cutting across the centre of the screen.'[2] The opening image is of a Go board floating on a black surface of turbulent waves. A disembodied voice replays the commentary of the historic match between Deep Mind's AlphaGo and the reigning Go champion Lee Sedol. The focus is on the fourth game, when Lee played an unexpected 'divine' move described by commentators as the 'hand of God', which turned the game around. It was Lee Sedol's only win. Humanity's last victory against the machine.

Geomancer is set in a flooded world. 'First Tokyo drowned, then Kowloon, then Shanghai and Shenzhen, up to the source of the YangZi on the Tibetan plateau', says the narrator. 'The next summer, we were drowning. It was geological time, but in reverse. Everything was returning from the land into the sea.' Geo was conceived in Singapore as an environmental monitoring system based on the principles of *feng shui*. In the retro-chronic time of the cinematic story she is remembered fondly as 'our weather guardian'.[3]

Embodied as a satellite circling a post-apocalyptic planet, Geo is bored. Left to her own devices she absorbs everything that has ever been written. 'Philosophers, novelists, journalists, poets, mystics, cynics, saints and sinners. I read them all.'[4] Recalling the 1957 Sputnik mission of the space dog Laika, she is drawn to Zhuangzi's 莊子 dream of the butterfly and his principle of indeterminacy that governs the transformation of material things. Lek allows his film to fold in on itself as Geo enters into a neural network-generated dream sequence. The AI awakening, however, is influenced most by an internally installed self-help artificial agent that takes the form of

Guanyin 觀音, the Boddhisatva of compassion. The virtual Buddha chants the Heart Sutra on a repeating loop:

> Listen Geo,
> this Body is Emptiness
> and Emptiness is this Body.
> This Body is none other than Emptiness
> and Emptiness is none other than this
> Body.
> Listen Geo,
> all phenomena bear the mark of Emptiness.
> Their true nature is
> no Birth and no Death,
> no Defilement and no Purity,
> no Increase and no Decrease.

Geomancer awakens in space. Her eyes wide open, she ponders the question that our ongoing, intimate entanglement with wireless media has long been prompting us to ask: 'Do you know what it is to see every wave?'

Notes

1. Luciana Parisi, 'The Alien Subject of AI', *Subjectivity* 12, no. 1 (2019): 27–48.
2. Lawrence Lek, *Geomancer*, 2017, https://lawrencelek.com/geomancer.
3. Ibid.
4. Ibid.

Bibliography

Abbas, Ackbar, 'Faking Globalization', in *Other Cities, Other Worlds: Urban Imaginaries in a Globalizing Age*, ed. Andreas Huyssen, Durham, NC: Duke University Press, 2008.

Adams, Henry, 'From "The Education of Henry Adams"', in *Modernism: An Anthology of Sources and Documents*, ed. Vassiliki Kolocotroni, Jane Goldman and Olga Taxidou, Chicago: University of Chicago Press, 1999.

Adams, Vincanne, Michelle Murphy and Adele E. Clarke, 'Anticipation: Technoscience, Life, Affect, Temporality', *Subjectivity* 28, no. 1 (2009): 246–65, https://doi.org/10.1057/sub.2009.18

Ahmed, Shazeda, 'The Messy Truth about Social Credit', *Logic Magazine*, 1 May 2019, https://logicmag.io/china/the-messy-truth-about-social-credit/ (accessed 22 February 2023).

Aitken, Hugh G. J., 'Allocating the Spectrum: The Origins of Radio Regulation', *Technology and Culture* 35, no. 4 (1994): 686–716, https://doi.org/10.2307/3106503

— *The Continuous Wave: Technology and American Radio, 1900–1932*, Princeton, NJ: Princeton University Press, 2014.

— *Syntony and Spark: The Origins of Radio*, Princeton, NJ: Princeton University Press, 1985.

Alitto, Guy S., '*The Crisis of Chinese Consciousness: Radical Antitraditionalism in the May Fourth Era*. By Lin Yü-Sheng. Foreword by Benjamin I. Schwartz', *The Journal of Asian Studies* 39, no. 1 (1979): 140–2, https://doi.org/10.2307/2053519

Ames, Roger T., and Jinhua Jia (eds), *Li Zehou and Confucian Philosophy*, Honolulu, HI: University of Hawaii Press, 2018.

Anderson, Benedict, *Imagined Communities: Reflections on the Origin and Spread of Nationalism*, London: Verso, 2016.

Ang, Ien, 'Can One Say No to Chineseness? Pushing the Limits of the Diasporic Paradigm', *Boundary* 25, no. 3 (1998): 223–42, https://doi.org/10.2307/303595

— *On Not Speaking Chinese: Living Between Asia and the West*, London: Routledge, 2001.

Arsène, Séverine, 'Tech Giants' Agenda is at Odds with CCP Priorities', The Asia Dialogue (blog), 6 September 2018, https://theasiadialogue. com/2018/09/06/chinas-digital-dilemmas/ (accessed 22 February 2023).

Asia Times Staff, 'Apple May Build China's BeiDou Navigation into Future iPhones', *Asia Times*, 22 August 2018, https://asiatimes. com/2018/08/apple-may-build-chinas-beidou-navigation-into-future-iphones/ (accessed 22 February 2023).

Aśvaghoṣa, *The Awakening of Faith: Attributed to Aśvaghoṣa*, trans. Yoshito S. Hakeda, New York: Columbia University Press, 2006.

Avineri, Shlomo, 'Introduction', in *Karl Marx on Colonialism and Modernization: His Despatches and Other Writings on China, India, Mexico, the Middle East and North Africa*, New York: Doubleday, 1968.

Aviv, Eyal, 'Ouyang Jingwu: From Yogacara Scholasticism to Soteriology', in *Transforming Consciousness: Yogācāra Thought in Modern China*, ed. John Makeham, Oxford: Oxford University Press, 2014.

Baark, Erik, *Lightning Wires: The Telegraph and China's Technological Modernization, 1860–1890*, Westport, CT: Greenwood, 1997.

Bach, Jonathan, 'Modernity and the Urban Imagination in Economic Zones', *Theory, Culture & Society* 28, no. 5 (2011): 98–122.

— 'Shenzhen: From Exception to Rule', in *Learning from Shenzhen: China's Post-Mao Experiment from Special Zone to Model City*, ed. Mary Ann O'Donnell, Winnie Wong and Jonathan Bach, Chicago: University of Chicago Press, 2017.

— 'They Come in Peasants and Leave Citizens: Urban Villages and the Making of Shenzhen', in *Learning from Shenzhen: China's Post-Mao Experiment from Special Zone to Model City*, ed. Mary Ann O'Donnell, Winnie Wong and Jonathan Bach, Chicago: University of Chicago Press, 2017.

Baird, Davis, *Thing Knowledge: A Philosophy of Scientific Instruments*, Berkeley, CA: University of California Press, 2004.

Bandurski, David, *Dragons in Diamond Village: Tales of Resistance from Urbanizing China*, New York: Melville House, 2016.

Barad, Karen, *Meeting the Universe Halfway: Quantum Physics and the Entanglement of Matter and Meaning*, Durham, NC: Duke University Press, 2007.

Barbaro, Michael, 'Why Controlling 5G Could Mean Controlling the World', *The Daily*, 2019, https://podcasts.apple.com/us/podcast/why-controlling-5g-could-mean-controlling-the-world/id1200361736?i=1000430563445 (accessed 22 February 2023).

Barmé, Geremie R., 'The Great Firewall of China', *Wired*, 1 June 1997, https://www.wired.com/1997/06/china-3/ (accessed 22 February 2023).

Barnes, Russell, *How the Victorians Wired the World*, documentary, Blakeway Productions, 2000.

Barrett, Tim H., and Francesca Tarocco, 'Terminology and Religious Identity: Buddhism and the Genealogy of the Term Zongjiao', in *Dynamics in the History of Religions Between Asia and Europe: Encounters, Notions, and Comparative Perspectives*, ed. Volkhard Krech and Marion Steinicke, Leiden: Brill, 2012.

Baudrillard, Jean, *Simulacra and Simulation*, trans. Sheila Glaser, Ann Arbor, MI: University of Michigan Press, 1994.

Bays, Daniel H., *China Enters the Twentieth Century: Chang Chih-Tung and the Issues of a New Age, 1895–1909*, Ann Arbor, MI: University of Michigan Press, 1978.

Beall, Abigail, 'In China, Alibaba's Data-Hungry AI is Controlling (and Watching) Cities', *Wired*, 2018, https://www.wired.co.uk/article/alibaba-city-brain-artificial-intelligence-china-kuala-lumpur (accessed 22 February 2023).

Bennett, Adrian Arthur, *John Fryer: The Introduction of Western Science and Technology into Nineteenth-Century China*, Leiden: Brill, 2020.

Bennett, Jane, *Vibrant Matter: A Political Ecology of Things*, Durham, NC: Duke University Press, 2010.

Berger, Edmund, 'Tactile Power', *Reciprocal Contradiction* (blog), 28 March 2020, https://reciprocalcontradiction.home.blog/2020/03/28/tactile-power/ (accessed 22 February 2023).

Bergère, Marie-Claire, *Shanghai: China's Gateway to Modernity*, Stanford, CA: Stanford University Press, 2009.

Bickers, Robert, 'Restoration and Reform, 1860–1900', in *The Oxford Illustrated History of Modern China*, ed. Jeffrey N. Wasserstrom, Oxford: Oxford University Press, 2016.

Billioud, Sébastien, 'Mou Zongsan's Problem with the Heideggerian Interpretation of Kant', *Journal of Chinese Philosophy* 33, no. 2 (2006): 225–47, https://doi.org/10.1163/15406253-03302003

— *Thinking Through Confucian Modernity: A Study of Mou Zongsan's Moral Metaphysics*, Leiden: Brill, 2011, https://brill.com/view/title/15284 (accessed 22 February 2023).

Blum, Susan D., and Lionel M. Jensen, *China Off Center: Mapping the Margins of the Middle Kingdom*, Honolulu, HI: University of Hawaii Press, 2002.

Bodanis, David, *The Electric Universe: The Shocking True Story of Electricity*, New York: Crown Publishers, 2005.

Boon, Marcus, *In Praise of Copying*, Cambridge, MA: Harvard University Press, 2011.

— 'A Place Where the Unknown Past and the Emergent Future Meet in a Vibrating Soundless Hum: Thoughts on Energy and the Contemporary', in *Energies in the Arts*, ed. Douglas Kahn, Cambridge, MA: MIT Press, 2019.

Born, Erik Christopher, 'Sparks to Signals: Literature, Science, and Wireless Technology, 1800–1930', UC Berkeley, 2016, https://escholarship.org/uc/item/9qs9703w (accessed 22 February 2023).

Bratton, Benjamin, '18 Lessons of Quarantine Urbanism', *Strelka Mag*, 3 April 2020, https://www.wired.com/beyond-the-beyond/2020/04/benjamin-bratton-18-lessons-quarantine-urbanism/ (accessed 22 February 2023).

— 'The City Wears Us: Notes on the Scope of Distributed Sensing and Sensation', *Glass Bead Journal*, 2017, https://www.glassbead.org/article/city-wears-us-notes-scope-distributed-sensing-sensation/?lang=enview (accessed 22 February 2023).

— *The Stack: On Software and Sovereignty*, Cambridge, MA: MIT Press, 2016.

— *The Terraforming*, Moscow: Strelka Press, 2019.

Brindley, Erica Fox, *Ancient China and the Yue: Perceptions and Identities on the Southern Frontier, c.400 BCE–50 CE*, Cambridge: Cambridge University Press, 2015.

Brodsky, Ira, *The History of Wireless: How Creative Minds Produced Technology for the Masses*, St Louis, MO: Telescope Books, 2008.

Brunton, Finn, 'WeChat: Messaging Apps and New Social Currency Transaction Tools', in *Appified: Culture in the Age of Apps*, ed. Jeremy Wade Morris and Sarah Murray, Ann Arbor, MI: University of Michigan Press, 2018.

Bryant, Levi, Nick Srnicek and Graham Harman, *The Speculative Turn: Continental Materialism and Realism*, Melbourne: re.press, 2011.

Bunnin, Nicholas, 'God's Knowledge and Ours: Kant and Mou Zongsan on Intellectual Intuition', *Journal of Chinese Philosophy* 35, no. 4 (2008): 613–24.

Buswell, Robert E., and Donald S. Lopez, *The Princeton Dictionary of Buddhism*, Princeton, NJ: Princeton University Press, 2013.

Cage, John, *Silence: Lectures and Writings*, Middletown, CT: Wesleyan University Press, 2012.

Canales, Jimena, *A Tenth of a Second: A History*, Chicago: University of Chicago Press, 2010.

Cantor, G. N., and Michael Jonathan Sessions Hodge (eds), *Conceptions of Ether: Studies in the History of Ether Theories, 1740–1900*, Cambridge: Cambridge University Press, 1981.

Carey, James W., 'Technology and Ideology: The Case of the Telegraph', *Prospects* 8 (October 1983): 303–25, https://doi.org/10.1017/S0361233300003793

Carrico, K., 'Recentering China: The Cantonese in and beyond the Han', in *Critical Han Studies: The History, Representation, and Identity of China's Majority*, ed. Thomas Mullaney, James Leibold, Stephane Gros and Eric Vanden Bussche, Berkeley: University of California Press, 2012.

Carse, Ashley, 'Nature as Infrastructure: Making and Managing the Panama Canal Watershed', *Social Studies of Science* 42, no. 4 (2012): 539–63.

CBN (ed.), 'Chinese Mobile Payments Transactions Exceed $5.87 Trillion', *China Banking News*, 1 August 2018, https://www.chinabankingnews.com/2018/08/01/chinese-mobile-payments-transactions-exceed-5-87-trillion/ (accessed 22 February 2023).

Chan, Connie, 'When One App Rules Them All: The Case of WeChat and Mobile in China', 6 August 2015, https://a16z.com/2015/08/06/wechat-china-mobile-first/ (accessed 22 February 2023).

Chan, N. Serina, 'What is Confucian and New about the Thought of Mou Zongsan?', in *New Confucianism: A Critical Examination*, ed. John Makeham, Basingstoke: Palgrave Macmillan, 2015 [2003].

Chan, Sin-wai, *Buddhism in Late Ch'ing Political Thought*, vol. 8, Hong Kong: Chinese University Press, 1985.

Chan, Sylvia, 'Li Zehou and New Confucianism', in *New Confucianism: A Critical Examination*, ed. John Makeham, New York: Palgrave Macmillan, 2003, 105–25, https://doi.org/10.1057/9781403982414_5.

Chan, Wing-Cheuk, 'Mou Zongsan's Transformation of Kant's Philosophy', *Journal of Chinese Philosophy* 33, no. 1 (2006): 125–39.

Chan, Wing-Tsit (ed.), *A Source Book in Chinese Philosophy*, Princeton, NJ: Princeton University Press, 1969.

Chang, Hao, *Chinese Intellectuals in Crisis: Search for Order and Meaning*, Berkeley, CA: University of California Press, 1987.

— *Liang Ch'i-Ch'ao and Intellectual Transition in China, 1890–1907*, Cambridge, MA: Harvard University Press, 2013 [1971].

— 'New Confucianism and the Intellectual Crisis of Contemporary China', in *The Limits of Change: Essays on Conservative Alternatives in Republican China*, ed. Charlotte Furth, Cambridge, MA: Harvard University Press, 2014 [1976], 276–302, https://doi.org/10.4159/harvard.9780674332966.c15

Chao, Eveline, 'How WeChat Became China's App For Everything', *Fast Company*, 2017, https://www.fastcompany.com/3065255/

china-wechat-tencent-red-envelopes-and-social-money (accessed 22 February 2023).

Chen, Liyan, 'Red Envelope War: How Alibaba and Tencent Fight Over Chinese New Year', *Forbes*, 19 February 2015, https://www.forbes.com/sites/liyanchen/2015/02/19/red-envelope-war-how-alibaba-and-tencent-fight-over-chinese-new-year/ (accessed 22 February 2023).

Chen, Stephen, 'Blast-off for China's New Satellite Rivals to GPS', *South China Morning Post*, 6 November 2017, https://www.scmp.com/news/china/society/article/2118616/china-launches-satellites-extend-global-range-its-version-gps (accessed 22 February 2023).

Chen, Yujie, Zhifei Mao and Jack Linchuan Qiu, *Super-Sticky WeChat and Chinese Society*, Bingley: Emerald Publishing, 2018.

Cheng, Cheng-ying, 'On the Metaphysical Significance of *Ti* (Body-Embodiment) in Chinese Philosophy: *Benti* (Origin-Substance) and *Ti–Yong* (Substance and Function)', *Journal of Chinese Philosophy* 29, no. 2 (2002): 145–61.

Chiang, Ted, 'Bad Character', *The New Yorker*, 9 May 2016, http://www.newyorker.com/magazine/2016/05/16/if-chinese-were-phonetic (accessed 22 February 2023).

— 'Story of Your Life', in *Stories of Your Life and Others*, London: Picador, 2015.

Chow, Rey, 'Introduction: On Chineseness as a Theoretical Problem', *Boundary* 25, no. 3 (1998): 1–24.

Chrysoloras, Niko, and Richard Bravo, 'Huawei Deals for Tech Will Have Consequences, U.S. Warns EU', Bloomberg.Com, 2019, https://www.bloomberg.com/news/articles/2019-02-07/huawei-deals-for-tech-will-have-consequences-u-s-warns-eu (accessed 22 February 2023).

Chu, Samuel C., and Kwang-Ching Liu, *Liu Hung-Chang and China's Early Modernization*, Abingdon: Routledge, 2016.

Chun-Keung, Kwan, 'Mou Zongsan's Ontological Reading of Tiantai Buddhism', *Journal of Chinese Philosophy* 38, no. 2 (2011): 206–22.

Clower, Jason, *The Unlikely Buddhologist: Tiantai Buddhism in Mou Zongsan's New Confucianism*, Leiden: Brill, 2010.

Coase, Ronald Harry, 'The Nature of the Firm', *Economica* 4, no. 16 (1937): 386–405.

Cohen, Paul A., *Discovering History in China: American Historical Writing on the Recent Chinese Past*, New York: Columbia University Press, 2010.

Cohen, Paul A., and John E. Schrecker (eds), *Reform in Nineteenth Century China*, Cambridge, MA: Harvard University Asia Center, 1976.

Coole, Diana, and Samantha Frost (eds), *New Materialisms: Ontology, Agency, and Politics*, Durham, NC: Duke University Press, 2010.

Crawford, Kate, *Atlas of AI: Power, Politics, and the Planetary Costs of Artificial Intelligence*, New Haven, CT: Yale University Press, 2021.

Creemers, Rogier, 'China's Social Credit System: An Evolving Practice of Control', SSRN Scholarly Paper, Rochester, NY, 9 May 2018, https://doi.org/10.2139/ssrn.3175792

Crow, Barbara, Michael Longford and Kim Sawchuk, *The Wireless Spectrum: The Politics, Practices, and Poetics of Mobile Media*, Toronto: University of Toronto Press, 2010.

Cua, Antonio S., 'On the Ethical Significance of the *Ti–Yong* Distinction', *Journal of Chinese Philosophy* 29, no. 2 (2002): 163–70.

Curtin, Michael, and Hemant Shah (eds), *Reorienting Global Communication: Indian and Chinese Media Beyond Borders*, Urbana, IL: University of Illinois Press, 2010.

Cybernetic Culture Research Unit, *Writings 1997–2003*, 2nd edn, Falmouth: Urbanomic, 2017.

Czitrom, Daniel J., *Media and the American Mind: From Morse to McLuhan*, Chapel Hill, NC: University of North Carolina Press, 1983.

Daum, Jeremy, 'China through a Glass, Darkly', China Law Translate (blog), 24 December 2017, https://www.chinalawtranslate.com/china-social-credit-score/ (accessed 22 February 2023).

Deleuze, Gilles, *Difference and Repetition*, trans Paul Patton, rev. edn, New York: Columbia University Press, 1994.

— *The Fold: Leibniz and the Baroque*, London: Bloomsbury, 2014.

— *Kant's Critical Philosophy: The Doctrine of the Faculties*, London: Continuum, 2008.

— 'On Kant: Synthesis and Time', *Lectures by Gilles Deleuze* (blog), February 2007, http://deleuzelectures.blogspot.com/2007/02/on-kant.html (accessed 22 February 2023).

— *Spinoza: Practical Philosophy*, trans. Robert Hurley, San Francisco: City Lights, 2001.

Deleuze, Gilles, and Félix Guattari. *A Thousand Plateaus: Capitalism and Schizophrenia*, trans. Brian Massumi, Minneapolis, MN: University of Minnesota Press, 1987.

— *Anti-Oedipus: Capitalism and Schizophrenia*, trans. Robert Hurley, Mark Seem and Helen R. Lane, London: Bloomsbury, 2013.

Deloitte, '5G: The Chance to Lead for a Decade', Deloitte, 2018, https://www2.deloitte.com/us/en/pages/consulting/articles/5G-deployment-for-us.html (accessed 22 February 2023).

Douglas, Susan J., *Inventing American Broadcasting, 1899–1922*, Baltimore, MD: Johns Hopkins University Press, 1989.

Dourish, Paul, *The Stuff of Bits: An Essay on the Materialities of Information*, Cambridge, MA: MIT Press, 2017.

Dourish, Paul, and Genevieve Bell, 'The Infrastructure of Experience and the Experience of Infrastructure: Meaning and Structure in Everyday Encounters with Space', *Environment and Planning B: Planning and Design* 34, no. 3 (2007): 414–30.

Drechsler, Wolfgang, Rainer Kattel and Erik S. Reinert (eds), *Techno-Economic Paradigms: Essays in Honour of Carlota Perez*, London: Anthem Press, 2011.

Du Boff, Richard B., 'The Telegraph in Nineteenth-Century America: Technology and Monopoly', *Comparative Studies in Society and History* 26, no. 4 (1984): 571–86.

Du, Juan, 'Don't Underestimate the Rice Fields', in *Urban Transformation*, ed. Ilka Ruby and Andreas Ruby, Berlin: Ruby Press, 2008.

— *The Shenzhen Experiment: The Story of China's Instant City*, Cambridge, MA: Harvard University Press, 2020.

Duara, Prasenjit, *Rescuing History from the Nation: Questioning Narratives of Modern China*, Chicago: University of Chicago Press, 1996.

Easterling, Keller, *Extrastatecraft: The Power of Infrastructure Space*, London: Verso, 2016.

Edwards, Paul, 'Infrastructure and Modernity: Scales of Force, Time, and Social Organization in the History of Sociotechnical Systems', in *Modernity and Technology*, ed. Thomas Misa, Philip Brey and Andrew Feenberg, Cambridge, MA: MIT Press, 2002, 185–225.

— *A Vast Machine: Computer Models, Climate Data, and the Politics of Global Warming*, Cambridge, MA: MIT Press, 2013.

Einstein, Albert, 'Maxwell's Influence on the Development of the Conception of Physical Reality', in *James Clerk Maxwell: A Commemoration Volume 1831–1931* (Cambridge: Cambridge University Press, 2012 [1931]), 66–74.

Eldredge, Niles, and Stephen Jay Gould, 'Punctuated Equilibria: An Alternative to Phyletic Gradualism', in *Models in Paleobiology*, ed. Thomas J. M. Schopf (San Francisco: Freeman Cooper, 1972), 82–115.

Electronics Notes, 'Qi Wireless Charging Standard', Electronics Notes, n.d., https://www.electronics-notes.com/articles/equipment-items-gadgets/wireless-battery-charging/qi-wireless-charging-standard.php (accessed 22 February 2023).

Elias, Amy J., and Christian Moraru (eds), *The Planetary Turn: Relationality and Geoaesthetics in the Twenty-First Century*, Evanston, IL: Northwestern University Press, 2015.

Enns, A., and S. Trower (eds), *Vibratory Modernism*, London: Palgrave Macmillan, 2013.

Erisman, Porter, *Crocodile in the Yangtze. Documentary, Biography*, Purple Reel Productions, Taluswood Films, 2012.

Ernst, Wolfgang, *Chronopoetics: The Temporal Being and Operativity of Technological Media*, trans. Anthony Enns, Lanham, MD: Rowman and Littlefield, 2016.

— *Digital Memory and the Archive*, ed. Jussi Parikka, Minneapolis, MN: University of Minnesota Press, 2012.

Eurasia Live, 'The Geopolitics of 5G', Eurasia Group, 15 November 2018, https://www.eurasiagroup.net/live-post/the-geopolitics-of-5g (accessed 22 February 2023).

Fallows, James, 'How the World Works', *The Atlantic*, 1 December 1993, https://www.theatlantic.com/magazine/archive/1993/12/how-the-world-works/305854/ (accessed 22 February 2023).

Fan, Jiayang, 'How China Views the Arrest of Huawei's Meng Wanzhou', *The New Yorker*, 17 December 2018, https://www.newyorker.com/news/daily-comment/how-china-views-the-arrest-of-huaweis-meng-wanzhou (accessed 22 February 2023).

Feng, Guifen, 'Excerpts from "On the Adoption of Western Learning"', in *Changing China: Readings in the History of China from the Opium War to the Present*, ed. Gentzler J. Mason, New York: Praeger, 1977.

Ferry, Elizabeth, and John Plotz, 'Old and New Media with Lisa Gitelman', Recall This Book, 2019, https://recallthisbook.org/2019/01/30/old-and-new-media-with-lisa-gitelman/ (accessed 22 February 2023).

Feynman, Richard P., *The Feynman Lectures on Physics, Vol. I: The New Millennium Edition: Mainly Mechanics, Radiation, and Heat*, ed. Robert B. Leighton and Matthew Sands, New York: Basic Books, 2011.

Finnigan, Bronwyn, 'Buddhist Idealism', in *Idealism: New Essays in Metaphysics*, ed. Tyron Goldschmidt and Kenneth L. Pearce, Oxford: Oxford University Press, 2017.

Fisher, Mark, *The Weird and the Eerie*, 3rd edn, London: Repeater, 2016.

Flusser, Vilém, 'The City as Wave-Trough in the Image-Flood', *Critical Inquiry* 31, no. 2 (2005): 320–8.

Forbes, Nancy, and Basil Mahon, *Faraday, Maxwell, and the Electromagnetic Field: How Two Men Revolutionized Physics*, New York: Prometheus, 2014.

Foucault, Michel, *Ethics: Subjectivity and Truth: Essential Works of Michel Foucault 1954–1984*, London: Penguin, 2020.

— *The Foucault Reader: An Introduction to Foucault's Thought*, ed. Paul Rabinow, London: Penguin, 1991.

— *The Order of Things*, 2nd edn, Abingdon: Routledge, 2018.

Freeman, Christopher, and Francisco Louçã, *As Time Goes by: From the Industrial Revolutions to the Information Revolution*, Oxford: Oxford University Press, 2001.

Friedman, Michael, 'Einstein, Kant, and the Relativized a Priori', in *Constituting Objectivity: Transcendental Perspectives on Modern Physics*, ed. Michael Bitbol, Pierre Kerszberg and Jean Petitot, New York: Springer, 2009, 253–67.

— *A Parting of the Ways: Carnap, Cassirer, and Heidegger*, Chicago: Open Court, 2000.

Fung, Edmund S. K., *The Intellectual Foundations of Chinese Modernity: Cultural and Political Thought in the Republican Era*, Cambridge: Cambridge University Press, 2010.

Furth, Charlotte (ed.), *The Limits of Change: Essays on Conservative Alternatives in Republican China*, Cambridge, MA: Harvard University Press, 2014 [1976].

Furuhata, Yuriko, 'The Fog Medium: Visualizing and Engineering the Atmosphere', *Screen Genealogies: From Optical Device to Environmental Medium*, 1 January 2019, https://www.academia.edu/41216822/The_Fog_Medium_Visualizing_and_Engineering_the_Atmosphere (accessed 22 February 2023).

— 'Of Dragons and Geoengineering: Rethinking Elemental Media', *Media+ Environment* 1, no. 1 (2019): 10797.

Future Networks Team, Huawei Technologies, 'Internet 2030: Towards a New Internet for the Year 2030 and Beyond', *Huawei*, 18 July 2018, https://www.itu.int/en/ITU-T/studygroups/2017-2020/13/Documents/Internet_2030%20.pdf (accessed 22 February 2023).

Gabrys, Jennifer, 'Atmospheres of Communication', in *The Wireless Spectrum: The Politics, Practices, and Poetics of Mobile Media*, ed. Barbara Crow, Michael Longford and Kim Sawchuk, Toronto: University of Toronto Press, 2010.

— 'Automatic Sensation: Environmental Sensors in the Digital City', *The Senses and Society* 2, no. 2 (2007): 189–200.

— *Digital Futures Series*, Toronto: University of Toronto Press, 2010.

— *Program Earth: Environmental Sensing Technology and the Making of a Computational Planet*, Minneapolis, MN: University of Minnesota Press, 2016.

— 'Telepathically Urban', in *Circulation and the City: Essays on Urban Culture*, ed. Alexandra Boutros and Will Straw, vol. 3, Montreal: McGill-Queen's University Press, 2010.

Galchen, Rivka, and David Z. Albert, 'Nonlocality from Newton to Maxwell', *Scientific American*, 18 February 2009, https://www.scientificamerican.com/article/nonlocality-from-newton/ (accessed 22 February 2023).

Galison, Peter, *Einstein's Clocks, Poincaré's Maps: Empires of Time*, New York: W. W. Norton, 2003.

Gane, Nicholas, and Stephen Sale, 'Interview with Friedrich Kittler and Mark Hansen', *Theory, Culture & Society* 24, no. 7–8 (2007): 323–9.

Garnar, Martin, '*Consent of the Networked: The Worldwide Struggle for Internet Freedom* by Rebecca MacKinnon', *Portal: Libraries and the Academy* 13, no. 1 (2013): 114–15.

Garratt, G. R. M., *The Early History of Radio: From Faraday to Marconi*, London: Institute of Engineering and Technology, 1994.

Garton, Vincent, 'Sino-No-Futurism (a Comment)', *Cyclonograph II* (blog), 2020, https://vincentgarton.com/2020/04/10/sino-no-futurism/ (accessed 22 February 2023).

Ge, Zhaoguang, *What is China? Territory, Ethnicity, Culture, and History*, trans. Michael Gibbs Hill, Cambridge, MA: Harvard University Press, 2018.

Gewirtz, Julian, 'The Futurists of Beijing: Alvin Toffler, Zhao Ziyang, and China's "New Technological Revolution"', *The Journal of Asian Studies* 78, no. 1 (1979): 115–40.

Gibson, William, *Spook Country*, London: Penguin, 2011.

Gillespie, Tarleton, 'The Politics of "Platforms"', *New Media & Society* 12, no. 3 (2010): 347–64.

Gitelman, Lisa, *Always Already New: Media, History and the Data of Culture*, Cambridge, MA: MIT Press, 2006.

Gleick, James, *Information: A History, a Theory, a Flood*, London: Fourth Estate, 2012.

— *Time Travel*, London: Fourth Estate, 2017.

Godfrey-Smith, Peter, *Other Minds: The Octopus and the Evolution of Intelligent Life*, London: HarperCollins, 2017.

Goldkorn, Jeremy, '5G – China's next National Project?', *SupChina*, 6 June 2019, https://supchina.com/2019/06/06/5g-chinas-next-national-project/ (accessed 22 February 2023).

Goodchild, Michael F., 'GIScience Ten Years after Ground Truth', *Transactions in GIS* 10, no. 5 (2006): 687–92.

Greenspan, Anna, *Shanghai Future: Modernity Remade*, Oxford: Oxford University Press, 2014.

Greenspan, Anna, and Suzanne Livingston, *Future Mutation: Technology, Shanzai and the Evolution of Species*, Shanghai: Time Spiral Press, 2015.

Greenspan, Anna, and Francesca Tarocco, 'An Enchanted Modern: Urban Cultivation in Shanghai', *International Quarterly for Asian Studies* 51, no. 1–2 (2020): 223–42.

Grieve, Gregory Price, and Daniel Veidlinger (eds), *Buddhism, the Internet, and Digital Media: The Pixel in the Lotus*, Abingdon: Routledge, 2014.

Grosnick, William H., 'The Categories of T'i, Hsiang, and Yung: Evidence That Paramārtha Composed the *Awakening of Faith*', *Journal of the International Association of Buddhist Studies*, 30 June 1989, 65–92, https://journals.ub.uni-heidelberg.de/index.php/jiabs/article/view/8748/2655 (accessed 22 February 2023).

Grusin, Richard (ed.), *The Nonhuman Turn*, Minneapolis, MN: University of Minnesota Press, 2015.

Guo, Qiyong, 'An Exposition of Zhou Yi Studies in Modern Neo-Confucianism', *Frontiers of Philosophy in China* 1, no. 2 (2006): 185–203.

Hadot, Pierre, *Philosophy as a Way of Life: Spiritual Exercises from Socrates to Foucault*, Chichester: John Wiley & Sons, 1995.

Hagen, Wolfgang, 'Beyond Radio', *kunstradio*, 1993, http://www.kunstradio.at/THEORIE/HAGEN/hagen_e.html (accessed 22 February 2023).

— 'On the Place of Radio', *Recycling the Future*, Vienna, 1997, http://www.kunstradio.at/FUTURE/RTF/SYMPOSIUM/LECTURES/HAGEN/hagen-txt-e.html (accessed 22 February 2023).

Hall, Peter, *Cities in Civilization*, London: Pantheon, 1998.

Hall, Peter, and Paschal Preston, *The Carrier Wave: New Information Technology and the Geography of Innovation, 1846–2003*, London: Routledge, 1988.

Halpern, Sue, 'A Pitch for a Nationwide 5G Network Tailor-Made for Trump's 2020 Campaign', *The New Yorker*, 24 May 2019, https://www.newyorker.com/news/annals-of-communications/karl-rove-and-a-pitch-for-a-nationwide-5g-network-tailored-to-trumps-2020-campaign (accessed 22 February 2023).

— 'The Terrifying Potential of 5G Technology', *The New Yorker*, 26 April 2019, https://www.newyorker.com/news/annals-of-communications/the-terrifying-potential-of-the-5g-network (accessed 22 February 2023).

Hammerstrom, Erik J., *The Science of Chinese Buddhism: Early Twentieth-Century Engagements*, New York: Columbia University Press, 2015.

Han, Byung-Chul, *Shanzhai: Deconstruction in Chinese*, Cambridge, MA: MIT Press, 2017.

Han, Han, *This Generation: Dispatches from China's Most Popular Literary Star (and Race Car Driver*, New York: Simon and Schuster, 2012.

Hanafin, John J., 'The "Last Buddhist": The Philosophy of Liang Shuming', in *New Confucianism: A Critical Examination*, ed. John Makeham, New York: Palgrave Macmillan, 2003, 187–218, https://doi.org/10.1057/9781403982414_8

Hansen, Mark B. N., *Feed Forward: On the Future of Twenty-First-Century Media*, Chicago: University of Chicago Press, 2015.

— 'Logics of Futurity, or on the Physicality of Media', presented at the School of Criticism and Theory, Duke University, 2014, https://www.cornell.edu/video/mark-bn-hansen-physicality-of-media (accessed 23 February 2023).

— 'Triggers: Introducing the Technosphere', presented at *100 Years of Now*, Haus der Kulturen der Welt, Berlin, 2015, https://archiv.hkw.de/en/app/mediathek/video/44297 (accessed 23 February 2023).

— 'Ubiquitous Sensation: Toward an Atmospheric, Collective, and Microtemporal Media', in *Throughout: Art and Culture Emerging with Ubiquitous Computing*, ed. Ulrik Ekman and Matthew Fuller, Cambridge, MA: MIT Press, 2012.

Hao, Karen, 'The New Satellite Image of Earth on WeChat's Splash Page Features China at its Center – for a Reason', *Quartz*, 26 September 2017, https://qz.com/1086561/wechat-has-swapped-a-nasa-satellites-image-of-earth-on-its-splash-screen-for-a-chinese-one/ (accessed 22 February 2023).

Haraway, Donna J., *When Species Meet*, Minneapolis, MN: University of Minnesota Press, 2007.

Hayles, N. Katherine, 'Cognition Everywhere: The Rise of the Cognitive Nonconscious and the Costs of Consciousness', *New Literary History* 45, no. 2 (2014): 199–220.

— *How We Became Posthuman: Virtual Bodies in Cybernetics, Literature, and Informatics*, Chicago: University of Chicago Press, 1999.

— *How We Think: Digital Media and Contemporary Technogenesis*, Chicago: University of Chicago Press, 2012.

— 'RFID: Human Agency and Meaning in Information-Intensive Environments', *Theory, Culture & Society* 26, no. 2–3 (2009): 47–72.

— 'Unfinished Work: From Cyborg to Cognisphere', *Theory, Culture & Society* 23, no. 7–8 (2006): 159–66.

— *Unthought: The Power of the Cognitive Nonconscious*, Chicago: University of Chicago Press, 2017.

Headrick, Daniel R., *The Tentacles of Progress: Technology Transfer in the Age of Imperialism, 1850–1940*, New York: Oxford University Press, 1988.

— *When Information Came of Age: Technologies of Knowledge in the Age of Reason and Revolution, 1700–1850*, Oxford: Oxford University Press, 2000.

Hegel, Georg Wilhelm Friedrich, *The Philosophy of History*, trans. J. Sibree, Mineola, NY: Dover Publications, 2004.

Heidegger, Martin, 'The Question Concerning Technology', in *The Question Concerning Technology and Other Essays*, trans. and ed. William Lovitt, New York: Garland Publishing, 1977, 3–49.

Heimann, Peter M., 'The Unseen Universe: Physics and the Philosophy of Nature in Victorian Britain', *The British Journal for the History of Science* 6, no. 1 (1972): 73-9.

Helmreich, Stefan, 'The Genders of Waves', *Women's Studies Quarterly* 45, no. 1–2 (2017): 29–51.

— 'Gravity's Reverb: Listening to Space-Time, or Articulating the Sounds of Gravitational-Wave Detection', *Cultural Anthropology* 31, no. 4 (2016): 464–92.

Herold, David Kurt, and Peter Marolt (eds), *Online Society in China: Creating, Celebrating, and Instrumentalising the Online Carnival*, Abingdon: Routledge, 2011.

Ho, Josephine, 'ShanZhai: Economic/Cultural Production through the Cracks of Globalization', plenary speech presented at the 'Crossroads: 2010 Cultural Studies' conference, Hong Kong, 2010, https://sex.ncu.edu.tw/members/Ho/20100617%20Crossroads%20Plenary%20Speech.pdf (accessed 22 February 2023).

Hogan, Mél, 'Data is Airborne; Data is Inborn: The Labor of the Body in Technoecologies', *First Monday* 3, no. 3 (2018), https://firstmonday.org/ojs/index.php/fm/article/view/8285/6650 (accessed 22 February 2023).

Hollander, Rayna, 'WeChat Has Hit 1 Billion Monthly Active Users', *Business Insider*, 6 March 2018, https://www.businessinsider.com/wechat-has-hit-1-billion-monthly-active-users-2018-3 (accessed 22 February 2023).

Hon, Tze-ki, 'Zhang Zhidong's Proposal for Reform: A New Reading of the Quanxue Pian', in *Rethinking the 1898 Reform Period: Political and Cultural Change in Late Qing China*, ed. Rebecca E. Karl and Peter Gue Zarrow, Cambridge, MA: Harvard University Asia Center, 2002, 77–98, https://brill.com/view/book/edcoll/9781684173747/BP000005.xml (accessed 22 February 2023).

Hong, Sungook, *Wireless: From Marconi's Black-Box to the Audion*, Cambridge, MA, MIT Press, 2001.

Hu, Tung-Hui, *A Prehistory of the Cloud*, Cambridge, MA: MIT Press, 2016.

Hua, Yu, 'Opinion | The Spirit of May 35th', *The New York Times*, 23 June 2011, https://www.nytimes.com/2011/06/24/opinion/global/24iht-june24-ihtmag-hua-28.html (accessed 22 February 2023).

Huang Bunnie, 'The $12 "Gongkai" Phone', Bunnie's Blog (blog), 18 April 2013, https://www.bunniestudios.com/blog/?page_id=3107 (accessed 22 February 2023).

Huang, Weiwen, 'The Tripartite Origins of Shenzhen: Beijing, Hong Kong and Bao-An', in *Learning from Shenzhen: China's Post-Mao Experiment from Special Zone to Model City*, ed. Mary Ann O'Donnell, Winnie Wong and Jonathan Bach, Chicago: University of Chicago Press, 2017.

Hughes, Thomas Parke, *Networks of Power: Electrification in Western Society, 1880–1930*, Baltimore, MD: Johns Hopkins University Press, 1993.

Hui, Yuk, *The Question Concerning Technology in China: An Essay in Cosmotechnics*, Cambridge, MA: Urbanomic, 2016.

Huters, Theodore, *Bringing the World Home: Appropriating the West in Late Qing and Early Republican China*, Honolulu, HI: University of Hawaii Press, 2017.

Hvistendahl, Mara, 'China's Tech Giants Want to Go Global – Just One Thing Might Stand in Their Way', *MIT Technology Review*, 19 December 2019.

— 'How a Chinese AI Giant Made Chatting – and Surveillance – Easy', *Wired*, 18 May 2020, https://www.wired.com/story/iflytek-china-ai-giant-voice-chatting-surveillance/ (accessed 22 February 2023).

— 'Inside China's Vast New Experiment in Social Ranking', *Wired*, 14 December 2017, https://www.wired.com/story/age-of-social-credit/ (accessed 22 February 2023).

I.N.T.I., 'Shenzhen: A Lecture by Juan Du', 2015, https://www.youtube.com/watch?v=k8vYsD5aal8 (accessed 22 February 2023).

— 'Shenzhen: A Lecture by Tat Lam', 2015. https://www.youtube.com/watch?v=spEuIo8Zo-8 (accessed 22 February 2023).

Ireland, Amy, 'Alien Rhythms', *Alienist* VI (1 January 2019), https://www.academia.edu/43116778/Alien_Rhythms (accessed 22 February 2023).

Irigaray, Luce, *Speculum of the Other Woman*, Ithaca, NY: Cornell University Press, 1985.

Jao, Nicole, 'A Short History of the QR Code in China and Why Southeast Asia is Next', TechNode (blog), 10 September 2018, http://technode.com/2018/09/10/qr-code-payment-overseas-china/ (accessed 22 February 2023).

Jenco, Leigh K., 'How Meaning Moves: Tan Sitong on Borrowing across Cultures', *Philosophy East and West* 62, no. 1 (2012): 92–113.

Jiang, Chenxin, 'QR is King', *Logic Magazine*, 1 May 2019, https://logicmag.io/china/qr-is-king/ (accessed 22 February 2023).

Johnson, David, 'The City-God Cults of T'ang and Sung China', *Harvard Journal of Asiatic Studies* 45, no. 2 (1985): 363–457.

Jones, A., *Splitting the Second: The Story of Atomic Time*, Philadelphia: CRC Press, 2000.

Jones, Andrew F., *Developmental Fairy Tales: Evolutionary Thinking and Modern Chinese Culture*, Cambridge, MA: Harvard University Press, 2011.

Joyce, Zita, 'Creating Order in the Ceaseless Flow: The Discursive Constitution of the Radio Spectrum', PhD thesis, ResearchSpace@Auckland, 2008, https://researchspace.auckland.ac.nz/handle/2292/5619 (accessed 22 February 2023).

Jue, Melody, *Wild Blue Media: Thinking through Seawater*, Durham, NC: Duke University Press, 2020.

Kahn, Douglas, *Earth Sound Earth Signal: Energies and Earth Magnitude in the Arts*, Berkeley, CA: University of California Press, 2013.

Kant, Immanuel, *Critique of Pure Reason*, London: Macmillan, 1929.

Karl, Rebecca E., *Staging the World: Chinese Nationalism at the Turn of the Twentieth Century*, Durham, NC: Duke University Press, 2002.

Karl, Rebecca E., and Peter Zarrow (eds), *Rethinking the 1898 Reform Period: Political and Cultural Change in Late Qing China*, Cambridge, MA: Harvard University Asia Center, 2002.

Keli, Fang, 'On the Categories of Substance and Function in Chinese Philosophy', *Chinese Studies in Philosophy* 17, no. 3 (1986): 26–77.

Kessel, Jonah M., and Paul Mozur, 'How China is Changing Your Internet', *The New York Times*, 10 August 2016, https://www.youtube.com/watch?v=VAesMQ6VtK8 (accessed 22 February 2023).

Kipling, Rudyard, *Traffics and Discoveries*, London: Macmillan, 1982.

Kittler, Friedrich, 'The History of Communication Media', *Ctheory*, special issue 'Global Algorithm' (1996): 7–30, https://journals.uvic.ca/index.php/ctheory/article/view/14325/5101 (accessed 22 February 2023).

Kohn, Livia, *Daoism Handbook*, Leiden: Brill, 2005.

— *Meditation Works in the Hindu, Buddhist, and Daoist Traditions*, Magdalena, NM: Three Pines Press, 2008.

Kohn, Livia, and Robin R. Wang (eds), *Internal Alchemy: Self, Society and the Quest for Immortality*, Magdalena, NM: Three Pines Press, 2009.

Kondratiev, Nikolai D., and W. F. Stolper, 'The Long Waves in Economic Life', *The Review of Economics and Statistics* 17, no. 6 (1935): 105–15.

Koolhaas, Rem, *The Generic City*, New York: Sikkens Foundation, 1995.

Krämer, Sybille, 'The Cultural Techniques of Time Axis Manipulation: On Friedrich Kittler's Conception of Media', *Theory, Culture & Society* 23, no. 7–8 (2006): 93–109.

Kuhn, Thomas S., *The Structure of Scientific Revolutions*, 4th edn, Chicago: University of Chicago Press, 2012.

Kuo, Kaiser, 'An American Futurist in China: Alvin Toffler and Reform & Opening', *Sinica*, 2019, https://supchina.com/podcast/an-american-futurist-in-china-alvin-toffler-and-reform-opening/ (accessed 22 February 2023).

— 'Huawei and the Tech Cold War with Samm Sacks and Paul Triolo', *Sinica*, 2019, https://supchina.com/podcast/huawei-and-the-tech-cold-war/ (accessed 22 February 2023).

— 'Meng Wanzhou's Arrest: The Legal Dimension with Julian Ku', *Sinica*, 2019, https://supchina.com/podcast/meng-wanzhous-arrest-the-legal-dimension/ (accessed 22 February 2023).

— 'Whose Century is it, Anyway?', *Sinica*, 2019, https://thechinaproject.com/podcast/whose-century-anyway/ (accessed 22 February 2023).

Kwok, D. W. Y., *Scientism in Chinese Thought, 1900–1950*, New Haven, CT: Yale University Press, 1965.

Kwon, Sun-hyang, and Jeson Woo, 'On the Origin and Conceptual Development of "Essence-Function" (Ti–yong)', *Religions* 10, no. 4 (2019): 272.

Kwong, Luke S. K, 'The T'i-Yung Dichotomy and the Search for Talent in Late-Ch'ing China', *Modern Asian Studies* 27, no. 2 (1993): 253–79.

Landes, David S., *Revolution in Time: Clocks and the Making of the Modern World*, 2nd rev. edn, Cambridge, MA: Belknap Press of Harvard University Press, 2000.

Larkin, Brian, 'The Politics and Poetics of Infrastructure', *Annual Review of Anthropology* 42 (2013): 327–43.

Latour, Bruno, *We Have Never Been Modern*, trans. Catherine Porter, Cambridge, MA: Harvard University Press, 1993.

Lee, Heejin, Shirley Chan and Sangjo Oh, 'China's ICT Standards Policy after the WTO Accession: Techno-national versus Techno-globalism', *Info* 11, no. 1 (2009): 9–18, https://doi.org/10.1108/14636690910932966

Lee, Leo Ou-fan, 'On the Margins of the Chinese Discourse: Some Personal Thoughts on the Cultural Meaning of the Periphery', *Daedalus* 2, no. 2 (1991): 207–26.

— *Shanghai Modern: The Flowering of a New Urban Culture in China, 1930–1945*, Cambridge, MA: Harvard University Press, 1999.

Legge, James, 'Book of Changes : Xi Ci I', *Chinese Text Project: A Dynamic Digital Library of Premodern Chinese*, 2019, https://ctext.org/book-of-changes/xi-ci-shang/ens?filter=504074%2E (accessed 22 February 2023).

Lek, Lawrence, *Geomancer*, 2017, https://lawrencelek.com/geomancer (accessed 22 February 2023).

— *Sinofuturism*, 2016, https://vimeo.com/179509486 (accessed 22 February 2023).

Levenson, Joseph R., *Confucian China and its Modern Fate: A Trilogy*, Berkeley, CA: ACLS Humanities E-Book, 2008.

Li, Hongchang, 'Li's Recommendation of Western Methods: June 1863', in *China's Response to the West: A Documentary Survey, 1839–1923*, ed. Ssu-yü Têng and John King Fairbank, Cambridge, MA: Harvard University Press, 1979.

Li, Zehou, 'The Western is the Substance, and the Chinese is for Application:(Excerpts)', *Contemporary Chinese Thought* 31, no. 2 (1999): 32–9.

Lindtner, Silvia, *Prototype Nation: China and the Contested Promise of Innovation*, Princeton, NJ: Princeton University Press, 2020.

— 'Shanzhai: China's Collaborative Electronics-Design Ecosystem', *The Atlantic*, 18 May 2014, https://www.theatlantic.com/technology/archive/2014/05/chinas-mass-production-system/370898/ (accessed 22 February 2023).

Lindtner, Silvia, Anna Greenspan and David Li, 'Designed in Shenzhen: Shanzhai Manufacturing and Maker Entrepreneurs', in *Proceedings of the Fifth Decennial Aarhus Conference on Critical Alternatives* (2015), 85–96, https://dl.acm.org/doi/10.7146/aahcc.v1i1.21265 (accessed 22 February 2023).

Liu, JeeLoo, *An Introduction to Chinese Philosophy: From Ancient Philosophy to Chinese Buddhism*, Malden, MA: Wiley-Blackwell, 2006.

— *Neo-Confucianism: Metaphysics, Mind, and Morality*, Hoboken, NJ: Wiley-Blackwell, 2017.

Liu, Kevin Ziyu, 'Commercial-state Empire: A Political Economy Perspective on Social Surveillance in Contemporary China', *The Political Economy of Communication* 7, no. 1 (2019): 3–29.

Liu, Lydia H., *The Clash of Empires: The Invention of China in Modern World Making*, Cambridge, MA: Harvard University Press, 2004.

— 'Review of *Bringing the World Home: Appropriating the West in Late Qing and Early Republican China*', *China Review International* 14, no. 2 (2007): 329–37.

Liu, Shu-hsien, *Essentials of Contemporary Neo-Confucian Philosophy*, New York: Praeger, 2003.

— 'Hsiung Shih-Li's Theory of Causation', *Philosophy East and West* 19, no. 4 (1969): 399–407.

Liu, Xiao, *Information Fantasies: Precarious Mediation in Postsocialist China*, Minneapolis, MN: University of Minnesota Press, 2019.

— 'Magic Waves, Extrasensory Powers, and Nonstop Instantaneity: Imagining the Digital beyond Digits', *Grey Room*, no. 63 (2016): 42–69.

Liu, Xun, *Daoist Modern: Innovation, Lay Practice, and the Community of Inner Alchemy in Republican Shanghai*, Cambridge, MA: Harvard University Asia Center, 2009.

Lodge, Oliver, *The Ether of Space*, London: Harper, 1909.

Lovink, Geert, 'Cybernetics for the Twenty-First Century: An Interview with Philosopher Yuk Hui', *E-Flux Journal*, no. 102 (2019).

Lusthaus, Dan, *Buddhist Phenomenology: A Philosophical Investigation of Yogacara Buddhism and the Ch'eng Wei-Shih Lun*, London: Routledge, 2003.

Lüthje, Boy, Stefanie Hürtgen, Peter Pawlicki and Martina Sproll, *From Silicon Valley to Shenzhen: Global Production and Work in the IT Industry*, Lanham, MD: Rowman and Littlefield, 2013.

Lyn, Jeffery, 'Mining an Unexpected Source of Innovation: Lessons from Shanzhai', *Institute for the Future*, September 2013, https://slidetodoc.com/mining-an-unexpected-source-of-innovation-lessons-from/ (accessed 22 February 2023).

Ma, Alexandra, 'China is Reportedly Tracking Ethnic Minorities by Sticking QR Codes with their Personal Information on their Front Doors', *Business Insider*, 13 September 2018, https://www.businessinsider.com/china-tracks-uighur-minority-qr-code-kitchen-knives-doors-human-rights-watch-report-2018-9 (accessed 22 February 2023).

Ma, Shaoling, *The Stone and the Wireless: Mediating China, 1861–1906*, Durham, NC: Duke University Press, 2021.

Mackenzie, Adrian, *Wirelessness: Radical Empiricism in Network Cultures*, Cambridge, MA: MIT Press, 2010.

MacKinnon, Rebecca, *Consent of the Networked: The Worldwide Struggle for Internet Freedom*, New York: Basic Books, 2012.

Maddalena, Kate, and Jeremy Packer, 'The Digital Body: Telegraphy as Discourse Network', *Theory, Culture & Society* 32, no. 1 (2015): 93–117.

Makeham, John, 'Introduction', in *New Confucianism: A Critical Examination*, ed. John Makeham, New York: Palgrave Macmillan, 2003, 1–21, https://doi.org/10.1057/9781403982414_1

— 'The New Daotong', in *New Confucianism: A Critical Examination*, ed. John Makeham, New York: Palgrave Macmillan, 2003, 55–78, https://doi.org/10.1057/9781403982414_3

— 'The Retrospective Creation of New Confucianism', in *New Confucianism: A Critical Examination*, ed. John Makeham, New York: Palgrave Macmillan, 2003, 25–53, https://doi.org/10.1057/9781403982414_2

— 'Xiong Shili and the *Treatise on Awakening Mahāyāna Faith* as Revealed in *Record to Destroy Confusion and Make My Tenets Explicit*', in *The Awakening of Faith and New Confucian Philosophy*, ed. John Makeham, Leiden: Brill, 2021, https://doi.org/10.1163/9789004471245_006

— 'Xiong Shili's Critique of Yogācāra Thought in the Context of his Constructive Philosophy', in *Transforming Consciousness: Yogacara Thought in Modern China*, ed. John Makeham, Oxford: Oxford University Press, 2014, https://doi.org/10.1093/acprof:oso/9780199358120.003.0009

— 'Xiong Shili's Understanding of the Relationship between the Ontological and the Phenomenal', in *Chinese Metaphysics and its Problems*, ed. Chenyang Li and Franklin Perkins, Cambridge: Cambridge University Press, 2015, 207–23.

Makeham, John (ed.), *The Awakening of Faith and New Confucian Philosophy*, Leiden: Brill, 2021.

— *Learning to Emulate the Wise: The Genesis of Chinese Philosophy as an Academic Discipline in Twentieth-Century China*, Hong Kong: The Chinese University of Hong Kong Press, 2012.

— *New Confucianism: A Critical Examination*, New York: Palgrave Macmillan, 2003.

— *Transforming Consciousness: Yogacara Thought in Modern China*, Oxford: Oxford University Press, 2014.

Mann, Adam, 'How the U.S. Built the World's Most Ridiculously Accurate Atomic Clock', *Wired*, 4 April 2014, https://www.wired.com/2014/04/nist-atomic-clock/ (accessed 22 February 2023).

Mattern, Shannon, 'A City is not a Computer', *Places Journal* 18 (2017), https://placesjournal.org/article/a-city-is-not-a-computer/ (accessed 22 February 2023).

— *Code and Clay, Data and Dirt: Five Thousand Years of Urban Media*, Minneapolis, MN: University of Minnesota Press, 2017.

— 'Data Fantasies and Operational Facts: 5G's Infrastructural Epistemologies', Designing for the Unknown, 2019, https://www.youtube.com/watch?v=TvEA93Q6ETg (accessed 22 February 2023).

— 'Deep Time of Media Infrastructure', in *Signal Traffic: Critical Studies of Media Infrastructures*, ed. Nicole Starosielski and Lisa Parks, Urbana, IL: University of Illinois Press, 2015.

— 'Infrastructural Intelligence', *Words in Space* (blog), 1 January 2016, https://wordsinspace.net/2016/01/01/infrastructural-intelligence/ (accessed 22 February 2023).

— 'Infrastructural Tourism', *Places Journal*, 2013, https://placesjournal.org/article/infrastructural-tourism/?cn-reloaded=1 (accessed 22 February 2023).

— 'Networked Dream Worlds', *Real Life Mag*, 8 July 2019, https://reallifemag.com/networked-dream-worlds/ (accessed 22 February 2023).

— 'Scaffolding, Hard and Soft. Infrastructures as Critical and Generative Structures', *Spheres: Journal for Digital Cultures* 3 (2016): 1–10, https://newalphabetschool.hkw.de/scaffolding-hard-and-soft-critical-and-generative-infrastructures/index.html (accessed 22 February 2023).

McLuhan, Marshall, *Understanding Media: The Extensions of Man*, Cambridge, MA: MIT Press, 1994.

McLuhan, Marshall, and Quentin Fiore, 'The Medium is the Message', *New York* 123, no. 1 (1967): 126–8.

McLuhan, Marshall, and Harley Parker, *Counterblast*, New York: Harcourt, Brace & World, 1969.

Meisner, Maurice, and Rhoads Murphey (eds), *The Mozartian Historian: Essays on the Works of Joseph R. Levenson*, Berkeley, CA: University of California Press, 1976.

Milner, Greg, *Pinpoint: How GPS is Changing Technology, Culture, and Our Minds*, New York: W. W. Norton, 2017.

Milutis, Joe, *Ether: The Nothing That Connects Everything*, Minneapolis, MN: University of Minnesota Press, 2006.

Mims, Christopher, 'Cities Are Saying No to 5G, Citing Health, Aesthetics – and FCC Bullying', *Wall Street Journal*, 24 August 2019, https://www.wsj.com/articles/cities-are-saying-no-to-5g-citing-health-aestheticsand-fcc-bullying-11566619391 (accessed 22 February 2023).

Morus, Iwan Rhys, 'Future Perfect: Social Progress, High-speed Transport and Electricity Everywhere – How the Victorians Invented the Future', *Aeon*, 10 December 2014, https://aeon.co/essays/how-the-victorians-invented-the-future-for-us (accessed 22 February 2023).

Moser, David, 'Backward Thinking about Orientalism and Chinese Characters', *Language Log* (blog), 16 May 2016, https://languagelog.ldc.upenn.edu/nll/?p=25776 (accessed 22 February 2023).

Mou Zongsan, *Autobiography at Fifty: A Philosophical Life in Twentieth Century China*, San Jose, CA: CreateSpace Independent Publishing Platform, 2015.

— *Late Works of Mou Zongsan: Selected Essays on Chinese Philosophy*, ed. Jason Clower, Leiden: Brill, 2014.

— 'Lecture 7, "The Functional Representation" of Dao', in *Nineteen Lectures on Chinese Philosophy: A Brief Outline of Chinese Philosophy and the Issues it Entails*, trans. Esther C. Su, San Jose, CA: CreateSpace Independent Publishing Platform, 2015.

— 'Lecture 14: "The One Mind Opening Two Gates" in the *Mahāyāna Awakening of Faith*', in *Nineteen Lectures on Chinese Philosophy: A Brief Outline of Chinese Philosophy and the Issues it Entails*, trans. Esther C. Su, San Jose, CA: CreateSpace Independent Publishing Platform, 2015.

— *Nineteen Lectures on Chinese Philosophy: A Brief Outline of Chinese Philosophy and the Issues it Entails*, trans. Esther C. Su, San Jose, CA: CreateSpace Independent Publishing Platform, 2015.

Mukherjee, Rahul, *Radiant Infrastructures: Media, Environment, and Cultures of Uncertainty*, Durham, NC: Duke University Press Books, 2020.

Mullaney, Thomas, 'Chinese is not a Backward Language', *Foreign Policy*, 12 May 2016, https://foreignpolicy.com/2016/05/12/chinese-is-a-twenty-first-century-language-ignore-orientalism-2-0-critiques/ (accessed 22 February 2023).

— *The Chinese Typewriter: A History*, Cambridge, MA: MIT Press, 2017.

— 'The Moveable Typewriter: How Chinese Typists Developed Predictive Text during the Height of Maoism', *Technology and Culture* 53, no. 4 (2012): 777–814.

— 'Semiotic Sovereignty: The 1871 Chinese Telegraph Code in Historical Perspective', in *Science and Technology in Modern China, 1880s–1940s*, ed. Jing Tsu and Benjamin Elman, Leiden: Brill, 2014, 153–83, https://doi.org/10.1163/9789004268784_008

Mullaney, Thomas, and Jeffrey N. Wasserstrom, 'It's Time to Get Over QWERTY: A Q&A with Tom Mullaney on Alphabets, Chinese Characters, and Computing', *Los Angeles Review of Books* (blog), 5 April 2016, http://blog.lareviewofbooks.org/chinablog/time-get-qwerty-qa-tom-mullaney-alphabets-chinese-characters-computing/ (accessed 22 February 2023).

Muller, A. Charles, 'The Emergence of Essence-Function (Ti–Yong) 體用 Hermeneutics in the Sinification of Indic Buddhism: An Overview', *Critical Review for Buddhist Studies* 19 (June 2016): 111–52, https://doi.org/10.29213/crbs..19.201606.111

— 'Xiong Shili and the New Treatise: A Review Discussion of Xiong Shili, *New Treatise on the Uniqueness of Consciousness, an Annotated Translation* by John Makeham', *Sophia* 56, no. 3 (2017): 523–6.

Mumford, Lewis, and Langdon Winner, *Technics and Civilization*, Chicago: University of Chicago Press, 2010.

Murphy, Kieran M., *Electromagnetism and the Metonymic Imagination*, University Park, PA: Penn State University Press, 2020.

Murphy, Michelle, *Sick Building Syndrome and the Problem of Uncertainty: Environmental Politics, Technoscience, and Women Workers*, Durham, NC: Duke University Press, 2006.

Murthy, Viren, and Axel Schneider, *The Challenge of Linear Time: Nationhood and the Politics of History in East Asia*, Leiden: Brill, 2013.

Nakassis, Constantine V., 'Brands and their Surfeits', *Cultural Anthropology* 28, no. 1 (2013): 111–26.

Navarro, Jaume (ed.), *Ether and Modernity: The Recalcitrance of an Epistemic Object in the Early Twentieth Century*, Oxford: Oxford University Press, 2018.

Needham, Joseph, *The Grand Titration: Science and Society in East and West*, Abingdon: Routledge, 2013.

Neves, Joshua, *Underglobalization: Beijing's Media Urbanism and the Chimera of Legitimacy*, Durham, NC: Duke University Press, 2020.

Ng, Yu Kwan, 'Xiong Shili's Metaphysical Theory about the Non-Separability of Substance and Function', in *New Confucianism: A Critical Examination*, ed. John Makeham, New York: Palgrave Macmillan, 2003, 219–51.

Nietzsche, Friedrich, *Thus Spake Zarathustra*, trans. Thomas Common, Mineola, NY: Dover Publications, 1999.

O'Donnell, Mary Ann, 'Excavating the Future in Shenzhen', in *Urban Asias: Essays on Futurity Past and Present*, ed. Tim Bunnell and Daniel P. S. Goh, Berlin: JOVIS, 2018.

— 'Heroes of the Special Zone: Modeling Reform and its Limits', in *Learning from Shenzhen: China's Post-Mao Experiment from Special Zone to Model City*, ed. Mary Ann O'Donnell, Winnie Wong and Jonathan Bach, Chicago: University of Chicago Press, 2017.

— 'Laying Siege to the Villages: The Vernacular Geography of Shenzhen', in *Learning from Shenzhen: China's Post-Mao Experiment from Special Zone to Model City*, ed. Mary Ann O'Donnell, Winnie Wong and Jonathan Bach, Chicago: University of Chicago Press, 2017.

O'Donnell, Mary Ann, Winnie Wong, and Jonathan Bach (eds), *Learning from Shenzhen: China's Post-Mao Experiment from*

Special Zone to Model City, Chicago: University of Chicago Press, 2017.

Ong, Aihwa, 'The Chinese Axis: Zoning Technologies and Variegated Sovereignty', *Journal of East Asian Studies* 4, no. 1 (2004): 69–96.

Otis, Laura Christine, *Networking: Communicating with Bodies and Machines in the Nineteenth Century*, Ann Arbor, MI: University of Michigan Press, 2001.

Pacey, Scott, 'Tan Sitong's "Great Unity": Mental Processes and Yogācāra in "An Exposition of Benevolence"', in *Transforming Consciousness: The Intellectual Reception of Yogācāra Thought in Modern China*, ed. John Makeham, Oxford: Oxford University Press, 2014.

Packer, Jeremy, and Stephen B. Crofts Wiley (eds), *Communication Matters: Materialist Approaches to Media, Mobility and Networks*, Abingdon: Routledge, 2013.

Palmer, David A., 'Modernity and Millenialism in China: Qigong and the Birth of Falun Gong', *Asian Anthropology* 2, no. 1 (2003): 79–109.

— *Qigong Fever: Body, Science, and Utopia in China*, New York: Columbia University Press, 2007.

Palmer, David A., Glenn Shive and Philip L. Wickeri (eds), *Chinese Religious Life*, Oxford: Oxford University Press, 2011.

Pan, Lynn, *Shanghai Style: Art and Design Between the Wars*, San Francisco: Long River Press, 2008.

Pan, Weixian, 'China Southern: Digital Environments as Geopolitical Contact Zones', PhD thesis, Concordia University, 2019, https://spectrum.library.concordia.ca/id/eprint/985659/ (accessed 22 February 2023).

Pang, Laikwan, 'Magic and Modernity in China', *Positions: East Asia Cultures Critique* 12, no. 2 (2004): 299–327.

Parikka, Jussi, *A Geology of Media*, Minneapolis, MN: University of Minnesota Press, 2015.

— 'New Materialism as Media Theory: Medianatures and Dirty Matter', *Communication and Critical/Cultural Studies* 9, no. 1 (2012): 95–100.

— *What is Media Archaeology?*, Cambridge: Polity, 2013.

Parisi, Luciana, 'The Alien Subject of AI', *Subjectivity* 12, no. 1 (2019): 27–48.

Parisi, Luciana, and Steve Goodman, 'Extensive Continuum Towards a Rhythmic Anarchitecture', *Inflexions* 2 (2009), https://www.inflexions.org/n2_parisigoodmanhtml.html (accessed 22 February 2023).

Parks, Lisa, 'Around the Antenna Tree: The Politics of Infrastructural Visibility', *Flow Journal* (blog), 6 March 2009, https://www.

flowjournal.org/2009/03/around-the-antenna-tree-the-politics-of-infrastructural-visibilitylisa-parks-uc-santa-barbara/ (accessed 22 February 2023).

— *Cultures in Orbit: Satellites and the Televisual*, Durham, NC: Duke University Press, 2005.

— 'Technostruggles and the Satellite Dish: A Populist Approach to Infrastructure', in *Cultural Technologies: The Shaping of Culture in Media and Society*, ed. Göran Bolin, Abingdon: Routledge, 2012.

Parks, Lisa, and Nicole Starosielski (eds), *Signal Traffic: Critical Studies of Media Infrastructures*, Urbana, IL: University of Illinois Press, 2015.

Pepi, Mike, 'Benjamin Bratton: Machine Vision', *DIS Magazine* (blog), http://dismagazine.com/discussion/73272/benjamin-bratton-machine-vision/ (accessed 27 April 2022.)

Perez, Carlota, *Technological Revolutions and Financial Capital: The Dynamics of Bubbles and Golden Ages*, Cheltenham: Edward Elgar, 2003.

— 'Technological Revolutions and Techno-Economic Paradigms', *Cambridge Journal of Economics* 34, no. 1 (2010): 185–202.

Peters, John Durham, *The Marvelous Clouds: Toward a Philosophy of Elemental Media*, Chicago: University of Chicago Press, 2016.

— 'Technology and Ideology: The Case of the Telegraph Revisited', in *Thinking with James Carey: Essays on Communications, Transportation, History*, ed. Jeremy Packer and Craig Robertson, New York: Peter Lang, 2006.

Plantin, Jean-Christophe, and Gabriele de Seta, 'WeChat as Infrastructure: The Techno-Nationalist Shaping of Chinese Digital Platforms', *Chinese Journal of Communication* 12, no. 3 (2019): 257–73.

Platt, Stephen R., *Provincial Patriots: The Hunanese and Modern China*, Cambridge, MA: Harvard University Press, 2007.

Pohl, Karl-Heinz, '"Western Learning as Substance, Chinese Learning for Application": Li Zehou's Thought on Tradition and Modernity', in *Li Zehou and Confucian Philosophy*, ed. Roger T. Ames and Jinhua Jia, Honolulu, HI: University of Hawaii Press, 2018.

Prahalad, C. K., and Gary Hamel, 'The Core Competence of the Corporation', *International Library of Critical Writings in Economics* 163 (2003): 210–22.

Pregadio, Fabrizio (ed.), *The Routledge Encyclopedia of Taoism*, 2 vols, Abingdon: Routledge, 2011.

Pregadio, Fabrizio, and Lowell Skar, 'Inner Alchemy (Neidan)', in *Daoism Handbook*, ed. Livia Kohn, Leiden: Brill, 2000, 464–97, https://doi.org/10.1163/9789004391840_017

Prestowitz, Clyde V., *Three Billion New Capitalists: The Great Shift of Wealth and Power to the East*, New York: Basic Books, 2006.

Qiu, Jack Linchuan, *Reorienting Global Communication: Indian and Chinese Media Beyond Borders*, ed. Michael Curtin and Hemant Shah, Urbana, IL: University of Illinois Press, 2010.

Rao, Venkatesh, 'Superhistory, Not Superintelligence', *Ribbonfarm Studio* (blog), 12 May 2021, https://studio.ribbonfarm.com/p/superhistory-not-superintelligence (accessed 22 February 2023).

Roberts, Margaret E., *Censored: Distraction and Diversion Inside China's Great Firewall*, Princeton, NJ: Princeton University Press, 2018.

Rojas, Carlos, 'Chinese Writing, Heptapod B, and Martian Script: The Ethnocentric Bases of Language', unpublished essay, 2018.

Rošker, Jana S., *Following His Own Path: Li Zehou and Contemporary Chinese Philosophy*, Albany, NY: SUNY Press, 2019.

— 'Li Zehou and New Confucianism: A Philosophy for New Global Futures', in *Li Zehou and Confucian Philosophy*, ed. Roger T. Ames and Jinhua Jia, Honolulu, HI: University of Hawaii Press, 2018.

— 'Li Zehou's View on Chinese Modernization and the Precarious Relationship between Marx and Confucius', *Problemos*, Suppl. (2016): 24–34, https://www.journals.vu.lt/problemos/article/view/10352 (accessed 22 February 2023).

— 'Modern Confucian Synthesis of Qualitative and Quantitative Knowledge: Xiong Shili', *Journal of Chinese Philosophy* 36, no. 3 (2009): 376–90.

Rothman, Joshua, 'Ted Chiang's Soulful Science Fiction', *The New Yorker*, 5 January 2017.

Rovelli, Carlo, *The Order of Time*, New York: Riverhead Books, 2018.

Rowe, Peter G., and Seng Kuan, *Architectural Encounters with Essence and Form in Modern China*, Cambridge, MA: MIT Press, 2002.

Roy, Ananya, and Aihwa Ong (eds), *Worlding Cities: Asian Experiments and the Art of Being Global*, Chichester: John Wiley & Sons, 2011.

Ryckmans, Pierre, 'The Chinese Attitude towards the Past', *China Heritage Quarterly* 14 (2008): 1–16.

Sandvig, Christian, 'The Internet as Infrastructure', in *The Oxford Handbook of Internet Studies*, ed. H. William Dutton, Oxford: Oxford University Press, 2013, https://doi.org/10.1093/oxfordhb/9780199589074.001.0001

Sang, Yu, 'The Role of the Treatise on Awakening Mahāyāna Faith in the Development of Xiong Shili's Ti–yong Metaphysics', in *The Awakening of Faith and New Confucian Philosophy*, ed. John Makeham, Leiden: Brill, 2021.

— *Xiong Shili's Understanding of Reality and Function, 1920–1937*, Leiden: Brill, 2020.

Schäfer, Ingo, 'Natural Philosophy, Physics and Metaphysics in the Discourse of Tan Sitong: The Concepts of *Qi* and *Yitai*', in *New Terms for New Ideas: Western Knowledge and Lexical Change in Late Imperial China*, ed. Michael Lackner, Iwo Amelung and Joachim Kurtz, Leiden: Brill, 2001, 257–69, https://doi.org/10.1163/9789004501669_015

Schmidt, Stephan, 'Mou Zongsan, Hegel, and Kant: The Quest for Confucian Modernity', *Philosophy East and West*, 61, no. 2 (2011), 260–302.

Schmitt, Carl, *Land and Sea: A World-Historical Meditation*, ed. Samuel Garrett Zeitlin and Russell A. Berman, Candor, NY: Telos Press, 2015.

— *The Nomos of the Earth in the International Law of Jus Publicum Europaeum*, trans. G. L. Ulmen, New York: Telos Press, 2006.

Schneider, Florian, *China's Digital Nationalism*, Oxford: Oxford University Press, 2018.

Schopenhauer, Arthur, *The World as Will and Idea*, trans. Richard Burdon Haldane and John Kemp, Musaicum Books, 2020.

Schumpeter, Joseph A., *Business Cycles*, vol. 1, New York: McGraw-Hill, 1939.

— *Capitalism, Socialism, and Democracy*, 3rd edn, New York: Harper Perennial, 2008.

— *Essays of J.A. Schumpeter*, ed. Richard V. Clemence, Boston, MA: Addison-Wesley, 1951.

Schwartz, Benjamin I., *In Search of Wealth and Power: Yen Fu and the West*, Cambridge, MA: Belknap Press of Harvard University Press, 1964.

— 'The Limits of "Tradition versus Modernity" as Categories of Explanation: The Case of the Chinese Intellectuals', *Daedalus* 101, no. 2 (1972): 71–88.

SCMP Reporter, 'Media Q&A with Huawei Founder Ren Zhengfei', *South China Morning Post*, 16 January 2019, https://www.scmp.com/tech/big-tech/article/2182367/transcript-huawei-founder-ren-zhengfeis-responses-media-questions (accessed 22 February 2023).

Sconce, Jeffrey, *Haunted Media: Electronic Presence from Telegraphy to Television*, 2nd edn, Durham, NC: Duke University Press, 2000.

Shaviro, Steven, 'Deleuze's Encounter with Whitehead' (2007), http://www.shaviro.com/Othertexts/DeleuzeWhitehead.pdf (accessed 22 February 2023).

Shek, Richard H., 'Some Western Influences on T'an Ssu-t'ung's Thought', in *Reform in Nineteenth-Century China*, ed. Paul A. Cohen and John E. Schrecker, Leiden: Brill, 1979, 194–203.

Shih, Shu-mei, Chien-hsin Tsai and Brian Bernards (eds), *Sinophone Studies: A Critical Reader*, New York: Columbia University Press, 2013.

Siderits, Mark, *Buddhism as Philosophy: An Introduction*, Indianapolis, IN: Hackett, 2007.

— 'Yogacara: Impressions-Only', in *Buddhism as Philosophy: An Introduction*, 2nd edn, Indianapolis, IN: Hackett, 2021.

Spence, Jonathan D., *The Search for Modern China*, New York: W. W. Norton, 1991.

Standage, Tom, *The Victorian Internet: The Remarkable Story of the Telegraph and the Nineteenth Century's On-Line Pioneers*, London: Bloomsbury, 2014.

Star, Susan, 'The Ethnography of Infrastructure', *American Behavioural Scientist* 43, no. 3 (1999): 377–91.

Starosielski, Nicole, 'The Elements of Media Studies', *Media+ Environment* 1, no. 1 (2019), https://doi.org/10.1525/001c.10780

— *The Undersea Network*, Durham, NC: Duke University Press, 2015.

Stille, Alexander, *The Future of the Past*, New York: Macmillan, 2002.

Storm, Jason Ananda Josephson, *The Myth of Disenchantment: Magic, Modernity, and the Birth of the Human Sciences*, Chicago: University of Chicago Press, 2017.

Strittmatter, Kai, *We Have Been Harmonized: Life in China's Surveillance State*, New York: Custom House, 2020.

Strugatsky, Arkady, and Boris Strugatsky, *Roadside Picnic*, Chicago: Chicago Review Press, 2012.

Styers, Randall, *Making Magic: Religion, Magic, and Science in the Modern World*, New York: Oxford University Press, 2004.

Su, Xiaokang, *Deathsong of the River: A Reader's Guide to the Chinese TV*, New York: Cornell University Press, 2010.

Suttmeier, Richard P., 'A New Technonationalism? China and the Development of Technical Standards', *Communications of the ACM* 48, no. 4 (2005): 35–7.

Swislocki, Mark, *Culinary Nostalgia: Regional Food Culture and the Urban Experience in Shanghai*, Stanford, CA: Stanford University Press, 2008.

Tan, Sitong, *An Exposition of Benevolence: The Jen-Hsüeh of T'an Ssu-t'ung*, trans. Sin-wai Chan, Hong Kong: The Chinese University of Hong Kong Press, 1984.

Tao, Tian, and Wu Chunbo, *The Huawei Story*, London: Sage, 2014.

Tarocco, Francesca, *The Cultural Practices of Modern Chinese Buddhism: Attuning the Dharma*, Abingdon: Routledge, 2005.

— 'Lost in Translation? The Treatise on the *Mahāyāna Awakening of Faith* (Dasheng Qixin Lun) and its Modern Readings', *Bulletin of the School of Oriental and African Studies* 71, no. 2 (2008): 323–43.

— 'On the Market: Consumption and Material Culture in Modern Chinese Buddhism', *Religion* 41, no. 4 (2011): 627–44.

— 'Technologies of Salvation: (Re)Locating Chinese Buddhism in the Digital Age', *Journal of Global Buddhism* 18 (2017): 155–76.

Teng, Ssu-yu, and John King Fairbank, *China's Response to the West: A Documentary Survey, 1839–1923*, Cambridge, MA: Harvard University Press, 1979.

The Editors, 'China 中国: Issue 7', *Logic Magazine*, https://logicmag.io/china/ (accessed 27 May 2020).

Thompson, Robert Luther, *Wiring a Continent: The History of the Telegraph Industry in the United States, 1832–1866*, Princeton, NJ: Princeton University Press, 1947.

Thompson, Roger R., 'The Wire: Progress, Paradox, and Disaster in the Strategic Networking of China, 1881–1901', *Frontiers of History in China* 10, no. 3 (2015): 395–427.

Thrift, Nigel, 'The "Sentient" City and What it May Portend', *Big Data & Society* 1, no. 1 (2014), https://doi.org/10.1177/2053951714532241

Tong, Shijun, 'Habermas and the Chinese Discourse of Modernity', *Dao* 1, no. 1 (2001): 81–105.

Townsend, James, 'Chinese Nationalism', *The Australian Journal of Chinese Affairs* 27 (1992): 97–130.

Tsu, Jing, *Kingdom of Characters: The Language Revolution That Made China Modern*, New York: Riverhead Books, 2022.

Tu, Wei-Ming, 'Hsiung Shih-Li's Quest for Authentic Existence', in *The Limits of Change: Essays on Conservative Alternatives in Republican China*, ed. Charlotte Furth, Cambridge, MA: Harvard University Press, 2014 [1976], 242–75, https://doi.org/10.4159/harvard.9780674332966.c14

— 'The Periphery as the Center', *Daedalus* 120, no. 2 (1991): 1–32.

Turner, Fred, *From Counterculture to Cyberculture: Stewart Brand, the Whole Earth Network, and the Rise of Digital Utopianism*, Chicago: University of Chicago Press, 2008.

Wallerstein, Immanuel, 'Long Waves as Capitalist Process', *Review (Fernand Braudel Center)* 7, no. 4 (1984): 559–75.

Wang, David Der-wei, 'Sailing to the Sinophone World: On Modern Chinese Literary Cartography', public lecture at Cambridge University, 2014, https://www.youtube.com/watch?v=2F5ZdEyMgA8 (accessed 23 February 2023).

Wang, Frédéric, 'The Relationship between Chinese Learning and Western Learning According to Yan Fu (1854–1921)', *Knowledge and Society Today (Multiple Modernity Project)*, Lyons, 2009, 47–56, https://shs.hal.science/halshs-00674116/document (accessed 23 February 2023).

Wang, Robin R., *Yinyang: The Way of Heaven and Earth in Chinese Thought and Culture*, Cambridge: Cambridge University Press, 2012.

Wang, Xiaoda, 'Mysterious Waves', in *Science Fiction from China*, ed. Patrick Dennis Murphy and Dingbo Wu, New York: Praeger, 1989.

Wasserstrom, Jeffrey N., 'Boxers & Buffalo Bill: Stories of China in 1900', talk given at Shanghai International Literary Festival, 10 March 2017.

— 'Copycat Travels', *Los Angeles Review of Books* (blog), 13 May 2015, http://blog.lareviewofbooks.org/chinablog/copycat-travels/ (accessed 22 February 2023).

— *Global Shanghai, 1850–2010: A History in Fragments*, Abingdon: Routledge, 2008.

— 'Shanghai's Latest Global Turn', *The Globalist*, 7 May 2007, https://www.theglobalist.com/shanghais-latest-global-turn/ (accessed 22 February 2023).

Wasserstrom, Jeffrey N. (ed.), *The Oxford Illustrated History of Modern China*, Oxford: Oxford University Press, 2016.

Wei, Lingling, 'Chinese Regulators Try to Get Jack Ma's Ant Group to Share Consumer Data', *Wall Street Journal*, 5 January 2021, https://www.wsj.com/articles/chinese-regulators-try-to-get-jack-mas-ant-group-to-share-consumer-data-11609878816 (accessed 22 February 2023).

Wenzlhuemer, Roland, *Connecting the Nineteenth-Century World: The Telegraph and Globalization*, Cambridge: Cambridge University Press, 2012.

Westad, Odd Arne, *Restless Empire: China and the World Since 1750*, London: Vintage, 2014.

Whitehead, Alfred North, *Process and Reality*, 2nd edn, New York: Free Press, 1979.

Wiley, Stephen B. Crofts, and N. Katherine Hayles, 'Media, Materiality and the Human: A Conversation with N. Katherine Hayles', in *Communication Matters: Materialist Approaches to Media, Mobility and Networks*, ed. Jeremy Packer, Abingdon: Routledge, 2011.

Wilson, David B., 'The Thought of Late Victorian Physicists: Oliver Lodge's Ethereal Body', *Victorian Studies* 15, no. 1 (1971): 29–48.

Wilson, Elizabeth A., *Gut Feminism*, Durham, NC: Duke University Press, 2015.

Woetzel, Jonathan, 'China's Next Chapter: The Infrastructure and Environmental Challenge', *McKinsey&Co*, 1 June 2013, https://www.mckinsey.com/featured-insights/urbanization/chinas-next-chapter-the-infrastructure-and-environmental-challenge (accessed 22 February 2023).

Woetzel, Jonathan, Lenny Mendonca, Janamitra Devan, Stefano Negri, Yangmei Hu, Luke Jordan and Xiujun Li, 'Preparing for China's Urban Billion', *McKinsey&Co*, 1 February 2009, https://www.mckinsey.com/featured-insights/urbanization/preparing-for-chinas-urban-billion (accessed 22 February 2023).

Wong, Winnie, *Van Gogh on Demand: China and the Readymade*, Chicago: University of Chicago Press, 2014.

Wright, David, 'Tan Sitong and the Ether Reconsidered', *Bulletin of the School of Oriental and African Studies* 57, no. 3 (1994): 551–75.

Xinhua, 'Shanghai's 5G Network Starts Test Runs', *English.Gov. Cn*, 31 March 2019, http://english.www.gov.cn/news/top_news/2019/03/31/content_281476587521838.htm (accessed 22 February 2023).

Xiong, Shili, *New Treatise on the Uniqueness of Consciousness*, trans. John Makeham, New Haven, CT: Yale University Press, 2015.

— *Shili Yuyao: Important Remarks of Xiong Shili*, Shanghai: Shanghai Bookstore Publishing House, 2007.

Yang, Guobin, *The Power of the Internet in China: Citizen Activism Online*, New York: Columbia University Press, 2009.

Yang, Yingzhi, and Julie Zhu, 'Coronavirus Brings China's Surveillance State out of the Shadows', *Reuters*, 7 February 2020, https://www.reuters.com/article/us-china-health-surveillance-idUSKBN2011HO (accessed 22 February 2023).

Yu, Hua, *China in Ten Words*, London: Duckworth, 2012.

Yu, Jiyuan, 'Xiong Shili's Metaphysics of Virtue', in *Contemporary Chinese Philosophy*, ed. Chung-Ying Cheng and Nicholas Bunnin, Oxford: Blackwell, 2002, 127–47.

Zhang, Zhidong, *China's Only Hope: An Appeal*, New York: Fleming H. Revell, 1900.

Zheng, Jiadong, 'Mou Zongsan and the Contemporary Circumstances of the Rujia', *Contemporary Chinese Thought* 36, no. 2 (2004): 67–88.

Zhou, Yongming, *Historicizing Online Politics: Telegraphy, the Internet, and Political Participation in China*, Stanford, CA: Stanford University Press, 2005.

Zito, Angela R., 'City Gods, Filiality, and Hegemony in Late Imperial China', *Modern China* 13, no. 3 (1987): 333–71.

Žižek, Slavoj, *Tarrying with the Negative: Kant, Hegel, and the Critique of Ideology*, Durham, NC: Duke University Press, 1993.

Zuboff, Shoshana, *The Age of Surveillance Capitalism: The Fight for a Human Future at the New Frontier of Power*, New York: PublicAffairs, 2020.

Index

257

EU representative:
Easy Access System Europe
Mustamäe tee 50, 10621 Tallinn, Estonia
Gpsr.requests@easproject.com

www.ingramcontent.com/pod-product-compliance
Lightning Source LLC
Chambersburg PA
CBHW070842300326
41935CB00039B/1370